STRATEGIC MANAGEMENT

TEXT AND CASES

STRATEGIC MANAGEMENT

TEXT AND CASES

Dr. C.B. Gupta
M. Com., Ph.D., MIMA
Former Head
Department of Commerce
Shri Ram College of Commerce
University of Delhi

S Chand And Company Limited
(ISO 9001 Certified Company)

S Chand And Company Limited

(ISO 9001 Certified Company)

Head Office: Block B-1, House No. D-1, Ground Floor, Mohan Co-operative Industrial Estate, New Delhi – 110 044 | Phone: 011-66672000

Registered Office: A-27, 2nd Floor, Mohan Co-operative Industrial Estate, New Delhi – 110 044 Phone: 011-49731800

www.**schandpublishing.com**; e-mail: **info@schandpublishing.com**

Branches

Ahmedabad	:	Ph: 27542369, 27541965; ahmedabad@schandpublishing.com
Bengaluru	:	Ph: 22354008, 22268048; bangalore@schandpublishing.com
Bhopal	:	Ph: 4274723, 4209587; bhopal@schandpublishing.com
Bhubaneshwar	:	Ph: 2951580; bhubaneshwar@schandpublishing.com
Chennai	:	Ph: 23632120; chennai@schandpublishing.com
Guwahati	:	Ph: 2738811, 2735640; guwahati@schandpublishing.com
Hyderabad	:	Ph: 40186018; hyderabad@schandpublishing.com
Jaipur	:	Ph: 2291317, 2291318; jaipur@schandpublishing.com
Jalandhar	:	Ph: 4645630; jalandhar@schandpublishing.com
Kochi	:	Ph: 2576207, 2576208; cochin@schandpublishing.com
Kolkata	:	Ph: 23357458, 23353914; kolkata@schandpublishing.com
Lucknow	:	Ph: 4003633; lucknow@schandpublishing.com
Mumbai	:	Ph: 25000297; mumbai@schandpublishing.com
Nagpur	:	Ph: 2250230; nagpur@schandpublishing.com
Patna	:	Ph: 2260011; patna@schandpublishing.com
Ranchi	:	Ph: 2361178; ranchi@schandpublishing.com
Sahibabad	:	Ph: 2771238; info@schandpublishing.com

First Edition 2014
Reprint 2020

ISBN: 978-93-843-1934-2 **Product Code:** H8STM60BMGT10ENAA14O

PRINTED IN INDIA

By Vikas Publishing House Private Limited, Plot 20/4, Site-IV, Industrial Area Sahibabad, Ghaziabad – 201 010 and Published by S Chand And Company Limited, A-27, 2nd Floor, Mohan Co-operative Industrial Estate, New Delhi – 110 044

PREFACE

India is one of the largest and fastest growing economies of the world. Business firms in India are undergoing transformation on account of globalisation, cut-throat competition, unprecedented technological advancements, rising customer aspirations and other environmental changes. Strategic management has been, therefore, prescribed as a compulsory paper in postgraduate, professional and undergraduate courses. This book has been designed and written as a textbook for these courses. The text has been organised into six parts. Nature, evolution and process of strategic management are explained in Part I. In part II, vision, mission, business definition, business model and other components of strategic Intent are described in detail. Part III contains strategy formulation at both corporate and business levels. SWOT analysis and strategic choice are the major contents of this part. In Part IV, issue in strategy implementation are discussed. Strategy evaluation and control are explained in Part V. Strategic issues in international business, E-business, technology and innovation, organisational change, small business, family business and non-profit organisation are discussed in Part VI of the book. Thus, the entire text is analysed in eighteen chapters.

Some of the distinctive features of the book are as follows:

- Chapter outline to indicate the topics covered in each chapter.
- Comprehensive coverage of the subject.
- Tables and diagrams to illustrate the text.
- Examples from Indian organisations.
- Summary at the end of every chapter for quick recapitulation.
- Test questions culled from MBA, M. Com., and BBA examinations.
- Case study at the end of every chapter.

I am indebted to the authors and publishers of leading works on the subject. I am sure the book would be useful to the concerned students, teachers and executives. Suggestions for improvements are welcome

Dr. C.B. Gupta

SOME SYLLABI ON STRATEGIC MANAGEMENT

University of Delhi
Master of Business Administration (MBA)
F-401 - Corporate Evolution & Strategic Management

Objectives

The objective of this course is to develop understanding about strategic processes and their impact on a firm.

Course Contents

Nature and Scope of Strategic Management; Strategic intent and vision; Concept of Core Competence, Capability and Organisational Learning; Process of Strategy Planning and Implementation; Strategy and Structure; Organisational Values and their Impact on Strategy; Power Games Amongst Competing Players; Chief Executive and Board; Work of top Management: Turnaround Management; Management of Strategic Change; Mergers and Acquisition; Strategic Management in an International Firm; Strategy and Corporate Evolution in India Context.

University of Delhi
Master of Business Administration (MBA)
F-302 - Business Policy & Strategic Analysis

Objectives

The objective of this course is to develop a wholistic perspective of an enterprise, critical from the point of view of top executives.

Course Contents

Business Policy: An area of Study; General Management point of view; Mission, objectives and policies; Environmental analysis & internal analysis; SWOT analysis; Tools and techniques for strategic analysis; Impact matrix; The experience curve; BCG matrix; GEC model; Industry analysis; Concept of value chain; Strategic profile of a Firm; Framework for analysing competition; Competitive advantage of a firm.

University of Delhi
Master of Business Administration (MBA)
3502 - Competitive Strategy

Objectives

The objective of this course is to develop indepth analysis for better understanding of the nature; of competition in different industry environment, policy environment and impact of external factors.

Course Contents

Basis for competition, Structural analysis of industries, Generic competitive strategies, Frame work for competition analysis, Market signals, Competitive moves, Technology of competitive advantage, Strategy towards buyers mid suppliers, Strategic groups within industries, Competitive strategy in fragmented industries, Competitive strategy in emerging industries, Competitive strategy in declining industries, Competitive strategy in global industries, Strategic analysis of integration capacity expansion, Strategies of entering into New Businesses, Portfolio techniques in competitor analysis, Techniques of conducting industry analysis.

University of Delhi
Master of Human Resource and Organisation Development (MHROD)
643 Strategic Management

Objectives

The main objective of this course is to develop the perspective for the overall management of the enterprise from the point of view of top management keeping in view the opportunities and threats posed by the environment.

Contents

Unit – I

Introduction: Business Policy as a field of study, Nature and scope of Strategic Management, Concept of Corporate Strategy and Tactics, Concept of Synergy and its relevance to strategy, Responsibilities of Top Management and the Chief Executive in formulating strategy; Overview of Decision Theories, Strategic Decision-making.

Unit – II

Formulation of Strategy: Corporate Mission and Objectives, Social Responsibility of Business Environmental Analysis: Corporate Appraisal; Basic Strategic alternatives: Stability, Retrenchment, Expansion, Diversification. Integration: Relating Economic Strategic to personnel Values: Matching Opportunities and Competence Making Choice of strategy.

Unit – III

Mergers and Acquisitions as a Strategic Alternative: Meaning, characteristics and causes of Mergers and Acquisitions (M & A). Rationale and Categories of M & A. Our Aspects of M & A – Industrial Relations. Organisation Culture. Compensation Management etc. Managing M & A as a successful strategic alternative.

Unit – IV

Implementation of Strategy: Interdependence of Formulation and Implementation of Strategy: Strategy and Corporate Organisation. Structure; Task. Responsibilities, Sub-division and co-ordination: Effective Design of Information System: Establishment of standards and Measurement of Performance. Motivation and Incentive System. An Overview of Functional Strategies. Human Resource Strategy; Strategy aspects of Recruitment Training. et. al.

Unit – V

Strategic HRM and International Experiences: Concepts and Importance of Strategic HRM in the Modern Business World. Understanding the success and failure of strategies HRM in the Modern Business World. Understanding the success and failure of strategies adopted by organisations in India and other countries through case analysis particular reference to HRM.

University of Delhi
Master of International Business (MIB)
Paper 541: Global Strategic Management

Content: The objective of this paper is to help the students understand strategy making process that is informed; integrative and responsive to rapid changes in an organisation's globally oriented environment and also to help them understand tasks of implementing strategy in a global market.

Content:

1. **Introduction:** Strategy making, strategy implementing and strategic managing; Roles of line managers, strategic planners and top management; Developing strategic vision and mission; Setting objectives and forming a strategy; Globalisation and Strategic management; Strategic flexibility and learning organisation.
2. **Environmental Scanning and Competitiveness Analysis:** Appraising company's, external strategic situation, company situation, competitive strategy and competitive advantage in global market.
3. **Situation specific Strategies:** Strategies for situations like competing in emerging industries, maturing or declining industries, fragmented industries, hyper-competitive industries and turbulent industries; Strategies for industry leaders, runner-up firms and weak business.
4. **Strategic Issues and Alternative in Globally Competitive Markets:** International entry options; Multi-country and global strategies; Concepts of critical markets, global market dominance and global competitiveness Corporate turnaround, retrenchment and portfolio restructuring strategies; Multinational diversification strategies; Outsourcing strategies; Techniques for analysing diversified companies.
5. **Corporate Diversification Strategies:** Building shareholder value; Roles of cost sharing and skills transfer in creating competitive advantage via diversification; Competitive advantages to diversified multinational corporations in a globally competitive business world.
6. **Strategy Implementation and Administration:** Organisation building; Budgets and support system commitment; culture and leadership; Issues in global strategy implementation; Strategy evaluation and control.
7. **Strategic Issues in Managing Technology and Innovation:** Social responsibility and ethics management.

University of Delhi
Master of Business Economics (MBE)
Semester - IV
Paper 19: Business Policy and Strategy

1. **Socio-Economic set up of Business in India:** Internal and External Perceptions.
2. **Strategic Management Decision:** Nature, Characteristics and Process of Strategic management decisions.
3. **Strategy Formulation:** Defying Company Mission & Goals, Assessing, External Environment, Industry Analysis, Internal Analysis of the firm.
4. **Policy Alternative and Grand Strategies:** Concentration, Market Development, product Development, Innovation, Interpretation, Joint Ventures, Diversification, Retrenchment, Divestiture and Liquidation.
5. **Strategic Analysis and Control at Corporate Level:** B.C.G Growth/Shares Matrix, the GE Nine Cell Planning Grid, SWOT Analysis, Behavioural Characteristics affecting Strategic Choice.
6. **Strategy Implementation:** Operationalising and Institutionalising the Strategy, Strategic Control.

University of Delhi
Mater of Commerce (M. Com)
6206: Strategic Management

Objective: The objective of this course is to help the students develop an understanding of the basic inputs in making and implementing corporate strategic decisions and also familiarise them with the issues and practices involved.

Course Outline:

1. **Introduction:** Concept and Role of Corporate Strategy. Levels of Strategy, Basic Model of Strategic Management. Approaches to Strategic Decision Making. Strategic Role of Board of Directors and Top Management. Strategic implications of social and ethical issues.
2. **Strategic Analysis:** Analysis of Broad Environment – Environmental Profile; Constructing Scenarios. Analysis of Operating Environment - Michael Porters Model of Industry Analysis. Analysis of Strategic Advantage – Resource Audit; Value Chain Analysis: Core Competence; SWOPT Analysis, Analysis of Stakeholder Expectations – Corporate Mission, Vision, Objectives and Goals.
3. **Strategic Choice:** Generating Strategic Alternatives. Strategic options at Corporate Level – Stability, Growth and Defensive Strategies. Enternal Growth strategics-Merges. Acquisition, joint Venture and strategic Alliance. Evaluation of Strategic Alternatives – Product Portfolio Models. Selection of a suitable Corporate Strategy – Concept of Strategic Fit. Strategic Options at SBU Level – Michael Porters'

Competitive Stratlogies; Operationalising Competitive Strategies.

4. **Strategic Implementation:** Strategic implementation issues. Planning and allocation resources. Organisation Structure and Design. Functional Strategies – Production, Human Resource, Finance, Marketing and R & D. Managing Strategic change. Strategic Control.
5. **Strategic Review:** Evaluating Strategy Performance – Criteria and Problems. Concept of Corporate Restructuring.

GGS Indraprastha University, Delhi
Master of Business Administration (MBA)
MS 213 – Strategic Management

This course aims at developing a holistic perspective of an organisation and making conversant the students with the process that facilitates decisions having strategic perspective.

Contents:

1. **Business Policy as an area of study:** Strategic Management Process – An Overview.
2. **Vision, Mission, Establishment of Organisational Direction:** Corporate Management and Chief Executive Officer.
3. **Formulation of Strategy:** Company's environment and its analysis; Tools and Techniques for Strategic Analysis, A Resource-Based Approach, Concept of Value Chain, SWOT, Industry Analysis; Strategic Alternatives and Evaluation Models – BCG Growth/Share Matrix; Stop Light Strategic Model; Directional Policy Matrix Model; Framework for Strategic Excellence Positions (SEPs).
4. **Strategic Alliances:** Types and motives of strategic alliances, risks and costs of alliances, selection of alliance partners, ethical dimensions of alliances.
5. **Implementing Strategy:** issues related to organisational structure, climate and culture, mergers and acquisitions, employee recruitment selection and development Process and criteria of strategy evaluation; Case Method of Study.

MBA, JIMS 3.1 Strategic Management

Objectives

The objective of this course is to develop understanding about strategic processes and their impact on a firm.

Course Contents

Nature and Scope of Strategic Management;

Strategic intent and vision;

Concept of Core Competence, Capability and Organisational Learning;

Process of Strategy Planning and Implementation;

Strategy and Structure;

Organisational Values and their Impact on Strategy;

Power Games Amongst Competing Players;

Chief Executive and Board;

Work of top Management;

Turnaround Management;

Management of Strategic Change;

Mergers and Acquisition;

Strategic Management in an International Firm;

Strategy and Corporate Evolution in Indian Context.

University of Delhi

Postgraduate Diploma in Global Business Operations

Semester IV

Business Policy and Strategic Management

The opening-up of economies and the increasingly integrated business world due to growing information technology make the global business extremely competitive, thus, requiring a fresh approach to strategy formulation. The objective of this paper is to expose the participants to the major dimensions of business strategy formulation.

1. **An Overview of Business Policy Formulation:** Nature and significance of strategic decisions, levels, of strategic decision, organisational framework for strategic management.
2. **Strategic Management Process:** Components of a strategic decision. Corporate vision, internal and external analysis.
3. **Strategic Considerations for Global Operations:** Complexity of global environment, planning for global operations, control problems in global operations.
4. **Strategy Implementation:** Organisational aspects, resource management, monitoring mechanism, managing change in strategy.

Himachel Pradesh University

M.Com – Business Policy

Objective:

The objective of the course is to help the participants develop an understanding of the basic inputs required in making & implementing business policy decision & also familiarise them with the issue & practices involved.

Contents:

Business Policy: Concept & scope, dynamic setting of corporate business goals & decision making social considerations in business policy.

Corporate Structure and Strategy: Concept functions and limitations strategic planning process formulation of organisational objective & their impact on strategic planning process.

Appraising Strategic Advantages of a Firm: Determinants of strategic advantage.

Preparing a strategic advantage profile. Alternative strategies and their evaluation by a firm.

Business policy in foreign collaboration.

Corporate Policies in Production Management: Marketing management, financial management & personnel management.

N.B: Case studies & other methods may be used to supplement lectures for this course.

Punjab Technical University
MBA – Strategic Management (MB – 401)

Max. Marks: 100

Internal Assessment: 40

External Assessment: 60

Unit–I

Definition, nature, scope, and importance of strategy; and strategic management (Business policy). Strategic decision-making. Process of strategic management and levels at which strategy operates. Role of strategists.

Defining strategic intent: Vision, Mission, Business definition, Goals and Objectives.

Environmental Appraisal: Concept of environment, components of environment (Economic, legal, social, political and technological). Environmental scanning techniques – ETOP, Quest and SWOT (TOWS). PEST.

Unit–II

Internal Appraisal: The internal environment, organisational capabilities in various functional areas and Strategic Advantage Profile. Methods and techniques used for organisational appraisal (Value chain analysis, Financial and non financial analysis, historical analysis, Industry standards and bench marking, Balanced scorecard and key factor rating). Identification of Critical Success Factors (CSF).

Unit–III

Corporate level strategies: Stability, Expansion, Retrenchment and Combination strategies. Corporate restructuring. Concept of Synergy.

Business level strategies: Porter's framework of competitive strategies; Conditions, risks and benefits of Cost leadership, Differentiation and Focus strategies. Location and timing tactics. Concept, Importance, Building and use of Core Competence.

Strategic Analysis and choice: Corporate level analysis (BCG, GE Nine-cell, Hofer's product market evolution and shell Directional policy matrix). Industry level analysis; Porters's five forces model. Qualitative factors in strategic choice.

Unit–IV

Strategy implementation: Resource allocation, projects and procedural issues. Organisation structure and systems in strategy implementation. Leadership and corporate culture, values, Ethics and social responsibility. Operational and derived functional plans to implement strategy. Integration of functional plans.

Strategic control and operational Control. Organisational systems and techniques of strategic evaluation.

Chartered Accountancy

PCE II – Paper 6(B)

Strategic Management (50 marks)

1. **Business Policy and Strategic Management:** Introduction, basic concepts, vision, mission and objectives. Short, medium and long term objectives.
2. **Environmental Scanning:** Internal and external environmental forces, industry analysis, identifying variables.
3. **Strategic Analyses:** Situational Analysis – SWOT Analysis, TOWS matrix, Portfolio Analysis – BCG Matrix.
4. **Strategic Planning:** Meaning, stages, alternatives, strategy formulation.
5. **Formulation of Functional Strategy:** Marketing strategy, financial strategy, operations strategy, logistics strategy, human resource strategy.
6. **Strategy Implementation and Control:** Organisational structures, establishing strategic business units, establishing profit centres by business, product or service, market segment or customer.
7. **Reaching Strategic Edge:** Business process reengineering, benchmarking, total quality. Management, six sigma, international perspective.

University of Delhi
BMS Course: Paper No. 8.3
Corporate Strategy

Learning Objective: To understand the concepts underlying how strategy is implemented in the business environment.

Unit–I

Introduction to Strategy: Nature & importance of business policy & strategy: Introduction to the strategic management process, Strategic Management & related concepts, Characteristics of corporate, business & functional level strategic management decisions. Company's mission statement, Statement, need for a mission statement, criteria for evaluating a mission statement formulation of a mission statement.

Unit–II

Environmental Analysis & Diagnosis: Analysis of company's external environment. Environmental impact on organisation's policy and strategy, organisation's dependence on the environment, analysis of remote environment, analysis of specific environment. Michael E. Porter's 5 Forces model, positioning against five force, Analysis of internal; Importance of organisation's capabilities, competitive advantage and core competence, Michael E. Porter's Value Chain Analysis.

Unit–III

Competitive Strategies: Perspectives to competition: industry, marketing & strategic group, competitive strategies – Michael E. Porter's generic competitive strategic, implementing competitive strategies – offensive & defensive moves.

Unit–IV

Corporate strategies: Formulating corporate strategies, introduction to strategies of growth, stability and renewal, types of growth strategies – concentrated growth, product development, integration, diversification, international expansion (multi domestic approach, franchising, licensing and joint ventures), strategic fundamentals of merger & acquisitions (M & A), types of renewal strategies – retrenchment and turnaround.

Unit–V

Strategic frameworks: Strategic analysis & choice, Strategic gap analyses, portfolio analyses MECF approach, BCG, GE, product market evolution matrix, experience curve, directional policy matrix, life cycle portfolio matrix, grand strategy selection matrix; Behavioural considerations affecting choice of strategy. Culture and strategic Leadership: Implementing & operationalising strategic choice, impact of structure, culture & leadership, functional strategies & their link with business level strategies.

GGS IP University, New Delhi
Sixth Semester
BBA 302: Business Policy & Strategy

OBJECTIVE:

The course aims to acquaint the student with the nature, scope and dimensions of Business Policy and Strategy Management process.

Course Contents

Unit–I

Introduction: Nature, scope and importance of the course on Business Policy; Evolution of this course – Forecasting, Long-range planning, strategic planning and strategic management.

Strategic Management Process: Formulation phase – vision, mission environmental factors; approaches to the environment scanning process – structural analysis of competitive environment; ETOP a diagnosis tool.

Unit–II

Environmental Analysis: Need Characteristics and categorization of environmental factors; approaches to the environmental scanning process – structural analysis of competitive environment; ETOP a diagnosis tool.

Unit–III

Analysis of Internal Resources: Strengths and Weakness; Resources Audit; Strategic Advantage Analysis; Value Chain Approach to Internal Analysis; Methods of analysis and diagnosing Corporate Capabilities – Functional Area Profile and Resource Deployment Matrix, Strategic Advantage Profile; SWOT analysis.

Unit–IV

Formulation of Strategy: Approaches to Strategy formation; formation; major strategy options – Stability, Growth and Expansion, Diversificaiton, Retrenchment, Mixed Strategy; Choice of Strategy – BCG Model; Stop-light Strategy Model; Directional Policy Matrix (DPM) Model, Product/Market Evolution – Matrix and profit Impact of Market Strategy (PIMS) Model;

Major Issues involved in the Implementation of strategy: Organisation structure; leadership and resource allocation.

CONTENTS

PART – I
CONCEPTUAL FRAMEWORK

PART – IV
STRATEGY IMPLEMENTATION

PART – VI
STRATEGIC MANAGEMENT IN SPECIFIED AREAS

PART – I

CONCEPTUAL FRAMEWORK

1. Nature and Evolution of Strategic Management
2. Strategic Management Process

1

CHAPTER

NATURE AND EVOLUTION OF STRATEGIC MANAGEMENT

CHAPTER OUTLINE

1.1. EVOLUTION OF BUSINESS POLICY AND STRATEGIC MANAGEMENT COURSE

Origin: As a field of study business policy originated in 1911 when an integrated course in management was introduced at Harvard Business School (USA) as a part of curriculum. The course was designed primarily for improving general management competence. However, this business policy course did not attract the attention of other business schools even in the USA. Almost fifty years later, business policy course became popular due to two expert studies sponsored by Ford Foundation and the Carnegie Corporation of New York. The reports on both the studies were published in 1959. These reports strongly recommended the introduction of business policy course in management education. The report sponsored by the Ford Foundation suggests that : "The capstone of core curriculum should be a course on 'business policy' which will give students an opportunity to pull together what they have learned in the separate business fields and utilise this knowledge in the analysis of complex business problems".[1]

1 Robert A. Gordon and James E. Howell, **Higher Education for Business**, Columbia University Press, New York, 1959.

Following these reports, the business policy course was made mandatory for all business schools in USA for recognition of management degree by the American Assembly of Collegiate Business Schools. Since then business policy has been introduced as an integral part of degree and diploma courses in management all over the world.

The evolution and development of business policy can also be traced through management practices. Hofer *et al* have identified four phases through which strategic management practices have developed ever time.[2]

1. **Paradigm of Adhoc Policy Making (Till mid-1930's):** Expansion of American firms both in terms of products and markets necessitated planning function. The focus, however, was on short-term planning of day to day operations. Budgeting and control systems replaced informal central and coordination. Policy formulation was confined to functional areas. The system of policy formulation was not integrated and ad hoc approach was adopted.
2. **Paradigm of Integrated Policy Formulation (1930's and 1940's):** Due to increasing complexity of environment in the form of technological innovation and competition, planned policy formulation became necessary. The focus shifted to integration of policies in different functional areas in the context of environmental changes. Still there was no direct participation of top management in planning and policy formulation.
3. **Strategy Paradigm (1940-1960's):** Rapid pace of environmental changes and increasing complexity of management prompted a critical look at the concept of business in relation to environment. The focus was more on strategic decisions based on competitors' actions. The environmental analysis focused primarily on competitive environment. In 1969 American Assembly of Collegiate Schools of Business (AACSB) made the business policy course mandatory.
4. **Paradigm of Strategic Management (1980's onwards):** Globalisation of economy changed in the complexity of competition. In the changed business scenario focus shifted to the strategic processes and top management assumed responsibility for resolving strategic issues. Under strategic management paradigm comprehensive analysis of environment is done to develop likely future business scenario. Top management formulates contingency strategies that are relevant to the scenarios.

The development of strategic management is not yet complete. Due to ever changing environment, more refined strategic management may be required in future. Top managers may have to shoulder more responsibility for managing discontinuous change.

Table 1.1: Evolution of Strategic Management

Dimensions	Time		Period		
	1960s	1970s	1980s	1990s	2000s
Main focus	Definition of strategy	Conceptualising strategic management	Economics view of strategy	Resource-based view of strategy	New paradigm of strategic management

2 CW Hofer, E.A. Murray Jr; Ram Charan and R.A. Pitts, Strategic Management — A Casebook in Policy and Planning, West Publishing, Minnesota, 1980.

Dominant Themes	Corporate strategy, planning and growth	Strategic management content and process	Competitive advantage development	Resources and capabilities development	Learning knowledge, and innovation
Strategic tools and techniques	SWOT analysis, experience curve, growth share matrix	Value chain	Five forces model, strategic choice	Core competence, value system	Integrated information technology systems
Main contributors	Chandler (1962), Ansoff (1965) Learned *et al* (1965)	Andrews (1971), Rumelt (1974), Mintzberg (1978), Ansoff (1979)	Porter (1980, 1986)	Wernerfelt (1984), Ghoshal (1986), Prahald and Hamel (1990), Barney (1991)	Hammel (2000), Pfeffer and Suttor (2000), Herrmann (2005), Kim and Mouborgne (2005)

1.2. OBJECTIVES OF BUSINESS POLICY AND STRATEGIC MANAGEMENT COURSE

Generally, the students of management start their career in a functional area. Only a very few of them reach the general management function or top level of management. Therefore, a question arises in their minds: Why should they study business policy and strategic management. This question can be answered by analysing the objectives of business policy course. These objectives may be described as follows:

1. **Knowledge:** The basic objective of any discipline is to impart knowledge. Business policy course provides knowledge in several dimensions:
   (*i*) The course helps to understand how environmental forces influence the functioning of an organisation.
   (*ii*) The study of business policy enables students to know the significance of strategy to an organisation and its top management.
   (*iii*) It stresses interrelationships among various subsystems in the organisation and the problems which top executives face in avoiding sub-optimisation of parts.
   (*iv*) The study of business policy is useful in understanding, how strategies are formulated and implemented to overcome organisational weaknesses and utilising the strengths.
   (*v*) The policy study provides understanding of the unique setting of operations in different industries.
   (*vi*) It enables the student to understand how specialised knowledge from different disciplines can be integrated to make suitable decisions and to solve complex problems.
2. **Skills:** To be successful managers need several types of skills though the relative importance of these skills may vary with the level of management. Business policy course helps in developing skills required for managing the total organisation. Top

level managers are responsible for monitoring environmental forces, making long range plans, and taking organisation wide decisions. Osmond[3] has identified eight specific skills that top level managers need. These skills relate to balancing, integrating, setting priorities, setting and developing standards, conceptualising, leading, matching oneself with one's job, and delegating.

Top managers require general management skills such as analytical skills, creativity, sense of high achievement, risk taking aptitude, leadership, personal mastery, building team work, and so on.

3. **Attitudes:** Business policy course is quite helpful in developing the attitudes, values and aspirations which are necessary for top management functions. These are given below:

   (*i*) Top managers make decisions on the basis of an overall view of all the relevant factors. They need a wholistic attitude and the mindset of a generalist.

   (*ii*) A top executive has to make decisions under the condition of partial ignorance. He aims at satisficing rather than maximising decisions. Tradeoffs have to be made in terms of the nature of the problem, timing of the decision and implementation of the solution.

   (*iii*) With the help of business policy course students can develop a professional orientation to management. Such orientation focusses on social responsibility and ethical considerations in policy formulation and implementation.

   (*iv*) Managers work in an environment of diversity and change. They should learn to work under uncertainty. They need to be creative so as to introduce innovative management practices. Policy course is helpful in developing such a mindset.

4. **Knowledge:**

   (*a*) Strategic management must have full and correct comprehension of internal and external environment changes which influence the company. Knowledge is the best means of evolving a sound strategy and policies to achieve it;

   (*b*) It must understand thoroughly the interrelationships inherent in sub-systems and how to avoid sub-optimisation of performance;

   (*c*) Learning the limitations of knowledge of functional areas for solving strategic problems.

   (*d*) Understanding different industries and companies;

   (*e*) Attitudes, values and ways of thinking of top management are such that they have a great impact on all processes and decision-making;

   (*f*) Understanding the best research and learning about the above subject.

5. **Skills:**

   (*a*) Sizing up the situation quickly and accurately, identifying core problems and issues, evaluating policy and strategy relevant to the environment, top management values, expectations, and financial position;

---

3. N. Osmond: "Top management Tasks, Roles and Skills" in Bernard Taylor and Keith Macmillan (eds.) Top Management, Longman, London, 1973; p. 84

(*b*) Analysing and identifying the opportunities and threats in the environment and the strengths and weaknesses of the company; preparing a situation audit required to formulating, evaluating and implementing business policies and strategies;

(*c*) Identifying policies and strategies which are quite appropriate to each situation and evaluating alternative courses of action;

(*d*) Recommending specific courses of action in regard to detailed strategy and plans changes in organisation, financial need, timing, labour and industrial relations;

(*e*) Sharpening analytical skills required in all the functional area like marketing and finance, in dealing with total company activities;

(*f*) Developing understanding of the use of tools and their main limitations; quantitative and qualitative tools must be understood in the proper manner; and

(*g*) Sharpening oral and written communication,

6. **Attitudes:**

(*a*) Strategic management must view the problems of top managers from the viewpoint of the "generalists". Instead of taking decisions based on one or more than one functional area, it must know how to use all disciplines and employ judgement where facts are not known;

(*b*) Decision-making must be pragmatic and result-oriented instead of waiting for "optimal results."

(*c*) Decision-making must be from the overall management point of view and not from the point of view of functional areas;

(*d*) Understanding the need for objectivity and professional management.

1.3. SIGNIFICANCE OF BUSINESS POLICY COURSE

Any field of study is significant in two ways. First for those who use the knowledge, skills and attitudes learnt from it, and second for the society. The first category consists of the top and middle level managers who participate in the strategic management process. Thus, business policy course is significant for the following:

1. **Top Management:** Top management of an organisation consists of chief executive, Board of Directors and other key strategists. They are responsible for the overall management of the organisation. They are expected to assess the environment, formulate corporate strategies, integrate, business level and functional strategies, mobilise and allocate resources, and evaluate and control overall performance. Business policy contributes to the effectiveness of top management in the following ways:

(*i*) Business policy course provides the knowledge, skills and attitudes which enable top managers to adopt the right approach to their functions. They can size up accurately and quickly the core issues involved in a problem.

(*ii*) Policy course equips top level managers to relate the organisation with its environment. They can learn how to exploit the opportunities and overcome the threats caused by environmental changes.

(*iii*) Top managers acquire the skills of integrating different sub-systems of the organisation. They learn to treat an organisation as an organic entity consisting of several sub-systems which interact with and influence one another.

(*iv*) Top executives can learn the criteria on the basis of which their effectiveness can be judged. Success in strategy formulation and implementation can be measured largely in qualitative terms.

2. **Middle Management:** At the middle level, managers are concerned with different functional areas such as manufacturing, marketing, finance and human resources. Business policy course is useful to them in the following ways:

(*i*) It enables functional heads to take a total view of the organisation and its relevant environment in the context of which they function. They can better relate the functioning of their respective departments with the corporate strategy.

(*ii*) Middle level managers can better approach the interdependence between different functions areas. Such understanding is helpful in integrating and coordinating the activities of different departments and units for achieving organisational effectiveness.

(*iii*) Managers at the middle level influence strategic decisions. They need to develop general management skills for making relevant proposals to the top management. Business policy course enables them to acquire such skills.

(*iv*) Policy course helps middle level managers to move to the top level. Departmental heads are busy in managing tangible tasks with clear priorities. But a chief executive has few clear priorities and sets the agenda. Middle level managers can inculcate the perspective of top level with the help of business policy course.

3. **Society:** Business policy course can contribute to the society in the following ways:

(*i*) Managers are vital organs of the society. They utilise the scarce resources of society. Business policy course enables them to make effective utilisation of resources and thereby better serve the needs of society.

(*ii*) A course in business policy helps in integrating different social interest groups. These interest groups are shareholders, employees, customers, government and so on. All of them have different aspirations, and put pressure on the organisation to seek maximum benefits. Business policy helps in optimising the satisfaction of these stakeholders.

(*iii*) Both stability and change are necessary for a happy society. It is necessary to integrate traditions and innovations to ensure continuity and progress in society. Business policy course can be useful in this task.

1.4. MEANING OF STRATEGIC MANAGEMENT

Some popular definitions of strategic management are given below:

Strategic management is defined as the set of decisions and actions resulting in formulation and implementation of strategies designed to achieve the objectives of an organisation.

—*Pearce and Robinson*

Strategic management is primarily concerned with relating the organisation to its environment formulating strategies to adapt to that environment, and assuring that implementation of strategies takes place.

—Steiner, Miner and Gray

Strategic management is that set of decisions and actions which leads to the development of an effective strategy, or strategies to help achieve corporate objectives.

—Glueck and Jauch

Strategic management is a systematic approach to a major and increasingly important responsibility of general management to position and relate the firm to its environment in a way which will assure its continued success and make it secure from surprises.

—H. Igor Ansoff

Strategic management is the formulation and implementation of plans and carrying out of activities relating to the matters which are of vital, pervasive, or continuing importance to the total organisation.

—A. Sharplin

Strategic management is the process which deals with fundamental organisational renewal and growth with the development of the strategies, structures and systems necessary to achieve such renewal and growth and with the organisational systems needed to effectively manage the strategy formulation and implementation processes.

—CA Hofer and others

Strategic management is the process through which organisations analyse and learn from their internal and external environments, establish strategic direction, create strategies that are intended to help achieve, established goals, and execute these strategies, all in an effort to satisfy key organisational stakeholders.

—Harrison and St. John

Strategic management is concerned with making decisions about organisation's future direction and implementing those decisions.

—Lloyd L. Byars

According to **Christensen, business policy** is "the study of the functions and responsibilities of top management, the crucial problems that affect success in the total enterprise and the decisions that determine the direction of the organisation and shape its future".

1.5. NATURE OF STRATEGIC MANAGEMENT

The main features of strategic management are as follows:

1. **A Process:** Strategic management is basically a process consisting of several activities which are performed in a systematic and sequential manner. This process is complex due to close interrelationships between different stages.

2. **Dynamic Rather than Static:** Strategic management is dynamic, continuous and flexible. Therefore, it must be considered as a whole. It is adaptive in nature as under it one keeps on asking "are we doing the right thing"? Strategic management is a continual and evolving process. It is not one time, static or mechanistic process.
3. **External Focus:** The focus of strategic management is on relating the organisation to its external environment. It involves determination of an organisation's future position.
4. **Open Systems Approach:** Strategic management emphasises that there is continuous interaction between an organisation and its environment. Therefore the organisation must adapt itself to its ever changing environment.
5. **Top Management Function:** Strategy formulation and its evaluation is primarily the responsibility of top management. Top managers must focus attention on strategic issues leaving operational management to middle and lower levels.
6. **Iterative Process:** Strategic management is not a rigid sequence of steps. Rather it is iterative because these steps may be performed in any order depending on the situation. Any stage in the strategic management process may be repeated over-time as per the demands of the situation
7. **Holistic:** Strategic management takes a totalistic or comprehensive view of the organisation. It is multidimensional or multifunctional. It is an integrated process that unifies inputs drawn from various functional areas. It is a cross functional process.
8. **Futuristic:** Strategic decisions are taken for future and are based on forecasts of future events. These decisions are made to improve the organisation's future positions in the industry and the society.
9. **Continuous:** Strategic management is an ongoing process of relating effectively the organisation's objectives and resources to opportunities in the environment. An organisation must modify its strategies and their implementation in accordance with changes in its external and internal environment.
10. **Analytical:** Strategic management is a sequential model that details out steps involved in it.
11. **Evolutionary:** Strategic management process is evolutionary.

1.6. BENEFITS OF STRATEGIC MANAGEMENT

Strategic Management can offer the following benefits:

1. **Financial Benefits:** Effective strategic management leads to better financial performance in terms of profits and growth. Research studies reveal that companies adopting strategic management out-performed those not adopting strategic management approach. Firms which adopt strategic management are able to realign their strategies to the needs of environment. They can take advantage of opportunities arising out of changes in the environment.

2. **Clarity in Objectives:** Strategic management focuses attention on organisational objectives and directs actions, towards those objectives. Once the objectives are clearly spelled out, people at all levels can move in the right action. Employees perform better when they know where the organisation is going and what they are expected to do. Strategies guide and direct action towards the goal and act as road map.

3. **Offsetting Uncertainty:** Strategic management involves forecasting the future and deciding the future course of action in the light of forecasting. During this process, an organisation acquires the capability to cope with future uncertainties. The organisation can successfully face the likely threats and reduce its risk by anticipating the future. Strategic management helps an organisation to be proactive in shaping its future.

4. **Minimum Resistance to Change:** Involvement of people at all levels in the process of strategy making increases acceptability of change. There is better awareness of the need for change and reasons behind changing the particular courses of action. This proactive approach facilitates innovation and changes.

5. **Improved Quality of Strategic Decisions:** Group interaction during the strategic management process facilitates generation and screening of strategic options. The best options are likely to be selected and acted upon.

6. **Prevention of Problems:** Environmental forecasting and strategic planning which are integral parts of strategic management enable an organisation to anticipate problems and take timely action and thereby prevent problems.

7. **Higher Employee Motivation:** Strategic management process helps to clarify roles thereby avoiding role ambiguity and role conflict. There is better understanding of priorities and operation of the reward system. The morale of employees improves and goal directed behaviour is likely to follow.

8. **Competitive Advantage:** Strategic management helps to improve the competitive position of the organisation. It enables the organisation to make optimum use of its competencies and resources and keeps it on the right track.

9. **Unifying Force:** Strategic management helps to unite and coordinate different parts of an organisation both horizontally and vertically.

10. **Resource Optimization:** Strategic management helps to ensure a rational allocation and use of resources.

11. **Criteria for Evaluation:** Strategic management clearly defines the desired level of performance. Actual performance can be judged in terms of critical success factors that are strategically important for the organisation.

12. **Public Image:** Companies which clearly know what they want to become and how enjoy the trust and confidence of their stakeholders.

Thus, strategic management helps to increase organisational effectiveness and thereby ensures the survival and growth of the organisation.

1.7. LIMITATIONS OF STRATEGIC MANAGEMENT

Strategic management suffers from the following limitations.

1. **Lack of Appreciation:** Managers often lack the mindset required for effective strategic management. They fail to isolate strategic issues. Their thinking about strategy is ambiguous and confused. Some executives focus attention on operating problems and short term achievements. A future oriented thinking can be developed only when managers properly understand the concept and role of strategic management.
2. **Complex and Dynamic Environment:** It is becoming more and more difficult to forecast due to increasing complexity and accelerating rate of change. In the absence of reasonably accurate forecasts, strategy formulation becomes difficult. However, the practical problem in the way of strategic management makes it all the more significant. Strategic management is as good as the information on which it is based.
3. **Rigidity:** Strategies are chosen and implemented in a given set of internal and external environment. Over-time people become accustomed to strategic plans. When changes in the environment require a change in strategy, internal inflexibilities relating to people and procedures serve as constraints.

   An open systems approach to strategic management can build flexibility in the system and thereby overcome this problem. This approach involves continuous adjustment in strategies on the basis of changes in the external and internal environment. A dynamic equilibrium is suggested between strategic direction on the one hand and the organisation's environment and capabilities on the other hand.
4. **Lack of Accuracy:** Strategic management is based on forecasts of future environment. It is very difficult to forecast distant future accurately. Greater is the error in forecasting, greater are the shortcomings in strategy formulation.
5. **Time Consuming:** Strategic management is lengthy and time consuming process. Comprehensive strategic planning requires considerable time, effort and cost.
6. **Problems in Implementation:** Strategy implementation is a complex process wherein several internal and external problems arise. The meaning and scope of the corporate strategy is not the same throughout the organisation. These are conflicts among different groups, divisions and departments of an organisation over goals, values and courses of action to be pursued. Strategic management is not a substitute for action.

   Thus, strategic management is not the pannacea for all problems of an organisation. But just as medicine is necessary to cure a patient despite its side effects, similarly strategic management is useful in spite of its limitations.

1.8. CONCEPTS OF STRATEGY, POLICY AND TACTICS

Strategy: The concept of strategy lies at the heart of the strategic management process. The term 'strategy' has been derived from the Greek Word *'strategos'* which means generalship, *i.e.,* the art of the army general. In management, however, the term 'strategy' has been defined differently by different writers. Some of the popular definitions of strategy are given below:

"Strategy is the determination of the basic long-term goals and objectives of an enterprise and the adoption of the course of action and the allocation of resources necessary for carrying out these goals".

—Alfred D. Chandler[4]

"A strategy is a unified, comprehensive, and integrated plan relating the strategic advantages of the firm to challenges of the environment. It is designed to ensure that the basic objectives of the enterprise are achieved".

— William F. Glueck[5]

"Strategy is the pattern of objectives, purposes or goals and major policies or plans for achieving these goals, stated in such a way as to define, what business the company is in or is to be in and the kind of business it is or is to be—"

—Learned 1969

"Corporate strategy is the pattern of decisions in a company that determines and reveals its objectives, purposes, or goals, produces the principal policies, and plans for achieving those goals, and defines the range of business the company is to pursue, the kind of economic and human organisation it tends to be and the nature of economic and non-economic contribution it tends to make to its shareholders, customers and communities".

—Kenneth Andrews, 1971

Igor Ansoff (1965) in his book *Corporate Strategy* has defined strategy as, 'The common thread among the organisation' activities and product markets that defines the essential nature of business that an organisation was or plans to be in future.

"Strategy is the creation of a unique and value position involving a different set of activities and, thus, a company that is strategically positioned performs different set of activities from its rivals or performs similar activities in different ways".

—Micheal A. Porter[6]

An analysis of these definitions reveals the following features of strategy:

(*i*) Strategy is a long-term plan through which an organisation seeks to achieve its objectives.

(*ii*) Strategy relates an organisation to its external and internal environment. It is the mediating force between an organisation and the world outside it.

(*iii*) Strategy serves as a common thread, a unifying force among different parts of an organisation.

(*iv*) Strategy is designed to move an organisation from its current position to the desired future position. Without a strategy, an organisation is like a ship without a rudder going around in circles.

(*v*) Strategy is forward looking. It defines in broad terms the actions which an organisation proposes to take in future.

(*vi*) Strategy requires acquisition, allocation and deployment of resources.

(*vii*) Strategy making involves significant risk and has a major impact on the organisation.

Policy vs. Strategy: A policy is a guideline for thinking and decision-making. It indicates the action to be taken in a contingent event of repetitive nature. For example, an organisation

---

4 Strategy and Structure MIT Press: Cambridge Mass, 1962, p. 13.

5 Business Policy and Strategic Management, McGrawHill: New York, 1980, p. 9.

6 "What is Strategy"?, Harvard Business Review, November-December, 1996, pp. 61-78.

may formulate a policy to promote employees on the basis of their performance. This acts as a standing guidelines for those who make promotion decisions.

There are several differences between policy and strategy:

(*i*) A policy is a guideline to the thinking and action of decision-makers while strategy provides the direction in which the organisation's resources are to be deployed and applied.

(*ii*) Policy is a contingent decision-whereas strategy is a rule for making-decision.

(*iii*) Policy decisions are taken under more precise conditions. Strategic decisions are made under the conditions where all the facts are not known.

(*iv*) Policy decisions can be delegated. In fact policy is implemented through subordinate managers. But strategy cannot be delegated downward because it requires last minute executive decisions. For example, whether or not to acquire a firm is a strategic decision.

(*v*) Strategy involves strategic decisions (why) while policy is concerned with routine matters (how).

Tactics *vs.* Strategy: Both strategies and tactics are concerned with formulation and implementation of courses of action to achieve certain objectives. The two however, differ in terms of their dimensions. These differences are as follows:

(*i*) Time Horizon: Strategy has a long-term perspective while the time horizon of tactics is short-term. The duration of strategy is flexible, whereas that of tactics is definite and uniform. Strategy is timed before action but tactics is timed during action.

(*ii*) Scope: Strategy is broad and general, on the other hand, tactic is narrowly focussed.

(*iii*) Objective: Strategy is designed to achieve grand objective but the objective sought in a tactic is limited. In other words, a strategy provides general and ongoing guidance whereas the guidance offered by tactics is specific and situational.

(*iv*) Formulation: Strategy formulation is an ongoing and irregular process. The process is continuous but the timing of strategic decision is irregular depending on the appearance of opportunity or crisis. Tactics follow a fixed and regular schedule. For example, budgets are prepared at regular intervals.

(*v*) Level of Decision Making: Strategic decisions are made at the top and divisional levels of management: On the other hand, tactical decisions are usually taken at lower or operating levels of management.

(*vi*) Degree of Uncertainty: Strategy formulation involves a higher degree of uncertainty because strategic decisions are taken under the conditions of partial ignorance. Element of uncertainty is low in tactical decisions which are taken within the framework of strategy.

(*vii*) Orientation: Strategy has an external or outside orientation as it attempts to link the organisation with its environment. On the other hand, tactics have an internal or inside orientation.

(*viii*) **Focus:** Strategy is focussed on the deployment of resources, whereas the focus of tactics is on the employment of resources.

(*ix*) **Significance:** Strategies determine the direction and future of an organisation. Tactics are less important as these have short-term and minor impact on the organisation.

(*x*) **Determinants:** Subjective factors such as the personal values of strategy makers influence strategy formulation. Tactics are relatively free from such factors because these are decided within the context of a strategy.

(*xi*) **Nature of Problems:** Strategic problems are usually unstructured while tactical problems are more structured.

(*xii*) **Information Needs:** Strategy formulation requires large amounts of information while tactics require less information.

(*xiii*) **Point of View:** Strategies are formulated from corporate viewpoint, whereas tactics are made from functional viewpoint.

Despite these differences, the lines of demarcation between strategy and tactics are blurred in practice. The plans considered as tactical at higher levels may be strategic at lower levels.

1.9. LEVELS OF STRATEGY

Strategy operates at three main levels

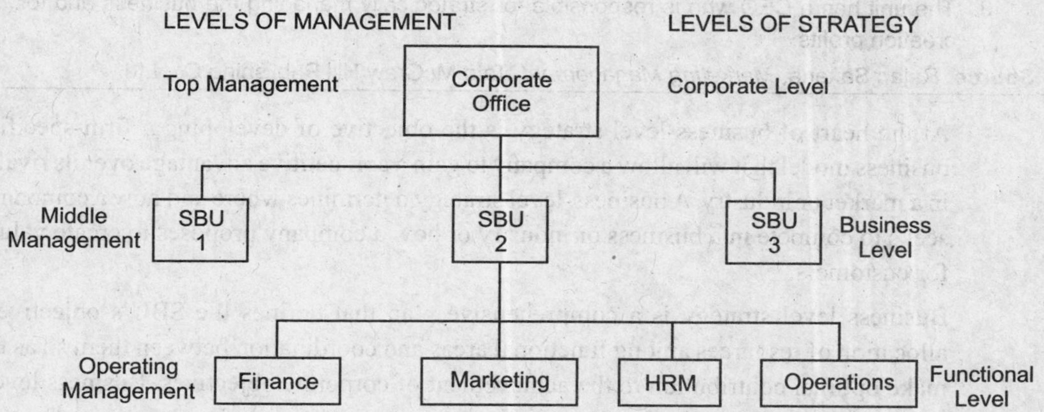

Fig. 1.1 Different Levels of Strategy

1. **Corporate Level Strategy:** Corporate or grand strategy is an overall plan of action concerned with the objectives of the organisation, acquisition and allocation of resources and coordination of strategic business units (SBUs) for optimal performance. Decisions relating to corporate strategy trend to be conceptual and value-oriented. These are taken at the top level of management. Diversification into new areas of business is an example of corporate strategy. Corporate level strategy is concerned with an organisation's reach (scope of activities), competition areas, management practices, synergy between activities and stakeholder value.

2. **Business Level Strategy:** In a single product company, the corporate level strategy serves the whole business and this strategy is implemented through functional strategies. Hero Motor Corp is a manufacture and seller of motorcycles and is, therefore, a single product company. A single strategy is neither adequate nor appropriate for multi-product line companies. ITC is a diversified company that operates in several businesses like tobacco products, hotels, paper, food, readymade garments, etc. These different businesses are organised as different divisions known as strategic business units or profit centres.

   A SBU is "any part of a business organisation which is treated separetely for strategic management purpose". Each SBU has a clearly defined product/market segment and has its own strategy. Physical and human resources are allocated to each SBU according to its needs and contribution to the achievement of overall objectives of the organisation.

Table 1.2: Characteristics of SBUs

For a product or service to be classified as a SBU, it is necessary that it must have following characteristics.

1. It can be a single business or collection of the related businesses (backward or forward integrated) which can be planned for profits and activities, independent of the rest of the company.
2. It has its own group of competitors competing with the business.
3. The unit has a CEO who is responsible for strategically managing the business and for creation profits.

Source: Rajan Saxena, *Marketing Management,* Tata McGraw Hill Publishing Co. Ltd.

   At the heart of business-level strategy is the objective of developing a firm-specific business model that will allow a company to gain a competitive advantage over its rivals in a market or industry. A business-level strategy determines where and how a company seeks to compete in a business or industry or how a company proposes to create value for customers.

   Business level strategy is a comprehensive plan that defines the SBU's objectives allocation of resources among functional areas and coordination between them so as to make optimal contribution to the achievement of corporate objectives. Business level strategies operate within the framework of corporate strategy. The business strategy of each SBU is designed to make the best use of its resources within the environment faced by it.

3. **Functional Level Strategy:** A functional strategy relates to a single functional area and the activities involved therein. It is a restricted plan providing objectives for a specific function, allocation of resources among different activities within that functional area and coordination between them for optimal contribution to the achievement of the SBU and corporate level objectives.

In addition to the three levels of strategy given above, companies may have strategies at social and operating levels. A **societal strategy** is above the corporate level and provides a broad view of how the company relates itself to the society. It serves as the basis for corporate level strategy. For example, the societal strategy of a corporation may decide to provide alternative sources of energy to the society at reasonable cost. On the basis of this societal strategy, the corporation may choose between nuclear every, solar energy and windmill energy. Societal strategies are reflected in the vision and mission statements.

Strategy is also used at operating level which is below the functional level. Each functional area may require a number of operational strategies. For example, the marketing strategy may be subdivided into product, pricing, distribution and promotion strategies. Functional and operating level strategies are concerned with the implementation of corporate and business level strategies.

A comparative view of strategies at three levels is given in Table 1.3.

Table 1.3: Characteristics of Strategy at Three Levels

Dimensions	Corporate Level	Business Level	Functional Level
1. Type of decision	Conceptual	Analytical	Operational
2. Time horizon	Long-term	Medium-term	Short-term
3. Degree of risk	High	Medium	Low
4. Impact	Critical	Major	Minor
5. Flexibility	High	Medium	Low
6. Profit potential	High	Medium	Low
7. Adaptability	Low	Medium	High

The strategy adoped by Tata Motors to promote Nano was badly flawed. A series of factors has impacted the Nano, right from the Singur issue to cars catching fire to clumsy marketing strategy. There was a bit of overconfidence at the start and not much marketing push from the company. The hype fizzled out even before Tata Motors could effectively roll out sizeable (number of) cars on the road.

Somehow it got slotted as a ₹ 1 lakh car or a cheap car Tata Motors did not intend to position it like that, but they did not do enough to manage perceptions.

The value engineering and innovation was brilliant. But it was never quite clear who the car was for. Was it to replace a two-wheeler for commuting, was it a second car for an affluent family or an aspirational first car for a 30 years old, or was it for all of these people?

Nano became a victim of its own hype. The marketing pitch is now aimed at breaking that image and giving the brand a more emotive personality as a mobility solution, a smart city car. The Nano Awesomeness ad campaign is a step in that direction.

Shree Cement Outpaces Rivals with Contrarian Strategy

"We bet on the low business cycle and were confident that demand would pick up—our strategy worked," says Bangur.

The company's strategy to augment capacity when demand is low and benefit when it picks up worked well, especially during the slowdown. In the past three years, when revenues of most large cement companies registered a compounded annual growth rate in the range of 3-24%, Shree Cement's sales grew at a compounded annual growth rate of 26%, indicating the benefit of timely expansion.

"We want to maintain cost-efficiency as our distinguishing factor from other cement companies, and want to maintain high productivity so that the cost of production of cement comes down,". — *Hari Mohan Bangur, MD Shree Cement*

1.10. CONCEPT OF STRATEGIC PLANNING

Strategic Planning is designed to find answers to three basic questions:

(*i*) Where are we now?

(*ii*) Where do we wish to reach and when?

(*iii*) How do we get from here to there?

In business, the term 'strategic planning' is used to refer to the process of deciding the objectives of the organisation as a whole, formulating strategies to achieve them and allocating resources to executive the strategies.

According to *Robert N. Anthony,* "Strategic planning is the process of deciding on objectives of the organisation, on changes in these objectives, on the resources used to attain these objectives and on the policies that are to govern the acquisition, use and disposition of these resources." These plans are made considering the impact of the prevailing external environment.

In the words of *Peter Drucker,* "Strategic, planning is the continuous process of making present entrepreneurial (risk taking) decisions systematically and with the greatest Knowledge of their futurity, organising systematically the efforts needed to carry out these decisions, measuring the results of these decisions against expectations through organised, systematic feedback".

In the context of social responsibility, strategic planning involves selecting and executing CSR strategy.

1.11. FEATURES OF STRATEGIC PLANNING

The definitions given above reveal the following characteristics of strategic planning:

(*i*) Strategic planning is planning for the company as a whole. Its focus is on defining and achieving the basic mission and overall goals of the organisation. It is comprehensive in nature.

(*ii*) Strategic planning is largely the responsibility of the top management. However, it is based on inputs received from all levels of management.

(*iii*) Strategic planning is mainly long-term in nature. However, it is different from long range planning as it considers changes in the environment, whereas long range planning builds on current goals and policies.

(*iv*) Strategic planning provides a framework for operational planning and day to day decision-making. It builds coherence in the organisation's goals, policies and programmes. A strategy ties all the parts of the organisation together.

(*v*) Strategic planning involves choice among the broad directions in which an organisation seeks to move.

(*vi*) Strategic planning relates the organisation to its external environment.

1.12. THE PROCESS OF STRATEGIC PLANNING

The strategic planning process can be divided into the following stages:

1. **Defining the Mission:** First of all the mission statement is prepared. It describes what the organisation wants to become and why it will exist? It states the company's preferred future to ensure clarity and consistency of purpose.

2. **SWOT Analysis:** At this stage, the strengths (S), Weaknesses (W), opportunities (O), and Threats (T) of the organisation are identified. Strengths are the inherent capabilities whereas weaknesses are the incapabilities. Strengths and weaknesses are identified by analysing the company's internal environment. Opportunities (O) are the favourable trends whereas Threats (T) are the unfavourable trends in the environment. Opportunities and threats are identified by analysing the external environment. SWOT analysis or strategic analysis is an indepth and systematic investigation.

Table 1.4: A Specimen of SWOT

Strengths	Opportunities
• Cutting edge technology	• Growing demand
• Large amount of funds	• Liberal Government policies
• Well trained and an experienced workforce	• Global customers
Weaknesses	**Threats**
• Rising attrition of labour	• Increasing competition
• Low level of motivation and morale	• Risks in global markets
	• Rising costs of inputs

3. **Identifying Strategic Alternatives:** In this phase, the alternative strategies that are available to exploit opportunities and overcome threats are identified. The key strategic areas and their priorities are decided.

4. **Choice of Strategy:** Various strategic alternatives are evaluated and compared in terms of cost, degree of risk and other relevant criteria. The alternative that is most appropriate for the organisation is selected.

5. **Implementation and Follow Up:** The strategy selected is executed. It involves developing action plans, allocating resources and executing the action plans.

1.13. STRATEGIC PLANNING VS. STRATEGIC MANAGEMENT

According to Pfeiffer, "strategic planning is the process by which the guiding members of an organisation envision its future and develop the necessary procedures and operations to achieve that future"[7] In the words of George Stainer (1979), " strategic planning is about fundamental decisions and actions on choices that must be made but it does not attempt to make future decisions".

Table 1.5: Some Principles for Strategic Planning

- Strategic planning is a line management function for which training in strategic analysis and participative skills is usually necessary.
- Strategic business units need to be defined so that one executive can control the key variables essential to the execution of his or her strategic business plan.
- A unit's concept of the business it is in must above all be formulated from the outside in so that it can most effectively engage the dynamics of its strategic environment.
- Action plans for achieving business objectives are the key to implementing and monitoring strategy. They require extensive lower-level participation and special leadership skills. Action plans are complete when underlying assumptions, allocation of responsibilities, time and resource requirements, risks, and likely responses have been made explicit.
- Participative strategy development, a prerequisite for successful strategy execution, often requires cultural change at the upper levels of corporations and their business units.
- The strategic planning system and other control systems designed to guide managerial and organisation behaviour must be integrated in a consistent whole if business strategies are to be executed well.
- Productivity improvement programmes are best treated as aspects of strategic business plans since productivity takes on significantly different meanings as the strategic balance between marketing and production shifts.
- Well-managed organisations must be both centralised and decentralised—centralised so that strategies and control systems can be integrated and decentralised so that units in each strategic environment can act and be treated with appropriate differentiation.
- Over-time, good strategic planning, one considered a separate activity, becomes a mindset, a style and a set of techniques for running a business—not something more to do but a better way of doing what has always had to be done.

Source: Daniel H. Gray, "Uses and Misuses of Strategic Planning, *Harvard Business Review,* Jan-Feb. 1986.

Strategic planning needs to be differentiated from strategic management. Strategic planning is narrower in scope than strategic management. The former is simply the process of formulating a long-term and comprehensive plan. On the other hand, strategic management involves formulation, implementation and evaluation of strategies. Unlike, strategic management, strategic planning is not a substitute for executive judgement. Strategic planning involves systems thinking, whereas strategic management involves strategic thinking.

---

7 William J. Pfeiffer, Applied Strategic Planning, Mcgraw Hill, New York, 1993.

Table 1.6: Difference between Strategic Planning and Strategic Management

Basis of Distinction	Strategic Planning	Strategic Management
1. Nature of the process	Strategic planning is a planning process	Strategic management is a management process
2. Flexibility	Disciplined and rigid	Disciplined and flexible
3. Type of thinking	Systems thinking	Strategic thinking
4. Focus	On the plan	On the people

Table 1.7: Distinction between Strategic Planning and Operational Planning

Basis of Distinction	Strategic Planning	Operational Planning
1. Focus	Goals	Tasks
2. Time Horizon	Long-term	Short-term
3. Level of Management	Top level	Operating level
4. Orientation	External	Internal
5. Resources	Future resources	Existing resources

SUMMARY

Evolution: (*i*) Beginning in 1911 at Harvard Business School (*ii*) Adhoc policy (till mid 1930s) (*iii*) planned policy (1930s – 1940s) (*iv*) Strategy (1940s – 1960s) (*v*) strategic management (1980s).

Objectives: (*i*) Knowledge (*ii*) Skills (*iii*) Attitudes.

Significance: (*i*) Top management (*ii*) Middle management (*iii*) Society.

Meaning of Strategic Management: The process of formulating, implementing and controlling strategies so as to achieve the strategic intent of an organisation.

Nature: (*i*) Process (*ii*) Dynamic (*iii*) External focus (*iv*) Open systems approach (*v*) Top level function (*vi*) Integrative process.

Benefits: (*i*) Financial gain (*ii*) Clarity of objectives (*iii*) Offsetting uncertainty (*iv*) Better strategic decisions (*v*) Problem prevention (*vi*) Employee motivation (*vii*) Competitive advantage (*viii*) Unifying force.

Limitations: (*i*) Lack of appreciation (*ii*) Complex and dynamic environment (*iii*) Rigidity (*iv*) Problems in implementation.

Strategy, Policy and Tactics: (*i*) Strategy is a unified and comprehensive plan designed to achieve the objectives (*ii*) Policy is a guideline for thinking and decision making (*iii*) Tactics are courses of action meant for implementation of strategy.

Levels of strategy: Corporate, business and functional levels.

Strategic Planning *Vs.* Strategic Management: The latter is a wider term consisting of the former.

TEST QUESTIONS

1. Trace the evolution of business policy and strategic management as a field of study.
2. Explain the objectives of business policy/strategic management course in terms of knowledge, skills and attitudes.
3. How is a course in business policy or strategic management significant for management and society? Explain.
4. Discuss the meaning and nature of business policy/strategic management.
5. What is strategic management? Discuss its benefits and limitations keeping in view the dynamic character of modern business.
6. Define strategic management and discuss its scope. Do you think that the scope of strategic management keeps on changing due to dynamic nature of modern business?
7. Differentiate clearly between strategy, policy and tactics with suitable examples.
8. Explain different levels of strategy, pointing out their characteristics.
9. What is strategic planning? How does it differ from strategic management?
10. Describe the different levels at which strategy operates and discuss the issues that are relevant for strategic decision-making.
11. How does a course in business policy/strategic management help in understanding an organisation and the environment in which it operates? Explain.
12. Business Policy course is supposed to integrate the knowledge of different functional areas of management and to develop certain skills and attitudes to make long-term strategic decisions. Bring out the scope and utility of the business policy course in the light of the above statement.
13. Define 'Business Policy'. What are the basic inputs required in making and implementing business policy decisions?
14. Does strategy only connote 'the way in which the ends are to be achieved'? Discuss. What, if any, is the alternative interpretation?
15. What are the basic elements of scope of a company? How does it help a company to identify its strategy? What is your opinion in the scope of Hindustan Computers Limited and Hindustan Unilever Limited?
16. Discuss the advantages of business games as a pedagogical tool over the case method in the field of strategic management. Demonstrate three major shortcomings of any such business game.
17. Describe the four paradigm shifts in the historical evolution of strategic management.
18. "A strategy is an action that managers in a firm take to achieve superior performance relative to rivals." Elucidate the above statement and bring out the important elements of a strategy.
19. "The strategy of a corporation is intended to maximise its competitive advantage". Explain this statement with suitable examples.

20. Do you agree with the view that strategy is the pattern of an organisation's response to its environment over a period of time? Give reasons for your answer.
21. Define 'corporate planning'. How will you distinguish between 'strategic planning' and 'operational planning'? Why is the need for coordination between strategic planning and operational planning?
22. Define strategic management. Why has strategic management become so important in today's corporations?
23. Define strategy and describe the various levels at which strategy operates.
24. "The purpose of strategy is to define the nature of relationship between a firm and its environment". Comment.
25. "In essence, strategy determines what an organisation will be, and how the organisation will reach that state of being" Elucidate.
26. "Strategic planning is a necessary but not sufficient condition for success of an enterprise". Do you agree Give reasons.
27. "Business policy is the study of the functions and responsibilities of senior management concerning the crucial problems that determine the direction of the total enterprise and shape its future". Explain.
28. "Business policy formulation must be a dynamic process". Explain.
29. "Strategic decisions are primarily concerned with external rather than internal problems". Discuss the nature of strategy making in the light of this statement.
30. Describe strategic management process model and explain each element of the model Consider a company of your choice in the automobile sector and discuss the strategic management process.
31. "Strategic management process should be viewed as a dynamic, continuous and flexible". Comment.
32. Mintzberg provides five dimensions of strategy. Explain his approach to strategy by giving suitable examples.
33. "Strategy is partly proactive and partly reactive". Do you agree? Give reasons.
34. "Environmental analysis cannot be complete without diagnosis of the results of analysis" Discuss.
35. "To what extent and how effectively diagnosis of environment is carried out depend upon the strategists and the environment". Explain.
36. A new company is proposed to be for the production and sale of household kitchen appliances. What are the environmental conditions which the company should consider and why.
37. Explain how would you use strategic groups maps to assess the market positions of key competitors?
38. How would you determine the degree of competitive pressures from sellers of substitute products? Explain.
39. In what ways can supplier bargaining power create competitive pressures?

CASE STUDY

Sometime in 2009, Raymond Apparel, a wholly-owned subsidiary of Raymond Limited, decided to slim down its brand portfolio. The first to come under the axe was Notting Hill, an economy apparel brand which was removed from shelves in metros and large cities, and was confined to Raymond stores in tier 4 and 5 towns. Next in line was children's wear brand Zapp which was pulled out in 2010, after a brief stint of four years in the market. The women and children's line of the casual fashion brand ColorPlus were removed recently.

The downsizing of its portfolio leaves the company with five brands — Raymond Premium Apparel, Park Avenue, Parx, Manzoni and ColorPlus (acquired in 2003 and operates as a separate company) – in its stable. Going forward, the company will concentrate on its thoroughbreds (Park Avenue, Parx and Color Plus), which clocked a combined revenue of ₹ 460 crore of total branded apparel revenue ₹ 550 crore in 2009-10.

To bring fresh energy into the 26 years old Park Avenue, the company has unveiled a new logo, with a modern typeface. Along with the logo change, it has unveiled a new-range (casual wear for the work–place) to add to the existing four (business, travel, leisure and evening) the brand currently offers. "The thrust will also be on the recently introduced Raymond Premium Apparel brand, the ready-to-wear extension of the textile business," says Shreyas Joshi, president, Raymond Apparel. Manzoni and Notting Hill will continue their life as niche brands.

The intent is clear: the company wants to divest unproductive ventures and focus on the core brands that are most profitable to the company. At the close of the financial year, the company hopes to notch up a 30 per cent growth over the previous year for its apparel business.

Analysts say the company's optimism isn't misplaced. Says Abhishek Ranganathan, analyst with MF Global Sify Securities, "Raymond has rationalised its business by exiting businesses that were not profitable. Now it is able to focus better. An improved retail network has increased visibility and improved sales. Its brands have also benefited from an uptake in consumer spending."

But why exit ventures that it entered with much fanfare? Did the company give its new product lines a fair chance?

Mind you, when Raymond entered the children and women's wear segments it knew pretty well it was getting into unfamiliar territory. Children's wear by itself is a tricky segment. The market is largely unorganised. Children outgrow their clothes quickly, making customers price sensitive. "The price points where Zapp operated didn't appeal consumers much. Given that margin in the children's wear business is low, being profitable is a big challenge.

With Notting Hill, the problem was achieving economies of scale. "Notting Hills, being an economy player, could not be stocked in all Raymond Shops in the metros because they have a premium image. Achieving scale through large retailers was not a viable solution because all these players have their private labels which they tend to push harder for obvious reasons. In Raymond stores in tier 4 and 5 cities, Notting Hill would still work as an 'aspirational brand' for customers accustomed to getting their clothes stitched to order.

Joshi acknowledges, "We decided to tap newer segments like women and children's wear, but realised we would be more successful if we achieved scale in what has been our forte — men's wear."

Of course, ready-to-wear men's clothing is big business. According to Cygnus Business Consulting and Research, while men's wear makes up 61 per cent of the overall branded ready-to-wear market (₹ 39,000 crore), women's wear and children's wear constitute 30 per cent and 9 per cent respectively. Branded ready-to-wear is only 25 per cent of the total apparel market. The market is growing at 10-15 per cent year-on-year, but competition is stiff with brands like Louis Philippe, Allen Solly, Peter England, Van Heusen (from Madura Fashion & Lifestyle), Arrow (from Arvind Brands) and Reid & Taylor, Belmonte (from S. Kumars) straddling different segments and price points. Retailer labels and lately international fashion labels such as Zara have joined the battle for space in the consumers' wardrobe.

With the product line rationalised, Joshi says the company has identified four clear segments for its brands. Park Avenue is positioned as a formal wear brand for men, with a range or women too. ColorPlus occupies the premium smart casual' space with offerings like trousers, shirts and knits, and Parx is positioned as the 'beyond work' brand with a young attitude and the product mix consists of t-shirts, trousers and jackets. And Raymond Premium Apparel, offering suits, trousers and shirts, will be an all occasion brand. The company will focus on three key areas to drive the unique appeal of each of its brands — product mix, retail experience and communication. As Joshi explains, "A white shirt irrespective of brand is a white shirt. What clearly makes the difference is the imagery in the mind of the consumer. This is driven by a mnemonic or logo, style and fit or the experience at the time of buying the product."

Product Focus

The three-pronged strategy is underway across its entire portfolio. For instance, Park Avenue is focusing on product design. "We study how body structures are evolving, lifestyles are changing. Earlier in formal wear shirts, the traditional colours were blue, white and cream; however, four years back, we introduced fashion colours (aqua green and blue, pink and purple) which met with fantastic results." Similarly, in suits, Park Avenue introduced slim fit and super slim fit suits. Other innovations done by the brand include non-iron and wrinkle-free shirts. Park Avenue will also introduce 'limited edition' products starting this season.

Joshi feels that the brand ColorPlus has very strong equity and has single-handedly built the smart casual category in India. He points out, "The brand differentiates itself through the unique mix of colours. We took the lead in introducing innovative washes and fabrics." The company toyed with the ColorPlus women's line briefly but decided women's wear is not really its cup of tea.

So why add women's wear to the Park Avenue brand? "In the casual space, the competition is much higher," says Joshi. "The dressing habit of Indian women in the formal wear space is slowly evolving. Women are looking for alternatives beyond kurta pyjama and saris. In casual wear, women continue to wear jeans, rather than trousers and shirts."

The company is betting its shirts on Raymond Premium Apparel, the newest brand in the portfolio. "With this brand we wish to capitalise on the strength of the Raymond brand, and its huge recall. It will help us move up the value chain," says Joshi. Manzoni will continue to operate as the bridge to the luxury space. "People look for maximum value at any price point. With Manzoni, our offerings are 25-30 per cent cheaper than any luxury brand," says Joshi. The difference between a Manzoni suit and a Raymond suit will be in the nature of the fabric. "For Manzoni, we source fabrics from all over the world. The fit and style also vary. I can't have a super slim fit at a Manzoni store, it would fail miserably as I don't have that type of consumer base walking in," adds Joshi. While rivals argue Raymond tends to slip on design, Joshi claims each of the company's brands has its own design team. "Our designers regularly visit fashion fairs in Italy to learn about fashion trends. We subscribe to a digital portal which does fashion trend forecasting," says Joshi.

Beyond the macro fashion trends, the preferences of consumers who visit the store are tracked extensively. "Through our point-of-sale systems, we track the sizes and colours that sell. In India, the tastes and preferences are quite unique and we also keep that in mind when launching the colour palette for a particular season.

Retail Push

Product is only one aspect, the other is retail. Rivals say the real strength of Raymond is its widespread distribution network. The company, with its legacy in the textile business, flaunts 560 Raymond Shops across the country — the largest for any branded apparel manufacturer. By end March, the company hopes to add 100 more stores. That's over and above its presence in multi branded outlets and department stores.

To reduce dependence on what the company calls its crown jewels (Raymond Shops), which now account for more than 50 per cent of overall sales, Raymond is keen to move more merchandise through exclusive stores to gain tighter control of its brands. Park Avenue with 16 exclusive brand outlets, hopes to reach 30 this year. Parx aims to reach 20, from its current 14. ColorPlus will continue to operate through 74 exclusive stores.

Observers say that there is another aspect that needs attention: the retail experience. Raymond needs to build a complete retail eco-system around its brands focusing on all aspects — from retail identity to visual display and staff training.

Joshi is only too aware and believes the company is taking concrete steps in this direction. For instance, the company will unveil a new retail design in August for Park Avenue and Parx, for ColorPlus it plans to have in-store demos where consumers can touch and feel the product. "The new retail concept for the Raymond Shop unveiled two years back has personalised sections for each brand," says Joshi. Raymond is also investing in pure retail initiatives such as Neckties and More and Made to Measure. Neckties and More, stocking accessories from all brands, are 100-200 square feet stores in malls and airports (Mumbai and Hyderabad) to tap impulse buying. "This model is also being extended to shop-in-shops and currently exists in 30 locations," says Joshi. This concept will be extended to Shirts and More in the future, which will be small format stores stocking shirts from all four brands.

The retail initiative is part of its larger brand building effort. The company spent 8 per cent of its turnover last year on advertising. The spend will be the same but the mix will be different this year. Traditionally, Park Avenue and Parx have used the print and outdoor media in a big way. Going forward, the focus will be on the electronic media. "For these two brands we will have models, as before, to carry off our brands, while for ColorPlus, we will focus on showcasing the product in all our communication; that has been our unique advertising style."

To improve appeal among younger consumers, Park Avenue is using Facebook which has 20,000 members and allows designers to 'interact with consumers. Going forward, Parx and ColorPlus will also focus on building communities around their brand.

Indeed, industry experts say Raymond needs to work more than ever before to build stronger identities for its brands. The Raymond textile brand which commands a strong brand equity was built at a time when competition was as good as absent. For apparel brands this is not the case. "The brand needs to create desire in consumers to buy the brand or consumer pull rather than depend on sales push," says an industry expert who wishes to stay anonymous.

Many of Raymond's peers are banking on 'imagery' to score points with younger audiences. If you notice, Raymond's communication also shows a lot of older people. "The Louis Philippe brand, for example, has built an aura of power and authority around it; Van Heusen is for the upwardly mobile executive who is successful; Allen Solly is for the unconventional person while the Arrow man wants to be impeccably dressed. What is the mindset of the Raymond brands?" asks Prateek Srivastava, group president (south) O & M.

That may not be too difficult — Raymond has 'heritage' on its side. Starting from the "You don't have to be a Raymonds' man… but it helps" campaign (which featured 'offbeat' celebrities like Vishwanathan Anand and Geet Sethi) to a culmination in "The Complete Man", the advertising for the brand has evolved brilliantly over the past couple of decades. And everyone acknowledges its then advertising agency Enterprise has played a huge role in building the brand.

What it will have to work on is segmenting its offerings on more concrete values, says a Delhi—based brand consultant. "When a consumer walks into a Raymond Shop which offers Raymond Premium Apparel shirts as well as Park Avenue shirts, how does one differentiate? It appears as though both brands are chasing the same segment:" he says. ColorPlus, which has a unique aspirational appeal, should stick to its knitting, he says. "The brand has experimented too much. They introduced product lines targeted at women and children, but that did not go down well with the consumer, forcing them to go back to their core lines."

Manzoni is in need of a vibrant, trendsetter image. "Consumers would rather spend a little extra on a Hugo Boss or Canali suit that have very strong aspirational appeal," notes Rao of Cygnus Business Consulting. "In the premium segment, it is not a value for money game," he adds. At the end of the day, it's all about desirability.

After all, in an increasingly competitive apparel space, it is not just the product but the branding and experience that will do the trick.

Questions

1. Why did Raymonds exit ventures that it entered with much fan fare?
2. Did the company give its new product lines a fair chance?
3. Point out any flawes in the company's strategy.
4. Suggest changes that you think should be made in Raymond's strategy.

2

CHAPTER STRATEGIC MANAGEMENT PROCESS

CHAPTER OUTLINE

2.1. Strategic Decision-Making
2.2. Approaches to Strategic Decision-Making (Modes of Strategy Making)
2.3. Schools of Thought of Strategy Formation
2.4. Process and Model of Strategic Management
2.5. Participants in Strategic Management
- Summary
- Test Questions
- Case Study

Decision-making is the task of every manager. But strategic decision-making is largely the responsibility of top management.

2.1. STRATEGIC DECISION-MAKING

Strategic decision-making is the core of strategic management. It influences the entire organization and has long-term implications. It involves commitment of large amount of resources. Take over of Corus Steel by Tata Steel, ITC's entry into food products, decision of Tata Motors to launch Nano car are examples of strategic decisions. Where are we now? Where we want to be? How can we get there from here? are examples of strategic decisions.

Table 2.1: The Characteristics of Strategic Decisions

Strategic decisions are concerned with:
• The scope of an organisation's activities. • The matching of an organisation's activities to its environment. • The matching of the activities of an organisation to its resource capability. • The allocation and reallocation of major resources in an organisation. • The values, expectations and goals of those influencing strategy. • The direction an organisation will move in the long run. • Implications for change throughout the organisation—they are therefore likely to be complex in nature.
Source: Gerry Johnson and Kevan Scholes, **Exploring Corporate Strategy**. Prentice-Hall, New York, 1988, p. 8.

Some of the issues involved in strategic decision making are given below

1. **Criteria for Decision-Making:** Strategic decisions are made to achieve major objectives. There are three broad viewpoints concerning the objective setting
   (*a*) **Maximisation:** The traditional or classical economists suggest maximisation of benefits as the criteria for decision-making.
   (*b*) **Satisficing:** According to behaviourists maximisation is not possible in practice due to several constraints. Therefore, the real criteria should be reasonably satisfactory rather than ideal decisions.
   (*c*) **Incrementalism:** Decision-making is a complex and continually evolving process. Therefore, an organisation has to move towards its goals in small and incremental steps.
2. **Rationality in Decision-Making:** In decision-making rationality means logic, and objective criteria based on facts and figures. According to the maximisation criteria a decision is rational when it yields maximum gain. The satisficing criteria suggests bounded rationality in decision-making. Incrementalists point out that the achievement of objectives depends on the bargaining between various interested coalition groups existing in the organisation.
3. **Creativity in Decision-Making:** Creative decision-making involves search for novel and untried alternatives. One of the objectives of the strategic management course is to develop the ability to think out of the box and find out creative solutions to problems.
4. **Value Oriented Decision-Making:** Several personal variables such as age, education, experience, risk taking capacity and moral values play a vital role in strategic decision-making. Strategic issues involve business ethics and the value system of strategy makers are important. Their moral values depend on the culture in which they are born and brought up.
5. **Variability in Decision-Making:** Every decision situation is unique and there are no set rules that can be applied in strategic decision-making. Therefore, in similar situations different decision-makers may arrive at different conclusions.
6. **Individual Versus Group Decision-Making:** Strategic decisions are made at top level of management. The Chief Executive is supposed to have a thorough understanding of his organization and its environment. But global firms are more complex and operate in a diverse and turbulent environment. Therefore, groups rather than individuals are given the responsibility of taking strategic decisions.

2.2 APPROACHES TO STRATEGIC DECISION-MAKING (MODES OF STRATEGY MAKING)

Mintzberg has identified three modes of strategy-making — entrepreneurial, planning and adaptive[1]. But Steiner et.al. have given five approaches – formal-structured, intuitive-anticipative, entrepreneurial-opportunistic, incremental and adaptive[2].

1. Henry Mintzberg, **Strategy-Making in Three Modes, California Management Review** Winter 1973, pp. 44-53
2. George A. Steiner, John B. Miner and Edmund R. Gray, **Management Policy and Strategy** Macmillan, New York, 1982, pp. 284-87

These two sets of classification can be reconciled to some extent. Entrepreneurial mode involves intuition and anticipation. Formal-structured approach is similar to planning mode. Incremental and adaptive approaches are by and large similar. Therefore, three main approaches to strategic decision-making are described below:

1. **Entrepreneurial-Opportunistic Approach:** Under this approach decision-making is an emergent rather than a formal process. Family-managed companies adopt the entrepreneurial approach. The basic features of entrepreneurial strategy-making are as follows:
   (*a*) The main objective is expansion and growth in turnover, assets and market share
   (*b*) Decision power is centralised in the promoters who are capable of making bold and unusual decisions in the face of environmental uncertainty
   (*c*) The focus of the entrepreneur is search for business opportunities and to capitalise them
   (*d*) The decisions lead the firm to make unusual leaps or lows depending on whether the decisions are right or wrong.

   The entrepreneurial approach is suitable when the key strategists have very high stake and are in a position to lead the organization from the front. Such strategists are highly ambitious, risk takers and visionary. Decisions made by them are unorthodox and path-breaking. Therefore their organizations outperform the competitors. However, if the strategy makers lack the necessary intuition and vision, their organizations are likely to fail badly.

EXAMPLES OF ENTREPRENEURIAL APPROACH

- During his morning walks, Akio Moita, chairman of Sony Corporation of Japan, needed a mini cassette player so that he could listen to his favourite music conveniently. Therefore, he asked his research and design engineers to design a Walkman. The engineers replied that the product would not succeed in the market. But he insisted on that and Walkman became a roaring success.
- The late Dhirubhai Ambani saw the business opportunity in high priced premium fabrics which was unheard at that time in India. Vimal brand fabrics made roaring success. Later on, he used the same approach to conceive several projects and Reliance ultimately became the largest private sector company in India.
- Brijmohan Lall Munjal, the chairman of Hero Motor Corp felt that motorcycles rather than scooter will be the future mode of personal transport due to rising fuel prices and speed-orientation. His vision tuned out to be true though most experts did not agree with him at that time. Today, Hero Motor Corp is the largest motorcycle manufacturer in the world.
- Sunrise Industries launched Yuva and Piyu brands of toilet cleaners in 1980s. Both the products failed in the market due to stiff competition from Hindustan Unilever and other existing competitors
- Suraj Automobiles launched diesel-based motorcycles. The product offered saving in fuel cost but failed in the market

2. **Formal-Structured Approach (Planning Mode):** In the formal approach, strategic decisions are made on the basis of the organization's purposes, environmental opportunities and threats, and the organization's strengths and weaknesses. In other words, various factors influencing the strategy are analysed before making the strategy. Therefore, this is a systematic and comprehensive approach involving anticipating of the future conditions. Decision-making is decentralised to the level of expertise.

Multinational corporations and other professionally managed firms usually follow the formal approach. The main advantage of this approach is that it generates adequate information which helps strategists to make decisions in complex situations. However, too much formalised and highly structured process may slow down decision-making. Path-breaking and unusual decisions are rare.

The degree of formalisation differs from one organisation to another. Large and high technology firms are operating in stable environment, i.e., usually characterised by greater formalisation than small and low technology firms operating in turbulent and highly competitive environment.

3. **Adaptive Approach:** In this approach the focus is on solving problems rather than exploiting opportunities. Decision-making is largely incremental and reactive. An attempt is made to adapt the organization to changes in its environment. The final decisions are largley compromises due to pressure from several stakeholders with conflicting interests.

The adaptive approach is followed in most of the public sector enterprises. Private sector firms lacking vision and intuition may also adopt this approach.

The main advantage of the adaptive approach is low risk because the firms using this approach follow industry leaders. But this approach does not work when there are rapid changes in the environment. By the time the organisation adopts one change, environment changes further. In the era of globalisation firms who follow the adaptive approach fail to gain a competitive advantage

Thus, each approach to strategic decision-making has its own merits and demerits. Several factors determine the approach which a particular organisation will adopt. Size, management style, environment, technology, etc. of the organisation are the main factors.

Strategic decision-making contributes to the strategic management process by:

(*i*) assisting the organisation adapting to its environment by monitoring changes in the environment;

(*ii*) improving integration between different parts of the organisation by means of common agenda (strategic intent);

(*iii*) monitoring the organisation's performance against the strategic priorities.

2.3 SCHOOLS OF THOUGHT ON STRATEGY FORMATION

As stated in the previous chapter, strategic management is in the midst of an evolutionary process. Several strands of thinking are emerging in the course of its development. Strategy formation is at the core of strategic management. Mintzberg and his associates[3] have identified ten schools of strategy formation. Two more schools have been suggested by Warren; and Kim and Maubougne. These twelve schools of throught on strategy formation are described below:

1. **The Design School:** Under this school of thought strategy formation is a process of conception. Strategy making is considered a deliberate process designed to match the organisation's strengths and weaknesses with the opportunities and threats in the environment. The chief executive as the main architect guides the process of strategy formation. The process tends to be simple and informal, and is based on judgment and thinking. This process is applicable to the organisation which operates in simple and stable environment. The design school developed during the late 1950s and 1960s. P

3. Henry Mintzberg, Bruce Ahlstrand and Joseph Lampel, **Strategy Safari: A Guided Tour Through the Wilds of Strategic Management**, The Free Press, New York, 1998

Selzrick (1957), Chandler (1962) and Andrews (1965) are the main contributors to the design school.

2. **The Planning School:** In this school, strategy formation is viewed as a formal and deliberate process. Strategy is seen as a plan divided into sub-strategies and programmes. Planners play the lead role in strategy formation. The planning school developed during 1960s. Ansoff (1965), E.P. Learned, C.R. Christensen and W.D. Guth are the major contributors to this school. Strategy based on the planning school tends to become too static and, therefore, does not work in a dynamic environment.

3. **The Positioning School:** This school perceives strategy formation as an analytical, systematic and deliberate process. Strategy is seen as the organisation's planned position based on the analysis of the industry in which it operates. The aim is to improve the organisation's competitive position in its industry. The positioning school developed during 1970s and 1980s. Schendel and Hatten (1970 s) Henderson, Schoeffler and porter (1980s) are the main contributors to this school. Certain key variables like power, politics and culture that shape strategy are overlooked in this school.

4. **The Entrepreneurial School:** Strategy formation in this school is viewed as a visionary process taking place within the mind of the founder. Strategy formation is considered intuitive, visionary and largely deliberate. Strategy is the outcome of the entrepreneurs's intuition, judgment, wisdom and experience. The entrepreneurial school developed during the 1950s. Schumpeter (1950) and Cole (1959) are the major contributors to this school. The entrepreneur/leader plays the lead role in strategy formation. A visionary founder may help the organisation to sail through storms but all organisations do not have charismatic leaders. Therefore, the entrepreneurial school does not have universal application. It ignores the interdependence of activities within an organisation.

5. **The Cognitive School:** Under this school, strategy formation is viewed as a mental and emergent process. Strategy is seen as the outcome of a mental perspective of the strategist. The cognitive school developed during the 1940s and 1950s. Simon (1947 and 1957) and March and Simon (1958) are the major contributors to this school. The lead role in strategy formation is played by the thinker-philosopher. This school stresses the creative side of strategy formation. But the school fails to suggest how strategy formation may be undertaken. However, research on cognitive biases in strategy making has grown.

6. **The Learning School:** This school views strategy formation as an emergent informal and messy process. Strategy is seen as a unique pattern. Close attention is paid to what does work. The complex world does not permit development of strategies all at once. Therefore, strategies emerge gradually as the organisation learns.

   The learning school developed during 1950s through 1990s. Lindblom (1954), Cyert and March (1963), Weick (1969) Guinn (1980), Senge (1990), Prahalad and Hamel (early 1990s) have been the major contributors of this school. The learner within the organisation whoever that might be plays the lead role in strategy formation. The learning school stresses upon organisational learning which helps to deal with complexity and impracticability in strategy formation. However, taking several small steps may not lead to a sound overall strategy but only to tactics.

7. **The Power School:** Under this school, strategy formation is viewed as a process of negotiation and politics between power holders within the organisation and/or between the organisation and its external stakeholders. The power school developed mainly during the 1970s and 1980s. Allison (1971), Pfeffer and Salancisk (1978), and Astley (1984) are the major contributors to this school. The power school presents a realistic view of

strategy formation. But the school over-emphasizes the role of power relationship in strategy formation. Moreover, the chosen strategy may not be optimal for the organisation as it is the outcome of coalition and bargaining.

8. **The Cultural School:** This school views strategy formation as a collective, ideological, deliberate and social process in which various groups and departments in an organisation are involved collectively. Strategy is considered as a unique and collective perspective which is the outcome of the organisation's culture. The cultural school developed mainly during the 1960s. Rhenman and Norman (1960s), Hedberg and Johnson are the major contributors to this school. The cultural school explains the role of values, beliefs and social process in strategy formation. The logic behind resistance to strategic change is also highlighted. But the school does not provide any significant clues for strategy formation as its focus is on status quo in the organisation.

9. **The Environmental School:** This school views strategy formation as a reactive process. Strategy is seen as some kind of a response to the challenges created by the external environment. The environmental school developed mainly during the late 1960s and the 1970s. Harman and Freeman (1977) and contingency theorists like Pugh et.al. (late 1970s) are the major contributors to this school. It highlights the role of external environment in strategy formation. But this school is reactive as it considers strategy merely a response to environmental changes.

10. **The Configuration School:** This school views strategy formation as a transformation process designed to transform the organisation from the current state to the desired state. Strategy is considered in relation to a specific context and-thus may take any process identified under any of the earlier nine schools of thought. Any actor suggested in the other nine schools may play the lead role in strategy formation. The process of strategy formation is integrative, episodic and sequential incorporating various elements of other schools. The configuration school developed during 1960s and 1970s. Chandler (1962), Mintzberg and Miller (late 1970s) and Miles and Snow (1978) are the major contributors to this school. The main merit of this school is that it integrates the contributions of other schools of thought. Whenever the organisational context changes, there is need for strategy formation to take the organisation from the existing context to the new context. But the school does not explain the configuration needed in the new context.

SCHOOL OF THOUGHT	VIEW OF STRATEGY FORMATION
Prescriptive Schools	
1. The Design School	A process of conception
2. The Planing School	A formal process
3. The Positioning School	An analytical process
Descriptive Schools	
4. The Entrepreneurial School	A visionary process
5. The Cognitive School	A mental process
6. The Learning School	An emergent process
7. The Power School	A process of negotiation
8. The Cultural School	A collective process
9. The Environmental School	A reactive process
Integrative Schools	
10. The Configuration School	A process of transformation

11. **The Dynamic Strategy School:** According to this school, the ultimate concern of strategic management is to improve performance of the organisation. Warren[4] developed this school which suggests that strategists have to find answers to the following questions:

(*i*) Why is the organisation following its current route?

(*ii*) What will the organisation achieve if it continues to do what it is doing?

(*iii*) How can it design a robust strategy to radically improve its performance?

According to Warren, the principles of strategic dynamics create an integrated strategic architecture or core architecture of the organisation.

The dynamic strategy school highlights where managerial actions are needed and what specific strategics can be adopted in future. It enables the members of an organisation to decide whether their actions are achieving the goals.

But it is very difficult to apply the prescriptions of this school in strategy formation.

12. **The Reconstructionist School:** This school views strategy formation on a worldwide basis. The beliefs and actions of firms reconstruct the market boundaries of the industry. According to Kim and Mauborgne[5] strategies based on competition in an industry are red ocean strategies. These strategies are based on the assumption that industry structure is given and firms have to compete within this structure. Blue ocean strategies overcome this problem by identifying and developing markets in which there is little or no competition. Therefore, strategists must identify and tap blue oceans.

The reconstructionist school is quite innovative. It suggests maximisation of customer value through differentiation while keeping cost low. But only innovative and risk-taking organisations can apply the blue ocean strategy.

2.4 PROCESS AND MODEL OF STRATEGIC MANAGEMENT

The process of strategic management consists of four broad phases (Fig. 2.1)

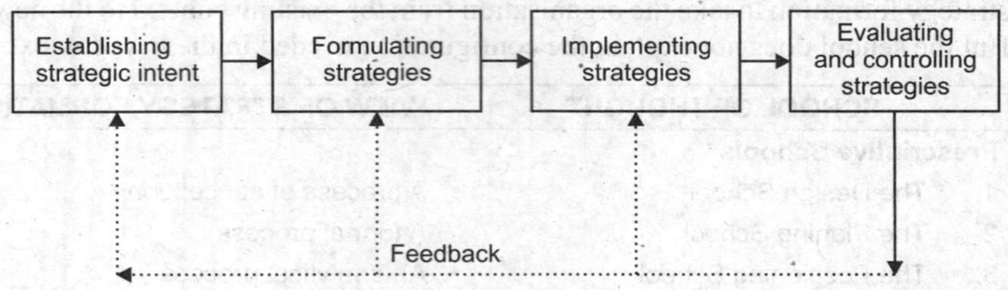

Fig. 2.1 Strategic Management Process

Each phase consists of several elements or sub-phases which are as follows:

1. **Establishing the Strategic Intent:** Strategic management aims to help the organisation realise its strategic intent. Strategic intent, represents what the organisation stands for and lays the foundation for the organisations strategic management. The main elements of strategic intent are as follows:

4 Kim Warren, *Competitive Strategy Dynamics,* John Wiley, New York, 2002

5 W. Chan Kim and Renee Mauborgne, *Blue Ocean Strategy: How to create Uncontested Market Space and Make the Competition Irrelevant*, Harvard Business School Press, Boston MA, 2005

(*i*) Creating and communicating the vision

(*ii*) Designing a mission statement

(*iii*) Defining the business

(*iv*) Choosing the business model

(*v*) Setting objectives

Vision represents what the organisation wants to be in future. **Mission** is the fundamental unique purpose that sets the organisation apart from other organisations and identifies its product market scope. It also prescribes how the organisation will deal with its various stakeholders. It relates the organisation to the society. **Business definition** is a statement of the business(es) the organisation engages or wishes to engage in future. **Business model** describes how the organisation creates value. **Objectives** are the end results which the organisation strives to achieve in future.

2. **Formulation of Strategies:** This phase of strategic management process involves the following activities:

(*a*) Analysis of external environment to identify the opportunities and threats for the organisation.

(*b*) Analysis of internal environment (organisational analysis) to identify the organisation's strengths and weaknesses.

(*c*) Identification of strategic alternatives in terms of corporate level strategies, and business level strategies.

(*d*) Strategic analysis and choice of strategy

3. **Implementation of Strategies:** The main activities involved in strategy implementation are as follows:

(*a*) Activating strategies

(*b*) Designing the structure, systems and process

(*c*) Behavioural implementation

(*d*) Formulating functional strategies

(*e*) Operationalising strategies

These activities constitute the action phase of the strategic management process.

4. **Evaluation and Control of Strategies:** The last phase of the strategic management process consists of the following activities:

(*a*) Evaluation of strategies

(*b*) Exercising strategic control

(*c*) Reformulating strategies

The various elements of the strategic management process are interrelated and interdependent. A simple model of strategic management process is given in Fig. 2.2

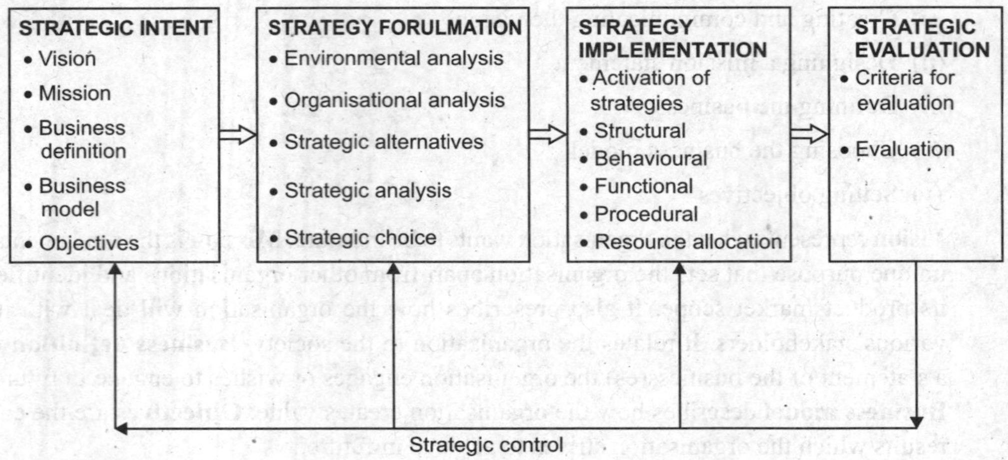

Fig. 2.2 Model of Strategic Management

The feedback from strategic evaluation helps in exercising strategic control which may involve reformulation of strategies and/or improving implementation of strategics. In this way, strategic management becomes an iterative process.

2.5 PARTICIPANTS IN STRATEGIC MANAGEMENT

Strategy formulation is largely the responsibility of top management because this level can take care of the total organisation and relate it to its environment. Top management consists primarily of the board of directors and the chief executive officer. Howerver, corporate planning staff, consultants and senior managers provide valuable inputs for strategy formulation. In strategy implementation managers at all levels are involved

2.5.1 Role of Board of Directors

Board of Directors has the authority to manage a company within the framework of the Companies Act, the Memorandum of Association and the Articles of Association. The main functions of the board of directors are as follows:

1. **Strategy Formulation:** The board of directors establishes the company's strategic intent and formulates corporate level strategies. It defines the broad direction in which the company will move and the long-term objectives which it will pursue.
2. **Designing Organisation Structure:** The board of directors designs the company's organisation structure in terms of SBUs, divisions and departments. It also appoints the chief executive and selects divisional/departmental heads.
3. **Financial Approvals:** The board of directors approves the company's master budget and distribution of its earnings. Through such approvals the board maintains control over the company's management
4. **Exercising Controls:** Board of directors is responsible to the shareholders for the management and performance of the company. Therefore, it has to keep effective checks and control over the company's functioning. The board of directors reviews the company's performance at periodic intervals (usually every quarter) and suggests suitable actions to improve performance.

5. **Trusteeship:** The board of directors has a fiduciary relationship with the company. Shareholders entrust the company's assets to the board of directors which must discharge its duties with honesty and sincerety for the benefit of shareholders. It must fulfil the trust and confidence shown by the shareholders.
6. **Legal Duties:** The Companies Act defines the legal functions and responsibilities of the board of directors. The directors face civil and criminal liabilities if they fail to comply with their legal duties.

The focus of board of directors on strategic functions and legal and routine functions depends on their involvement in the process of strategic management. Wheelan and Hunger have explained such involvement in the form of a continuum[6] (Table 2.3).

Table 2.3 Degree of Board's involvement in Strategic Management

Low (Passive) Phantom ⟵	Rubber Stamp	Minimal Review	Nominal Participation	Active Participation	⟶ High (Active) Catalyst
Never know what to do	Permits executives to make all decisions and approves what they decide	Reviews selected issues brought before him	Involved to a limited degree to review management's performance, decisions or programmes	Approves, questions, and makes final decisions on mission, objectives, strategy, policies; performs fiscal and management audits	Takes the leading role in establishing and modifying mission, objectives strategy and policies; has very active strategy committee

In real life, board of directors in most companies in India acts as a rubber stamp. The promoter/founder and his family/relatives take most of the strategic decisions. These decisions are then approved in meeting of board of directors to meet the legal requirements. An individual or small group controls the board of directors and acts as an extra-constitutional authority. Most of the directors in the board are friends, relatives, business associates of the promoter group. They do not oppose the group and thereby the group dominates strategic decision-making.

Tatas-Group Executive Council

The $ billion Tata Group has a Group Executive Council (GEC).

"The GEC provides strategic and operational support to the Chairman of Tata Sons with the mandate to own and drive the delivery of the core purpose of Tata Sons, which is long term value creation for all stakeholders. The GEC also works closely with and partners the Boards, CEOs and senior management of the various Tata companies."

2.5.2 Role of Chief Executive

Chief executive is the strategist and the chief architect of the organisation's purpose. He acts as the organisation builder and leader of the management team.

6. Thomas J. Wheelan and J. Daniel Hunger, **Strategic Management and Business Policy,** Addison Wesley. Reading MA, 1983,

The main functions of the chief executive are as follows:

1. **Strategic Planning:** The chief executive identifies business opportunities and makes strategic decisions. He lays down corporate goals and formulates long-term plans.
2. **Guidance and Direction:** The chief executive guides and directs all the functional heads of the organisation by (*a*) explaining and interpreting the strategies and policies formulated by the board of directors, (b) issuing orders and instructions to departmental heads.
3. **Coordination:** The chief executive ensures cooperation and coordination among all the departments of the company. He ensures that various departmental/divisional heads work together as a team towards the achievement of organisational purpose.
4. **Staffing:** The chief executive selects heads of divisions/departments, fixes their pay structure and decides their promotions/transfers.
5. **Review and Control:** The chief executive appraises the performance of different divisions/departments and suggests appropriate remedial measures. He prepares progress and control reports for the board of directors
6. **Public Relations:** The chief executive is the spokesman and representative/public face of his company. He works to maintain cordial relations with shareholders, banks, financial institutions, trade unions, trade associations, government and other stakeholders.

Thus, the chief executive performs general management functions rather than looking after functional aspects of the company. He assists the board of directors in the strategic management of the organisation.

Chief executive is the executive head of a company Traditionally, one person acts as the chief executive and is responsible for overall functioning of the company. He may be assisted by staff specialists such as legal adviser, personal secretary, executive assistant, etc. In big companies a small group rather than a single person serves as the chief executive.

This group is called plural executive. This is done because one person cannot effectively perform different roles of the chief executive.

However, a company may not like too much concentration of power in an individual. Multiple chief executive system is also helpful in solving the problem of succession. People with complementary skills and experience can be selected for the chief executive group.

In a large corporation, top management functions may be grouped into two divisions — management division and operating division.

The Chief Executive Officer (CEO) looks after the management division whereas the Chief Operating Officer (COO) handles the operating division.

SUMMARY

Strategic Decision-making: (*i*) Criteria–Maximisation, satisficing, optimising (*ii*) Rationality (*iii*) Creativity (*iv*) Value orientation (*v*) Variability (*vi*) Individual vs. group.

Approaches: (1) Entrepreneurial-opportunistic (2) Formal-structured (3) Adaptive

Schools of Strategy Making: Design, planning, positioning, entrepreneurial, cognitive, learning, power, cultural, environmental, configuration, dynamic strategy, reconstructionist school

Process: (1) Establishing strategic intent (2) Strategy formulation (3) Strategy implementation (4) Strategy evaluation and control

Participants: (1) Board of Directors – strategy formulation, organising, financial approval, controlling, trusteeship, legal duties (2) Chief Executive – Strategic planning, guidance and direction, coordination, staffing, review and control, public relations

TEST QUESTIONS

1. What is strategic decision-making? Explain the main issues involved in strategic decision-making.
2. Discuss various approaches to strategic decision-making, pointing out the suitability of each approach.
3. Explain different schools of thought on strategy making, with suitable examples.
4. Describe the main phases involved in the process of strategic management.
5. Explain the role of Board of Directors and Chief Executive in strategic management.
6. Discuss in brief the process of strategic management. Briefly explain the levels at which strategy operates.
7. Write a detailed note on role of top management under the new paradigm of strategy formulation.
8. "Strategic planning is a necessary but not sufficient condition for success of an enterprise." Do you agree? Give reasons.
9. Discuss the alternative approaches for formulating corporate strategy. What factors should the top management keep in mind in strategy making?
10. Give important reasons due to which firms use strategic management. How according to rational-analytical and intuitive-emotional approaches, a decision maker formulates strategy?
11. "In complex situations, decision-making in organisations is rarely rational-analytical." Critically examine this statement.
12. "The purpose of strategy is to define the nature of relationship between a firm and its environment." Comment on this statement and explain the importance of the various elements of the strategic management process for the success of an organisation.
13. Discuss alternative models of strategy formulation. Under what conditions is it preferable to start with objectives and identify 'gaps' in different strategic aspects of an organisation.
14. Explain the term 'corporate strategy'. What are the stages involved in formulating a corporate strategy?
15. What do you mean by 'strategic planning'? Outline the broad phases in the strategic planning process. How is strategic planning linked with operational planning?
16. "In essence strategy determines what the nature of a business is or will be and further it determines how the enterprise will reach that state." Elucidate with relevant examples.
17. How can the planning process be managed so that strategies are realistic?

18. Describe the work of top management in the post-liberalisation regime in India. Critically examine the role of the Board of Directors in providing direction to companies.
19. Explain the strategic management process in detail. Also explain the varicus levels at which strategy operates in an organisation.
20. What are the characteristics which make a decision strategic?
21. Define a Strategic Business Unit (SBU). What is its importance in organisational portfolio analysis?
22. What makes a decision strategic? Briefly explain Henry Mintzberg's modes of strategic decision-making. Why is the planning mode superior to the other modes of strategic decision-making?
23. "In practice, the strategies of most organisations are probably a combination of the intended (planned) and the emergent." State the main criticism of the formal strategic planning model and show the relationship between planned strategy and realised strategy.
24. In what respects strategic decisions are different from operating decisions? Explain the routes to strategic advantage.
25. What is a strategic decision? Briefly describe the various approaches to strategic decision-making.
26. Examine the strategic role of Board of Directors and CEO of a company in view of 'Satyam Episode'.
27. "Strategic management process should be viewed as dynamic, continuous and flexible". Comment.
28. Define Strategic Group. Briefly describe various types of strategic groups.
29. What is a strategic group? How is it important to categorise firms of an industry into strategic groups?
30. Define strategic management. Discuss the steps in strategic management process.
31. Why is formulation of strategy important? Explain the steps involved in the strategic management process.
32. What is the importance of formulating strategy to an organisation? Explain the levels of strategy formulation in a diversified company.
33. "Top management has a number of functions to perform and not any specific function, therefore, top management has to be a team." Critically examine the statement for a multi-division large company.
34. Analyse the role of the Board of Directors in the strategy–making and executing process.
35. Explain the nature of strategic decision-making. How do strategic decisions differ from administrative decisions and operating decisions?
36. Distinguish between entrepreneurial, adaptive and planning modes of strategy-making. Which mode do you think is the best?
37. "Strategy making in terms of precise modes is difficult for, in reality, it may be necessary to combine or alternate the modalities of strategic decision making". Elucidate.

CASE STUDY

The Diary of Kiran Nag, Chairman & Managing Director, Swadeshi Bank.

April 1, 2010

It has finally happended. I received a telephonic confirmation yesterday from the Union Ministry of Finance about my appointment, with immediate effect, as the **Chairman** and **Managing Director of Swadeshi Bank.** I will have to take charge in a day or two. I must say that I have had a rewarding 5-year term as the head of **Swatantra Bank between** 2005 and 2010—a period of **dramatic change in the banking** industry in this country.

I know that Swadeshi Bank been in business since **1945**; introduced home-savings accounts and lockers **in 1951,** and was also the **first nationalised bank** to offer **credit cards here**. While it should have seized leadership in a number of areas, it **failed** to do so. Naturally, it has the image of a **stodgy, old, slow-moving institution today**. My brief is clear: make the **elephant dance**. It is, by no means, an easy task. After all, there are so many fleet-footed players today. Just how do I transform Swadishi Bank into a modern **commercial bank**?........I shall have to rise to the **challenge**.

April 8, 2010

At the Management Committee meeting this morning, we reviewed the **financials**. Swadeshi Bank has been **incurring losses** in the **last 4 years**. Of course, the other nationalised banks too have had to bleed their balance-sheets to clean them up thanks to the new norms on bad debts. The ratio of our Non-Performing Assets (NPAs) to **Total Advances is 16 p.c**, but our fundamentals are sound. We have a huge network of branches, and brand **equity in the small scale sector**. 200 units that have grown into bigger corporations **continue to bank with us**. I can see two pockets of excellence: **fund management**, and **export finance**. The key to survival lies in identifying our strengths and building on them. That will be my biggest challenge at Swadeshi Bank.

April 10, 2010

How things change! I had joined Swatantra Bank as an officer 5 years before 14 banks—including my own—were nationalised by the Government in 1969. For the next two decades, we rode the boom. We took banking to the masses and in the process created a vast infrastructure. That has become both an asset and a liability now. Suddenly, we have been overtaken by technology, which has rendered the concepts of time and space **redundant**.

The new private sector banks enjoy ***one advantage:*** an unmatched degree of **automation,** which enables them to cut **their transaction costs** as well as leverage their expertise in specialised areas like retail banking, corporate finance, and investment banking. They pose a **threat** to the profitability of the **nationalised banks**.

We have also had to contend with an increasing number of Non-Banking Finance Companies (NBFCs) in our resource mobilisation efforts. There are other forces at work too. Increasingly, disintermediation has resulted in corporates tapping both the domestic and the global markets directly. And while banks are getting **involved in long-term project financing,** where they have to compete with the **Development Financial Institutions,** the latter are trying to make inroads into **short-term financing**—the mainstay of commercial banks like us.

April 13, 2010

We, at nationalised banks, have to ask ourselves whether we want to be **everything** to **everybody**, or choose a particular segment that will guard us against **competition**. With the array of services that we already provide—**project finance, retail finance, housing finance, export finance**, and **asset management**—it is easier to upgrade Swadeshi Bank into a **one-stop shop**, where we meet **all the customers' requirements under one roof**. The limitations: our costs could **spin out of control,** and new products may have to be cross-subsidised. Universal banking is not the best option when cost and profitability are the biggest stumbling blocks. It would be prudent, I suspect, to exploit **niches** instead.

Swadeshi Bank: The Financials

Figure ₹ in Crores.

	2005–06	2006–07	2007–08	2008–09	2009–10
Deposits	9,125	11,267	12,354	14,676	16,956
Advances	6,357	6,475	5,299	8,702	9,837
Interest Income	1,234	1,112	1,345	1,967	2,222
Other Income	149	145	156	245	287
Interest Costs	1,035	1,222	1,179	1,161	1,422
Employee Costs	305	343	376	479	623
Operating Expenses	133	137	161	159	166
Net Profits	**30**	**– 383**	**– 712**	**– 84**	**– 74**
No. of Employees	51,462	51,378	51,259	51,146	51,065
No. of Branches	**3,105**	**3,124**	**3,126**	**3,187**	**3,202**

April 15, 2010

I met the Indian head of the London-based consultancy firm, Sigma Inc.—which has a special cell that is involved in **restructuring** banks all over the world. We discussed how we could identify the **core competency** of a bank. I told him that we had a number of competencies—**a large assetbase, a huge network of branches, privileged access to Public Sector Unit (PSU) accounts**. But the consultant quickly pointed out that these were not core competencies, and were not sustainable in the long-run since the other nationalised banks had them too. Instead, he listed three parameters that would help identify a core competence at Swadeshi Bank:

- It should provide access to a wide variety of markets.
- It must make a significant contribution to customer satisfaction and shareholder value
- It should be an attribute that would be difficult for our competitors to emulate.

The best way to go about the exercise is to narrow down on **20-30** capabilities, of which **5-6** could be focused on.

April 17, 1210

I brought this issue up at the Management Committee meeting this morning. It was agreed unanimously that our top managers should spend a significant portion of their time in

developing a strategic architecture for Swadeshi Bank. This architecture would first establish the **objectives of competence-building**, identify the **focus areas** and **technologies** that each would require, and provide a **route-map for the future**. One we do that, we would have a rationale for product and market-diversification. And it would give us the leeway to manage uncertainties in the implementation phase.

It was agreed that the bank's senior managers should ponder over the following question: **Who will be our future customers**? **What kind of distribution and delivery channels will we have in place? What will be the competition like tomorrow? Will it be price, service, technology, or talent** that will be the **basis of competition? What will be the characteristics of our competitive strategy? Where will our margins come from?**

Evidently, competence can only be developed through foresight. We should be able to anticipate the shape of things in the banking industry in the next 10 years, ensure that it evolves in a way that is advantageous to Swadeshi Bank, and develop skills to help us attain leadership in certain segments of the business.

April 20, 2010

At Swatantra Bank, during the **last 3 years** of my tenure, I ensured the **automation** of more than half of our **2,500** branches. We became the first nationalised bank to offer hi-tech delivery-mechanisms like ATMs. Infotech applications were clearly aimed at providing customer value. I can think of building one particular **capability at Swadeshi** Bank: **treasury management.** The **bank has a formidable pool of talent in dealing-room** operations, enabling **it to participate simultaneously in the debt**, foreign exchange, and equity markets.

April 24, 2010

There is an excessive **dependence on interest income** at Swadeshi Bank. This has to change. One of my priorities is to sharpen the bank's focus on **fee-based income**. The ratio of fee income to total income for 1996-97 was 18.44 per cent in the case of Konark Bank—which is less than 3 years old—while it was about 9 per cent for Swadeshi Bank. With spreads coming under increasing pressure, we will have to find other ways of increasing our Other Income.

April 29, 2010

During the brainstorming sessions with my senior managers at the bank's holiday home, we identified seven broad areas of action that Swadeshi Bank should simultaneously work on. It may help us evolve some core competencies, which should direct the bank's advance into the future. The focus areas:

- **Mindset.** Swadeshi Bank must move from a **product-centric mindset** to a **customer-centric** philosophy. The idea is to develop products to meet the needs of our present and future customers.
- **Infotech.** Infotech accelerates growth. We should create delivery systems that will match the priorities of the customer of the future.
- **Marketing.** Swadeshi Bank should move from traditional banking such as deposit-mobilisation and lending, to marketing a diversified range of financial services under one roof.

- **Credit Risk Management.** It is an area that our bank must capitalise on. The deregulation of interest rates has brought in an element of risk that was absent in an administered rate regime.
- **Exchange Risk Management** skills are in demand now, be it currency futures, options, or swaps. At our bank, we cannot ignore this lucrative niche.
- **Fee-based Income.** We must derive income from non-fund-based activities, like guarantees and underwriting. To enlarge our fee-based business, we should venture into profitable areas like housing finance and leasing.
- **Talent Search.** People management has not been a strong point at Swadeshi Bank. Instead of grooming people from scratch, we must attract top-notch managerial talent from other organisations.

May 1, 1996:

Although I am convinced that Swadeshi Bank has effective systems and control in place, but we need to **strengthen** our business systems. I am inclined to appoint Sigma India as our consultants who are expected to reengineer the bank's processes and bring about a radical redesign of systems to achieve improvements in **cost management, customer services, and time cycles.**

May 2, 1996:

Sooner or later, Swadeshi Bank will divest a part of its equity to the public. Then, we will be accountable to our new shareholders. So, it is necessary to get our focus right on the following issues:

- Developing business strategies.
- Reducing the level of NPAs.
- Providing value-added products and services.
- Placing an emphasis on product profitability
- Differentiating services to secure a competitive edge.
- Devising innovative sources of funds.
- Building cost efficiencies.

May 5, 1996:

I talked to **Mrinal Dasgupta**, the president of the Swadeshi Bank Employees Union, about the need for **downsizing** the workforce. But he left unconvinced saying that the 51,065-strong union would oppose any such plan.

May 6, 1996:

As **retail banking is** emerging as a new growth area, I have set up a committee to identify the opportunities in personal banking. It will take us at least 6 months to firm up our plans.

May 10, 1996:

I received a call this morning from **Rajesh Shah, a merchant banker** whom I have known for many years. He hinted that if Swadeshi Bank were to think in terms of **a merger** with any other bank—he even suggested Swatantra Bank as a possible partner—he would be glad to handle the formalities. I felt I had been hit by a thunderbolt. With spreads coming under increasing pressure, and competition hotting up, the banks will be compelled to build economies of scale through mergers. Only the fittest will survive.

Liberalisation has led to a shakeout in a number of industries. And banking is no exception. It would be strategic to strike **an alliance** with a global bank. That will reduce the **time and cost involved** in building competencies from scratch. And, apart from giving us access to better technology and product-expertise, a **strategic alliance** will give us credibility and capability.

May 12, 1996:

I now realise why our competitors, especially the private banks, have opted for strategic alliance with global majors. My apprehension is that Swadeshi Bank, which has a large workforce and is unfocussed, could face problems in finding the right partner. Besides, any foreign bank will insist on acquiring a stake in Swadeshi Bank. Unless we are on a strong financial footing, it will be difficult to drive a hard bargain.

Questions:

(*a*) Examine the main problems plaguing Swadeshi Bank.

(*b*) Make a SWOT analysis of the Bank, bringing out clearly its strengths and weaknesses, opportunities and threats.

(*c*) What are the key areas for the survival of Swadeshi Bank that must be addressed to on a priority basis by the new Chairman and Managing Director?

(*d*) Critically examine the possibility of a strategic alliance with an international partner for Swadeshi Bank.

PART – II

Strategic Intent

3 CHAPTER HIERARCHY OF STRATEGIC INTENT

CHAPTER OUTLINE

Organisations exist and function to realise some dreams and aspirations. These dreams and aspirations are expressed in their strategic intent. Organisations state at many levels what they wish to achieve. Therefore, there is a hierarchy of strategic intent. Establishment of strategic intent is the first phase of strategic management process and it serves as the base for other phases.

3.1 CONCEPTS OF STRATEGIC INTENT, STRETCH, LEVERAGE AND FIT

The concept of strategic 'intent' was coined by Hamel and Prahalad[1] in 1989. They attributed the lead of Japanese firms over their American and European counterparts to "an obsession to win", an obsession of having ambitions that may even be out of proportion to their resources and capabilities. This obsession to win or the quest for global leadership was called 'strategic intent'. Hamel and Prahalad defined strategic intent as follows:

"On the one hand, strategic intent envisions a desired leadership position and establishes the criterion the organisation will use to chart its progress.... . At the same time, strategic intent is more than simply unfettered ambition ..... The concept also encompasses an active management process that includes: focussing the organisation's attention on the essence

1. Garry Hamel and C.K. Prahalad, "Strategic Intent" **Harvard Business Review,** May June, 1989, pp. 63–76.

of winning, motivating people by communicating the value of the target, leaving room for individual and team contributions, sustaining enthusiasm by providing new operational definitions as circumstances change and intent consistently to guide resource allocations".

The strategic intent of an organisation represents what the organisation wants to become in future. It reflects the desired end result. It has wide implications and meaning for strategic management of an organisation. The main functions of strategic intent are as follows:

1. **Desired Destiny:** Strategic intent reflects what the organisation wants to become in future.
2. **Sense of Direction:** Strategic intent implies what the organisation should do and why it should do. It serves as a unified guide to its activities.
3. **Sense of Discovery:** Strategic intent implies a unique competitive position that will differentiate the organisation from its rivals.

   The hierarchy of strategic intent has significant implications for strategic management of an organisation. It serves as the charter of goals the organisation wants to achieve. **Second,** it indicates the direction in which the organisation should move in future. **Third,** it is a powerful means of communicating the organisation's intent down the line of command. **Fourth,** it helps to create a result oriented culture in the organisation. **Lastly,** it serves as a means of integrating the efforts of individuals and groups in the organisation.

Examples of Strategic Intent

The late Dhirubhai Ambani, former chairman of Reliance Group of Industries dreamt of making Reliance the biggest private sector firm in India. He had the strategic intent of being a global leader by being the lowest cost producer of polyester products. He achieved this status through a relentless pursuit of scale, vertical integration and operational effectiveness.

"To become the leader in the document market in India by helping improve the customer work processes, positively impacting productivity and costs while digitally empowering them to transform their work. In other words, 'helping people find better ways to do great work'— Xerox India.

Hamel and Prahalad[2] also introduced the concepts of stretch and leverage. Strategic "stretch" means a misfit between the resources and aspirations of an organisation. Strategic "leverage" refers to concentrating, accumulating, contemplating, conserving and recovering resources in such a manner that a meagre resource base is stretched to meet the aspirations that the organisation dares to have. The idea of stretch is opposite to the idea of 'fit' that means matching the resources of the oragnisation to its aspirations and environment.

The concept of strategic fit is central to the positioning school of strategy making. Under this school, strategy is a compromise between environmental opportunities and organisational capabilities. On the other hand, the concepts of stretch and leverage are central to the learning school of strategic making. Under this school both environment and capabilities are treated as flexible that can be modified. In other words, strategic intent under the idea of fit is realistic while it is realistic under the ideas of stretch and leverage.

---

2. Gary Hamel and C.K. Prahalad, " Strategy as Stretch and Leverage", **Harvard Business Review,** March April, 1993, pp. 75-84

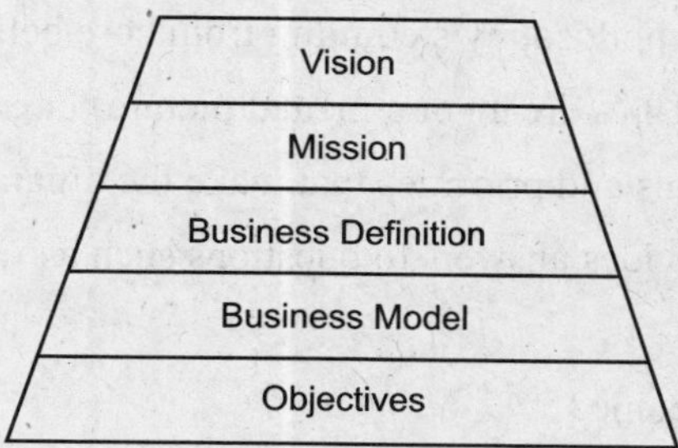

Fig. 3.1 Hierarchy of Strategic Intent

Strategic intent of an organisation is established in the form of a hierarchy consisting of several layers. At every successive lower layer, the generalised intent is converted into more specific intent. Different layers of strategic intent are interrelated and interdependent and form a continuum[3]. [Fig. 3.1].

3.2 VISION

Nations, organisations and individuals all have a vision. For example, a nation like India may have the vision to become a developed country by 2025. Similarly, an MBA student may have the vision of retiring as the chief executive of a large diversified multinational corporation, or to become a start up entrepreneur. In the context of an organisation, vision means a mental image or articulation of its future. It is the position that an organisation would like to attain in the distant future.

Different experts have defined vision in different ways. According to Kotter, vision is a "description of something (an organisation, a corporate culture, a business, a technology, an activity) in the future"[4]. In the words of Miller and Dess, vision means "the category of intentions that are broad, all–inclusive and forward thinking"[5].

El-Namaki defines vision as, " a mental perception of the kind of environment an individual, or an organisation, aspires to create within a broad time horizon and the underlying conditions for the actualisation of this perception[6].

These definitions reveal the following features of vision:

(*i*) Vision reflects the organisation's intentions or desires or expectations

(*ii*) Vision is a mental picture of the desired future. It indicates where the organisation will be in future rather than where it is now. It is not a history of the organisation's proud past.

(*iii*) Vision sets out a core set of principles that the company stands for and criteria for measuring organisational success.

(*iv*) Vision is long term representing what an organisation ultimately wants to become.

3. Alex Miller, **Strategic Management'** McGraw Hill, MA, 1998, pp. 41 – 42
4. John P. Kotter, **A Force for Change: How Leadership Differs from Management,** The Free Press, London, 1990.
5. A. Miller and G.G. Dess, **Strategic Management,** McGraw Hill, New York, 1996, p.p 6.
6. M.S.S. El-Namaki, "Creating a Corporate Vision", **Long Range Planning**, 25(6), 1992, pp. 25–29.

(*v*) Vision is the guiding philosophy stemming from core beliefs and values.

(*vi*) Vision may be implicit (a dream or a mental picture) or explicit (a written statement).

(*vii*) Vision is a set of ideals and priorities that make the organisation special and unique.

Vision statement provides answers to questions such as:

- Who are we?
- What we want to become?
- Where are we headed?

Examples of Vision

Reliance Industries Limited: To achieve global leadership in polymers, fibres, and resin businesses through innovative research and technology development in materials, products, and applications through efficient, disciplined, target-oriented, and cost-effective research and development activities.

Tata International: To be the "Leading International Business Company" of the country and " International Arm" of Tata Group with a significant overseas reach, presence and linkages, and with focus on facilitating globalisation of Tata Group's core business.

Bank of Baroda: To become "a technology enabled customer centric financial services organisation".

Hindustan Unilever Ltd: To meet everyday needs of people everywhere.

Life Insurance Corporation (LIC) of India: Vision 2020 – At the centre of this vison is the welfare of the nation along with the welfare of its stakeholders – the policyholders, employees, agents and the society in general. The company's vision for the year 2020 is to provide 'A Policy in Every Pocket'. It implies that every insurable Indian should have one policy by the end of the year 2020.

ITC Limited: Sustain ITC's position as one of India's most valuable corporations through world class performance, creating growing value for the Indian economy and the Company's stakeholders.

3.2.1 Essentials of a Good Vision

A good vision must fulfil the following requirements.

1. **Realistic:** A vision is meaningful for the organisation only when it is based on reality. Mere daydreaming is useless but a dream that can be converted into reality is required. Vision should be realistic so that people believe that it is achievable. However, The vision should be idealistic or challenging enough so that it cannot be achieved without stretching.
2. **Credible:** A vision becomes relevant to the members of the oragnisation when it is believable. A credible vision can aspire them to excel and provide direction to their actions.
3. **Attractive:** A vision must be attractive so as to inspire and encourage members of the oragnisation. It must make them part of the future that is envisioned for the organisation.

4. **Unique:** A good vision reflects uniqueness and distinctive competence of the organisation.
5. **Appropriate:** A good vision is consistent with the core values and beliefs, and environment of the organisation.
6. **Charter:** A good vision is a set of core values and principles. It should reflect what the organisation stands for. It also needs to indicate the priorities of the organisation.
7. **Motivational:** A good vision should inspire members of the organisation and encourage commitment from them.
8. **Articulated:** A good vision is well articulated and well understood by those who are responsible to convert it into reality.

3.2.2 Benefits (Role) of Vision

Vision stands at the top of the hierarchy of strategic intent. A written statement of vision offers the following advantages:

(*i*) Vision indicates the destination. It provides clues as to where the organisation is heading for in future and what it stands for.

(*ii*) Vision is a source of inspiration to members of the organisation. It encourages them to give their best towards the organisation's success.

(*iii*) Vision helps in the creation of a common identity and a shared sense of purpose.

(*iv*) A good vision encourages risk-taking and experimentation.

(*v*) A good vision fosters long-term thinking.

(*vi*) A good vision represents integrity. It is truly genuine and can be used for the benefit of people.

(*vii*) It differentiates the organisation from its counterparts.

Thus, vision creates a sense of commonality that permeates the organisation and gives coherence to diverse activities. It helps to focus the collective energy of people.

3.2.3 Developing Vision (Envisioning)

The process of developing a vision is called envisioning. It consists of the following steps:

(*i*) Conducting Vision Audit: First of all, the current status and momentum of the organisation is assessed. Answers are sought to key questions such as: Does the organisation have a clear vision? In which direction the organisation is moving? Do the strategists know where the organisation is headed?

(*ii*) Identifying the Context: Vision is the desired future position. Therefore, it is necessary to identify the broad direction of the future environment in which the organisation will operate. Key questions asked at this stage are: What must the vision achieve? What are the boundaries and constraints? What critical issues must be addressed in the vision?

(*iii*) Developing the Future Scenarios: The likely future trends in the environment are called scenarios. It is not possible to predict accurately the distant future environment.

Therefore, alternative scenarios are developed. The organisation will have to behave in accordance with the particular scenario that actually occurs.

Tradition, fear of ridicule, stereotypes, complacency, shortsightedness are the hurdles in evisaioning.

(*iv*) **Generating the Alternative Visions:** Possible visions are developed for different scenarios. These alternative visions reflect different directions in which the organisation may move.

(*v*) **Choosing the Final Vision:** Alternative visions are evaluated in the light of scenarios and organisation's capabilities. That vision is finally selected which is most likely to lead to success.

3.2.4. Components of Vision

According to Collins and Porras[7] a good vision consists of two major elements: core ideology and envisioned future. The core ideology or corporate philosophy defines the *enduring* character of an organisation. It consists of core or corporate values (what the organisation stands for) and core purposes (reason for existence). The envisioned future or tangible image also consists of two elements: long-term audacious goal, and a vivid description of its achievement.

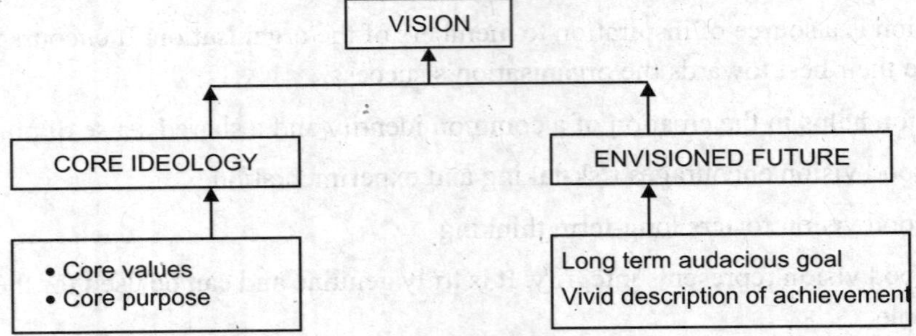

Fig. 3.2 Components of Vision

Core ideology or guiding philosophy reflects the basic tenets, values and principles which remain constant over a long-time period.

1. **Core Values:** Core values refer to the deeply held values of an organisation. These are independent of industry environment. Core values do not change even if industry in which the company operates changes. Excellent customer service, innovation, integrity, transparency are examples of core values.
2. **Core Purpose:** The core purpose means the reason for the existence of the organisation. It is relatively unchanging and endures for a long-time period. The core purpose sets the company apart from its competitors. For example, the purpose of a marketing research firm may be "to provide information that helps clients to better understand their markets".
3. **Visionary Goals:** The lofty objectives which an organisation wants to pursue are its visionary goals. These represent the milestones that a company will reach in future. These goals should be challenging. Visionary goals are of the following types:

7. J. C. Collins and J. I. Porras, " Building your Company's Vision," **Harvard Business Review**, Sept. Oct. 1996, pp 65–77.

(*a*) **Target:** Quantitative and qualitative goals such as Ford's goal to 'democratize the automobile'.

(*b*) **Common enemy:** Overtaking a rival *e.g.* goal of Reliance Industries 'to be the biggest private sector company'.

(*c*) **Role mode:** To become like another firm in a different industry *e.g.* 'to become the Nike of the motorcycle industry'.

(*d*) **Internal transformation:** For example, General Electric set the goal of becoming number one or two in every market it serves.

Once a visionary goal is reached, it should be replaced, otherwise the company may fall behind. For example, after placing the automobile within the reach of common man, Ford did not set a new visionary goal. General Motors overtook Ford in the thirties.

3.3 MISSION

Mission is the second level in the hierarchy of strategic intent. It describes the reason for the existence of an organisation. Every organisation exists to satisfy some needs of the society. Mission is a statement which defines the role that an organisation plays in the society. For example, a publisher exists to satisfy the information needs of the society.

According to Thompson[8], "Mission is the essential purpose of the organisation concerning particularly why it is in existence' the nature of the business(es) it is in, and the customers it seeks to serve and satisfy". In the words of Pearce and Robinson[9]. "The company mission is defined as the fundamental unique purpose that sets a business apart from other firms of its types and identifies the scope of its operations in product and market terms". Collins and Porras define mission as "a clear and Compelling goal that serves to unify organisation's efforts"[10].

Mission provides answers to questions such as: What is our business? What it will be? What it should be? Mission also represents the image which the organisation seeks to project and sets it apart from its counterparts. Mission defines the product-market scope of a company.

Mission Statement of Dabur

1. **Customer:** We believe in providing our consumers with innovative products within easy reach.
2. **Product:** We focus on growing our core brands across categories through continuous innovation in products.
3. **Geographical Domain:** We intend to build a platform to enable Dabur to become a global ayurvedic leader.
4. **Technology:** We intend to improve operational efficiencies by leveraging technology.
5. **Concern for Survival:** We will provide superior returns, relative to our peer group, to our shareholders.

Dabur
Celebrate Life!

8. J. L. Thompson, **Strategic Management: Awareness and Change,** International Thompson Business Press, London, 1997, p.6.
9. John A. Pearce and Richard B. Robinson, **Strategic Management,** AITBS, Delhi, 1999, p.73
10. James C. Collins and Jerry I. Porras, **Built to Last: Successful Habits of Visionary companies Harper Business**, New York, 1994

6. **Philosophy:** We are determined to be the best at doing what matters most.
7. **Self-Concept:** We believe in teamwork, and in the principle of mutual trust and transparency.
8. **Concern for Public Image:** We are dedicated to be responsible citizens with a commitment to environmental protection.

3.3.1 Difference Between Vision and Mission

Vision and mission are different in the following ways:

1. **Nature:** Vision is a view of what an organisation wants to become in distant future. On the other hand, mission states what an organisation is and why does it exist *i.e.* what is its business.
2. **Focus:** Vision focusses on long-term concept and high achievement level for the organisation. The focus of mission is on what the organisation proposes to do for its stakeholders.

Examples of Mission

Hero Motorcop: It is our mission to strive for synergy between technology, systems and human resources to produce products and services that meet the quality, performance and price aspirations of our customers. While doing so, we maintain the highest standards of ethics and societal responsibilities. This mission is what drives us to new heights in excellence and helps us to forge a unique and mutually beneficial relationship with all our stakeholders. We are committed to move ahead resolutely on this path.

HCL Infosystems: "To provide world-class information technology solutions and services to enable our customers to serve their customers better".

LIC: Zindagi ke Saath Bhi Zindagi ke Baad Bhi

ITC Limited: To enhance the wealth generating capability of the enterprise in a globalising environment delivering superior and sustainable stakeholder value.

HUL: Unilever's mission is to add Vitality to life. We meet everyday needs for nutrition, hygiene and personal care with brands that help people feel good, look good and get more out of life.

BHEL: To maintain leading position as suppliers of quality equipment, system and services in the field of conversion, transmission, utilization and conversion of energy for application in the areas of electric power, transportation and industries.

Dabur India: Be the preferred company to meet the health and personal grooming needs of our target consumers with safe, efficacious, natural solutions by synthesising our deep knowledge of ayurveda and herbs with modern science.

3.3.2. Advantages (Role) of Mission

A clearly defined mission helps in strategy formulation in the following ways:

(*i*) It helps in deciding the unified direction in which the organisation will proceed. Strategic decisions can be geared in that direction.

(*ii*) It helps to clarify the aspirations of the organisation and its stakeholders. Strategic decisions can be aligned to these aspirations.

(*iii*) Mission serves as a guide in dealing with various internal and external stakeholders.

(*iv*) It ensures uniformity of purpose. It helps in integrating different subsystems of the organisation as well as in integrating the organisation with its environment.

(*v*) Mission helps in developing a positive image of the organisation in the society.

(*vi*) It provides standards for allocation of resources.

3.3.3 Formulating a Mission Statement

A mission statement is a written description of an organisation's mission. An explicit mission statement helps to communicate the philosophy, character and image of the organisation to people inside and outside it. Moreover, various sections of society who are aware about the mission know how to interact with the organisation.

A mission statement defines the basic reason for the existence of an organisation. It reflects the philosophy, identity, character and image of the organisation.

The main elements of a mission statement are as follows:

1. **Organisation's Self-Concept:** The self-concept of an organisation is based on its perception of how society will respond to it. It defines the organisation's role in the industry. For example, the self-concept of Reliance Industries is: "Growth is the way of life."

2. **Organisations's Philosophy:** The philosophy or etho or creed of an organisation is a set of assumptions, beliefs, values, aspirations and priorities. It serves as a guide in strategic decision making. 'Concern for all stakeholders' is for example the philosophy of ITC Limited.

3. **Organisation's Image:** The image which an organisation wants to project in public mind is an integral part of mission statement. For example, Wipro Limited says, "We will adhere to the highest level of business integrity and ethics in all our dealings."

4. **Organisation's Business:** Some companies mention the nature of their business in terms of products/services, market segment, and technology.

5. **Organisaiton's Objectives:** In some cases basic objectives like survival, growth and profitability are included in the mission statement. Reliance Industries Limited states: "We are committed to enhance our shareholder value."

3.3.4 Essentials of a Good Mission Statement

A good mission statement must fulfil the following requirements:

1. **Clear:** A mission statement should be clear enough to lead to action. It should not just be a high sounding set of platitudes meant for image building. For example, the mission of Hindustan Unilever Limited (HUL) "to add vitality to life" is clear.

2. **Precise:** A mission statement should not be too broad to be meaningless, nor should it be too narrow to restrict growth. For example, " Mobility is our business" is too broad while " manufacturing cycles" is too narrow.
3. **Feasible:** A mission statement should be realistic and achievable in view of the organisation's capabilities. It should always aim high but should not be impossible as otherwise it will not be credible.
4. **Inspiring:** A mission statement should be motivating for people both inside and outside the organisation. They should feel it worth-while working for the organisation or being its customers. For example, Bank of Baroda's mission of "pursuing best global practices for delivering added value to customers" inspires its employees to serve its customers well.
5. **Focus on Customer Rather Than the Product:** Mission statement should focus on needs and wants of customers which define a business. The mission and purpose of every business is to satisfy the customer. It should look at the business from the outside viewpoint of the customer.
6. **Distinctive:** A good mission statement must create a distinctive image of the organisation and set it apart from its counterparts. If all car firms define their mission in the same manner, then there will be little difference between them. Maruti Suzuki's mission of "providing value for money" is distinctive.

3.4 BUSINESS DEFINITION

A business definition means a clear statement of the business or businesses the organisation engages at present or wishes to pursue in future. It specifies the arena in which the organisation will function and compete. A company's business is defined by what needs it is trying to satisfy, to which customer groups it is targeting and by the technologies it will use and the functions it will perform in serving the target market.

Defining the business is necessary because an organisation cannot operate in all the segments of an industry. It can do well when it does different things or does the same things differently. While defining its business, an organisation should focus on its chosen field of business activity. For example, Reliance Industries initially focused on high-priced premium clothing (Vimal brand) in the textile industry.

Another aspect to be considered in business definition is differentiation *i.e.* how an organisation differentiates itself from its counterparts. Differentiation may be in terms of quality, price, delivery or service. For example, Nirma differentiates on the basis of price while Hindustan Unilever uses quality as the differentiation factor.

Business may be defined at corporate level or SBU level. In case of a single business company, business definition is simple. But a large conglomerate such as ITC Limited has to define its business at both corporate and SBU levels.

Similarly, Bharat Heavy Electricals Limited (BHEL) has defined its business at the corporate level as well as at the product category levels (energy, industry, and transportation sectors). At the product category level, business is defined in terms of market segment.

When a company takes up activities outside the scope of its business definition, it may face the crisis of identity. But when a diversification or acquisition is guided by overall business definition, there may be synergy.

Examples of Business Definition

Hindustan Unilever Limited: To meet everyday needs of people everywhere with branded products.

Hero Cycles: To provide functionally valuable bicycles that common people can afford to buy.

Bharti Airtel: To provide multiple forms of reliable, efficient, and inexpensive telecommunication devices.

Indian Oil Corporation: To provide various types of safe and cost-effective energy.

3.4.1. Dimensions of Business Definition

According to Abell[11], a business can be defined along three dimensions of customer groups, customer functions and alternative technologies.

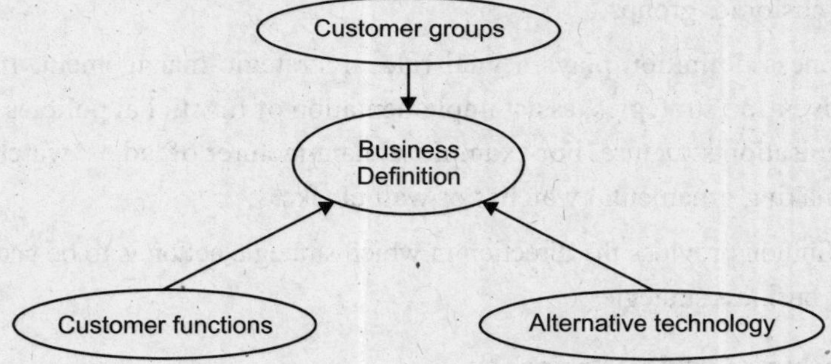

Fig. 3.2 Dimensions of Business Definition

1. **Customer Groups:** Individual customers and industrial users could be the customer groups. These groups relate to who is being satisfied. Customer groups may be classified on the basis of income – low, middle and high income groups.
2. **Customer Functions:** What is being satisfied indicates customer functions. In case of watches, customer functions could be finding time, recording time, using watches as a fashion accessory, gift items or pieces of art. Thus, customer functions are based on what the product or service does for the customers.
3. **Alternative Technologies:** These refer to the ways in which a particular function could be performed for a customer. In case of watches, mechanical, quartz, digital and analogue could be alternative technologies. The core competence of a firm lies in its skills used to provide value to customers. While defining business, the focus must be on the customer.

   Thus, business definition provides the framework within, which a business can operate. It also lays down the direction in which the business can expand or grow. For example, a

11. Derek F. Abell, **Defining the Business: The Starting Point of Strategic Planning,** Prentice Hall, New Jersey, 1980, p. 30.

business serving a specific group of customers can expand to serve other customer groups as well. Similarly, a firm satisfying a set of needs can expand to satisfy complementary needs. The alternative technologies can be expanded to adopt other means of satisfying customer needs. In this way, business definition makes the activities of a business meaningful.

The foregoing three dimensions may be described as the 'who', 'what' 'and 'how' of business definition. The 'who' aspect refers to the customer groups that are targeted by a business. Customer groups may be identified on the basis of demographies (age, income, gender, occupation), geographies (rural/ urban, northern/southern India), or lifestyle (traditional/ modern). The 'what' aspect means the customer functions or needs. Customer needs include basic needs (food, clothing and shelter) and higher-order needs (security, education, leisure status, etc.). Firms design products and services to satisfy customer needs. The 'how' aspect of business definition implies the alternative technologies used to provide products and services to the identified customer groups.

A clear business definition plays a vital role in strategic management. It can guide the choice of objectives and strategies, assist implementation of functional policies and suggest an appropriate organisation structure. For example, a manufacturer of ladies' watches may extend its business by making ornamental watches or wall clocks.

Business definition provides the direction in which strategic action is to be taken and there-by forms the core of business strategies.

3.4.2. The Product/Service Concept

A product/service concept refers to the manner in which a firm assesses the user's perception of its product or service. Such a perception is based on how the product or service performs functions to satisfy customer needs. A business firm seeks to enhance its competitive advantage by offering products/services that provide value to customers.

Examples of Product/Service Concept

1. HCL Ltd. Perceived a computer not as a sophisticated awe-inspiring machine but as a commodity for daily use. This product concept prompted the company to advertise the computer as a consumer durable available through an innovative hire-purchase scheme.
2. Idea Cellular perceived the mobile phone not just a device for making phone call but a multiuse item that can perform a variety of functions such as pay bills, buy tickets, unlock car, take photos, etc.

A carefully and innovatively defined product/service concept is helpful for strategic management in many ways. Products are transient and intermediary mechanisms through which a company provides value to customers. Therefore, firms should focus on skills, capabilities and technologies. With shortening lifecycles of products, the lifecycles of skills become longer. Innovative firms can gain a competitive advantage.

Table 3.1 Some Broad and Narrow Definitions

Broad Definitions	Narrow Definitions
Transportation	Rail roads
Beverages	Soft drinks
Footwear	Women footwear
Home decor	Furniture
Travel and Tourism	Luxury buses

Criteria of an Effective Business Definition

An effective business definition should meet the following criteria:

(*i*) An effective business definition should include a statement of products, markets and functions;

(*ii*) The business definitions should be as precise as possible.

(*iii*) The statement should also indicate the kind of management desired and policies necessary to attain the mission; and

(*iv*) The statement should provide the necessary direction for the formulation of strategies.

3.5 BUSINESS MODEL

The term business model has been defined as "a representation of a firm's underlying core logic and strategic choices for creating and capturing value within a value network"[12].

Business model indicates how the strategies it pursues will allow the company to gain a competitive advantage and achieve superior profitability. In simple terms it specifies how the company makes money. For example, the business model of an economy airline is characterised by e-ticketing, no-frills service, uniform planes, etc.

Examples of Business Model

- Companies operating in the same industry compete with one another but rely on different business models. In the information technology industry Tata Consultancy Services (TCS) uses a traditional fixed-price, fixed time business model in which clients make payments on the basis of time related milestones. On the other hand, Infosys and Wipro depend on a time and material business model under which clients pay on an ongoing basis, according to the volume of work done rather than the time elapsed.

  Source: P. Srinivasan and V. Babu, "India's Famous IT Brigade," **Business Today**, December 4, 2005, p. 100

- Two brothers – B. Saundararajan and G.B. Sundararajan – created and perfected a business model revolving around chickens in 1984. Their chicken-and-egg story model was simple – win the confidence of the farmers, provide a logistic platform for them and provide a link with retailers to sell the merchandise. The model clicked and "Suguna Poultry"

12. Scott M. Shafer, Smith H. Jeff and Jane C. Linder, "The Power of Business Models, "**Business Horizons**, 48(3), pp-199-207.

evolved into a ₹ 4200 crore company. The two brothers started a poultry farm in 1986 in Udumalpet, Tamilnandu. They call their business model as "contract broiler farming" under which farmers who own land and resources can become breeders of Suguna's Ross breed of chicks. The brothers now operate in 13 states, work with 18,000 farmers and have 250 offices across the country with 5,500 employees. They produce 7.5 million chickens per week equivalent to 18% of the Indian market share. They sell to KFC, McDonalds and 22,000 retail shops across the country through 600 distributors.

- Our business model is that we use a master franchise is the market, with local management, local knowledge – they can make these decisions locally and move very quickly to find opportunities—**Domino's**

Business model of an organisation is closely related to its strategy. It can be helpful in analysing and communicating the strategic choices. A business model is a down-to-earth prescription for strategy implementation. The success of Wal-Mart (world's biggest retailer), Google (a search engine). Amazon.com (a virtual bookseller) and several other firms is largely due to their unique business models. McDonald is a global success because its business model is so simple and replicable the world over. The conglomerates of the sixties collapsed because they tried to manage too many businesses in too many different industries. Enron crumbled because tried to run an energy company as a financial institution. "Keep it simple", stupid is a good rule for business models.

Thus, a business model outlines a firm's value proposition for its stakeholders and the system it uses to create and deliver value to its customers. It is a mental model of how a company's strategies form a congruent whole enabling it to gain a competitive advantage.

3.6 GOALS AND OBJECTIVES

Meaning: Goals and objectives refer to the end results which an organisation strives for. These two terms are used interchangeably. But strictly speaking, goals are different from objectives. Goals represent what an organisation wishes to accomplish in a future time period. On the other hand, objectives specify how the goals shall be achieved. Goals are mainly generalised and qualitative whereas objectives are more specific and quantitative. Objectives are measurable and comparable and operatioalise the goals. Objectives have a short term orientation while goals are mainly long term. If profitability is a goal, objective may be 25 per cent return on investment.

Nature: The main features of objectives are:

(*i*) Objectives are the **reason for an organisation's existence.** Every organisation exists to achieve certain objectives.

(*ii*) Objectives are **multiple.** In the words of Peter Drucker' "to manage a business is to balance a variety of needs and goals..... objectives are needed in every area where performance and results directly and vitally contribute to the survival and growth of the business"[13].

(*iii*) Objectives at different levels of an organisation constitute a **hierarchy** or **ends-means chain.** Higher level objectives are the ends and lower level objectives serve as the means.

13. Peter F. Drucker, **The Practice of Management**, William Hineman, London, 1954, pp 62-63.

Corporate objectives may be called strategic objectives (*e.g.* market share, profitability social change, corporate image, etc) while objectives in functional areas like finance (ROI), marketing, etc may be called business process objectives.

Fig. 3.4. Hierarchy of Objectives OR Ends-Means Chain

(*iv*) Objective vary in time span *e.g.* yearly, half yearly, quarterly objectives.

(*v*) Objectives require change due to changes in environment, organisational capabilities, expectations of stakeholders, life cycle of the organisation, etc.

Table 3.2. Key Result Areas (KRAs)

1. ***Market Standing*** — the specification of market segments and the share of each segment sought.
2. ***Innovation*** — the extent of business involvement in developing new products and services.
3. ***Productivity*** — the way the firm is going to measure its efficiency. (Options include processing and output discussed earlier).
4. ***Physical and financial resources*** — the acquisition and efficient use of resources (inputs).
5. ***Profitability*** — identification of desired levels of profitability to be used (10 per cent ROI, 7 per cent profit margin).
6. ***Manager performance and development*** — criteria for evaluating the performance of managers and the design of training and development programmes to assist managers in reaching their potential.
7. ***Worker performance and attitude*** — criteria for evaluating the performance of operative employees and organisational efforts to maintain positive employee attitudes towards their jobs and the firms.
8. ***Public responsibility*** — the role of the firm in meeting the needs of society and actions to be taken to enhance the firm's public image.

Source: Peter F. Drucker, **Management Tasks, Responsibilty and Practices,** Harper & Row, New York, 1974, p.100

(*vi*) There are two main approaches to setting objectives – top down approach and bottom up approach.

3.6.1 Role of Objectives

Objectives play a significant role in strategic management in the following ways:

1. **Define Relationship:** Objectives define the relationship of an organisation with its environment. These reflect its commitment to various stakeholders.
2. **Operationalise Vision and Mission:** Objectives help an organisation to pursue its vision and mission. Long-term goals and short-term targets are the milestones to reach the mission and vision.
3. **Provide Basis for Decision Making:** Objectives direct the attention of decision makers to those areas where strategic decisions are needed. Clearly defined objectives facilitate unified planning. Objectives serve as a guide to strategy formulation.
4. **Motivate People:** Objectives serve as a source of inspiration for members of an organisation. They work hard to achieve the objectives and get a sense of accomplishment.
5. **Facilitate Decentralisation:** Objectives indicate the contribution each unit or individual is expected to make. They enable higher level managers to delegate decision-making authority to managers at operating levels.
6. **Serve as Control Standards:** Objectives in the form of time-bound targets serve as standards against which performance can be assessed. They put pressure on employees and help to ensure accomplishment.
7. **Assist Voluntary Coordination:** Clearly specified and mutually agreed upon objectives help integrate individual and group efforts. People tend to work within their own areas of discretion and adjust according to the needs of one another. Unity of purpose leads to unity of action.

The importance of objectives can be summed up as: "If you don't know where you want to reach, no path will take you there."

In the absence of clear-cut objectives, an organisation is like a ship which has no radar and compass.

The unchanging purpose of business, like any human activity, is not to go somewhere but to discover who we are and what we can become.

The hardest part of building a company is working silently over long periods of time and keep the faith in goals that are far away.

3.6.2 Factors Influencing Objective setting

According to Glueck and Jauch,[14] organisational objectives are set on the basis of the following factors:

1. **Forces in the Environment:** These refer to various stakeholders such as shareholders, employees, customers, suppliers, government and society. Each of these stakeholders has certain expectations from the organisation. The interests of these various stakeholders

14. Willian F. Glueck and Lawrence R. Jauch, **Business Policy and Strategic Management** McGraw Hill, New York, 1984.

may be conflicting. The objectives of an organisation emerge out of integration of these expectations. Stakeholders having higher bargaining power or control may exercise greater influence on organisational objectives. The importance attached to different objectives may change over time with change in the expectations of stakeholders.

2. **Organisational Resources:** The objectives of an organisation are dependent on its resources or capabilities. Material and human resources serve as constraints on objective setting.
3. **Internal Power Relationships:** Power politics within the organisation also influences objective setting. Board of Directors, Chief Executive and other strategists who wield considerable power decide the priority of objectives.
4. **Value System of Top Executives:** Values refer to enduring beliefs about what is good or bad, desirable or undesirable. These affect the organisation's philosophy regarding strategic management in general and objectives in particular. For example, entrepreneurial or monetary values may give emphasis to profitability whereas philanthropic values may focus on social objectives.
5. **Management's Awareness:** Managers who are aware of the past objectives may focus on these objectives. Organisations usually operate on the basis of continuity and change their objectives in incremental rather than radical manner.

Thus, objective setting is a complex process which is based on consensus building. Vision and mission help in building consensus and serve as the foundation for setting objectives

Objectives of Bharat Heavy Electricals Limited

Growth: To ensure a steady growth in Business so as to fulfil national aspirations and expand international operations.

Profitability: To provide a reasonable and adequate return on capital employed primarily through improvements in operational efficiency, capacity utilisation and productivity, and generate adequate internal resources to finance the company's growth.

Image: To build up a high degree of customer confidence by sustaining international standard of excellence in product quality, performance and services particularly in regard to supply of spares and after-sale-service; to fulfil the expectations which stakeholders like Government as owner, employees, customers, and the country at large have from BHEL.

Continuity: To invest in human resource development, sustained research and development, strive for excellence in management, and other long-term objectives to ensure a leadership status for BHEL.

3.6.3 Issues in Objective Setting

The basic issues involved in objective setting are as follows:

1. **Periodicity:** Objectives are set for different time periods – long term, medium term and short term. Most of the organisations set objectives for long term and short term. Long-term objectives (*e.g.* growth) are, by nature, less certain and, therefore, stated in a general way. On the other hand, short-term objectives are relatively more certain and are set in specific terms. Short-term objectives are generally derived from long term objectives.
2. **Specificity:** Objectives may be stated at different levels of specificity which range from broadly stated goals to specifically stated targets. Many organisations set overall corporate objectives as well as functional and operational objectives. The level of

specificity should be such that members of the organisation clearly understand what is to be achieved. For example, a company may set the objective of doubling its turnover in four years and net profits in three years.

3. **Multiplicity:** An organisation strives to achieve several, rather than a single one objective simultaneously. The issue of multiplicity of objectives is concerned with organisational levels (higher or lower), importance (primary or secondary), ends (growth or survival), functions (finance or marketing) and nature (organisational or personal). Another issue related to multiplicity is the number and type of objectives to be set. Too few or too many objectives are both unrealistic. Objectives should be set in all the key result areas (KRAs). Peter Drucker has identified eight such areas: market standing, innovation, productivity, physical and financial resources, profitability, manager performance and development, worker performance and attitude, and public responsibility.[15]
4. **Reality:** Organisations tend to have two sets of objectives – official and operational. Official objectives are those which organisations prefer to attain while operational objectives are those which they seek to attain in reality. Official objectives are meant for image building.
5. **Quality:** Objectives may be set in good or bad forms. Good objectives are those which provide specific direction for action and a tangible basis for evaluating performance. "To be market leader in our industry" is a bad objective because it is not measurable. This objective may be restated as: "To increase market share by 20 per cent during the next four years". This objective is measurable and verifiable.

3.6.4 Essentials of Valid Objectives

Good objectives must fulfil the following requirements.

1. **Understandable:** Objectives must be understandable by those who are responsible for achieving them. Otherwise no action may be taken or a wrong action might be taken.
2. **Clear and Specific:** To say that " our company seeks to increase sales" is vague. On the other hand, "our company seeks to increase sales by ten per cent next year" is concrete and specific.
3. **Time-Bound:** Objectives should have a time frame so that managers know the duration within which objectives have to be achieved.
4. **Measurable:** Objectives must be such that performance can be compared and controlled with them. For example, a company which wants to be attractive to work for can use measures like number of job applications received per hire, average emoluments offered, employee turnover per year. Objectives should be result oriented rather than activity oriented.
5. **Challenging:** Objectives should be set at challenging but realistic levels. They should be neither too easy nor unachievable.
6. **Interrelated:** Objectives set in different areas must be balanced with each other. Otherwise they may be a source of conflict between departments or divisions. Short-term objectives should be consistent with long-term objectives.

---

15. Peter F. Drucker, *op. cit*

3.6.5 Changes in Objectives

Objectives of an organisation are not static but dynamic. These have to be changed when the existing objectives have been achieved or cannot be achieved. It may not be desirable to pursue the existing objectives due to changes in the environment. Objectives may be expanded or substituted by new objectives. Changes in organisational objective may become necessary due to the following reasons:

1. **Change in Aspiration Level:** An organisation is used as a means of satisfying the personal ambitions of its founders and other key strategists. For example, Reliance Industries Limited worked to achieve the ambition of its founder late Dhirubhai Ambani to become the biggest industrialist of India. Changes in the top management team may require a change in organisational objectives.
2. **Change in Environment:** An organisation has to work within the framework of external environment. The environment changes over time. Any major change in enivonment requires a change in organisational objectives. For instance, Indian companies had to change their objectives and strategies to withstand competition from foreign companies after liberalisation in 1991. Product innovation, cost reduction, quality improvement, human resource development became important objectives.
3. **Pressure from Stakeholders:** The objectives of an organisation are often the outcome of bargaining between its shareholders, employees, customers, government, suppliers, etc. When the bargaining power of a particular stakeholder group increases considerably, it may necessitate a change in organisational objectives.
4. **Change in Organisation's Life Cycle:** Like human beings, an organisation passes through different stages in its lifecycle[16]. There is a shift in its objectives from one stage to another. (Table 3.3)

Table 3.3: Organisational Lifecycle, Objectives, and Strategic Focus

Lifecycle stage	Organisational objectives	Strategic focus
Birth	Survival–create new entity	Identify an entrepreneurial idea and find resources
Infancy	Define mission and search environment	Define products, markets, and functions to offer
Youth	Quantitative growth	Increase market share, claim more territory
Youth adult	Achieve uniqueness and establish niche	Redefine products, markets , and functions
Adult	Qualitative growth, gain reputation	Reap reward, mine markets for benefits
Maturity	Stabilise and contribute to society	Maintain position with stability
Old age	Survival	Procreate and retrench parts that are no longer healthy

The time which is taken to reach a particular stage of its lifecycle differs from one organisation to another. For example, ITC Limited, set up in 1913, is still hungry for expansion while many leasing companies established in 1980s have completed their lifecycle and have exited.

16. William F. Glueck and Laurence R. Jauch, *op. cit.* p. 62.

3.7 STAKEHOLDERS APPROACH TO ORGANISATIONAL OBJECTIVES

Cyert and March suggest that objective setting is a continuous coalition and bargaining process in which several stakeholders participate. While setting its objectives and deciding their priorities, an organisation must identify its major stakeholders and their expectations. It must reconcile and integrate these expectations into its objectives. For example, the profitability objective helps to meet the expectations of shareholders while social commitment objective is necessitated by the expectations of the society. Coalition and bargaining are the two key elements in this objective setting process.

1. **Coalition:** The alliance between two or more individuals or groups for a common goal is called coalition. The purpose of a coalition is to increase power against other individuals or groups. An organisation is considered a coalition of several groups. For example, shareholders, managers and financiers may join together to dominate objective setting in a company.
2. **Bargaining:** Negotiation of an agreement between two or more parties is known as bargaining. It is a process of give and take or compromise so as to reach a final settlement. Management wants to control costs and labour wants increase in wages. The two sides bargain to arrive at a compromise. Similarly, there may be bargaining between different divisions/departments over allocation of resources.

3.8 BALANCED SCORECARD APPROACH TO OBJECTIVE SETTING

The Balanced Scorecard Approach developed by Kaplan and Norton[17] is a strategic planning and performance management system. It focuses attention on measuring a wide range of non-financial and operational objectives so as to avoid undue emphasis on short-term financial objectives. The balanced scorecard model is shown in Fig. 3.5

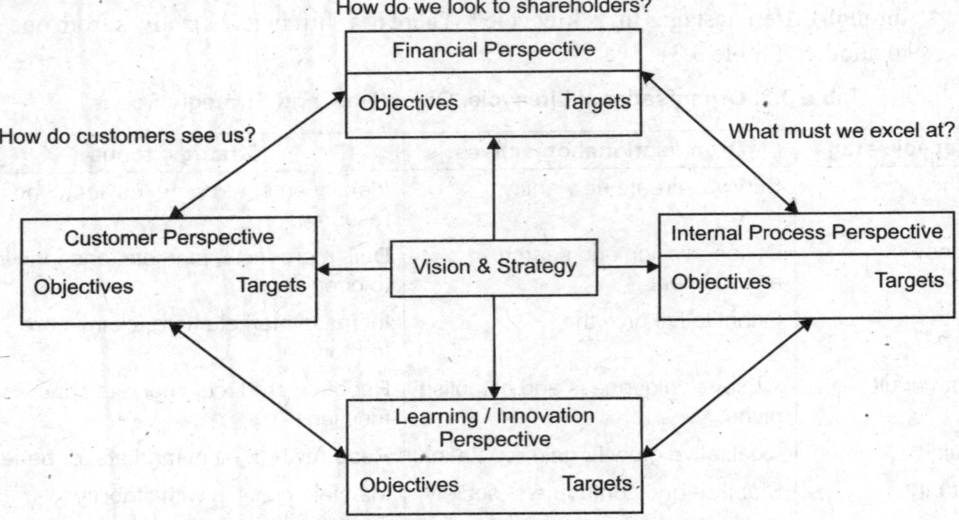

Fig. 3.5. The Balanced Scorecard Model Source: Based on R.S. Kaplan and D.P. Norton, The Strategy-focused orientation: How Balanced Scorecard Companies Thrive in the New Business Environment, Boston, Harvard Business School Publishing , 2000

17. Robert S. Kaplan and David P. Norton, **The Balanced Scorecard: Translating Strategies into Action,** Harvard Business School Press, Boston, 1996

Once the strategic intent is established the specific, measures relating to the four perspectives, can be identified. For example, revenue growth may be measure for financial perspective. The specific strategies and the activities needed to implement them are mapped. Kaplan and Norton used, 'strategy map' which is a visual representation of strategy. The four perspectives are connected to each other in a 'cause and effect' manner. Thus, the relationship between the strategic intent and strategic objectives becomes clear. (Fig. 3.6)

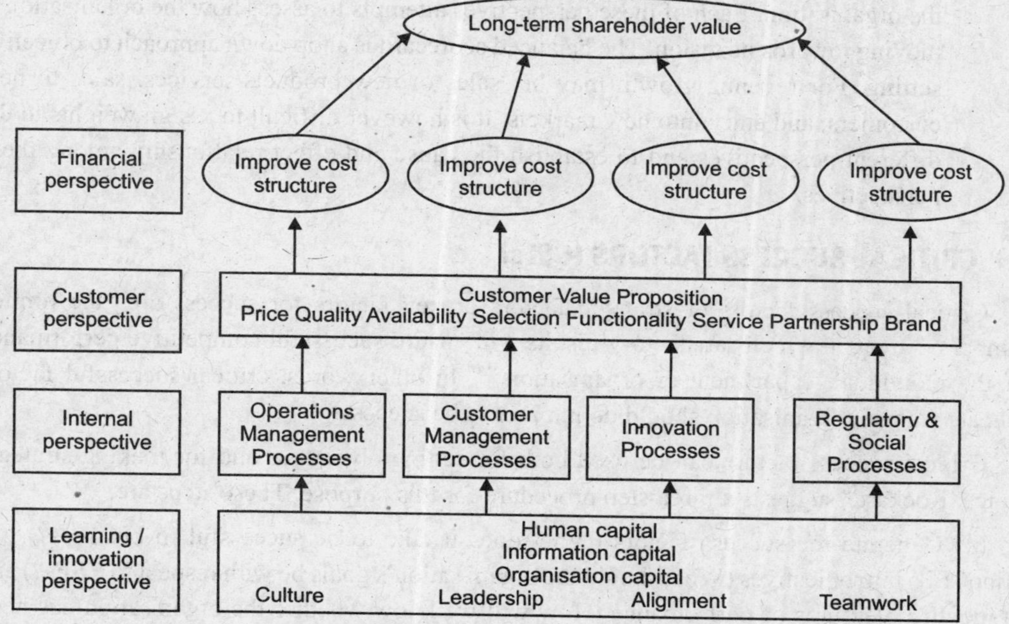

Fig. 3.6. A Typical Strategy Map

Source: Based on R. S. Kaplan and D.P. Norton : op. cit.

In order to measure performance in the four areas metrics can be set up. For example, metrics and cost benefit figures are also included in the financial perspective

1. **Financial Perspective:** The financial measures derived from the strategic intent are included in this perspective. Revenues, earnings, return on capital and cash flow are examples of these measures. Additional finance related variables such as risk management and cost benefit figures are also included in the financial perspective.
2. **Customer Perspective:** The organisation's ability to provide quality goods and services, effective delivery and overall customer satisfaction are measured in this perspective. Market share, customer satisfaction and customer loyalty are examples of these measures.
3. **Internal Business Perspective:** The mechanisms through which performance expectations are achieved are called internal business processes. In order to meet these expectations and organisational objectives, an organisation must identify the key business processes at which it has to excel. Productivity, quality and efficiency are examples of measures that lead to financial success and satisfied customers.

4. **Learning and Growth Perspective:** An organisation must be able to manage its business and adapt to change. Its employees must acquire new skills and capabilities to face the challenges of environmental changes and customer expectations. Employee morale, knowledge, employee turnover and suggestions, share of revenue from new products are examples of these measures.

   The four perspectives given above help in prioritising the key strategic objectives of the organisation. Each of these perspectives attempts to assess how the organisation is moving towards its vision. The balanced scorecard is a top down approach to objective setting. For revenue growth may be: sales of new products/services, sales to new customers, and entry into new markets. It is however difficult to assign weights to the different perspectives and to establish the cause and effect relationship among these perspectives.

3.9 CRITICAL SUCCESS FACTORS (CSFs)

Critical success factors or strategic factors or key factors for success are "the limited number of areas in which satisfactory results will ensure successful competitive performance for the individual, department or organisation"[18]. In other words, critical successful factors indicate what an organisation should do in order to be successful.

Critical success factors can be used both for setting objectives and for making strategic choice. Rockart[19] suggests a three-step procedure for this purpose. These steps are:

(*a*) Generate the success factors (What does it take to be successful in business?), (*b*) refineCSFs into objectives (What should the organi sation's goals be with respect to CSFs?) and (*c*) identify measures of performance (How will we know whether the organisation has been successful on this factor?). CSFs help to pinpoint the key result areas to determine objectives in those areas and to identify measures of performance.

CSFs differ from industry to industry, depending on the following factors:

1. **Industry Characteristics:** An industry's specific characteristics define its own CSFs. For example, in sugar, steel, loose tea and other commodity-based industries, sales promotion is not a CSF but it becomes a CSF in fast moving consumer goods in which products are sold on brand basis. Similarly, high capital investment is a CSF in petroleum, civil aviation and other highly capital-intensive industries while this is not a CSF in soft ware development.
2. **Competitive Strategy and Industry Position:** The CSFs of an industry arise out of the competitive strategies of various firms. Different firms compete on the basis of their relative position in the industry. Some firms are industry leaders and create their own CSFs. For example, advertising became a CSF in textiles industry largely due to Reliance Industries Limited.

18. John F. Rockart and Christine V. Bullen, " A Primer on Critical Success Factors" in C.V. Bullen (ed.), **The Rise of Managerial Computing,** Dow Jones Irwin, Homewood Ill., 1986.
19. John F. Rockart, " CEs Define Their Own Data Needs," **Harvard Business Review** March-April 1979, p. 89.

3. **Environment:** Population growth, economic position, government regulations and other environmental factors also determine CSFs. For example, customer service emerged as a CSF after deregulation and the entry of private telecommunication firms in India.
4. **Temporal Factors:** These factors create temporary CSFs such as death of the chief executive, division in family business, etc.

Table 3.4: Critical Success Factors In Some Industries

Shoe Manufacturing: High product quality, low cost, flexible product mix, sophisticated retailing, product image
Food Processing: High quality product, packaging, efficient distribution network, sales promotion.
Toothpaste Industry: Quality (form, foam, flavour and freshness) widearea distribution network, high level of promotion, brand loyalty
Automobile Industry: Styling, strong dealer network, manufacturing cost control, ability to meet environmental standards
Courier Service: Speed, dispatch, reliability and price

5. **Managerial Position:** Manufacturing mangers, for example, have CSFs in terms of product quality, inventory control and cash control. Customer relationship management may be a CSF for managers in marketing and sales departments.

3.10 KEY PERFORMANCE INDICATORS

In order to measure CSFs, key indicators of performance are needed. Key performance indicators (KPIs) are the measures in terms of which performance can be measured and compared. KPIs are related to the CSFs and ultimately to the vision of the organisation. For example, an organisation may define its vision as "to be the leader in the industry". To operationalize this vision, it may determine KPIs such as market share. Similarly KPIs for the CSF of high quality product may be product reject rate, recall rate after delivery and number of complaints. Thus, KPIs help to quantify the critical success factors. Right KPIs also. enable employees to understand how are they contributing to organisational goals.

Key performance indicators make it clear what is important and what is to be done to achieve objectives. These help to measure progress towards organisational objectives. KPIs also act as motivators for employees. An organisation can use KPIs to benchmark its performance over time and against its competitors in the same industry.

SUMMARY

Strategic Intent: Desired future position – destiny, sense of direction and discovery

Stretch, Leverage and Fit: (1) Stretch means extra effort to optimise the resources and capabilities. (2) Leverage is concentrating, accumulating and conserving resources so as to realise aspiration. (3) Fit is the match between capabilities and aspirations.

Vision: Desired picture of the organisation's position in distant future. **A good** vision is realistic, credible, attractive, unique, appropriate, charter, motivational and well articulated. **Vision** indicates ultimate destination, source of motivation, unifying force, encourages risk taking, fosters long term thinking, differentiates, integrity. **Developing** vision involves (1) vision audit (*ii*) vision context (*iii*) future scenarios, (*iv*) alternative visions (*v*) choice of final vision.

Core ideology (core values and core purpose) and envisioned future (long-term audacious goals and vivid description of achievement) are the elements of vision.

Mission: The reason for the existence of an organisation and its fundamental unique purpose. **Advantages:** provides direction, clarifies aspirations, guides stakeholder relations, unifying force, improves public image: **Formulation:** (*i*) self-concept (*ii*) philosophy (*iii*) image (*iv*) business (*v*) objectives. **Essentials:** clear, precise, feasible, inspiring, distinctive.

Business Definition: Customer groups, customer functions, alternative technologies; the product/service concept.

Business Model: Underlying core logic and strategic choice for creating value.

Business Objectives: End results to be achieved, objectives are multiple and form a hierarchy. Define relationship, operationalism mission, basis for decision making, motivate, help decentralise, assist coordination, provide standards for control.

Factors Influencing Objectives: (*i*) environmental forces (*ii*) organisational resources (*iii*) power relationships (*iv*) value system (*v*) managerial awareness.

Issues in Objective Setting: Periodicity, specificity, multiplicity, reality, quality.

Essentials of Valid Objectives: (*i*) understandable (*ii*) clear and specific (*iii*) time bound (*iv*) measurable (*v*) challenging (*vi*) interrelated

Changes in Objectives: Due to changes in (*a*) aspirations (*b*) environment (*c*) stakeholder's pressure (*d*) organisation's lifecycle

Stakeholders' Approach to Objectives: (*i*) coalition (*ii*) bargaining

Balanced Scorecard: (*i*) Financial perspective (*ii*) customer perspective (*iii*) internal business perspective (*iv*) learning and growth perspective.

Critical Success Factors (CSFs): (*i*) industry characteristics (*ii*) competitive strategy and industry position (*iii*) environment (*iv*) temporal factors (*v*) managerial position

Key Performance Indicators (KPIs): Help operationalise CSFs, make clear what is to be done, motivate employees, help benchmark organisation's performance.

TEST QUESTIONS

1. What do you mean by 'strategic intent'? Differentiate between the concepts of 'strategic stretch' 'leverage' and, strategic fit', with appropriate examples.
2. What is meant by 'Hierarchy of Strategic Intent'? Give its elements in the context of an Indian multinational corporation.
3. What do you understand by the term "vision"? What is its role in strategic management?
4. Explain the essentials of a good vision statement. State the steps involved in developing a vision statement.
5. What is meant by the term "Mission"? Describe its role in strategic management.
6. Explain the steps involved in formulating a mission statement. What are the essentials of a good mission statement?

7. Define and distinguish between Vision, Mission and Purpose.
8. What is Mission? Why do companies write their mission? Prepare the mission statement of any global firm with which you are aware.
9. What is Vision? Why do companies write their vision? Write the vision statement of any global firm with which you are aware.
10. What is meant by 'Business Definition'. State its dimensions. Define the business of any Indian conglomerate.
11. "The mission statement is a declaration of an organisation's reason for being. It answers the pivotal equation: What is our mission?" Elucidate this statement and discuss the nature and importance of a mission statement.
12. "Vision, mission, business definition and objectives are not mutually exclusive components of the strategic management process rather these are highly interdependent and inseparable". Explain
13. What do you understand by Business Model? Compare the business models of any three companies in the same industry.
14. What are the objectives of business organisation? How are these established?
15. What are the causes and consequences of conflict among objectives? Suggest measures for resolution of conflict among organisational objectives.
16. As a consultant in a global firm in which areas would you prefer to formulate objectives and why?
17. Identify the major areas in a business organisation in which goals are to be set. Discuss each one of them in detail.
18. What do you understand by objectives of an organisation? How can a firm determine its objectives?
19. What are the goals of business organisations? How are they established?
20. The ends for which corporate enterprises strive are referred to as 'mission' 'objectives' and 'goals'. How would you distinguish between these terms?
21. How is strategic intent different from unrealistic targets? Suggest ways to operationalise strategic intent of a company in pharmaceutical sector.
22. How is 'mission' different from scope? Take the example of a company from the FMCG sector to illustrate the difference.
23. "It is more important to have a vision than to have a mission in the 21st century." Do you agree? Give reasons. Explain your understanding of vision and mission from either Hindustan Unilever Limited or ITC Limited.
24. Discuss the Balanced Scorecard Approach' to objective setting. How is this approach related to a firm's Vision and Mission?
25. Define 'objectives' and explain the main characteristics of objectives.
26. What do you mean by multiple objectives? What is the hierarchy of objectives?
27. Distinguish between:

    (*a*) Strategic intent and core competence

(*b*) Strategy model and business model

28. Explain the role of objectives in strategic management. What are the factors influencing objectives of an organisation?
29. What are the major issues in objective setting. Discuss the essentials of valid objectives.
30. Why an organisation needs to change its objectives? Explain the stakeholder' approach to objective-setting.
31. What is Balanced Scorecard? Describe its role in objective-setting.
32. What are Critical Success Factors? Why do they differ from industry to industry?
33. What do you understand by Key Performance Indicators? How are these useful in strategic management of an organisation?
34. What is meant by the "Mission" of an organisation? Describe its role in strategy formulation. State the features of a good mission statement.
35. What do you mean by the term "Vision"? Describe its role in strategy formulation. State the features of a good vision statement.
36. Define and illustrate mission statement. Are mission and vision same or different?
37. "The business definition clarifies the nature of existing products and functions the company presently provides." Elucidate this statement and bring out the difference between vision, mission and objective.
38. "A vision is too abstract to be of any practical value." How far do you agree with this view? Give reasons for your answer.
39. "A mission statement should always aim high but it should also be realistic and achievable." How far do you agree with this statement? Cite at least two corporate examples and explain the characteristics of a mission statement.
40. What do you understand by corporate objectives? What are the areas in which the corporation might establish objectives?
41. Explain 'business objectives'. Why do we determine objectives first before starting the business and how do these differ from goals?
42. (*a*) Why is it necessary for any organisation to identify its 'Mission'?

    (*b*) Give two suitable examples to indicate the relationship between 'Mission' and 'Strategy'.
43. "In India today, every corporation has to consider adopting a number of diverse objectives rather than single objective like profit". Why? Explain.
44. "Goal setting may be influenced by constraints perceived by decision makers reflecting the organisation's capabilities". In the light of this statement explain the factors affecting goal setting.
45. How do realities of external environment and organisation's capabilities affect the choice

of strategic goals?

46. A company manufacturing pre-recorded music cassettes seeks your help in formulating its business mission'. Prepare a draft mission statement for the company.

47. "Vision and mission statements help guide stakeholder expectations". Discuss.

48. "Tata Motors represent a classic case of strategic stretch, leverage and fit". Elaborate.

CASE STUDY

Marico Ltd. is a leading Indian family group operating in consumer products, skin care services and ayurvedic products businesses. Marico has four business segments: domestic FMCG, international FMCG, Kaya Skin solutions and Sundari Spa Skin products. It occupies the leading or second position in most of its brands and brand extensions such as Parachute, Saffola, Sweekar, Hair & Care, Kaya and Sundari serving the hair oil, edible oils and sikn care segments of the FMCG industry. Manufacturing takes place in its seven plants at different places in India and sourcing is done from sub-contractors. Consumption of Marico's products takes place mainly in the urban and semi-urban areas of India and by expatriates outside India. As an FMCG company, Marico has implemented supply chain planning and management systems.

Marico's strengths lie in factors such as a well-established distribution network and low operational costs. Externally, the factors helping Marico are intense competition between organised and unorganised segments and wide availability of raw materials in India. Mario attempts to leverage its national competitive advantage to operate in SAARC countries under its regionalisation strategies and in the Middle East under its inter nationallisation strategies. Franchising and acquisitions are the main drivers of its regional and international expansion.

Marico consciously tries to avoid head-on competition with formidable MNCs such as the Hindustan Unilever by differentiating on the basis of unique ethnic Indian products and services. Its business model is based on focused growth across all its brands and territories, driven by offering better value propositions to consumers, market expansion and widening of the distribution network. It lays emphasis on sales volume and growth rather than sales value, thus adopting a long-term perspective.

The domestic FMCG sector has some of the well-known brand sin India such as Parachute and Saffola. Parachute hair oil relies on converting users of loose hair oil sold in India consumer markets and perceived as low quality with the risk of being 'adulterated', to users of packaged and branded hair oil. Saffola operates on the health platform with claimed benefit for a healthy heart. Both brands rely on the differentiation platforms of branded, quality and reliable products with moderately high prices.

Marico's International FMCG sector has a subsidiary in Bangladesh, an acquisition in Egypt, franchisees in and exports to the Middle Eastern countries such as Oman, Saudi Arabia and UAE that have a substantial Indian expatriate population. Sales have also been initiated in other countries such as the US and Malaysia. Products are sold with minor customisation to suit local conditions and customer preferences.

The Kaya Skin solutions sector adopts a focused differentiation strategy by seeking to provide dermatological services for high-quality, premium skin care through its clinics located in India and some Middle Eastern countries. It aims to provide a high-end solution to the innumerable beauty salons that have mushroomed in Indian cities and towns. This business is in a take-off stage.

Sundari embarked in the US by acquisition and spread to European cities as a specialty range of skin products, capitalising on the increasingly popular ayurvedic solutions for skin care.

As an FMCG company, Marico attempts to keep a continual supply line of improved and new products in its various businesses. In 2005, it crossed the ₹1000-crore sales benchmark and intends to reach ₹2500-crore mark in 2010.

Questions:

(*a*) Explain the 'business definition' of Marico. What business model is it following to accomplish its strategic objectives?

(*b*) Identify and explain the business level strategies adopted by Marico to push its various brands.

(*c*) Why is Marico concentrating more on uncontested markets? Do you agree with the view that business level strategies operate under the corporate strategies? Give reasons for your answer.

PART – III

STRATEGY FORMULATION

4. Environmental Analysis and Appraisal
5. Organisational Analysis and Appraisal
6. Corporate Level Strategies
7. Business Level Strategies
8. Strategic Analysis and Choice of Strategy

4 CHAPTER

ENVIRONMENTAL ANALYSIS AND APPRAISAL

CHAPTER OUTLINE

By establishing the hierarchy of strategic intent, an organisation knows what it wants to achieve. Now it has to decide how it will achieve. This question can be answered by formulating strategies. The first stage in the process of strategy formulation is analysis and appraisal of the environment in which the organisation will operate.

4.1. CONCEPT OF ENVIRONMENT

The concept 'environment' is often used in two ways: (a) external forces which lie outside the organisation, and (b) internal forces which lie inside the organisation. But in this chapter we are concerned only with the external environment.

The external environment consists of all those forces, factors, institutions and groups which lie outside an organisation and interact with it directly or indirectly.

"Environment factors or constraints are largely, if not totally, external and beyond the control of individual industrial enterprises and their managements. These are essentially the 'givens' within which firms and their managements must operate in a specific country and they vary, often greatly, from country to country.".

4.2. NATURE OF ENVIRONMENT

The main characteristics of business environment are as follows:

1. **Complexity:** The environment consists of several factors and forces which interact with each other. Greater the number and diversity of environmental forces, higher is the degree of their complexity. The range of environmental forces and their heterogeneity has increased since globalisation. Today's business firms operate in a highly complex environment.
2. **Dynamism:** The environment is dynamic as it is changing continuously. The rate of change in the environment is fast and unpredictable. When the rate of change is high and variable, environment becomes volatile or turbulent.

The complexity and volatility of environment may be combined to determine environmental uncertainty. Such a combination yields four quadrants (Fig. 4.1).

Degree of Change

Degree of Complexity		Stable	Dynamic
	Simple	Stable, predictable environment. Few products and services. Limited number of customers, suppliers and competitors. Minimal need for sophisticated knowledge.	Dynamic, unpredictable environment. Few products and services. Limited number of customers, suppliers and competitors. Minimal need for sophisticated knowledge.
	Complex	Stable, predictable environment. Many products and services. Many customers, suppliers and competitors. High need for sophisticated knowledge.	Dynamic, unpredictable environment. Many products and services. Many customers, suppliers and competitors. High need for sophisticated knowledge.

uncertainty

Fig. 4.1 Environmental Complexity and Dynamism

(*i*) **Stable-Simple:** Organisations operating in such an environment generally provide few products with a limited number of customers, suppliers and competitors. In addition, the sources of raw materials are few and easily identifiable. Both the degree of change and the degree of complexity are low. Decisions can, therefore, be made with some certainty about the end results.

(*ii*) **Stable-Complex:** In this quadrant the degree of change is low but the degree of complexity is high. In other words, the number of customers, competitors and suppliers has increased. The degree of knowledge associated with serving these customers is high.

(*iii*) **Dynamic-Simple:** An organisation operating in this environment faces high degree of change. But the number of customers, competitors and suppliers is limited. For example, a clothing manufacturer selling to retail outlets faces rapidly changing styles of clothing.

(*iv*) **Dynamic-Complex:** Here the environment is highly unpredictable. The number of customers, competitors and suppliers is also large. Electronics and computer software firms face such an environment.

As the environment moves from stable-simple to dyanmic-complex, information about the environment decreases and the effects or specific organisational actions become increasingly unknown.

Thus, environment is multifaceted or multidimensional. It exercises a far reaching impact on the survival, growth and profitability of organisations. There is a continuous interaction between an organisation and its environment. This interaction can be analysed in several ways. **First,** the organisation can be considered as an **input-output system.** It takes human, capital, technical and other inputs from the environment. These inputs are transformed into outputs (goods, services, profits, wages, etc.) which are given back to the environment. **Second,** the organisation may be thought of as a **coalition** of several groups both within and outside the organisation. These groups of **stakeholders** (shareholders, employees, customers, suppliers, government, society, etc.) contribute to the success of the organisation and want a share in its success. **Third,** changes in the environment create opportunities and threats for the organisation. The success of an organisation depends on how well it exploits the opportunities and faces the threats.

The organisation-environment interaction has important implications for strategic management.

(*i*) The environmental influence process is very complex because different elements of environment are interconnected. The influence is probabilistic rather than deterministic. For example, the structure of an organisation and employee attitudes depend on the environment. But the organisation structure also influences employee attitudes. Thus, the influence is both direct and indirect and there is no simple cause-effect relationship between environmental forces and organisational variables.

(*ii*) The environmental forces may affect different parts of the organisation in different ways. The effect may be direct on some parts and indirect on other parts. For example, any change in the taxation policy may affect the finance department directly but it may have only an indirect effect on marketing and production departments.

(*iii*) Different organisations may perceive the same environmental force in different ways depending upon its internal situation. For example, an innovative firm may treat a technological change as an opportunity while a non-innovative firm may consider it a threat.

(*iv*) Environment-organisation interface is multilateral rather than unilateral. Organisations can collectively influence their environment. For example, trade associations and chambers of commerce lobby with the government to create business-friendly policies, rules and regulations.

4.3. COMPONENTS OF ENVIRONMENT

The external environment may be classified into two broad categories—

(*a*) Micro or direct action or task or specific environment, and

(*b*) Macro or indirect action or general environment.

Micro or specific environment refers to those groups with which the organisation comes into direct and frequent contact in the course of its functioning. They directly affect a particular organisation. Micro environment consists of the following:

(*i*) **Customers:** They are the people who pay money to acquire the organisation's products and services. An organisation's survival depends upon its ability to identify its customers and meet their needs. Customers determine the nature and prices of products and services. The need to meet customer requirements thereby influences the organisation's interactions with its competitors and suppliers.

The needs, preferences, attitudes and buying behaviour of customers in India are changing. They are increasingly paying attention to product quality, price, safety and convenience. Therefore, both manufacturers and distributors are more concerned about quality, speed of delivery and customer service.

(*ii*) **Competitors:** They are the business firms which compete with the organisation for resources. An organisation that fails to meet the needs of its customers as effectively as do competitors cannot survive for long. In many cases it is not customers but competitors who determine what products or services can be sold and at what price. Today an organisation must be innovative and efficient in order to cope with its competitors. It must face not only the direct competitors but also the suppliers of substitute products and services For example, an airline faces direct competition from other airlines and indirect competition from railways, bus operators and taxi operators.

(*iii*) **Suppliers:** They are the people and groups which supply inputs to the firm. An organisation must acquire raw materials, labour, equipment, etc., in order to produce products and services. In the case of raw materials, an organisation must ensure a steady supply of high quality at the minimum possible price. It may have to avoid becoming overly dependent on a single supplier. The acquisition of human resources depends on variations in labour market, trade unions and labour laws.

Cost, availability and reliability of raw materials, parts, components and sub-assemblies have become increasingly important. Manufacturers are also more concerned about cost, availability and reliability of energy, human resources, plant and machinery, infrastructure and other inputs. Companies are paying increasing attention to supplier environment in strategy formulation. They complain that shortage and high cost of raw materials, power and capital are affecting their profitability and growth.

(*iv*) **Investors:** They are the owners and creditors who provide finance. An organisation can obtain financial resources from shareholders, debentureholders, banks and financial institutions. During periods of prosperity, an organisation can easily sell shares and debentures. But during recession, it might have to depend on borrowing from institutions. Interest rates and issue charges determine the cost of funds.

(*v*) **Distributors:** These are the agents, wholesalers and retailers who distribute and sell the organisation's products and services.

Macro or general environment refers to the forces which indirectly influence all business firms. The main elements of macro environment are described below:

1. **Economic Environment:** The economic environment consists of various factors related to the means of production and distribution. Some of major components of economic environment are as follows:
   (*i*) Economic system of the country—capitalism, socialism or mixed economy.
   (*ii*) State of economic development.
   (*iii*) Economic planning—five year plans and annual budgets.
   (*iv*) Economic policies—industrial, monetary and fiscal policies.
   (*v*) Economic indices—national income and its distribution, rate and growth of GDP, rate of savings and investment, per capita income, value of exports and imports, balance of payments position,
   (*vi*) Infrastructure—banks and financial institutions, capital and money markets, transportation and communication facilities, etc.

   Indian companies recognise the significance of economic environment on their strategies. Annual reports of most companies contain an assessment of general economic environment and its impact on their operations and performance.

Some Economic Trends in India

- There has been a slowdown in the economy. The GDP growth has declined from 9.5 per cent in 2008 to 4.5 per cent in 2013.
- India is emerging as the third largest economy after USA and China.
- Infrastructure in terms of roads, power, ports, etc. is in adequate.
- There exist great economic disparities between Bharat (villages) and India (cities). However, the poverty rate has declined from 50 per cent in 1977-78 to about 20 per cent in 2008-09.
- Competition has increased tremendously owing to liberalisation, privatisation and globalisation (LPG) and the entry of a large number of multinational corporations.
- India's market is highly hetrogenous. Therefore, market segmentation is quite difficult.
- Consumers are becoming increasingly aware and discerning and seek value for money spent.
- Debt funded consumption is rising sharply in real estate and consumer durable sectors.
- Rural India has emerged as a huge market not only for fast moving consumer goods but also for automobiles, TVs, refrigerators, washing machines, etc.
- Organised retail is growing in the form of shopping malls, etc.
- Shortage of power, poor infrastructure and high cost of raw materials are affecting economic growth.

2. **Political and Legal Environment:** The political and legal environment consists of factors related to public affairs and regulations of economic activities. The main elements of political and legal environment are as follows:
   (*i*) The political system — political parties and their ideologies,
   (*ii*) The political structure, its goals and stability.
   (*iii*) Political processes — elections and their funding.

(*iv*) Political philosophy — government's role in business.

(*v*) The constitutional framework — Directive Principles and Fundamental Rights.

(*vi*) Legislative, executive and judiciary.

(*vii*) Defence and foreign policies and external relations.

(*viii*) Centre-State relations

(*ix*) Regulations concerning licensing, prices, distribution, imports and exports, foreign investment and technology, pollution, small scale sector, consumer protection, labour, patents and trade marks, capital markets, etc.

(*x*) Bureaucracy and red tape.

Political and legal environment can be both promotional and regulatory. Promotional environment includes various facilities and incentives that stimulate business activities. Regulatory environment consists of restrictions on business activities.

Some Politico-Legal Trends in India

- India is a democratic country with a stable political system.
- Coalition governments have replaced one-party government. Compulsions of a coalition government have slowed down the pace of economic reforms. Most economic decisions are based on political considerations.
- Business houses fund political parties and some industrialists have joined political parties.
- There are widespread ideological conflicts due to which building political consensus on economic reforms is quite difficult.
- There exists political unrest in the form of Naxel movement, etc. in many states of the country.
- Indian economy is mainly planned and controlled. But the regulatory environment has become more liberal particularly for foreign direct investment. Still India remains an over-regulated and under-governed country.
- Judiciary has become more active which is resisted by legislators and bureaucracy.
- Political corruption is widespread. Bureaucracy and red-tapism are high.
- There exists a love and hate relationship between industry and government.

3. **Socio-Cultural Environment:** The socio-cultural environment consists of factors related to society, its customs, traditions, beliefs and values. Its main elements are as follows:

(*i*) Demographic factors — size, density and distribution of population, age and sex composition, birth and death rate, rural-urban migration or mobility.

(*ii*) Social customs, beliefs, attributes, values, expectations, etc.

(*iii*) Life styles, consumer habits and work ethics.

(*iv*) Family structure and size, class structure.

(*v*) Role and position of men, women, children and aged in family and society.

(*vi*) Education levels, awareness and consciousness of rights, attitudes towards minorities and disadvantaged groups.

(*vii*) Social concerns such as environmental pollution, corruption, consumerism, use of mass media, role of business in society, etc.

(*viii*) Expectations of society from business and its attitudes towards business.

(*ix*) Religious beliefs and customs.

Socio-cultural environment influences strategic management process in terms of deciding mission and objectives, decisions concerning products and markets, etc. Most strategists do not give high priority to socio-cultural environment because it changes slowly and does not have an immediate and direct impact on business.

Some Socio-Cultural Trends in India

- Family structure and values are changing rapidly in metros. Nuclear family is replacing the joint family system. Respect for elders, neighbours, etc. is declining.
- Educational levels and literacy rate are rising.
- Mass media (TV, twitter, e-mail, etc.) has become quite powerful. Use of internet for banking, shopping, ticketing, entertainment, education, etc. is increasing rapidly.
- Crimes against women are increasing
- Population growth is declining but gender disparity is rising.
- Migration from rural to urban areas is increasing.
- India has a demographic dividend (an advantage due to increasing population in the 15-60 age group India is one of the youngest countries in the world.
- Social instability, unemployment, under-employment, labour over supply threaten economic growth.
- India is a highly diverse society due to a large number of religions, castes, ethnic groups, languages.
- Middle class has emerged as a very large and powerful group in India.
- Indians are now paying greater attention to personal grooming. They are adopting foreign life styles and eating out is increasing.

4. **Technological Environment:** The technological environment consists of factors related to technology, machinery, and knowledge used in the design, production and distribution of goods and services. Its main elements are as follows:

(*i*) Sources, cost and transfer of technology.

(*ii*) Stage of technological progress, rate of change in technology, research and development facilities.

(*iii*) Man-machine system, impact of technology on people and environment.

(*iv*) Restrictions on transfer of technology, time taken in technology absorption, incentives and facilities for technological innovations.

Technology defines business and can change competitive cost position of an organisation. It can create new markets and new business segments. Technological environment can also collapse or merge previously independent businesses by eliminating or reducing their segment cost barriers.[1]

1 B. Petrov, "The Advent of the Technology Portfolio", **Journal of Business Strategy,** Fall 1982, pp 70-75.

Table 4.1: Trends in Technology and their Effects

Trends in Technology	Effects
Technology is changing fast	Customers will expect and accept new ideas
Technology is getting cheaper	Competition will come from unexpected quarters
Technology is becoming easily available	Product life cycles will be shorter
Technology is touching lives in more and more areas	New things will make old products, skills, knowledge obsolete necessitating continuous change.

Some Technological Trends in India

- Transfer of foreign technology to India takes place largely through foreign direct investment and foreign collaborations.
- Several foreign companies have established R & D facilities in India.
- Some Indian companies have acquired R & D facilities abroad.
- India has emerged as the hub of information technology industry.
- Knowledge-based industries and service sector are growing rapidly.

Table 4.2: Some Technological Developments and their Impact

Development	Impact
Television, Fax	The way in which customers are targeted, approached, convinced
CAD, Solid modeling, Advanced materials	Wider possibilities, faster development times
CNC, Microelectronics, Micro-hydraulics, Robotics	Shrinking of the factories. Manpower reduction, Lower cycle times
ERP systems, Communications technology	Comprehensive planning systems, systematic rigidity. Global sourcing changes in motivating to employees
Communications technology	Changes in motivating offerings to employees
Faster computers, Smarter applications	Extremely fast adolescence
Communication technology	Global financing, Rapidly fluctuating markets.

5. **International Environment:** The international or global environment consists of all those factors that operate at the transnational and cross-cultural levels. Its main elements are as follows:
   (*i*) The process, content and direction of globalisation.
   (*ii*) The process of and trends in global trade and forces.
   (*iii*) Global economic organisations and forums; and regional economic blocks.
   (*iv*) Global financial system and international accounting standards.
   (*v*) Global markets and international competitiveness
   (*vi*) Global demographic patterns and trends.
   (*vii*) Global information systems and communication networks and media.
   (*viii*) Global technological and quality systems and standards.

(*ix*) Global legal and arbitration system.

(*x*) Global human resource trends and globalisation of management.

Large Indian firms are making attempts to align themselves to emerging global trends. They are adopting global business practices and international accounting and reporting standards. India's corporate sector is taking greater interest in the World Trade Organisation (WTO), International Monetary Fund (IMF), World Economic Forum (WEF) and other international agencies.

Some Global Trends

- Markets and production are internationalising
- Well educated Indians are migrating abroad and are increasingly occupying top positions in global firms.
- There is also a reverse 'brain drain' as many Indians working abroad are coming back to work in India due to economic slowdown in USA and Europe and increasing opportunities in India.
- Several Indian companies have raised capital abroad and are listed on stock exchanges in USA and Europe.
- Indian companies are increasingly acquiring firms in USA, Europe, Middle East, etc.

4.4. CONCEPT AND ROLE OF ENVIRONMENTAL ANALYSIS

Environmental analysis or environmental scanning or **external analysis** is the process through which an organisation monitors various environmental forces to identify opportunities and threats which it is likely to face. The main features of environmental analysis are as follows:

(*i*) **Holistic:** Environmental analysis is a holistic exercise because it takes a total rather than piecemeal view of environmental forces. No doubt environment is divided into different components for the sake of comprehension. But finally the analysis of these components is aggregated to have a total view of the environment.

(*ii*) **Exploratory:** Environmental analysis is an exploratory or heuristic process. It attempts to estimate what could happen in future on the basis of present trends. Possible alternative futures are identified on the basis of different assumptions. The probabilities of these alternative futures are also estimated to arrive at more rational conclusions.

(*iii*) **Continuous:** Environmental analysis is an ongoing rather than an intermittent exercise. Continuous scanning of the environment is necessary to identify the trends. More relevant trends are analysed in detail to understand their impact on the organisation.

Environmental analysis plays a vital role in strategy formulation. In the absence of environmental analysis, no meaningful strategy can be formulated. Organisations which regularly monitor their environment outperform those which do not analyse their environment. For example, ITC, TCS, Reliance Industries Limited and other companies which give very high priority to environmental scanning have achieved high growth rates over decades. **Environmental analysis** is crucial for strategic management in the following ways:

1. Environmental changes create opportunities and threats for an organisation. On this basis of understanding the opportunities and threats, the organisation can take appropriate strategic decisions to exploit the opportunities and ward off the threats.

2. Environmental analysis serves as an early warning system. By anticipating the likely threats, the strategists can take timely action before the damage is done. They are not caught unaware.
3. Environmental analysis helps the strategists to identify the most promising alternatives and eliminate the options that are inconsistent with environmental trends. As a result strategic decision-making becomes easier.

The environment facing business firms is complex and ever changing. Therefore, environmental scanning is essential for strategic decision-making.

4.5. INDUSTRY ANALYSIS

An organisation must thoroughly understand the specific industry in which it operates or plans to operate because the factors relating to that industry directly affect its working. An industry means a group of firms offering products or services that are close substitutes of each other. For example, firms which manufacture two-wheelers (motorcycles, scooters, mopeds) and four-wheelers (passenger cars) constitute the automobile industry because these products perform the same function—personal transport. On a broader level, commercial vehicle (taxis, three-wheelers, tempos, trucks, etc.) manufacturers may also be included in automobile industry.

Industry analysis involves the analysis of the following industry related factors:

1. **Industry Setting:** The pattern of industries in terms of their stage of evolution, stage of maturation and geographical dimension form the setting of an industry. On the basis of these characteristics, Porter[2] has classified industries into the following categories:
   (*i*) *Fragmented Industry:* A fragmented industry is one which is scattered at numerous places with each place serving the local markets. There are several problems in the expansion of the industry beyond certain geographical areas due to non-mechanised production technology. Pottery and non-mechanised farm equipments are examples of fragmented industry. The firms in such an industry have a narrow competitive advantage because they cater to a small area.
   (*ii*) *Emerging Industry:* In such an industry market for the product exists in latent form and it materialises later. Most of the industries were emerging ones in the initial stages. For example, computer industry, at one point of time, was emerging in the form of abacuses, slide rules, adding machines and other means of calculation. In an emerging industry, buyer preferences are evenly scattered. A company has three options to differentiate its product and gain a competitive advantage: (*a*) the product may be designed to meet the preferences of one part of the market, (*b*) two or more products may be launched simultaneously for two or more parts of the market, (*c*) the new product may be designed for the middle of the market.
   (*iii*) *Maturing Industry:* As an industry grows and matures, several competitors enter it and they cover all segments of the market. Competitors grow faster than the industry. Therefore, they cut each other's market shares through product differentiation and other means. For example, firms producing oral care products in India are cutting the market shares of each other.

2 Michael E. Porter, **Competitive Advantage : Creating and Sustaining Superior Performance,** The Free Press, New York, 1985.

(*iv*) *Declining Industry:* After maturing, an industry may start declining in terms of total market size. Decline may start due to decline in need for the product and/ or availability of substitute product. For example, demand for washing soaps has declined due to detergent based washing. Firms in a declining industry may come out with emerging products or may leave the market. In a declining industry, a firm may consider reducing capacity, reduce costs, improve service link through to end users, maintain competitive advantage, harvest/sell.

(*v*) *Global Industry:* In a global industry the strategic positions of competing firms depend on their overall global positions. A global firm has a competitive advantage over domestic firms due to differentiation based on cost, quality, product features, brand image, etc. After economic liberalisation, more and more industries are becoming global.

2. **Industry Structure:** The economic and technical forces operating in an industry are called industry structure. It also includes the number of competitors and the extent of product differentiation. There are five types of industry structures:

(*i*) *Pure Monopoly:* In this structure there is only one seller in the market. Therefore, there is no need for product differentiation. Indian Railways and State Electricity Boards are examples of pure monopoly.

(*ii*) *Pure Oligopoly:* There are few sellers which have no product differentiation. Therefore, any price change by one seller affects the other sellers. For example, in the heavy commercial vehicles industry in India, Tata Motors and Ashok Leyland are the major players which compete on the basis of price and location.

(*iii*) *Pure Competition:* In case of pure or perfect competition, there is a large number of sellers with no product differentiation. They compete on price basis and no single seller has control over price. Sugar, steel, cement and other commodity industries are characterised by pure competition.

(*iv*) *Differentiated Oligopoly:* There are few sellers with differentiated products. Differentiation is based on price, quality, product design, delivery, after-sale service, etc. For example, in consumer durables the number of competitors is limited and each competitor's product is positioned on some unique selling proposition.

(*v*) *Monopolistic Competition:* There is a large number of sellers with differentiated products. Firms with a highly differentiated product have high customer loyalty and enjoy monopoly power. But there is competition due to several sellers. Thus, there is a combination of both monopoly and competition. Each industry structure provides different opportunities and threats and, therefore, requires a different strategy.

3. **Industry Attractiveness:** Industry attractiveness refers to the profitability position of the industry. An industry is considered attractive when there is enough scope for earning profit. Industry attractiveness depends on the following factors:

(*i*) *Nature of Demand:* The total market size and its rate of growth determines the industry's present and future business scope. The industry becomes attractive if the demand is large and increasing due to increase in population and income, changes in tastes, etc. On the other hand, when the demand is declining owing to substitute products, etc. the industry is unattractive. In case seasonal and cyclical fluctuations phenomena affect demand, industry becomes less attractive.

(*ii*) *Industry Potential:* Total sales potential also affects attractiveness of an industry. A high volume industry has more potential because it can accommodate a large number of players. For example, in the oral care industry, toothpaste segment has more potential than tooth powder segment.

(*iii*) *Profit Potential:* Profit potential refers to the possibility of earning the targeted volume of profit. Sales volume and profit margin influence the profit volume. Knowledge-based industries (e.g., information technology, consultancy, etc.) and industries with product differentiation generally offer more scope for higher profitability.

(*iv*) *Entry and Exit Barriers:* An industry is more attractive when entry barriers are high and exit barriers are low. Numerous entry barriers restrict future competition and few exit barriers reduce the cost of exit from the industry.

4. **Industry Performance:** An industry's performance is measured in terms of the following factors:

(*i*) *Profitability:* Profits in relation to sales or investment is a common measure of industry performance. Both sales and investment should be considered for comparison between industries. For example, a low capital-intensive industry may show less profitability in relation to sales than a high capital-intensive industry.

(*ii*) *Operating Efficiency:* Ratio between inputs and outputs indicates operating efficiency. Man-machine ratio, labour productivity, technology level, quality of raw materials, availability of power and infrastructure are the main determinants of efficiency.

(*iii*) *Technological Advancement:* Development and use of new technologies influences industry performance. Firms which use latest technology have a competitive advantage due to lower costs and better quality.

(*iv*) *Innovation:* In some industries the rate of innovation is higher than in other industries. Frostfree refrigerator, teleshopping, mobile banking and other innovations help to improve industry performance.

Industry environment exercises a significant influence on strategies. The environment differs from industry to industry and over time. For example, an embryonic or sunrise industry will require a different strategy than a mature or sunset industry. Moreover, business strategies must be aligned with changing environment of the industry. Demand conditions and competitive equations in an industry change over time.

4.6. COMPETITION ANALYSIS

Analysis of competition in an industry helps to identify the exact nature of opportunities and threats in that industry. Porter[3] has given a model of five forces that shape competition in an industry.

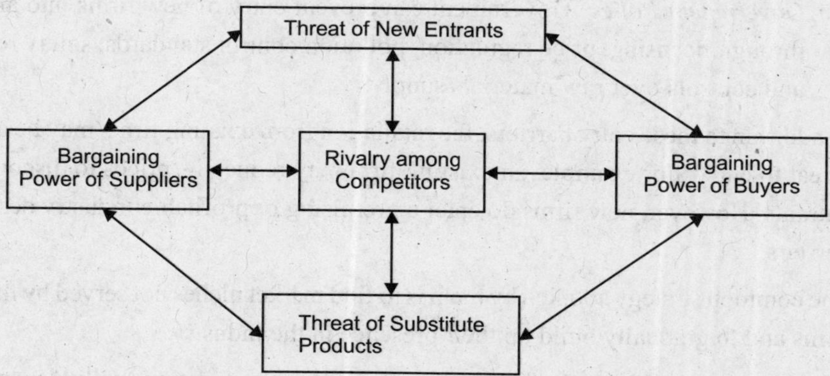

Fig. 4.2 Five Forces Model of Competition

1. **Threat of New Entrants:** An industry that is considered profitable tends to attract new entrants. Such new firms often make large investments, add to the existing production capacity and desire to gain substantial market share. The possibility of new firms entering into an industry depends on two factors: the entry barriers to an industry and the expected retaliation from the existing firms. When entry barriers are high, the chance that new firms will enter into an industry is low. Barriers to entry arise due to the following factors:

   (*i*) *Economies of Scale:* Economies of scale in production, marketing, etc. give lower cost advantage to existing firms. The new firms which want to enter the industry have to either come on a large scale or to accept a cost disadvantage.

   (*ii*) *Capital Requirements:* The need to invest huge capital in order to compete may prevent new entrants particularly when the projects involve long gestation periods.

   (*iii*) *Product Differentiation:* Unique product features, advertising, customer service, etc. create brand loyalty of customers towards existing firms. New entrants have to spend heavily to overcome customer loyalty.

   (*iv*) *Access to Distribution Channels:* The existing firms might have developed close long-term relationships with wholesalers and retailers. The new entrants may not have access to distribution channels and may have to gain access at higher costs.

   (*v*) *Cost Disadvantages Independent of Scale:* The existing firms may have cost advantages not available to potential rivals, irrespective of their size. These

3 Michael E. Porter "How Competitive Forces Shape Strategy", **Harvard Business Review,** March-April 1979, pp. 137-145.

advantages may arise from experience, proprietary technology, exclusive access to raw materials, favourable location, low cost assets, etc. Per unit costs decline with experience and new entrants with no experience face higher costs than the existing firms.

(*vi*) *Government Policy:* Government can prevent entry of new firms into an industry through licensing, price regulation, pollution control standards, safety regulations and controls over raw materials supply.

In addition to these entry barriers, the retaliation from existing firms may be a potential threat to entry. For example, an existing firm may reduce its prices to discourage new entrants. However, new firms do enter a promising or profitable industry despite entry barriers.

The common strategy adopted by them is to find market niches not served by the existing firms and to gradually build up their presence in the industry.

2. **Rivalry among Competitors:** Firms within an industry are mutually dependent. The desire to capture a larger market share leads to rivalry among them. When such rivalry is high there is intense competition among them. The rivalry among competing firms is high when:

(*i*) the number of competitors is large and all of them are trying to increase their market shares;

(*ii*) none of the competitors is in a position to dominate the industry;

(*iii*) there is less or no product differentiation and buyers can easily switch over from one brand to another;

(*iv*) the rate of growth in supply is higher than the rate of growth in demand;

(*v*) the product is perishable creating urgency to sell as quickly as possible;

(*vi*) high exit barriers prevent firms from leaving despite low or negative returns; exit barriers may arise due to economic, strategic and emotional factors. Economic factors are huge investment in assets with no alternative usage and high fixed costs of exit, such as high severence pay under agreement or high retrenchment compensation. Strategic factors refer to linkages between different businesses of the company such as sharing a common resource pool or the firm being its own supplier or buyer. Sentimental attachment to a business, e.g., being an ancestral business, loyalty to employees/distributors, etc. is an example of emotional factors.

3. **Bargaining Power of Buyers:** Powerful buyers may force an organisation to reduce prices, improve quality and improve customer service so as to get more value for their money. Buyers have a high bargaining power under the following conditions.

(*i*) Buyers are few in number but each buyer purchases in large volume.

(*ii*) The product bought is standardised or undifferentiated so that buyers can easily find alternative suppliers who are willing to supply at a lower price.

(*iii*) The product purchased constitutes a significant proportion of the buyer's cost, as for example, industrial products like TV picture tubes and automobile components.

(*iv*) Buyers have a low profit margin making them more price sensitive.

(*v*) The product is not important for the quality of buyers' product.

(*vi*) Buyers have the ability to integrate backward and create their own source of supply.

4. **Bargaining Power of Suppliers:** Powerful suppliers may raise prices and reduce quality or level of service. Such actions are likely to reduce the profitability of firms in the industry. Suppliers have a high bargaining power under the following conditions:

(*i*) There are few suppliers and many buyers.

(*ii*) The products/services supplied are unique and are not commonly available.

(*iii*) The substitutes of the products/services are not freely available.

(*iv*) The supplier can easily switch over from one buyer to another.

(*v*) The supplier has low dependence on the products/services supplied.

(*vi*) The buyer purchases in small quantities and, therefore, is not important to the supplier.

(*vii*) The supplier is able to integrate forward and thereby use his own supplies for producing the end product/service.

5. **Threat of Substitute Products;** Products or services that are apparently different but satisfy the same customer needs are known as substitutes. For example, tea and coffee are substitute products. Similarly, postal and courier services are substitutes. Easy availability of substitutes at same price poses a threat to the industry. Firms in such an industry cannot charge high prices. Substitutes, therefore, affect the profitability and growth of the industry. For instance, polysack industry has caused a huge loss to jute industry because the former offers better packaging material at about the same price. The threat of substitutes is high in case of more profitable products because greater attention is paid to develop substitutes for such products.

The central theme of Porter's hypothesis is location of clusters, i.e., the group of companies specialising in a specific area and location at one place. Clusters affect competition in these basic ways:

- Companies become more productive.
- Rate of innovation increases.
- Rate of growth is enhanced with regard to new businesses.
- The knowledge and motivation is almost next door. Clusters also attract more talent.

The Competition Trap

Too often companies try to outrun competitors, rather than carving their own path, and pursuing distinctive strategies. This leads to a misguided focus on current competitors and the market *status quo*, rather than a focus on flexibility, adaptability, and fast action. If you fall into this trap, you become oblivious to new market opportunities and exposed to unexpected developments.

- Competition takes the focus off what you are doing.
- Competition is the easy way out of not taking risks.
- Competition puts you at the mercy of someone else's pace.
- Competition creates a scarcity of mindset.
- Competition robs you of your potential.

You can break out of this trap by focusing on yourself and your own initiative. Be so busy that you don't have time to know what the competition is up to. You don't want to succeed for the sake of beating someone else. You want to succeed for the sake of helping others and your family.

4.7. APPROACHES TO ENVIRONMENTAL SCANNING

Kubr[4] has suggested the following approaches which can be adopted for scanning the environment.

1. **Systematic Approach:** Under this approach, a highly systematic and formal procedure is used to collect, process and interpret information about the environment. In order to monitor the environment, information concerning markets, customers, government policies and regulations and other environmental factors influencing the organisation and its industry is collected on a continuous basis. Proactive organisations with a high degree of sensitivity to the environment use this approach. The anticipated changes in the environment and their data collection and processing are well structured.

2. **Adhoc Approach:** Under this approach, special surveys and studies are conducted about specific environmental issues. For example, an organisation planning to undertake a special project may conduct a survey to develop new strategies. The impact of unforseen changes in the environment may also be investigated. Reactive organisations which are less sensitive to the environment often adopt an adhoc and informal approach to environmental scanning.

3. **Processed-form Approach:** Under this approach, processed information available from different internal and external sources is used. For example, data contained in government publications (Census Report, etc.) may be used.

   The approach adopted by a particular organisation depends on the nature of the environment (stable or dynamic), concern for the environment (low or high concern), importance of environment (directly relevant or general environment), etc.

---

4 M. Kubr (Ed), **Managing a Management Development Institution,** International Labour Organisation, Geneva, 1982, pp 88-89.

4.8. SOURCES OF INFORMATION FOR ENVIRONMENTAL SCANNING

Timely collection of relevant information is absolutely essential for proper scanning of the environment. The major sources of environmental information are as follows:

(*i*) **Internal Sources:** Files, reports, databases, and other documents and employees of the company are internal sources of data.

(*ii*) **Secondary Sources:** Newspapers, magazines, journals, books, annual reports of other companies, government publications, publications of trade associations and chambers of commerce, trade and telephone directories and commercial databases are secondary sources or publications.

(*iii*) **External Agencies:** Customers, suppliers, marketing intermediaries, industry associations and government agencies are included in this category. Information from these agencies can be collected verbally or in writing.

(*iv*) **Mass Media:** Radio, television and Internet are the mass media.

(*v*) **Formal Studies:** Company's employees, market research agencies, consultants and educational institutions may conduct surveys and studies to collect data.

(*vi*) **Business Espionage:** An organisation may collect data through spying and surveillance through competitors' employees, industrial espionage agencies, etc. This source is considered unethical but is used.

Before using a particular source, the organisation should check its reliability, time and cost involved, etc.

4.8.1. Forecasting

For strategy formulation, information is needed about future trends in the environment. Therefore, forecasting is essential. Forecasting is the process of estimating systematically the relevant future events on the basis of their past and present trends. The main steps involved in this process are as follows:

1. **Developing Framework for Forecasting:** First of all a sound framework is created for forecasting. Past records serve as the basis for estimating the future events at both micro and macro levels. In addition to past records, present trends also have to be considered. For example, inflation is increasing and growth rate is falling in India.
2. **Estimating Future Events:** The trends of future business and the company's market share can be estimated. The likely behaviour of the industry and the firm's business are judged by using various techniques of forecasting.
3. **Comparing Actual and Projected Results:** Differences or deviation between actual and projected results are identified and measured. These deviations may occur due to errors in forecasting or changes in environment. Plans may have to be modified or even abandoned on account of such deviations.
4. **Refining the Process:** Forecasting is an ongoing rather than a one-time process. Therefore, it is necessary to refine and adjust it to meet the changing business needs.

Qualitative factors affecting business trends need to be interpreted. But considerable experience is needed for this purpose.

4.8.2. Scenario Development

Scenarios are descriptions of possible future situations. These are prepared after projecting the likely future events.

Strategic decisions are usually made on the basis of incomplete information or under conditions of partial ignorance. Contingent strategies can be developed to meet the needs of different scenarios. Therefore, strategists need to develop alternative scenarios and adopt one of them as the most probable. They must watch signals that might confirm or reject that scenario[5]. In case the scenario is confirmed, there may be no need to modify the strategy. Otherwise the strategy has to be modified or abandoned and an alternate strategy may be required. The process of scenario development involves the following steps:

1. **Preparing the Background:** First of all, the background on which scenarios may be developed is prepared. This is done by creating a preliminary model for environmental analysis indicating various industry trends.
2. **Selecting the Critical Factors:** The critical indicators are selected out of the various trends identified at the first stage. A search is made for the potential events which are likely to affect the trends in future.
3. **Analysing the Behaviour of Indicators:** The past behaviour of each major indicator is analysed and the reasons thereof are identified.
4. **Verifying Future Events:** The probability and potential impact of future events are assessed.
5. **Forecasting the Indicators:** On the basis of experts' opinions, each major indicator is forecast. Trend Impact Analysis (TIA) and Cross Impact Analysis (CIA) are used for this purpose. TIA is the analysis of relevant factors affecting the major trends. CIA is the analysis of the impact of these trends. In case of any discrepancy, a fresh forecast is made. This process continues until there is a consensus among the experts on the likely behaviour of future events.
6. **Writing the Scenarios:** Alternative scenarios are prepared for each strategic action. The number of scenarios to be prepared depends on the nature of the industry, nature of environment, and the duration of future period. For example, more scenarios are needed in case of an emerging industry, fast changing environment and five years period than in case of a matured industry, stable environment and two years period.

4.9. FACTORS AFFECTING ENVIRONMENTAL ANALYSIS

There are numerous factors in the environment but only some of them are relevant to an organisation. Only those environmental factors are relevant which have an impact on the

5 Paul J.H. Shoemaker, "Scenario Planning: A Tool for Strategic Thinking", **Sloan Management Review,** Winter 1995, pp 25-40.

organisation. Strategists can identify the high priority environmental factors (called issues by Boulton[6]) by constructing a matrix that combines two variables: impact on the organisation, and probability of impact.

Table 4.3 Identifying High Priority Environmental Factors

Probability of Impact	Degree of Impact on Business		
	High	Medium	Low
High	Critical	High priority	Low priority
Medium	High priority	High priority	Low priority
Low	To be watched	High priority	Low priority

The factors which are most likely to have a high degree of impact on the organisation are critical and require immediate attention. The factors having medium to high impact are the high priority ones. The factors having high degree of impact but a low probability of impact need to be kept under watch. Lastly, the remaining factors are of low priority but require monitoring because the conditions might change over time.

The choice of environmental factors also depends upon the following factors:

1. **Organisation-Related Factor:** The nature, age, size, competitive power, complexity, etc. of the organisation have an impact on environmental analysis. For example, new, large and less powerful organisations require more information than old, small and more powerful organisations. Similarly, organisations operating in multiple products and/or unrelated products and with geographically dispersed operations need more information than single product and concentrated organisations.
2. **Strategist-Related Factors:** Strategists play a central role in strategy formulation. Therefore, their age, education, experience, motivation level, attitudes, sense of responsibility and the ability to face time pressure have a major impact on environmental analysis. For example, forward looking and long-term oriented managers seek more information than those who believe in *status* quo and short-term.
3. **Environment-Related Factors:** How does an organisation scan its environment also depends on the nature of environment. A more thorough scanning is required when the environment is complex, volatile, hostile and diverse.

4.10. METHODS AND TECHNIQUES OF ENVIRONMENTAL SCANNING

Several techniques are used for scanning the environment. Some of these are described below:

1. **Environmental Threat and Opportunity Profile (ETOP):** The ETOP is the most useful technique of structuring the results of environmental analysis. ETOP or Environmental Impact Matrix is a summary of the environmental factors and their likely impact on the organisation.

6 William R. Boulton, **Business Policy: The Art of Strategic Management,** MacMillan, New York, 1984, p. 120.

The preparation of ETOP involves the following steps:

(i) *Selection of Environmental Factors:* First of all, relevant components of the environment are selected. Each major factor is divided into sub-factors. For example, economic environment may be divided into economic policies, economic indices, market environment, etc.

(ii) *Assessment of Importance:* The importance of each selected factor/sub-factor is assessed in qualitative (high, medium, low) or quantitative (3, 2, 1) terms.

(iii) *Measurement of Impact:* The positive and negative impact of each factor is measured as opportunity and threat respectively.

(iv) *Combination of Importance and Impact:* The importance and impact of each factor together indicate clearly the situation.

ETOP can be prepared in two forms: matrix form or descriptive form. In matrix form, importance and impact of each environmental factor are expressed in quantities. In descriptive form the impact is expressed as being positive or negative. Table 4.4 is in matrix form while Table 4.5 gives ETOP in descriptive form.

Table 4.4 Environmental Threat and Opportunity Profile

Environmental Factors	Degree of importance			Degree of impact		
	High (3)	Medium (2)	Low (1)	High ±3	Medium ±2	Low ±1
1. Economic – Sub-factors						
2. Political and Legal – Sub-factors						
3. Socio-cultural – Sub-factors						
4. Technological – Sub-factors						
5. International – Sub-factors						

Table 4.5 ETOP of . . . . . .

Environmental Factors	Type and Degree of Impact
1. Economic	Both positive and negative, high degree
2. Political and Legal	More positive than negative, high degree
3. Socio-cultural	Both positive and negative, high degree
4. Technological	More positive than negative, high degree
5. International	Both positive and negative, high degree

ETOP provides a clear picture of where the organisation stands in relation to its environment. It indicates the opportunities and threats which the organisation is likely to face. Such an understanding is very useful in formulating appropriate strategies which will help the organisation to take advantage of the opportunities and to counter the threats in its environment.

2. **P.E.S.T. Analysis:** The acronym P.E.S.T. stands for Political, Economic, Social and Technological environment. These environmental factors create opportunities and threats for an organisation. Some strategists rearrange these variables as Social, Technological,

Economic and Political and use the acronym S.T.E.P. analysis. Each category of these factors contains innumerable elements. But the more common elements are as follows:

(*i*) *Political Analysis:* It involves analysis of:

- Political system and stability
- Legal framework concerning business
- Political parties and their ideology
- Risk of military invasion
- Foreign relations with other nations
- Bureaucracy and red tape
- Political corruption

(*ii*) *Economic Analysis:* It consists analysis of:

- Economic system
- Economic policies
- Economic indices
- Financial markets
- Industrial infrastructure

(*iii*) *Social Analysis:* It includes analysis of:

- Demographics
- Class structure
- Family system
- Education levels
- Cultural values, attitudes and interests
- Entrepreneurial spirit

(*iv*) *Technological Analysis:* It involves analysis of:

- Level of technological progress
- Rate of technology diffusion
- Transfer of foreign technology
- Impact of technology on costs, quality and value chain

3. **Q.U.E.S.T.:** The acronym Q.U.E.S.T. represents Quick Environmental Scanning Technique.

4.11. LIMITATIONS OF ENVIRONMENTAL SCANNING

Environmental scanning is not a foolproof exercise. It suffers from several shortcomings:

(*i*) Complete accuracy in environmental scanning is impossible because long-term future events are analysed. More turbulent is the environment greater may be the degree of error.

(*ii*) It is very difficult to judge what is the relevant environment. Too much focus on the relevant factors may lead to overlooking issues in the general environment that may be significant.

(*iii*) The basic purpose of environmental analysis is to identify the trends that really matter for strategy formulation. Strategists may use the information for their own goals through manoeuvring.

(*iv*) Environmental scanning may create such an overload of data that timely action is not taken. This is called 'paralysis by analysis'.

(*v*) In practice, environmental scanning may become a line or staff function devoid of organisational realities.

SUMMARY

Concept of Environment: All the forces, factors, institutions and groups that lie outside an organisation but affect its functioning and performance.

Nature of Environment: Complex and dynamic, input-output system, coalition of stakeholders, opportunities and threats.

Components of Environment: (1) Micro environment – customers, competitors, suppliers, investors, distributors, employees; (2) Macro environment – economic, political and legal, socio-cultural, technological, and international factors.

Concept and Role of Environmental Analysis: Holistic, exploratory, continuous; serves as an early warning system, reveals opportunities and threats, serves basis of policy formulation.

Industry Analysis: (*i*) Industry setting – fragmented, emerging, maturing, declining and global industry; (*ii*) Industry structure – pure monopoly, pure oligopoly, pure competition, differentiated oligopoly, monopolistic competition; (*iii*) Industry attractiveness – nature of demand, industry potential, profit potential, entry and exit barriers; (*iv*) Industry performance – profitability, operating efficiency, technological advancement, innovation.

Competition Analysis: Five forces model of competition – Threat of new entrants, bargaining power of suppliers, rivalry among existing firms, threat of substitutes, bargaining power of suppliers.

Approaches to Environmental Scanning: Systematic, adhoc, processed form.

Sources of Information: (*i*) internal (*ii*) external (*iii*) mass media (*iv*) formal studies (*v*) business espionage – forecasting, scenario building.

Factors Affecting Environmental Analysis: Organisational, strategist related and environmental factors.

Methods and Techniques of Environmental Scanning: ETOP, PEST, STEP, QUEST.

Limitations of Environmental Scanning: Inaccuracy, relevancy, misuse, overload of information, line or staff function.

TEST QUESTIONS

1. Describe and discuss the different aspects of environmental analysis and diagnosis necessary for identifying the opportunities and threats for an Indian conglomerate operating in India, USA and Europe.
2. Why is environmental analysis necessary for strategy formulation? Explain the components of micro-environment of an organisation.
3. Describe the different aspects of environmental scanning necessary for identifying opportunities and threats.
4. Discuss the elements of competitive environment which should be analysed for strategy formulation. What are the various sources of collecting environmental information?
5. Identify five major factors to scan the environment for a firm contemplating to enter petro-chemicals business. How would you determine their relative significance and what sources would you tap to obtain information on the same?
6. Explain the factors which influence attractiveness of an industry.
7. "Environmental analysis cannot be complete without diagnosis of the results of analysis which implies assessment of the relative significance of opportunities and threats identified in the process of analysis. How well the diagnosis is carried out depends upon the role and characteristics of the strategists and the nature of environment." Explain fully.
8. Explain ETOP as an instrument of environmental analysis. What aspects of the economic environment should strategies take into account while formulating the strategic objectives of a large company in the electronic goods industry?
9. Which among the environmental factors should the strategies be concerned with? Discuss in the light of empirical findings.
10. What factors are considered important by the Indian firms in scanning the business environment? Critically review the techniques used by these firms for forecasting economic and technological factors.
11. Explain the rationale of environmental analysis for strategic management. What key questions would you ask in analysing the socio-economic environment?
12. Discuss in detail the various components of operating environment. List important techniques used for environment analysis.
13. Explain Michael Porter's Five Forces Model of competition with the help of suitable examples. How does it help in strategy formulation?
14. Apply Porter's Five Forces Model to the Indian organised retail industry. What are the weaknesses of this model?
15. Discuss how Porter's national diamond of competitive advantage framework can help a multinational firm in making decisions with respect to its value chain?

16. Give a detailed account of how Porter's five forces model may be used for industry structure analysis. Carry out industry structure analysis of telecommunications industry in India using this model.
17. Discuss the role played by entry barriers in the Porter's five forces model of competition. Also discuss how entry barriers may differ in the case of 'experience goods' and 'credence goods' as opposed to 'several foods'.
18. "The study of external environment in formulating strategies is multidisciplinary in nature". Discuss.
19. Describe the value chain for a firm in the fast food business. How can it improve its effectiveness? Indicate how it can increase value addition for its buyers and suppliers of inputs.
20. Discuss the relevance of industry structure in formulating corporate strategy.
21. Explain Porter's approach to industry analysis through the five forces model given by him.
22. Why is environmental analysis necessary for strategy formulation? Explain the components of micro-environment.
23. Explain the role of environmental analysis in strategic management. What, according to Michael Porter, determines the level of competitive intensity in an industry? Discuss with the help of suitable examples.
24. A corporation is most concerned with the intensity of competition within its industry. What, according to Michael Porter, determines the level of competitive intensity in an industry? Discuss with the help of suitable examples from the corporate world.
25. What aspects of the economic environment should strategists take into account while formulating the strategic objectives of a large company in the electrical goods industry?
26. Assume you have just become personal assistant to the chief executive of a major pharmaceutical company. She knows you have recently undertaken a business management degree and asks if you would prepare a brief report summarising how scenario planning might be useful to a company in the pharmaceutical industry.
27. Carry out a five forces analysis of an industry or sector. What are the key competitive forces at work in that industry? Are there any changes that might occur that would significantly affect bases of competition in the industry?
28. Critically examine the various factors in external environment which must be kept in mind while deciding business strategy. Explain with suitable illustrations.
29. Explain Porter's model of competitive strategies. Is it possible for a company to have a sustainable competitive advantage when its industry becomes hyper competitive?
30. Explain Porter's five forces model for analysing the industry. According to Porter's discussion of industry analysis, is Pepsi-Cola a substitute of Coca-Cola?
31. What do you mean by Business Environment Analysis? Explain the main techniques of such analysis.

32. What do you understand by structural analysis of an industry? Is it helpful in developing strategy? What are the major shortcomings of this technique?
33. What is the purpose of environmental scanning? Describe the main components of environment which an organisation should monitor.
34. Distinguish between environmental analysis and environmental diagnosis.
35. How would you determine the degree of competitive pressures stemming from buyer bargaining power?
36. "External environment of a firm is too volatile to be predicted these days". Discuss, suggesting ways to overcome this fluidity.
37. "In India strategic planning for large enterprises is affected more by government policies than any other environmental factor". Examine this statement.

CASE STUDY

ESS BEE Company was established in 1989 in Mumbai to manufacture cycles. Initially the company served few markets of South India. They company due to its higher efficiency emerged as low cost manufacturers within a period of five years from its inception and managed to cover 40 per cent market share of the markets it served. The company managed to obtain a licence from the Government of India in 1993 to manufacture mopeds and in the same year it started the manufacturing. In 1995, the company entered a joint venture programme with a Japanese company for the manufacturing of mopeds and scooters. The company is currently manufacturing two brands of scooters, namely, 'Lady Bird' and 'Flying Queen'. Both the brands of the company have succeeded in gaining a market share of 21 per cent and 26 per cent respectively in highly competitive markets. The company' mission is to become industry leader and set trends for the followers.

India being one of the most populated countries in the world is considered the most attractive market for the automobile industry today. Consequently the competitive structure of the Indian automobile industry is bound to change in the future. Presently there are four major competitors for the company. However, the number of competitors is expected to go up with the arrival of three global players who have already sought permission from the Government of India for the manufacturing of two-wheelers. These global companies enjoy the benefits of having strong international brands and the proven ability to market those brands. Further, the ability to produce more efficiently due to having larger operations and the ability to transfer resources across company areas produce a strong competitive advantage for the global companies. However, the domestic companies possess in-depth knowledge of the local taste and preference which they can use as a source of competitive advantage. The presence of the global players has led to an increase in capabilities of the existing players in two-wheelers segment. To meet the growing demands of competition, many companies have already redesigned works, jobs and business processes in their organizations. At the same time the Society of Indian Automobile Manufacturers reports that auto-vehicle manufacturers are expected to invest US $ 5.7 billion in Indian market from 2005 to 2010 to meet the challenges of growing competition.

ESS BEE Company has core competencies in resources and the capabilities which it has never used so far as its sources of competitive advantage. However, presently the company is having conpetitive advantage in a large network of distribution and service across the country. The company is also known for its research and development capabilities in the country and currently its R & D division is working on a new brand which is expected to be a combination of design, outlook and technology. The company intends to launch this brand in the market within a period of six months.

Hero Honda, one of the strong competitors in the industry, with a greater understanding of local taste and preferences has been able to meet the growing expectations and needs of the customers. In fact, this company has been producing least cost and fuel-efficient two-wheelers for the last two decades and has been able to earn a market share of more than 40 per cent of the two-wheeler market, Meanwhile, Satum Automobiles, a strong competitor with a highly skilled and trained workforce has recently established a network of dealers, separate from ESS BEE Company dealers, who are committed to provide a level of personalized customer service unmatched in the industry.

The two-wheeler industry of India has turned global and is becoming highly competitive. Consequently, domestic firms have to respond to the changing environment of the industry. In fact, the firms have to leave behind their practice of subsidized inefficiency and have to take necessary measures to transform their way to functioning in order to compete with the strongest firms in the world in their local markets.

Questions

1. Identify and discuss the impact of changing environment on the competitive structure of the industry.
2. Discuss the core competencies of major competitors in the industry.
3. What is your perception about Resource-Based View? How could such a view help domestic companies to compete with multinational companies in local market?

5

CHAPTER

ORGANISATIONAL ANALYSIS AND APPRAISAL

CHAPTER OUTLINE

Environmental analysis reveals opportunities and threats which the organisation is likely to face in future. In order to exploit these opportunities and to counter the threats, the organisation must have relevant capabilities. An organisation's strengths and weaknesses can be identified through organisational analysis and appraisal.

5.1. CONCEPT OF ORGANISATIONAL ANALYSIS

Organisational analysis is the process of evaluating systematically an organisation's capabilities which can give it a competitive advantage in the market. The capabilities enable the organisation to achieve strategic advantage for long-term success. Organisational analysis is also known as internal analysis, corporate appraisal, self-approval, company analysis, etc.

Organisational analysis is the analysis of internal environment which refers to all factors within an organisation that influence its capability to achieve its strategic intent. The purpose of organisational analysis is to determine the capabilities of an organisation in terms of its strengths and weaknesses.

To analyse itself, an organisation may adopt a highly systematic approach or an ad hoc approach. Proactive organisations which have formal strategic planning systems adopt a systematic approach. On the other hand, reactive organisations use the ad hoc approach in response to a crisis. In this approach, occasional studies are undertaken to determine organisational capability.

Both secondary and primary sources are used for collecting information needed for organisational analysis. Employees opinions, company files and documents, financial statements are the internal sources of information. External sources include newspapers, magazines, journals, government publications, trade and industry reports, etc. The help of consultants and research agencies may also be sought.

Several factors relating to the organisation, internal environment and strategists affect organisational appraisal. The size, complexity and diversity of the organisation determine the quality of appraisal. Similarly, organisational appraisal depends on cohesiveness of management team and power politics. The philosophy, attitudes and ability of strategy makers also determine how well the organisation will be appraised.

5.2 NEED FOR ORGANISATIONAL ANALYSIS

Organisational analysis plays a vital role in strategic management. It is required for the following purposes.

(*i*) Analysis of the external environment enables the organisation to think of what it **might choose to do**. Organisational analysis is needed to decide **what it can do.**

(*ii*) An organisation tries to succeed by focussing on its strengths and overcoming its weaknesses. These strengths and weaknesses can be identified through organisational analysis. On the basis of its strengths and weaknesses, the organisation can concentrate on those businesses in which it is most likely to be successful.

(*iii*) Knowledge of weaknesses helps the organisation to take relevant action for overcoming the weak areas. It may rearrange and rellocate its resources to convert weaknesses into strengths. Alternatively, the organisation may withdraw itself from the operations wherein it is weak.

(*iv*) Strategy formulation requires matching strengths and weaknesses with environmental opportunities and threats. By appraising itself, an organisation can identify the capabilities it must develop to compete in the market place.

5.3 PROCESS OF ORGANISATIONAL ANALYSIS

The process of organisational analysis consists of the following steps:

1. **Identifying the Key Factors:** First of all the key factors for organisational analysis are identified. The analysis should cover all important aspects of the organisation. The structure, management pattern, personnel, finance, marketing, manufacturing, research and development are the key aspects of an organisation.

2. **Assessing the Importance of Factors:** All the factors identified for analysis are not equally important. Their relative importance is assessed in terms of their contribution towards the achievement of key results. Another method used to judge the importance of organisational factors is their relationship with the critical success factors (CSFs). These are those factors which are crucial for the success of an organisation.

3. **Evaluating Strengths and Weaknesses of Key Factors:** The strength of a key factor can be measured in terms of its contribution towards the achievement of organisational objectives. The weakness of a factor means its negative contribution. Another method of evaluating strengths and weaknesses is to make a comparative analysis of these factors with those of the competitors.

4. **Preparing Organisational Capability Profile:** The organisational capability profile shows the strengths and weaknesses of an organisation in qualitative (very strong, strong, average) or quantitative (5, 4, 3, 2, 1) terms. Strengths and weaknesses may also be expressed in positive (3, 2, 1) and negative (–1, –2, –3) quantities.

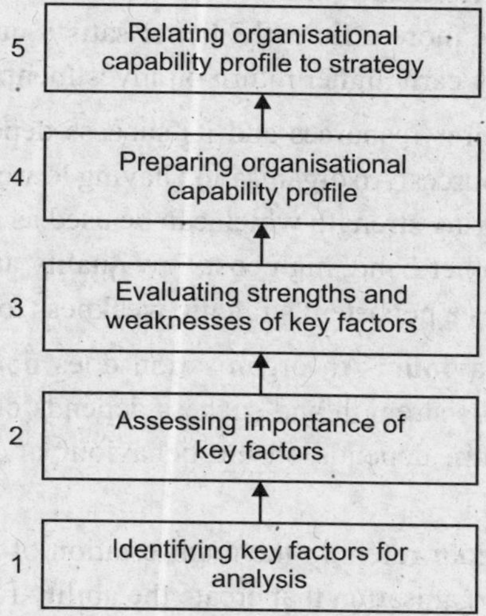

Fig. 5.1. The Process of Organisational Analysis

5. **Relating Oganisational Capability Profile to Strategy:** Organisational analysis becomes meaningful when strengths are related to strategy. The organisation can concentrate on areas of its strengths. It may undertake activities which convert its weaknesses into strengths. In the long run an organisation can succeed through, synergistic advantages gained by relating its capability to the environmental forces.

5.4 HIERARCHY OF STRATEGIC OR COMPETITIVE ADVANTAGE

The strategic advantage of an organisation is developed through its resources, behaviour strengths, weaknesses, synergistic effects, competencies and capability. [Fig.5.2].

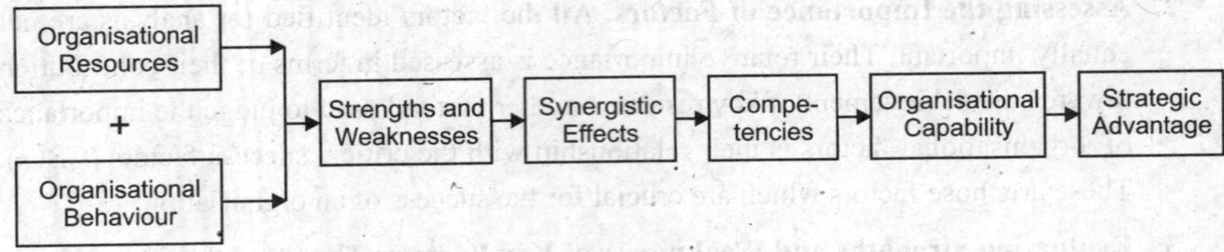

Fig. 5.2. Framework for Developing Strategic Advantage

1. **Organisational Resources:** According to Barney[1], an organisation is a bundle of tangible and intangible resources. These resources include all physical, human and financial resources. Geographic location, plant and machinery, technology, raw material are examples of physical resources. Human resources include intelligence, experience, training, judgment, relationships, etc. of members of the organisation. Formal structures, systems and processes are also important resources. Valuable, scarce, inimitable, durable and non-substitutable resources enable an organisation to achieve strategic advantage and to achieve superior performance in the long run. Organisations which possess superior resources can produce more efficiently, better satisfy customers, deliver better value for money and thereby earn higher return on investment.

   An organisation acquires resources and its success depends on the cost, quality and adequacy of these resources. An organisation having low cost, high quality and abundant resources has an enduring strength which can be used as a strategic weapon against the competitors. On the other hand, high cost, low quality and inadequacy of resources is a handicap that creates a persistent strategic weakness to the organisation.

2. **Organisational Behaviour:** An organisation does not become capable merely by acquiring resources. Its strength and success depends on efficient utilisation of these resources which in turn depends on the behaviour of individuals and groups in an organisation.

   Organisational behaviour refers to the manifestation of various forces and influences operating within an organisation that create the ability for, or place constraints on, the usage of resources. Several forces and influences such as management philosophy, organisational climate and culture, organisational politics and use of power shape organisational behaviour. If resources are considered the hardware of an organisation, behavior is its software. The two together create its strengths and weaknesses

3. **Strengths and Weaknesses:** A strength is an inherent capability which an organisation can use to gain strategic advantage over its competitors. On the other hand, a weakness is an inherent limitation or constraint which creates a strategic disadvantage for the organisation. For example, low cost of capital is a strength and inexperienced management is a weakness. Strengths and weaknesses do not exist in isolation but combine within a functional area, and also across different functional areas, to create synergistic effects.

---

1. J. B. Barney, "Firm's Resources and Sustained Competitive advantage, **Journal of Management,** Vol. 17 No 1 (1991), pp. 99-120

4. **Synergistic Effects:** Synergy occurs when two elements complement each other. It is popularly known as 2 + 2 = 5 effect. It other words, synergy means the whole is more/ less than the sum of its parts. Synergistic effects occur in an organisation in many ways. For example, when marketing and production departments support each other there is operating synergy. Within a functional area *e.g.* marketing, when product, pricing, distribution and promotion support each other there is marketing synergy. Synergistic effect can also be negative (2 + 2 = 3). For example, conflict-between marketing and production areas leads to negative synergy or dysergy.

   Synergistic effects influence the type and quality of the internal environment of an organisation and may lead to the development of competencies.

5. **Competencies:** An organisation's competencies are its unique qualities that enable it to withstand competitive pressures in the marketplace. The ability of an organisation to compete with its rivals depends on its unique qualities. Competencies may exist in the forms of unique resources, core capabilities, embedded knowledge, invisible assets, etc. In order to analyse organisational competencies, it is necessary to understand the concepts of core competence and distinctive competence.

   (*i*) *Core Competence*: According to Prahalad and Hamel[2], core competence is an enduring strength that:

   (*a*) makes a significant contribution to the perceived customer benefits of the end product;

   (*b*) provides potential access to a wide variety of markets; and

   (*c*) is difficult for the competitors to imitate.

   For example, Honda Motors of Japan has core competence in auto engines, Sony Corporation has core competence in miniaturisation, Cannon has core competence in optics and Reliance Industries in skilful management and project execution. These companies enjoy long-lasting advantages because competitors cannot easily imitate their competencies. Their core competencies have enabled these companies to offer different products in diverse markets. For example, Honda offers world class cars, motor cycles, scooters, generators etc. Similarly, Sony sells pocket TVs, mobiles, digital watches, tape recorders, walkmans, etc.

   Core competencies cannot 'however, be taken for granted. These can be lost or diminish over time due to new technologies. Core competencies may turn into core rigidities due to strategic commitment. According to Ghemawat[3], strategic commitment means an organisations's commitment to a particular way of doing business. Once a company has made a strategic commitment' it finds it difficult to respond to new competition when doing so requires a break with its commitment. An organisation may become a prisoner of its own excellence and may suffer from dependence on core competencies.

---

2. C. K Prahalad and Gary Hamel, "The Core Competence of the Corporation" **Harvard Business Review**, May-June 1990, pp. 79-81.
3. Pankaj Ghemawat, **Commitment: The Dynamics of Strategy**, The Free Press, New York, 1991

Critics also argue that a narrowly defined core competence may restrict an organisation's freedom to move in a new direction when new opportunities arrive in the business environment. For example, economic liberalisation in India in 1991 opened up new opportunities in telecommunications, banking, insurance and several other sectors. Organisations that stick to a single core competence deprive themselves of new opportunities. That is why Mukesh Ambani, Chairman of Reliance Industries' said, "We do not believe in core competence; we believe in building competence around people and processes to create value"[4] Large and diversified business houses like Tatas, Birlas, Ambanis can have core competence in several areas. For example, Tatas are a 'salt to software' 'tea to trucks' and 'hotels to houses' conglomerate.

(*ii*) *Distinctive Competence*: A distinctive competence is a unique capability which an organisation possesses exclusively or relatively in a large measure. It has been defined as "any advantage a company has over its competitors because it can do something which they cannot or it can do something better than they can"[5]. Low cost production, ability to mobilise huge amount of resources, unique products/services are examples of distinctive competence. Hindustan Unilever and ITC have distinctive competence in the form of Indiawide distribution network. Distinctive competence is important for strategy making because it gives a company the competitive edge in the marketplace and helps it to capitalise upon a business opportunity.

Superior product quality (Maruti's more fuel-efficient ALTO 800 car), a market niche by supplying specialised products/services to particular market segment (Flipkart online retailing), access to low cost finance, superior research and development, are other examples of distinctive competence.

Core and distinctive competencies serve a useful purpose when these are used to build up organisational capability.

6. **Organisational Capability:** The capability of an organisation means its inherent capacity or potential to use its strengths and to overcome its weaknesses so as to exploit the opportunities and face the threats in its external environment. In the absence of capability, even unique and valuable resources may be worthless. According to several thinkers in strategic management, capabilities are the outcomes of an organisation's knowledge base or the skills and knowledge of its employees. Organisational capability is significant for strategy making due to two reasons. **First,** it indicates an organisation's capacity to meet environmental challenges. **Second,** it reveals the potential that should be developed in the organisation to achieve success.

4. Quoted in Ashok V. Desai, "A Rival of Your Size", **Business world**, October 9, 2000, p. 16.
5. A. Sharplin, **Strategic Management,** Mc Graw Hill, New York, 1985, pp.93-94.

7. **Strategic and Competitive Advantage:** Strategic advantages (*e.g.* shareholder value, market share, etc.) are the outcomes of organisational capabilities. On the other hand, strategic disadvantages are the shortcomings due to lack of organisational capabilities. Both can be measured in absolute terms. For example, higher the profitability greater is the strategic advantage.

   Comparative advantage is a special type of strategic advantage. It is a relative term and is compared with respect to rivals in the industry. For example, a company has a comparative advantage when its profitability is higher than that of its rivals. "Competitive advantage exists when there is a match between the distinctive competencies of a firm and the factors critical for success within its industry that permits the firm to outperform its competitors."[6]

Thus, strategic advantage is a broader concept and competitive advantage is one of its parts. An organisation does not achieve a competitive advantage merely by having some capability. What is important is how the capability is used. Organisational capability is measured in specific context and it may turn into organisational incapability due to significant changes in the context. For example, Raymonds having capability in textiles diversified into cement sector, sustained losses, and exited from it.

5.5 STRATEGIC FACTORS IN ORGANISATIONAL ANALYSIS (ORGANISATIONAL CAPABILITY FACTORS)

Organisational analysis involves the identification of factors which indicate organisational capabilities. These factors are known as organisational capability factors or competitive advantage factors or strategic factors. Organisational capability factors are the strengths and weaknesses existing within an organisation which are critical for the formulation and implementation of strategy. For the sake of convenience organisational capability factors may be analysed under the following heads:

1. **Capability Factors in Finance:** Financial capability factors are concerned with the availability, usage and management of funds. Some of the important factors which influence an organisation's financial capability are as under:

   (*i*) *Sources of funds-related factors* – financing pattern (capital structure), cost of funds, financial leverage, reserves and surplus, relationship with provider of funds, etc.

   (*ii*) *Usage of funds-related factors*—fixed assets, current assets, loans and advances, dividend distribution

   (*iii*) *Management of funds-related factors* – accounting and budgeting systems, financial control system, tax planning, return risk and management, etc.

   Major strengths and weaknesses in finance are given in Table 5.1

6. Peter D. Bennett (ed.), **Dictionary of Marketing Terms**, American Marketing Association, Chicago, 1988, p.35.

Table 5.1: Strengths and Weaknesses in Finance

Strengths	Weaknesses
1. High-level creditworthiness	Low-level creditworthiness
2. Low cost of capital	High cost of capital
3. Sound capital structure	Defective capital structure
4. Sound financial planning	Poor financial planning
5. Tax concessions	High incidence of taxes
6. Cordial relations with shareholders and lenders	Lack of cordial relations with shareholders and lenders
7. Efficient accounting and budgeting systems	Lack of efficient accounting and budgeting systems
8. Sound dividend policy	Unsound dividend policy
9. Effective internal audit and financial controls	Ineffective internal audit and financial controls

Some examples of how financial strengths and weaknesses influence.

- Reliance Industries can afford to plan a capital investment of more than ₹5000 crore due to its easy access to equity and debt. It has very low cost of funds through convertible debentures, Yankee Bond issue in global financial markets. Its relations with banks and financial institutions are very cordial. It has an efficient capital budgeting system.
- Hindustan Unilever has financed all its expansion plans through internally-generated funds. It is a debt-free company.
- Unitech is debt-ridden company and its financial structure is skewed. It has deployed its funds in long gestation period projects and interest-burden is quite heavy.

2. **Capability Factors in Marketing:** The main factors that influence the marketing capability of an organisation are as follows:

   (*i*) *Product related factors* – product mix, branding, product positioning, differentiation, packaging, etc.

   (*ii*) *Price related factors* – pricing policies, price competitiveness, value for money pricing, price changes, etc.

   (*iii*) *Place related factors* – distribution network, transportation and logistics, relations with intermediaries, etc.

   (*iv*) *Promotion related factors* – promotion mix, promotional tools, customer relationship management, etc.

   (*v*) *Integration and control related factors* – market standing, company image, marketing information system, marketing organisation, etc.

   Typical strengths and weaknesses in marketing area are given in Table 5.2

Table 5.2: Strengths and Weakness in Marketing

Strengths	Weaknesses
1. Favourable Company and product image	Poor company and product image
2. Wide variety of products	Single or narrow product line
3. High market share	Low market share
4. Low prices – price protection	High prices – price control
5. Wide and efficient distribution network	Narrow and inefficient distribution network
6. Effective sales promotion	Weak sales promotion
7. Large, advertising budget	Small advertising budget
8. Motivated and hard working sales force	Demotivated and inexperienced sales force
9. Sound marketing information system	Poor marketing information system
10. High quality customer service	Poor customer service

Marketing strengths and weaknesses of some companies are given below:

- Hindustan Unilever is known for its marketing capability. It has a countrywide distribution network with a large number of clearing and forwarding (C & F) agents, wholesalers and retailers. It has prominent brands in its kitty, most of them provided by its parent company. HUL spends more then 7.5 per cent of its revenues on promotional activities.
- Parle enjoys a strong image and appeal among Indian consumers. Several of its biscuits and confectionery brands are market leaders in their category. The company enjoys a high market share with its biscuit brands such as Parle-G, Monaco and Krackjack and confectionery brands such as Kismi, Mangobite, Malady and Poppins.
- Philips India adopted premium pricing strategy for its colour televisions on the premise of popularity of its brands in electrical and electronic segments. But customers could not relate quality of Philips TV sets with higher price due to several quality-price-performance offerings from its competitors like LG, Samsung, Sony, etc.
- Several studies reveal that ineffective marketing is one of the major causes of industrial sickness in the small scale sector.

3. **Capability Factors in Operations:** Operations capability factors relate to the production of products and services. Major factors influencing an organisation's operations capability are as under:

   (i) *Production system related factors* – plant location, capacity and its utilisation, plant layout, product/service design, materials supply system/degree of automation, extent of vertical integration, etc.

   (ii) *Operations and control system related factors* – production planning, inventory management, cost and quality control, maintenance systems and procedures, etc.

(*iii*) *Research and development related factors* – product development, R & D staff, technical collaboration and support, patent rights, level of technology used, etc.

Typical strengths and weaknesses in operations are given in Table 5.3.

Table 5.3: Strengths and Weaknesses in Operations

Strengths	Weaknesses
1. Favourable plant location	Unfavourable plant location
2. High level of capacity utilisation	Low level of capacity utilisation
3. Good inventory management	Poor inventory management
4. High degree of vertical integration	Low degree of vertical integration
5. Reliable supply of materials and parts	Unreliable supply of materials and parts
6. Effective cost and quality control system	Weak cost and quality control system
7. Technical collaboration with reputed foreign firms	Lack of technical collaboration
8. High calibre of R & D staff	Low calibre of R & D staff

Strengths and weaknesses in the area of operations of some companies are given below:

- Reliance Industries got access to global technology for its petrochemical plants through technical collaboration with Dupont (USA), ICI (UK), Novacor (Canada) and Crest (Netherlands). Its high level of vertical integration serves as an entry barrier to new entrants in petrochemicals.
- ICICI Bank has used information technology to offer value to its customers. In its operating process, more than 20 per cent transactions take place on the Internet, about 65 per cent through ATMs and less than 15 per cent in branches. As a result ICICI Bank is narrowing the gap between itself and the largest bank, State Bank of India, though the latter has much more number of branches than ICICI Bank.
- JK Tyres introduced radial tyres in India but has not been able to take advantage of being the first one. Its competitors such as Bridgestone and others having access to latest tread patterns proved to be better.
- Hero Cycles became the lowest cost producer of bicycles due to favourable location. Its suppliers are located in the same city (Ludhiana) where the company has its plant. Its component manufactures have a cost advantage due to lower overheads.

4. **Capability Factors in Human Resource:** In any organisation, human resources make use of non-human resources. Human resource capabilities relate to the acquisition and use of human resources, skills and all allied aspects that influence strategy formulation and implementation. Some of the important factors which determine human resource capability are given below:

(*i*) *Factors related to the human resource system* – human resource planning, recruitment and selection, training and development, human resource mobility, appraisal and compensation management, etc.

(*ii*) *Factors related to employee retention* – company's image as an employer, career development opportunities for employees, working conditions, employee benefits, employee motivation and morale, etc.

(*iii*) *Factos related to industrial relations* – union-management relationship, collective bargaining, grievance handling system, employee participation in management, etc.

Major strengths and weaknesses in human resource area are given in Table 5.4

Table 5.4: Strengths and Weaknesses in Human Resource

Strengths	Weaknesses
1. Highly skilled and committed personnel	Low skilled and less committed personnel
2. High motivation and morale	Low motivation and morale
3. Receptiveness to change	Resistance to change
4. Low employee absenteeism and turnover	High employee absenteeism and turnover
5. Excellent opportunities for training and development	Lack of opportunities for training and development
6. Genuine concern for the employees and their families	Lack of concern for the employees and their families
7. Good industrial relations	Poor industrial relations

Some examples of human resource capability and their impact are as under:

- Infosys Technologies is considered a good employer and employees are its greatest strength. It recruits people with good academic record, attitudes for teamwork and high learnability. The company spends about 3 per cent of its resources on training and development and has a very attractive employee stock option scheme.
- Steel Authority of India Limited (SAIL) recruited 1.7 lakh employees, much more than what it actually required due to faulty human resource planning. This resulted in heavy losses to SAIL due to huge wage/salary bill. Moreover, availability of ample idle time created complacency among employees. On the advice of its consultants (McKinsey & Co.), SAIL pruned its workforce to one lakh employees and paid heavy compensation under the Voluntary Retirement Scheme (VRS).

5. **Capability Factors in Information Management:** Information is a valuable resource and can provide a competitive advantage to the organisation. Information system is concerned with collection, processing, storage and dissemination of information relevant for decision-making. Some of the factors that influence information management capability are as follows:

(*i*) *Factors related to acquisition and retention of information* – sources, quantity, quality, timeliness and cost of information, capacity to retain and protect information.

(*ii*) *Factors related to processing and synthesis of information* – computer systems, software capability, database management, synthesising capability.

(*iii*) *Factors related to retrieval and usage of information* – availability of right information in the right format, capacity to assimilate and use information.

(*iv*) *Factors related to transmission and dissemination of information* – speed of transmission, willingness to accept information, etc.

(*v*) *Factors related to integration and support* – availability of appropriate IT infrastructure, investment in state-of-the-art system, competence of computer professionals, top management, support, etc.

Major strengths and weaknesses in information management are given in Table 5.5.

Table 5.5: Strengths and Weaknesses in Information Management

Strengths	Weaknesses
1. Easy access to information sources at low cost	Lack of access to information at reasonable cost
2. Availability of high tech equipment and professionals	Non-availability of high tech equipment and computer professionals
3. Widespread use of computerised information system	Limited use of computerised information system
4. Wide coverage and networking of computer system	Lack of good coverage and net working of computer systems
5. High security of information systems	Low security of information systems
6. Positive attitudes to sharing and disseminating information	Negative attitudes to sharing and disseminating information
7. Top management support to IT and its application	Lack of top management support

Some examples of companies with information system capability are given below:

- Infosys Technologies has linked its various software development centres, located at different places in India and abroad, through computerised networks. It has similar networking with its clients too. As a result, its staff can share relevant information among themselves as well as with the clients.
- All branches of ICICI Bank spread throughout the country are interlinked through computerised networks. This creates value for a customer as he can operate his account from any place even if he does not have an account in the branch located at that place.
- Hero Motor Corp. has interlinked its different functional areas such as production, purchase, inventory management, marketing and finance. This information chain ensures instant coordination for sound product management.

6. **Capability Factors in General Management:** General management involves integration and direction of the functional capabilities. Some of the major factors that influence general management capability are as under:

   (*i*) *Strategic management system related factors*—processes relating to developing strategic intent, – strategy formulation and implementation, strategy evaluation, rewards and incentives for top managers, etc.

(*ii*) *Top management related factors*—values, norms, personal goals, competence, experience, orientation and risk propensity of general managers.

(*iii*) *External relationships related factors*—public image as a corporate citizen, sense of social responsibility, rapport with government and regulatory agencies, public relations, etc.

(*iv*) *Organisational climate related factors*—organisational culture, powers and politics management of change, balance of vested interests, etc.

Major strengths and weaknesses in general management are given in Table 5.6

Table 5.6: Strengths and Weaknesses in General Management

1. Favourable corporate image	Unfavourable corporate image
2. Transformational leadership	Transactional leadership
3. Entrepreneurial orientation and high propensity for risk taking	Managerial orientation and low propensity for risk taking
4. Sound organisational culture and climate	Poor organisational culture and climate
5. Good rapport with government and regulatory agencies	Poor rapport with government and regulatory agencies
6. Effective management of organisational change	Ineffective management of organisational change

Some examples of companies with or without general management capability are given below:

- Hindustan Unilever Limited (HUL) has exceptional capability in general management. It is considered a leadership laboratory. As a result, it has produced a large number of chief executives both for itself and its parent company, Unilever.
- Amul is a household name in India. Gujarat Cooperative Milk Marketing Federation (GCMMF), the producer of Amul brand milk and milk products, is a success story in the cooperative sector. Its legendary founder, Verghese Kurien, is called the father of White Revolution in India. His vision and the top management team of GCMMF has made it.
- Infosys Technologies is neither India's biggest IT company nor does it have the widest market segment coverage. Yet, it enjoys reputation due to its legendary founders and their philanthropy. It has become a global leader in IT industry. It is known for transparency, international accounting and reporting standards and other dimensions of good governance.

There are plenty of reasons why size matters. Besides the obvious economies of scale and the strong bargaining power with suppliers, being big makes it easier, especially with today's flexible production lines, to offer an ample product range that can exploit every niche. And the biggest car making groups are better able to spread the heavy cost of complying with ever tougher environmental regulation in the largest economies. But size itself is no guarantee to success.

5.6 METHODS AND TECHNIQUES OF ORGANISATIONAL ANALYSIS

Analysis and appraisal of an organisation is a çomprehensive and future-oriented process. Its focus is on what the organisation needs to do so as to exploit the forthcoming opportunities and to counter the threats in its external environment. The methods and techniques used in organisational analysis and appraisal may be classified as follows:

1. **Internal Analysis**
   (*a*) VRIO Framework
   (*b*) Value chain Analysis
   (*c*) Quantitative Analysis
   - Financial analysis
   - Non-financial analysis

   (*d*) Qualitative Analysis
2. **Comparative Analysis**
   (*a*) Historical Analysis
   (*b*) Industry Norms
   (*c*) Bench Marking
3. **Comprehensive Analysis**
   (*a*) Key Factor Rating
   (*b*) Balanced Scorecard
4. **SWOT Analysis**

5.6.1 Internal Analysis

The internal analysis of an organisation involves investigation into its strengths and weaknesses by focussing on factors which are relevant to it. Techniques used for internal analysis are described below:

1. **VRIO Framework:** The acronym VRIO stands for Valuable, Rare, Inimitable and Organised for usage. These terms are explained below:

   (*a*) *Valuable:* These are the capabilities that enable the organisation to generate revenues by capitalising on opportunities and/or to reduce costs by neutralising threats. The ability to provide high quality after-sale service to customers and the ability to develop rapport with the government are examples of valuable capabilities.

   (*b*) *Rare:* These are the capabilities that one or a few firms in the industry exclusively possess. An unique location and a highly motivated workforce are examples of rare capabilities. Coca-Cola's brand name is a rare capability. Both Honda and Toyota have rare capability to build quality cars at a relatively low cost.

(*c*) *Inimitable:* These are the capabilities which competitors either cannot duplicate or can duplicate only at a very high cost. Excellent corporate image and the ability to acquire/merge new businesses are examples of inimitable capabilities.

(*d*) *Organised for usage:* These are the capabilities which an organisation can use through its appropriate structure, business processes, control and reward system. The availability of competent R & D personnel and research laboratories to continually bring out innovative products is an example of organised for usage capabilities. Many firms have valuable and rare capabilities but they fail to exploit these capabilities. For example, for many years Novell had a significant competitive advantage in computer networking based on its core Net Ware product. But its inability to innovate in the face of changing markets and technology led to Novell's decline during 1995-1999. Similarly Xerox failed to exploit its innovation capability for quite some time. Suppose a firm adopts differentiation through superior R & D. It can evaluate whether its R & D capability is valuable (high quality R & D equipment), rare (highly qualified research staff), inimitable (R & D skills) and organised (integration of R & D resources, structure and systems).

An organisation can develop a sustainable strategic advantage through the four types of capabilities given above (Table 5.7). The organisation should emphasise the capabilities that give it strengths.

Table 5.7: How Capabilities Contribute to Strengths and Weaknesses

Are the capabilities valuable?	Are the capabilities rare?	Are the capabilities costly to imitate?	Are the capabilities organised for usage?	Are the capabilities strengths or weaknesses?
No	—	—	No	Weakness
Yes	No	—	Yes	Strength
Yes	Yes	No	Yes	Strength and distinctive competence
Yes	Yes	Yes	Yes	Strength and sustainable distinctive competence

Source: Adapted from J. B. Barney, **Gaining and Sustaining Competitive Advantage,** Addison Wesley, Reading MA, 1997, p.163.

2. **Value Chain Analysis:** Every organisation performs several activities. These activities are interrelated and form a chain. Each activity in the chain creates some value and involves cost. Thus, a value chain is a set of interlinked and value-creating activities performed by an organisation. Value chain analysis[7] is used to measure how each activity in the chain creates value.

---

7. Michael E. Porter, **Competitive Advantage: Creating and Sustaining Superior Performance,** The Free Press, New York, 1985.

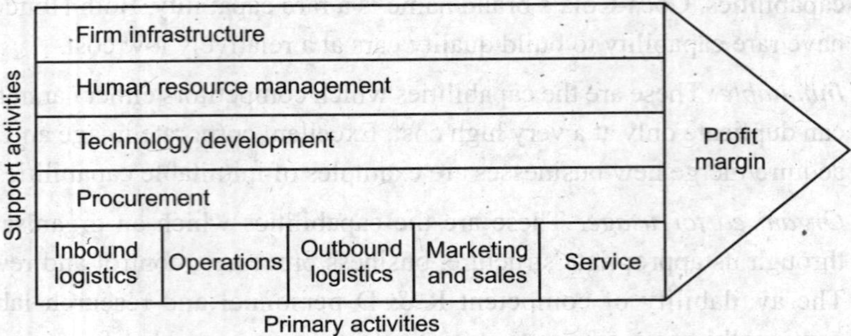

Fig. 5.3. Porter's Generic Value Chain

Primary Activities: These activities are directly related to the creation of a product or service. Primary activities consist of the following:

(*i*) *Inbound logistics:* All the activities used for receiving, storing and transporting inputs into the production process are known as inbound logistics. These activities are materials handling, transportation, warehousing and inventory control.

(*ii*) *Operations:* All activities involved in the transformation of inputs into outputs are called operations. These include assembling, fabricating, machining, testing, packaging, etc.

(*iii*) *Outbound logistics:* All the activities used for receiving, storing nad transporting finished products are known as outbound logistics. Collecting, order processing, physical distribution and warehousing are the activities.

(*iv*) *Marketing and sales:* These consist of activities used to market and sell products/ services to customers. Pricing, advertising, promoting and distributing are examples of such activities.

(*v*) *Service:* These are the activities used for enhancing and maintaining a product's value. Installation, repair, maintenance and customer training are the typical service activities.

Support Activities: These activities provide support to the primary activities. Support activities consist of:

(*i*) *Firm infrastructure:* All activities for general management of the organisation to achieve its objective are called firm infrastructure. These include accounting, finance, legal, secretarial, general management and managing government relations.

(*ii*) *Human resource management:* These comprise recruitment, selection, training, deploying and retaining the human resources of an organisation.

(*iii*) *Technology development:* Typical activities in this category are research and development, product and process design, equipment design, etc. These activities are used for creating, developing and improving products or services.

(iv) *Procurement:* Obtaining raw materials, parts, supplies, machinery, equipment and other purchased items are included in procurement.

The value chain provides a systematic view of all the activities performed by an organisation and interrelationship/interaction between them. The value created by an activity in the value chain can be estimated by assessing its contribution and cost. Profit margin that an organisation earns depends on how effectively it manages the value chain.

The value chain analysis is a useful method of identifying the areas in which the strengths and weaknesses of an organisation reside. Those activities in the value chain that create more value to the customer at less cost are the strengths. On the other hand, the activities that create less value at more cost are the weaknesses.

Value chain analysis suffers from following limitations:

(*i*) The technique is simple but difficult to apply.

(*ii*) The concept of value is vague and difficult to measure. It remains theoretical until the customer actually pays for what is offered.

(*iii*) In order to estimate the cost of any activity in the chain, activity-based costing is required and traditional cost accounting methods are not adequate.

(*iv*) Data from varied sources has to be collected for the analysis. When cost figures or other data are not available for the same period, the analysis becomes very difficult.

(*v*) Value chain analysis applies to manufacturing organisations and needs to be adopted for application to service organisations.

(*vi*) Due to globalisation, old value-creating activities have become less useful. In many cases, information technology and collaboration among different organisations have taken their places[8].

(*vii*) In Porter's model, value creation is taken as linear while it has become multidimensional in the present situation. Value grid[9] which allows firms to move beyond immediately recognisable opportunities across industry lines is better than value chain.

Value Chain Analysis of Hero

Hero Cycles is the biggest cycle manufacturer in the world. Its strategy is based on overall cost leadership and mass marketing. Its value chain is as follows:

Primary Activities:

(*i*) **Inbound logistics** – raw materials, components and other materials (tyres, tubes, etc.) are brought into the plant at low cost. The company saves costs in several ways: procurement from small scale local manufacturers, cash discount due to cash purchase, low technology and vendor training, minimum inventory as components are readily available locally through tie-ups.

8. Joe Peppard and Anna Rylander, "From Value Chain to Value Network: Insights from Mobile Operators," **European Management Journal,** 24(2), 2006.
9. F. K. Pil and M. Holweg, "Evolving from Value Chain to Value Grid, "**MIT sloan Management Review**, 47(4), 2006, p.p.72-80.

(*ii*) **Operations** – higher productivity through hard-working and loyal workers and automation

(*iii*) **Outbound Logistics** – transpotation of bicycles to stockists within one week of their manufacturing through trucks helps to reduce costs due to lower freight and just-in-time inventory

(*iv*) **Marketing and Sales** – manufacturer-stockist-customer distribution channel helps to reduce the number of intermediaries and to reduce marketing costs

(*v*) **Service** – bicycle being a simple product, so not much is needed.

Support Activities

(*i*) **Firm Infrastructure:** Zero interest burden and computerised operations help to save money.

(*ii*) **Human resource management:** Every worker is treated as colleague, even the chairman takes rounds and calls workers by their names, yearly lunch meetings with workers and their families creates belongingness and loyalty among employees, on the job training.

(*iii*) **Technology development:** Information, and R & D to make cycles functionally useful.

(*iv*) **Procurement:** centralised procurement system.

Thus, all activities in the chain create value to customers and the company. As a result Hero Cycles enjoys a great competitive advantage

3. **Quantitative Analysis:** Both financial and non-financial aspects are covered in quantitative analysis which is easy and verifiable.

(*i*) *Financial Analysis:* In order to assess strengths and weaknesses in different functional areas, ratio analysis and economic value added analysis are used.

(*a*) **Ratio Analysis** is a traditional and popular technique. Under it the liquidity, profitability, leverage and activity aspects of the organisation are assessed. Various ratios are calculated and compared over a period of time. However, ratio analysis has limited use in strategic management as it suffers from several limitations.

(*b*) **Economic Value Added (EVA) Analysis** is a relatively new technique developed by Stern Stewart & Co.(USA). EVA measures profitability in terms of the returns on capital above the cost of servicing the capital employed. It is the wealth created by the company for its owners and is expressed as the difference between after-tax operating profits and the cost of capital. When the EVA is positive, the organisation has the required strength.

(*c*) **Activity Based Costing (ABC)** attempts to measure the cost of each activity in the value chain. Like EVA, it helps to identify the areas where the organisations's strengths and weaknesses lie.

(*ii*) *Non-Financial Analysis:* There are several aspects of an oragnisation which cannot be measured in financial terms. Non-financial analysis is used to assess these aspects. Employee absenteeism and turnover, advertising recall rate, production cycle time, service call rates, number of patents registered per annum, inventory turnover rate, etc. are such aspects.

4. **Qualitative Analysis:** Those aspects of an organisation which cannot be expressed in quantitative terms are assessed through qualitative analysis. Corporate image, corporate

culture, learning ability, employee morale, etc. are examples of these aspects. Qualitative analysis can be used to support and reinforce quantitative analysis. The former is considered as 'soft' while the latter is viewed as 'hard'. But qualitative analysis should not be based on emotions or fancy. It should be rigorous. Ansoff[10] has suggested grid approach for qualitative analysis.

Table 5.8: Ansoff's Grid Approach

Organisational factors	Degree of			
	Facilities	Personnel skills	Organisational capabilities	Managerial capabilities
• General Management • Finance • R & D • Production • Marketing				

5.6.2 Comparative Analysis

Strengths and weaknesses provide a competitive advantage to the organisation when these are unique and exclusive. Therefore, an organisation should compare its capabilities with those of its competitors. Comparative analysis can be made over a time period, on the basis of industry norms and through bench marking.

1. **Historical Analysis:** In historical analysis an organisation's strengths and weaknesses are compared over different time periods. It reveals whether the strengths are improving or declining. Areas which show continuous improvement are durable strengths. Hofer and Schendel[11] have developed a functional-area profile and resource deployment matrix for historical analysis (Table 5.9).

Table 5.9: Functional-area Profile and Resource Deployment Matrix

Functional Area	Resource deployment Percentage outlays				Focus of efforts			
	2013.	2014	2015	2016	2013	2014	2015	2016
R & D and Engineering Manufacturing Marketing Finance Management								

The matrix shows financial outlay and efforts focus in various functional areas over four years. This will indicate improvement/decline in strengths.

---

10. H. Igor Ansoff, **Implementing Strategic Management,** Prentice Hall International,/London, 1984
11. Charles W. Hofer and Dan **Schendel, Strategy Formulation: Analytical Concepts**, West Publishing Co; St. Paul, Minnesota, 1988.

Historical analysis suffers from some **limitations**. **First,** it reveals improvement/decline but not the reasons behind them. **Second,** measurement of performance on a small base could show dramatic but illusory improvement. For example, many IT firms earned more than 100 per cent increase in profit over the previous year but their base is very thin and gestation period is very short. **Third,** historical analysis indicates improvement with respect to a company's own performance and not in comparison with its competitors.

2. **Industry Norms:** Every industry has certain norms or standards for key parameters of performance. The performance levels of a firm can be compared with the norms of the industry in which the firm operates. For example, cost levels of Maruti Suzuki may be compared against cost standards in the car industry.

   A more selective approach can be to compare with firms that follow similar strategies. These firms are known as a strategic group. According to Miller and Dess[12], a strategic group is "a cluster of competitors that share similar strategies and, therefore, compete more directly with one another than with other firms in the same industry".

   Industry norms, however, suffer from following **limitations:**

   (*i*) Comparisons on the basis of industry norms may yield erroneous conclusions concerning an organisation's capability as these are averages.

   (*ii*) Firms in the same industry differ in many respects and may not be fully comparable.

   (*iii*) It is difficult to get industry norms because competitors closely guard information.

   In spite of these limitations, industry norms can reveal the areas in which an organisation requires improvement.

3. **Benchmarking:** A benchmark means a reference point for the purpose of measurement and comparison. "Benchmarking is the process of identifying, understanding and adapting outstanding practices from within the same industry or from other businesses to help improve performance"[13]. The basic purpose of benchmarking is to match and even surpass the best performer. The key questions in benchmarking are: What to benchmark, and whom to benchmark. These questions can be answered by knowing the types of benchmarking. On the basis of what to benchmark, benchmarking is of the following types:

   (*i*) Performance benchmarking involves comparison of an organisation's performance with that of the best performer.

   (*ii*) Process benchmarking involves comparison of an organisation's methods and practices with those of the best organisation.

   (*iii*) Strategic benchmarking involves comparison of an organisation's strategies with those of the best organisation

   On the basis of whom to benchmark, there are four types of benchmarking:

   1. **Internal benchmarking** means comparison between departments/units of the same organisation.

---

12. A. Miller and G.G. Dess, **Strategic Managment,** Mc Graw Hill, New York, 1996, p.73
13. Sarah Cook, **Practical Benchmarking: A Manager's Guide to Creating Competitive Advantage,** Kogan Page, London, 1995.

2. **Competitive benchmarking** means comparison with the rival organisations.
3. **Functional benchmarking** means comparison of function against non-competing organisations.
4. **Generic benchmarking** means comparison of own processes with the best practices anywhere or any organisaton at the global level.

Benchmarking by Indian Firms

1. **Product quality improvement** – Tata Motors Jenson & Nicholson, NTPC, BHEL, SAIL, IOC are some of the companies which have improved their product quality by modifying their operations after benchmarking against global leaders in their industries.
2. **Customer service improvement** – HDFC, Modi Xevx, Thermax, Kirloskar cummins, IFB, Infosys and many other firms have bench-marked those practices which can improve customer service.
3. **Comprehensive practices** – Reliance, Hindustan Unilever, Maruti Suzuki, etc. have benchmarked their technology supplier or foreign partner/parent firm to improve overall performance. Reliance Industries observes: "Global benchmarking has always been a *mantra* for all of us, here at Reliance. We have now geared ourselves up to raise our levels of productivity and efficiency for capital, assets, people, and the entire organisation, well beyond comparable global benchmarks."

Benchmarking is a popular technique of assessing organisational capability. But it suffers from some **limitations**. **First,** it is a time-consuming and expensive process. **Second**, it can be useful only when done on a continuous basis. **Third,** it is difficult to find comparable organisations for benchmarking in different industries and sectors.

5.6.3 Comprehensive Analysis

Each of the techniques given above has its own use but fails to provide a comprehensive picture of organisational strengths and weaknesses. Comprehensive analysis is required to overcome this limitation. The techniques used in comprehensive analysis are given below:

1. **Key Factor Rating:** In this method the key factors as discussed under section 5.5 are analysed to judge their positive and negative impact on the functioning of the organisation. The rating of key factors in the finance area is illustrated in Fig. 5.4

FACTORS HAVING POSITIVE IMPACT

↑ Sound capital structure
↑ Ample reserves and surplus
↑ Cordial relations with banks and financial institutions
↑ Sound accounting and budgeting systems

FACTORS HAVING NEGATIVE IMPACT

↓ Tight cash flow position
↓ Time and cost overruns
↓ High incidence of taxes

Fig. 5.4 Equilibrium Analysis for key Factors in Finance

Key factor rating provides a very comprehensive or holistic view of performance but it suffers from some limitations. **First,** it is an unwieldy technique. It requires considerable information from different parts of the organisation and is, therefore, time-consuming. **Second,** this method is subjective because managers assign rating on the basis of their judgment. **Third,** the key factor rating needs to be calibrated with the on going audit processes in the organisation.

2. **Balanced Scorecard:** Balanced scorecard discussed in Chapter 3 is the most comprehensive method of analysing an organisation's strengths and weaknesses. It integrates different perspectives with vision and strategy to provide a comprehensive and balanced picture of organizational performance.

   The four key performance measures identified in balanced scorecard are as under[14].

   (*i*) *Financial Perspective*—How do shareholders look at us?

   (*ii*) *Customer Perspective*—How do customers see us?

   (*iii*) *Internal Business Processes Perspective*—What must we excel at?

   (*iv*) *Learning and Innovative Perspective*—Can we continue to improve and create value.

   When used together, these perspectives help in judging whether the organisation is moving towards its vision. A balanced view of the organisation's strengths and weaknesses can be obtained by keeping score in the four critical areas of performance. It can be used for deciding the key areas of performance and focus attention to build capabilities in these areas.

3. **Business Intelligence Systems:** Data from various internal and external sources are used to evaluate the company's strategic directions and operational performance. Data mining, data warehouses and analytical reports are used.

5.6.4 SWOT Analysis

The acronym SWOT stands for the following:

1. **Strength (S):** A strength is a competence which enables an organisation to gain an advantage over its competitors.

2. **Weakness (W):** A weakness is a limitation or constraint which creates a competitive disadvantage for the organisation.

3. **Opportunity (O):** An opportunity is a favourable condition in the environment.

4. **Threat (T):** A threat is an unfavourable condition in the environment.

Strengths and weaknesses can be identified through organisational appraisal or analysis of the internal environment. Environmental appraisal or analysis of the external environment reveals opportunities and threats.

---

14. Robert Kaplan and David Norton, "The Balanced Scorecard: Measures That Drive Performance", **Harvard Business Review,** January-February 1992pp. 71-80.

SWOT analysis is also known as **WOTS** and **TOWS** analysis. It helps in understanding the internal and external environment. It is very useful in strategy formulation as the organisation's strengths and weaknesses can be matched with the opportunities and threats. An effective strategy makes use of strengths to capitalise on the opportunities and minimisse the impact of weaknesses to neutralise the threats. After SWOT analysis, an organisation has to decide how to maximise its strengths and minimise its weaknesses. It can also decide how to exploit the opportunities and to counter the threats.

SWOT analysis is made in the form of a four-cell matrix (Fig. 5.5)

STRENGTHS	WEAKNESSES
• Good corporate image • Favourable location • Wide distribution network • Ample reserves & surplus • ISO 2000 quality certification	• Inexperienced management • High cost of production • High prices • Poor relations with banks and financial institutions
OPPORTUNITIES	**THREATS**
• Liberal government policies • Existence of niche target market • Reliable foreign partners • Increasing education levels	• Intense competition • Political instability • Stagnant demand • Rising customer expectations

Fig. 5.5. A Typical SWOT Matrix

Main **advantages** of SWOT analysis are as follows:

(*i*) It is simple to use.

(*ii*) It is inexpensive.

(*iii*) It provides a comprehensive picture of environment.

(*iv*) It is flexible and can be adapted to different types of organisations.

(*v*) It serves as the basis for strategic analysis.

SWOT analysis suffers from some **limitations.**

1. It may give an oversimplified view of reality.
2. It does not indicate relative importance of different variables.
3. It may be affected by the evaluator's perception and judgment.
4. There is a change of confusion between opportunities and strengths, and threats and weaknesses.
5. It provides a static picture.

SWOT analysis can be divided into two major parts – ETOP and SAP. ETOP is a list of opportunities and threats in the external environment. It has been described in Chapter 4. SAP indicates an organisation's strengths and weaknesses against its competitors. SWOT analysis combining ETOP and SAP is given in Table 5.10.

Table 5.10: SWOT Analysis of a Car Company

ETOP	IMPACT	SAP	IMPACT
1. Economic	↑	Operations	↑
2. Socio-cultural	↓	Marketing	↑
3. Politico-legal	↑	Finance	↑
4. Technological	→	Personnel	→
5. Global	↓	General Management	↓
Up arrows indicate favourable impact; down arrows indicate unfavourable impact; while horizontal arrows indicate a neutral impact.			

Table 5.11: SWOT Analysis of Infosys

Strengths	Weaknesses
• Sound management • Qualified manpower • Wide networks • Expertise in new technologies • Strong reputation	• High attrition rate • High cost structure • Dependence on service
Opportunities	**Threats**
• Growing demand • Collaborative possibilities • Scope for diversification	• Growing competition • Economic slowdown in Europe and USA • Lack of global parity in telecom tariff

5.7 STRUCTURING ORGANISATIONAL APPRAISAL

The information obtained through organisational analysis and appraisal can be summarised in two formats – organisational capability profile, and strategic advantage profile.

5.7.1 Organisational Capability Profile (OCP)

Organisational capability profile is a summary of an organisation's strengths and weaknesses in key result areas. Information in this summary statement should be presented in quantitative terms so as to show the degree of a strength/weakness. The values to different capabilities may be assigned along a scale ranging from +5 to –5. A summarised form of OCP is given in Table 5.12.

Table 5.12: Organisational Capability Profile

Capability Factors	Weakness (–5)	Neutral 0	Strength (+5)
1. Financial Capability			
(*a*) Sources of funds			
(*b*) Usage of funds			
(*c*) Management of funds			

2. Marketing Capability			
(*a*) Product factors			
(*b*) Price factors			
(*c*) Promotion factors			
(*d*) Distribution factors			
3. Operations Capability			
(*a*) Plant location			
(*b*) Production system			
(*c*) Cost structure			
(*b*) R & D system			
4. Human Resource Capability			
(*a*) Quality of personnel			
(*b*) Training and development			
(*c*) Compensation system			
(*d*) Industrial relations			
5. Information Management Capability			
(*a*) Acquisition, processing and storage of information			
(*b*) Retrieval, usage and sharing of information			
(*c*) Transmission and dissemination of information			
(*d*) Reporting system			
6. General Management Capability			
(*a*) Top management team			
(*b*) Organisational culture			
(*c*) External relations			

OCP helps an organisation to identify gaps in capabilities so that appropriate action can be taken to overcome the weakness.

5.7.2 Strategic Advantage Profile (SAP)

Strategic advantage profile describes an organisation's competitive position in the industry. While OCP has internal orientation, SAP is externally-oriented. SAP gives "a picture of the more critical areas which can have a relationship with the strategic posture of the firm in future"[15].

The preparation of SAP involves the following steps:

(*i*) Identify the factors (called critical success factors) which are important for success in the industry.

(*ii*) Measure the organisation's position on these factors in comparison to its competitors.

---

15. W. F. Glueck and L. R. Jauch, **Business Policy and Strategic Management,** McGraw Hill New York, 1984, p. 135.

(*iii*) Judge the sustainability of each competitive advantage/disadvantage of the organisation. Competitive advantage may turn into a disadvantage due to changes in the environment.

SAP of a motorcycle company is given in Table 5.13

Table 5.13: Strategic Advantage Profile of a Motorcycle Company

Capability Factor	Competitive Strength (+)	Competitive Weakness (–)	Sustainability High-Medium-Low
1. Finance	Low cost of capital	High debt equity ratio	
2. Marketing	Rapidly growing demand	Narrow distribution network	
3. Operations	Favourable location	Poor R & D system	
4. Human Resource	High quality personnel	Poor industrial relations	
5. Information Management	Fully computerised system	Limited scope for e-commerce	
6. General Management	Experienced top management team	—	

Three years after Rajiv Bajaj took charge, it was all smooth sailing till the tide turned at Bajaj Auto. Its newest launch XCD, a 125 cc bike targeted at the computer segment, bombed, sales of the Discover dipped and overall volume plunged. After weeks of introspection, Bajaj conceded his company didn't have a coherent strategy. He learnt that people don't actually buy products, they buy brands.

Take sports bike Pulsar, for instance. Its attributes are clear: it's big, fast, expensive, powerful, and its strong point is definitely not mileage. Bajaj's competitive edge has been its consistent focus on 'brands', 'positioning' and creating 'exciting segments' for two-wheeler enthusiasts.

SUMMARY

Concept: Organisational appraisal is the process of evaluating an organisation's strengths and weaknesses.

Need: (*i*) to concentrate in areas of strengths (*ii*) to decide what can be done (*iii*) to overcome weaknesses (*iv*) to match strengths and weaknesses with opportunities and strengths.

Process: (*i*) identify key factors (*ii*) assess their importance (*iii*) evaluate strengths and weaknesses of key factors (*iv*) prepare OCP (*V*) relate OCP to strategy.

Competitive/Strategic Advantage: (*i*) organisational resources (*ii*) organisational behaviour (*iii*) strengths and weaknesses (*iv*) synergistic effects (*v*) competencies (*a*) core competence (*b*) distinctive competence (*vi*) organisational capability (*vii*) strategic and competitive advantage.

Strategic Factors (Organisationsal Capability Factors): (*i*) Finance (*ii*) Marketing (*iii*) Operations (*vi*) Human resources (*v*) Information management (*vi*) General management.

Methods and Techniques: (*i*) Internal analysis (*a*) VRIO Framework (*b*) Value chain analysis (*c*) Quantitative analysis (financial, and non-financial) (*d*) Qualitative analysis (*ii*) Comparative analysis (*a*) historical analysis (*b*) industry norms (*c*) benchmarking (*iii*) Comprehensive analysis (*a*) Key factor rating (*b*) balanced scorecard (*iv*) SWOT analysis.

Structuring Appraisal: (1) OCP (2) SAP.

TEST QUESTIONS

1. Why is it essential to consider both external and internal environment while formulating corporate strategy? Briefly explain the process of environmental scanning.
2. A company has decided to compete on the basis of superior technology of its products. What parameters should be used to assess if it has the requisite competence?
3. What are the factors that can contribute to an organisation possessing sustainable competitive advantage? Discuss. Illustrate your arguments with an example drawn from the Indian auto industry?
4. What do you understand by the concept of 'value chain'? How can it be used to identify organisational strengths, weaknesses and sources of competitive advantage?
5. What is the difference between resources and capabilities? What are the steps a firm should take to promote the development of distinctive capabilities?
6. Make a critical appraisal of strategic advantage of a firm and discuss the various determinants of strategic advantage.
7. What is strategic advantage? How would you determine the strategic advantage of a company?
8. What is the importance of identifying strategic advantage? Prepare a strategic advantage profile of a large private sector company in India.
9. Define SWOT analysis. Give the SWOT analysis for any multinational corporation with which you are familiar.
10. Discuss the Balanced Scorecard model and apply it to an organisation of your choice.
11. What is core competence of a company? How can you identify it? What in your opinion is the core competence of the following companies: (*i*) ICICI Bank (*ii*) Proctor and Gamble, and (*iii*) Bajaj Auto Ltd.
12. Identify three major parameters to identify strength in the areas of (*i*) finance, (*ii*) human resources, and (*iii*) physical facilities for a firm which is in services sector.
13. "Assessment of the internal capabilities of a firm centres round an appraisal of performance in different functional areas." Elucidate the statement.

14. What is SWOT analysis? How does it help in strategy formulation? Write the SWOT analysis of Hindustan Unilever Limited.
15. Explain the Critical Success Factors Approach and Business Scorecard as techniques of organisational analysis.
16. Identify the Critical Factors for Survival and Growth for the following organisations engaged in:
    (*a*) manufacture of capital-intensive plant and machinery
    (*b*) producing basic material such as cement
    (*c*) insurance business
    (*d*) manufacture of synthetic fibres
    (*e*) trading in consumer products.
    In each case explain why you consider the stated factor as critical.
17. "Assessment of SAP of an organisation centres round appraisal of performance in different functional areas." Discuss.
18. How should the executives of a super bazar go about assessing the strengths and weaknesses of their organisation in the process of strategic planning?
19. Briefly describe Value Chain Analysis and its importance in strategic management.
20. What is value chain Analysis? How does it help the company in identifying strengths and weaknesses?
21. Explain Hofer's Product Market Evolution and shell Directional Policy Matrix for corporate analysis.
22. What are the strategic groups? Select an industry of your choice and demonstrate the procedure for constructing a strategic group map. What are the implications of strategic group analysis for the identification of opportunities and threats within an industry?
23. "The value chain is an excellent framework by which strategic managers can determine the strengths and weaknesses of each activity vis-a-vis the firm's competitor's." Explain.
24. What is core competence? How can it be related to strategic advantage? Illustrate the concept of strategic advantage profile.
25. What is Strategic Advantage Profile (SAP)? How and why is it prepared?
26. "HMT once considered time-keeper of the nation has been outperformed by TITAN in the field of wrist watches." How will you respond to this statement? How can companies avoid competitive failure and sustain their competitive advantage in the long run?
27. What is sustainable competitive advantage?
28. Explain Porter's Value Chain Approach for diagonising a company's strengths and weaknesses.
29. What is BCG Matrix? Explain its components and their role in the choice of strategy with appropriate examples from Indian industry.

30. What is Balanced Scorecard? Describe the steps in the implementation of Balanced Scorecard.
31. Describe SWOT analysis technique for environmental scanning. What is the importance of this analysis in strategic management of an organisation?
32. What do you understand by corporate synergy? How does synergy take place in the organisations?
33. What do you understand by SWOT analysis? Describe Strategic Factor Analysis summary for analysing the strategy of a company. Illustrate with the help of an example.
34. Why is it important to undertake internal capability analysis? Outline important techniques of organisational appraisal.
35. Explain BCG matrix and GE Matrix approaches of portfolio analysis to develop strategies.
36. "Organisations can't survive in today's competitive would without getting synergic benefits in business operation." Explain.
37. Discuss various methods of obtaining corporate synergy for better profitability.
38. What are the benefits of SWOT analysis? Outline the factors to be considered in environmental scanning.
39. Why is it important to analyse organisational capabilities? What techniques are used for organisational appraisal?
40. What factors should be kept in mind while undertaking internal analysis of an organisation?
41. What is benchmarking? Explain the benefits of benchmarking to an organisation.
42. (*a*) In what ways can a company revamp value chain to achieve cost advantage over competitors?

    (*b*) Why should a firm go for adopting outsourcing strategies? What are the pitfalls of outsourcing?
43. "The matching of external threats and opportunities with strategic advantage factors provides the necessary basis for strategy making." Explain
44. "A firm must possess distinctive and scarce resources and capabilities in order to gain competitive advantage." Discuss.
45. Discuss three tools of strategic internal audit used for doing an organisational analysis. Which of these tools would you recommend for use by a firm in aviation sector?
46. "Situational ground realities matter more than theoretical strategic assumptions." Do you agree? Give reasons.
47. "It is the shareholders who own the firm – hence their interests must be paramount." Critically discuss. How should the balanced scorecard approach to strategic goal setting be relevant to this discussion?
48. "No core competence can yield competitive advantage forever." Discuss.

49. How can the concept of value chain help in making diversification decisions? Discuss.
50. "Balanced Scorecard is a better measure than financial measures to measure performance." Discuss.
51. How can a firm translate its proficient performance of value chain activities into competitive advantage?
52. Explain with example the concepts of competence, core competence and distinctive competence.

CASE STUDY

During the 1990s, in the mature and saturated fast food industry, competition for customers between the different hamburger chains has been intense. McDonald's, the industry leader, has been under pressure to maintain its profit margins, because, as the price of fast food has fallen, price wars have periodically broken out. Taco Bell started a major price war when it introduced its $.99 taco, for instance, which pushed McDonald's and other burger chains such as Burger king and Wendy's to find ways to lower their costs and prices. As a result of price competition, all the burger chains were forced to learn how to make a cheaper hamburger, and they have been able to lower their prices. With most fast food restaurants now offering comparable prices, the focus of competition between the burger chains has shifted to other aspects of their products. First the major chains are all introducing bigger burger patties. The battle was started by burger king. Which is still waging an aggressive campaign to increase its market share at the expense of McDonald's.

In 1994, Burger king added a full ounce of beef to its 1.8 ounce regular patty and followed this with an intense advertising campaign based on the slogan, "Get Your Burger's Worth." directed at McDonald's burger, which was more than 40 per cent lighter. The campaign worked for Burger king, and the chain's market share rose by 18 per cent in 1995. As a result, in May 1996, McDonald announced that it would enlarge its regular patty by 25 per cent to beat back the challenge from Burger king from Wendy's, which has always offered a larger burger (and whose "Where the Beef?") slogan helped it gain market share in the 1980s.

Developing bigger burgers is only one part of competitive strategy in the fast food industry, however. The main burger chains are constantly experimenting with new and improved kind of burgers to appeal to customers – burgers that add cheese, bacon, different kind of vegetables, and exotic sauces – they are also trying whole meal offerings, such as McDonald's "value Meals" to provide a competitive package to attract customers. Furthermore, recognizing the competition from other kinds of fast food chains, such as those specialising in chicken or Mexican food, the burger chains have moved to broaden their menus. McDonald; for example, offers chicken dishes, pizza, and salads; it also allows restaurants to customize their menus to suit tastes of customers in the region in which they are located. Thus, McDonald's restaurants in New England have lobster on the menu, and those in Japan serve sushi. Product development is a major part of competitive strategy in the industry.

Another major competitive strategy that Burger king and McDonald's have adopted is market penetration. Opening up new restaurants to attract customers. Because all the big chains have thousands restaurants each, many analysts thought that the market was saturated, meaning that it would not be profitable to open new restaurants. However, McDonald's in particular has opened hundreds of restaurants in new locations such as gas stations and large retail stores (for example Wal-Mart), all of which are profitable and have helped it protect its market share and maintain its margins.

Finally, a major aspect of the burger chains competitive strategy has been to take their core competencies and apply them on an international level by building global restaurant empires. Indeed, so important have global operations become that both MeDonald's and Burger king earn a significant part of their profits from their foreign operations. It the mature fast food industry developing new competitive strategies to fend off attacks by other companies within the industry and to protect and enhance competitive advantage is a never-ending task for strategic managers. Even McDonald's is currently experiencing many problems because of the intense competition in the industry.

Questions:

(*i*) Describe the nature of competition and the industry environment of the fast food industry.

(*ii*) What strategies are fast food restaurants pursuing today to protect their competitive position?

6

CHAPTER

CORPORATE LEVEL STRATEGIES

CHAPTER OUTLINE

After environmental appraisal and organisational appraisal, an organisation can identify the strategic alternatives. These alternatives exist at three levels – corporate level, business level and functional level. Strategic alternatives at the corporate level are known as **corporate** strategies or **grand** strategies. These are the possible directions in which an organisation can move. Corporate strategies involve decisions concerning allocation of resources among different businesses, transfer of resources from one business to another, and managing a portfolio of businesses. According to Glueck and Jauch, "Strategic alternatives revolve around the question of whether to continue or change the business the enterprise is currently in or improve the efficiency and effectiveness with which the firm achieves its corporate objectives in its chosen business sector."[1]

Corporate level strategies may be classified as follows:

1. Growth / Expansion Strategies
   (*a*) Concentration Strategies
   (*b*) Integration Strategies
   (*c*) Diversification Strategies.
   (*d*) Cooperation Strategies
2. Stability Strategies
   (*a*) No Change Strategy
   (*b*) Pause / Proceed with Caution Strategy
   (*c*) Profit Strategy
3. Retrenchment Strategies
   (*a*) Turnaround Strategy
   (*b*) Restructuring Strategy
   (*c*) Divestment Strategy
   (*d*) Liquidation Strategy
4. Combination Strategies
   (*a*) Simultaneous Combination
   (*b*) Sequential Combination
   (*c*) Simultaneous-cum-Sequential Combination

Most organisations seek to grow and expand. Therefore, **growth strategies** are the most popular corporate strategies. Companies aim at sustained growth. Some of them grow slowly while others grow substantially. For example, Reliance Industries Limited (RIL) has grown very rapidly. These days companies have adequate opportunities for growth due to a growing world economy, increasing demand, expanding customer aspirations and emergence of new technologies.

According to Glueck, "A growth strategy is one that an enterprise pursues when it increases its level of objectives upward in significant increment, much higher than an extrapolation of its past achievement level: The most frequent increase indicating a growth strategy is to raise the market share and or sales objectives upward significantly."[2]

1 W.F. Glueck and L. R. Jauch, *Op.cit.* p. 209

2 William F. Glueck, ***Business Policy and Strategic Management***, McGraw Hill, New York, 1980, p.207

Table 6.1: Why Companies Seek Growth

1.	In the long run, growth is essential for the very survival of an organisation, particularly in a volatile environment. The new entrants may push out the organisation that does not grow.
2.	Growth provides economies of large scale operations. Cost per unit declines on account of economies of large scale. The organisation gains a competitive advantage due to lower costs and high degree of specialisation.
3.	Growth brings intangible benefits such as greater prestige, employee satisfaction and social standing.
4.	Highly motivated and achievement oriented promoters and chief executives want recognition through rapid growth. For example, Reliance Industries Limited grew fast to realise the dream of its founder Dhirubhai Ambani to make Reliance the biggest private sector company in India.
5.	Sustained growth can provide an organisation control over the market or leadership position in the industry concerned. In uncertain times, companies become risk-averse and struggle to gain traction in their growth initiatives, However, at these times focusing on growth is more necessary than ever.

6.1 CONCENTRATION STRATEGIES

Expansion in the present business is known as concentration or intensification or concentric expansion. It involves more investment in a product line for an identified market. The company expands production capacity and increases market share. In other words, concentration is the "stick to the knitting" strategy because the company confines itself to doing what it is best at doing. There are three variants of concentration strategy[3]:

PRODUCT / MARKET	PRESENT	NEW
PRESENT	Market Penetration	Product Development
NEW	Market Development	Diversification

Fig. 6.1 Ansoff's Product Market Matrix

(i) **Market Penetration:** In this strategy, the firm attempts to sell more of the existing product in the existing market. It increases its market share through higher usage of the product by existing customers. Price reduction, free gifts, improvement in quality/packaging, better promotion and distribution may be used for this purpose. For example, Indigo and other budget airlines in India achieved very high growth rate through low pricing and aggressive promotion.

(ii) **Market Development:** Under this strategy, the firm attempts to sell the existing product to new markets. It may attract new users, find new geographical markets (*e.g.* rural buyers or exports), and/or new segments (offering the product at different price to a different group of customers). For example, several FMCG firms such as ITC, Hindustan Unilever and Dabur launched low priced sachets of their products in rural areas.

3 H. I. Ansoff, "Strategies for Expansion", ***Harvard Business Review***, 1957 (5), pp. 113–124.

(*iii*) **Market Development:** Here, the firm sells new products in the existing market. The basic product may remain the same but new features, size, price, package, etc. are added to it. For example, the tourism industry introduced medical tourism to increase sales revenue.

Concentration strategy offers the following **advantages**:

1. Concentration is an easy means of growth as it requires minimum changes. The organisation deals with the known business and therefore faces less problems.
2. It enables the company to acquire an indepth knowledge of the business and thereby achieve the benefits of specialisation.
3. By focussing its resources on one line of business, the company can gain a competitive advantage.
4. Concentration involves minimum risk because the firm does what it has been doing.
5. Past experience is a good guide and decision-making is easy due to high level of predictability.

Concentration strategy suffers from some **limitations**:

(*i*) In concentration strategy, the firm is totally dependent on one industry. It is like 'putting all the eggs in one basket'. Recession in the industry, entry of several competitors, saturation of demand and other adverse conditions can significantly reduce the industry attentiveness.

(*ii*) Product obsolescence, emergence of new technology, etc can pose threats to the firm.

(*iii*) Concentration may create inertia when the organisation does too much of the known business. It may lose interest and find the business less challenging.

(*iv*) Concentration requires large investment in capacity expansion which may create cash flow problem in the initial stage. When the business matures, the firm may have cash surplus with little scope for further investment in the existing business.

(v) Concentration strategy can be successfull when the industry has a high growth potential, the company has adequate funds for capacity expansion and possesses the competencies needed to develop new markets and new products.

Example of Concentration Strategy

- Xerox India offered multifunctional devices for print job service (market penetration). It launched several new office products such as laser printers (product development). It educated small business entrepreneurs in the usage and benefits of its products (market development).
- Bajaj Auto has concentrated on two-and three-wheelers. It has increased its turnover through market penetration (selling more in urban areas), market development (selling to well-to-do customers in rural areas) and product development (state-of-the-art motorcycles and mopeds).
- Britannia Industries is scripting a new growth strategy which focusses on high margin products and innovations amid stiff competition from ITC and Parle.

6.2 INTEGRATION STRATEGIES

Integration strategy involves widening the scope of a firm's business definition. The firm may move up or down its value chain to serve the same group of customers. It may undertake another business adjacent to its existing business. Integration is of two types—horizontal and vertical.

6.2.1 Horizontal Integration

Under horizontal integration the firm launches the same type of products at the same level of production/marketing process. For example, a cement manufacturing company takes over its competitor. The firm remains in the same industry and continues to serve the same markets and customers through its present products by means of the same technology. A firm may adopt horizontal integration strategy to expand geographically, to increase its market share and/or to secure economies of scale.

Example of Horizontal Integration

- By taking over the United Western Bank, the IDBI Bank increased its retail network from 181 to 410 branches. It added agricultural credit financing to its industrial credit financing. It also gained access to lower cost deposit base.

Horizontal integration offers the following **advantages**:

(*i*) Cost per unit is reduced through economies of large scale operations.

(*ii*) Integration of two or more similar firms helps in better utilisation of assets/resources.

(*iii*) The firm can offer a wider range of products and obtain the benefit of product differentiation.

(*iv*) Horizontal integration helps to increase the market power of the firm

(*v*) When the firm acquires a competitor the degree of competition is reduced.

(*vi*) A firm can replicate its successful business model through horizontal integration.

The **drawbacks** of horizontal integration are as follows:

1. Horizontal integration in the form of mergers may not increase the firm's value.
2. Too much increase in size through horizontal integration may become unmanageable.
3. The firm may face legal problems under the Competition Act.

6.2.2 Vertical Integration

Vertical integration means the combination of technologically distinct production and distribution processes into one organisation. The firm either becomes its own supplier or distributor. Vertical integration is of two types—backward and forward. In **backward integration,** the firm starts manufacturing the raw materials. For example, a cloth mill may add a spinning mill. **Forward integration** occurs when the firm starts using its own output. For example, a cloth will may add a readymade garment manufacturing unit.

Example of Vertical Integration

- Reliance Industries started as a cloth manufacturer. It went for backward integration by manufacturing filament yarn, petrochemicals and hydrocarbons. By launching garment manufacturing units and exports of readymades it adopted forward integration. Thus, it became a fully integrated textile firm.

Vertical integration offers following **advantages**:

(*i*) Backward integration ensures uninterrupted inhouse supply of raw materials.

(*ii*) The cost of raw materials is reduced through inhouse manufacturing. Quality of raw material can also be maintained.

(*iii*) Forward integration helps to save the cost of selling and offers an inhouse market for the product.

(*iv*) The firm can change the mix of various inputs used in the production process.

(*v*) The firm may be able to differentiate itself from others by offering a wide range of value addition.

(*vi*) Vertical integration can increase entry barriers. A fully integrated firm enjoys competitive advantage in the form of lower costs and risks.

(*vii*) The firm gains better control over its value chain through access to and control of supply and demand.

Vertical integration suffers from some **limitations**:

(*i*) Vertical integration increases costs of coordinating different stages of value chain.

(*ii*) It reduces the flexibility of operations. Inefficiency or fluctuation of inhouse supplier or customer can affect the entire chain. Changeover to outside supplier or customer is costly.

(*iii*) Uneven productivity across different stages of the value chain may lead to underulilisation of resources or excess capacity. It is difficult to maintain proper balance between upstream and downstream units.

(*iv*) When the main product fails or becomes obsolete, the firm faces huge risk.

(*v*) Inhouse supply and demand may reduce the incentives for efficient working. This problem can be overcome through transfer pricing.

(*vi*) Vertical integration requires additional capital investment.

HCL FORAYS INTO HEALTHCARE

Shiv Nadar-led HCL Corporation, the holding company of the HCL Group, announced its entry into the healthcare sector with the launch of a new company, HCL Healthcare, which plans an initial investment of ₹ 1,000 crore.

The helathcare startup is aiming to roll out a chain of multi-specialty clinics, HCL Avitas, as the healthcare delivery arm of HCL Healthcare, in affiliation with US-based Johns Hopkins Medicine International.

HCL Healthcare has acquired a controlling stake in Bharat Family Clinic, a primary healthcare provider. Bharat runs two health and wellness clinics in and around Delhi.

“We will invest as much as the wellness and preventive healthcare market needs with an aim to treat 50,000 patients daily, and have its primary focus on middle-class patients.

“By the year 2020, we aim to provide patient-centred care for over 20 million people,” said Shikhar Malhotra, vice-chairman of HCL Healthcare and Nadar’s son-in-law.

The company said that it hopes to create the largest health network in India.

Jyothy Labs' Henkel Bet Pays Off in 2 Years

In 2011, when Jyothy Laboratories, which makes soaps, detergents, fabric whiteners and home insecticides, announced that it's acquiring stake in loss-making Henkel India, its stock tanked almost 20%. Every equity research outfit thought it was a crazy thing to do and put a 'Self' recommendation on it.

Henkel India's revenues were ₹ 400 crore and it was making a loss of ₹ 600 crore, while Jyothy's revenues were at ₹ 600 crore and its profit after tax, ₹ 74 crore. They had 7 strong brands which had survived for more than 25 years, but were just not managed well. Henkel India's operating margins were at –4.4% then.

Their optimism wasn't misplaced, and in less than two years of acquisition, the company turned around Henkel India. Henkel was spending too much on ads, and its sales were more geared towards urban India. At the same time, our strength was in rural areas. This all-India brand recognition made it easy to take Henkel's products to the rural markets.

The company trimmed Henkel's staff to 50 from 475. Many of them retired voluntarily as they were expats and didn't want to work for an Indian company.

All this helped the company achieve 8% efficiency, which means on a top line of ₹ 1,200 crore, it saved almost ₹ 100 crore. This helped it improve profitability and at the same time allowed high ad spends. In the last two years, it has almost doubled its ad spends from 5-6% of sales to 10% now.

6.3 DIVERSIFICATION STRATEGIES

Diversification means entry into a business which is new to the firm either marketwise or technologywise or both. The firm may make new products or serve new markets or may enter totally unrelated business. Diversification is of two types—concentric and conglomerate.

1. **Concentric or Related Diversification:** When a firm's new business is in any way related to its existing business in terms of customer groups, customer functions or alternative technologies, it is called concentric or related diversification. Thus, concentric diversification is of three types:

   (*a*) **Marketing-related Diversification:** The new and old products both can be distributed through the same channel. For example, a book publisher may go into publishing magazines or a sewing machine manufacturer may launch household appliances and kitchenware.

   (*b*) **Technology-related Diversification:** In this case the new and old products both use the same technology. For example, a firm which offers hire-purchase services to institutional customers may start financing purchase of consumer durables by households.

   (*c*) **Marketing and Technology-related Diversification:** Under this strategy, the firm introduces a similar product-service with the help of similar technology./ For example, Syntax, a producer of synthetic water tanks-launched prefabricated, synthetic doors and windows which are all sold through hardware stores. In this case the distribution channel and technology (plastic processing and engineering) used both for old and new products are similar.

Examples of Concentric Diversification

- Larsen and Toubro has grown consistently through related diversification. It is mainly an engineering and construction company. But it has diversified into several related businesses such as electrical and electronics, machinery and industrial products, etc.
- Themax diversified into energy conservation equipment, a related business.
- Sintex industries, a traditional plastic goods market, entered the monolithics business in 2007, which provided two main unique advantages: it helped build structures faster, and at a 10-15% cheaper cost. The concept became a favourite with various state governments and government agencies implementing low-cost housing projects for the economically weaker sections of the society. At its peak in 2011, business was growing in double-digits, contributing nearly one-third to the company's total revenues with margins of over 20%.

Concentric diversification offers the benefits of synergy. It helps to

(*a*) save transferation costs and taxes

(*b*) increase market power by offering a complete range of products

(*c*) provide economies of scale

(*d*) ensure better use of resources and capabilities

2. **Conglomerate or Unrelated Diversification:** Conglomerate means a combination of two or more businesses which are related neither by technology nor by marketing. Companies diversify into unrelated businesses to diversify risks, to make profitable use of surplus capital, etc.

Examples of Conglomerate Diversification

- Tata Group is a conglomerate of more than twenty businesses from salt to software. It operates in hotels, airlines, steel, software, foods and beverages, chemicals, electricals, electronics, textiles, automobiles, and several other businesses.
- Aditya Birla Group is in several unrelated businesses such as cement, aluminium, copper, carbon black, chemicals, fertilisers, mining, gas, software, retail, textiles, telecom, financial services, etc.
- ITC began as a tobacco company. Over the years it has diversified into paper and paperboards, foods and beverages, readymades, hotels, soaps and cosmetics, information technology, etc. ITC diversified into unrelated businesses because growth in tobacco, products was blocked by increasing opposition to smoking and anti-smoking legislation.
- Reliance Industries is in textiles, petrochemicals, gas, retail, telecom, financial services, etc.
- Themax diversified during 1980s in unrelated areas such as software, financial engineering and electronics.
- Jain Irrigation Systems is proposing to add spice to its basket ranging from irrigation to energy solutions.

Conglomerate diversification offers several **benefits**:

(*i*) It helps to minimise risks due to investment in different industries.

(*ii*) It enables a firm to take advantage of emerging opportunities due to economic liberalisation and globalisation.

(*iii*) It helps to maximise returns through investment in profitable businesses and selling out unprofitable businesses.

(*iv*) It facilitates creation of business empires.

(*v*) Competencies can be leveraged in corporate restructuring and turnaround management.

Table 6.2: Merits and Demerits of Diversification

Merits	Demerits
1. Minimises risks by spreading investment in several businesses	1. Considerable managerial and financial competencies are needed for success
2. Enables capitalising on emerging business opportunities	2. A wide variety of skills are required for different unrelated businesses
3. Helps to grow when growth in existing businesses is restricted due to regulatory and other environmental factors	3. Administrative costs of managing, coordinating and controlling a wide portfolio of businesses are high
4. Better use of resources through synergy	4. Risk of regulations
5. Increasing organisational capability by adapting to rapidly changing environment	
6. Helps to buildup a balanced portfolio of business so as to face cyclical and seasonal fluctuations	
7. Adds to power and prestige	

6.4 COOPERATION STRATEGIES

Competing or rival firms can benefit through mutual cooperation when they have complimentary capabilities. Strategic alliances, joint ventures, mergers and acquisitions are cooperative strategies.

6.4.1 Strategic Alliances

A strategic alliance is a cooperative arrangement in which two or more independent firms combine their resources and capabilities for mutually agreed common objectives. It may be made to develop, manufacture or distribute products or services. The main characteristics of a strategic alliance are as follows[4]:

(*a*) Two or more firms unite to pursue a set of agreed upon goals, but remain independent subsequent to the formation of the alliance;

(*b*) The partner firms share the benefits of the alliance and control over the performance of assigned tasks; and

(*c*) The partner firms contribute on a continuing basis, in one or more key strategic areas, for example, technology, product and so forth.

(*d*) Liberalisation and globalisation have led to the growth of strategic alliances. Indian firms lack resources and capabilities needed for growth. It takes time and funds to develop capabilities. Therefore, they form alliances with other firms for sharing technology, distribution network, global brand name, managerial expertise, etc.

4 M. Y. Yoshino and U. Srinivasa Rangan, ***Strategic Alliances—An Entrepreneurial Approach to Globalisation,*** Harvard Business School Press, Boston, 1995.

Strategic Alliances in India

- Taj Group of hotels formed an alliance with British Airways. Under this alliance the two promoted each other. Taj Group gives priority to clients who travel by British Airways which, in turn, helps in booking Taj Group of hotels.
- Bharti Airtel, India's largest telecom company by market cap and revenues, has entered into an infrastructure-sharing deal with the telecom arm of Reliance Industries, creating a somewhat unlikely alliance between two groups usually perceived to be bitter rivals.

  The deal will give the telecom unit, Reliance Jio, pan-India access to Bharti's nationwide infrastructure while giving Bharti access to the optic fibre capacity created by Jio in future.

  Consequently, RIL might be able to launch telecom and broadband services in the near future ridiing on Bharti's infrastructure, much earlier than if it had to build its own infrastructure. "It has cut Reliance Jio's time to market by several years,"

  Airtel, for its part, will see its cash flows boosted by lease rentals from Jio.

  "The sharing could extend to roaming on 2G, 3G and 4G, and any other mutually benefiting areas relating to telecommunication", both the companies said in a statement, reflecting the expansive contours of the deal between the two.
- Indian Overseas Bank entered into a strategic alliance with TTK Group to offer a range of services to **NRIs**, including healthcare to dependents and property services in India.
- Renault and Nissan celebrated 15 years of their alliance. The combination of Nissan's technology and cash and Renault's management has kept both firms alive.
- HCL Technology, India's fourth largest IT services provider, recently announced an applications service alliance with larger rival Computer Sciences Corporation (CSC) that the companies have said will benefit both.

  History says otherwise. From EDS to Cognizant, such alliances tend to either not work or benefit one partner at the expense of the other. In this case, HCL is likely to come out smiling whereas it is not clear how the larger US-based company will benefit.

  "The main obstacle is, it's very difficult to make this kind of partnership work." From CSC's perspective, there's potential here to bring in a competitor into client accounts and then lose the clients, which is what usually happens, especially when you have a formidable player like HCL.

Reasons for Strategic Alliances

1. **To Enter New Markets:** A company having a successful product or service may find it difficult to enter a new market. It may enter into an alliance with a foreign firm to gain entry into the foreign market. Several multinationals have, for example, entered into strategic alliances with Indian firms. Global alliances help to overcome entry barriers (legal and trade barriers) in foreign markets. Some countries allow entry of foreign firms only with participation of local firms. For example, foreign firms entered into insurance sector in India by forming strategic alliances with Indian firms.
2. **To Reduce Manufacturing Costs:** Strategic alliances are a means of pooling resources so as to gain economies of scale and to make better utilisation of resources. These in turn help to reduce manufacturing costs. For example, a firm may enter into an alliance with its suppliers to ensure regular supply of raw materials at reasonable cost.

3. **To Develop New Products:** Development of a new product involves huge costs. Firms may collaborate to share the costs and benefits of new products.
4. **To Develop and Diffuse Technology:** Two or more firms may leverage their technical expertise to develop new technology. They learn thereby new ways of doing things.
5. **To Preempt Competition:** Competitors quickly imitate new products and services. Firms enter into strategic alliances to preempt such imitation.

   The basic advantage of a strategic alliance is synergy which creates a win – win situation for all partners. It is based on the theme "if you can't do it alone, join hands with others".

Limitations of Strategic Alliances

(*i*) A strategic alliance can be successful only when there is mutual trust and commitment between the partners. In most cases the initial trust turns into suspicion and the alliance fails.

(*ii*) Partners expect much from an alliance. When the expected results do not materialise they get frustrated and the alliance is broken.

(*iii*) In a strategic alliance, business secrets of partners may become known to each other. After the alliance is over, these partners may become competitors and use such information against each other. Alliances are typically complicated and can come unstuck when the benefits to both sides become unclear.

Thus, suspicion and misunderstanding among partners, conflicting goals and interests, lack of adequate preparation, hasty implementation of plans, etc are the main pitfalls in strategic alliances.

Some of the steps that can be taken for successful management of strategic alliances are as follows:

(*a*) Clearly define the strategy to be adopted and align it with the corporate strategies of the partners.

(*b*) Clearly spell out in writing the operational responsibilities of the partners.

(*c*) Ensure trust and commitment of partners on a continuous basis.

(*d*) Allow adequate time and opportunity to the partners to know and understand each other.

(*e*) Reconcile or blend the cultures of the partners

(*f*) Lay down a strategy for amicable exit from the alliance

Types of Strategic Alliances

On the basis of their focus, strategic alliances are of five types[5]:

1. **Technology Development Alliance:** This type of alliance is formed to reduce costs and risks involved in development of new technology. The partners pool their R & D capabilities by sharing information and ideas through networking.
2. **Operations and Logistics Alliance:** Partners form such an alliance to improve efficiency of manufacturing through exchange of information.

---

5. Michael E. Porter and Mark B. Fuller, "Coalitions and Global Strategy" in Porter (ed.), ***Competition in Global Industries***, Harvard Business School Press, Boston, M.A. 1986, pp. 330–338.

3. **Marketing, Sales and Service Alliance:** Under such an alliance, partners share their distribution network and after-sale service facilities to increase sales revenue and to reduce marketing costs.
4. **Single Country or Multicountry Alliance:** Partners in an alliance may belong to the same country or to different countries. Multicountry alliances have become popular on account of globalisation.
5. ***X* and *Y* Alliance:** In *X* alliance, the partners perform different activities. For example, one may manufacture and the other may distribute. This type of alliance is formed between partners having different types of skills. When partners have similar types of skills and perform similar functions, it is called *Y* alliance. Such an alliance provides economies of scale.

6.4.2 Joint Ventures Strategy

A joint venture is a new company formed jointly by two or more independent companies. Each partner contributes a distinctive competence such as finance, technology, managerial expertise, etc. A joint venture is usually formed between two or more firms with complementary skills.

A joint venture differs from a strategic alliance in three ways. **First,** a joint venture is a new company whereas no new company is formed in a strategic alliance. **Second,** a joint venture has a distinct identity and continues for a long time while a strategic alliance has no separate identity and is of temporary nature. **Third,** in a joint venture all partners contribute equity while in a strategic alliance there is no equity from any partner.

Types of Joint Ventures

Joint ventures are of the following types:

1. A joint venture between two companies belonging to the same country and the same industry. For example, NTPC and Indian Railways created a joint venture named Bharatiya Rail Bijlee Company to meet the needs of rail network across India. NTPC contributed 74 per cent equity and Indian Railways provided the balance 26 per cent.
2. A joint venture between two companies belonging to different industries. For example, Biocon Ltd. of India set up a joint venture with Neo Pharma of Abu Dhabi to produce and sell bio-pharma unitcals in the Gulf. Nissan Motors (Japan), Renault (France) and Mahindra & Mahindra (India) entered into a joint venture to manufacture Sedan Tram cars in Chennai in India.
   - The Tata Group has inked a joint venture with Telestra Tradeplace and Malaysia's AirAsia to launch a low cost carrier,
   - Britain's TescoPlc and Tata Groups's Trent Hypermarker Limted (THL) have set up a 50 : 50 joint venture to open super markets in India.
3. A joint venture between two companies from different countries but belonging to the same industry *e.g.* Hero Group of India and Honda Motors of Japan.
4. A joint venture between two companies belonging to different countries and different industries.
5. A joint venture between Government of India and a foreign company (*e.g.*, Suzuki Motors of Japan).

Advantages of Joint Ventures

Gopalan[6] has identified the following reasons behind joint ventures:

1. **Technology:** In a global joint venture the foreign partner can bring in advanced technology while the Indian partner has good understanding of the local market. Such joint ventures are popular in automobiles and telecommunications. TTK Group in association with LIG of London set up TTK LIG for making condom.
2. **Geography:** A foreign company having presence in several key global markets enters India through a joint venture. Several Indian firms have entered into joint ventures with global insurance firms such as Prudential, Standard Life, etc.
3. **Regulation:** When a highly regulated sector is opened up for private firms, joint ventures spring up. For example, India allows 26 per cent equity participation in insurance sector. Bajaj, Birla, Tata, ICICI have formed joint ventures with foreign firms after the opening of the insurance sector.
4. **Sharing Risk and Capital:** Capital-intensive sector like heavy engineering requires huge investment and involves high risks. Joint ventures are formed to share risk, capital investment and technological expertise.
5. **Intellectual Exchange:** In legal, accounting, audit and consultancy professions, joint ventures are formed to exchange information and knowledge.

   Thus, minimising risk, sharing investment, gaining access to high-class technology, entry into new businesses, effective use of resources through combined expertise are the main benefits of joint ventures.

Drawbacks of Joint Ventures

Gopalan[7] has identified the following reasons for failure of joint ventures:

1. **Change of Strategy:** As a market a country may lose its strategic advantage. For example, Bell Canada sold its stake in Tata Cellular to the Indian partner when the company lost interest in the Indian market.
2. **Regulatory Changes:** When a host government does not hike FDI limit or reduces it, the foreign partner may lose interest in the joint venture. For example, FDI limit of 26 per cent in insurance is not attractive for foreign firms.
3. **Success of Joint Venture:** When the joint venture is doing very well, the foreign partner becomes very keen on increasing its holding. For example, Suzuki of Japan bought out government of India's stake in Maruti joint venture.
4. **Partners Hampering Growth:** A partner way hamper the growth prospects and both the partners may feel they would be better off on their own. For example, Tatas sold their holding in Tata Telecom to Avaya Inc., the other partner.
5. **Lack of Transparency:** When a partner withholds information considerable mistrust occurs between the partners. Hutchison-Essar joint venture failed due to lack of

6. K. Gopalan, "The Art of Living Together," ***Business Today***, December 17, 2006, pp 112–118
7. *Ibid*

transparency. Tata Unisys (Tatas and Unisys), Proctor and Gamble, Godrej and LML (Piaggio and Singhanias) are some of the joint ventures that failed due to different approaches of partners.

Joint venture is a high-risk, high-reward strategy. It can be successful, when both the partners trust each other, have strong commitment, and work in close cooperation to make it work. Joint ventures are useful for gaining access to new business under the following conditions[8]:

(*i*) For a single firm the activity is uneconomical to do.

(*ii*) Risk of business has to be shared.

(*iii*) Distinctive competence of two or more firms can be pooled together.

(*iv*) Hurdles like trade barriers, political and cultural roadblocks, etc have to be surmounted

Strategic Issues in Joint Ventures

The key issues in setting up joint ventures are as follows:

1. **Defining Objectives:** The first basic issue is to decide what the joint venture will do and how it will add value for the partners. In many cases a clash of interests arises and necessary safeguards should be provided for to avoid such a clash.
2. **Choosing the Partner:** Some of the criteria for choice of partner are technical, financial and managerial capabilities, In addition, the intention, sincerity and commitment of partner should be considered. A joint venture should not merely be a marriage of convenience.
3. **Deciding Shareholding:** Government regulations, desire for control of joint venture, etc are considered while deciding equity participation by the partners. Such participation should serve the interests of joint venture as well as those of the partner.
4. **Selecting Management Pattern:** A key question is who will constitute and head the board of directors? Shareholding pattern, and mutual agreement between the partners can provide answer to this question.

6.4.3 Merger Strategy

Merger and acquisition is a strategy for external growth of the organisation. A merger means an amalgamation or integration of two or more firms. The combining firms lose their separate identities and form a new and bigger firm. For example, ACC was created through a merger of eleven cement firms. Similarly, Indian Explosives, Alkalie and Chemicals; and Crescent Dyes and Chemicals were merged to form ICI India Limited.

Types of Mergers

1. **Horizontal Merger:** In this type of merger, two or more organisations engaged in the same business combine together. ACC is an example of horizontal merger.

8. A. A. Thompson Jr. and A. J. Stickland III, ***Strategic Management: Concepts and Cases***. Business Publication, Texas, 1984, pp. 92-93.

2. **Vertical Merger:** It takes place when two or more organisations at different levels of business in the same industry amalgamate. For example, a footwear company combines with a leather tannery or a chain of retail stores selling footwear.

3. **Concentric Merger:** When the combining firms are related to each other in terms of customer groups, customer functions or alternative technologies, there is a concentric merger. For example, a footwear company may combine with a hosiery firm making socks or a firm manufacturing leather bags.

4. **Conglomerate Merger:** Under it the combining firms are totally unrelated. For example, a footwear firm may combine with an automobile firm.

   The opposite of a merger is known as reverse merger, demerger or spinoff. In a demerger, unrelated business/division of a diversified firm is spinned off into a stand-alone firm and the shares of the demerged unit are distributed freely among the existing shareholders of the original firm. For example, Zee Telefilms was demerged into three firms: Zee Entertainment Enterprises, Zee News and Wire and Wireless India.

Reasons for Mergers

A merger is beneficial for both the merging company and the merged company.

Benefits to the Merging Company:

(*i*) Provides quick entry into markets and industries which involve huge risk and large investment, or wherein government regulations restrict entry.

(*ii*) Helps in faster growth than what is possible through internal expansions. Growth offers economies of scale which can provide a competitive edge.

(*iii*) Facilitates diversification of operations.

Reduce competition and dependence. Horizontal mergers reduce competition while vertical mergers reduce dependence on outsiders for supply of raw materials and distribution of products.

(*v*) When one firm has tax liability while the other firm has accumulated losses, their merger helps to save taxes.

(*vi*) Merger of firms with complementary capabilities offers benefits of synergy in marketing, operations and management.

(*vii*) Merger of firms having seasonal businesses helps to stabilise sales revenue and profits. For example, a firm manufacturing fans and coolers may combine with a firm manufacturing heaters, gysers, etc.

Filling Gaps Through Mergers

- Product line gap—acquisition of Tomco by Hindustan Unilever
- Distribution gap—alliance between P&G and Godrej Soaps
- Usage gap—converting non-users into users
- Competitive gap—increasing market share and market power

Benefits to the Merged Company

(*i*) A loss-making firm can liquidate itself through merger.

(*ii*) A company whose management cannot revive it can grow by merging with a highly efficient firm.

(*iii*) A firm which has acquired a distinctive competence may not be able to manage growth beyond a certain size. It may merge with another firm to sustain its growth.

(*iv*) A firm faced with management crisis (top management succession problem) may find it beneficial to merge with another firm

Thus, mergers help in improving efficiency, gaining synergy, achieving strategic alignment and diversification

Why Mergers Fail and How to Avoid Them

Mergers, particularly conglomerate and concentric types, often fail due to various reasons. Some of these reasons are as follows:

(*i*) Mistake in assessing the synergistic effects of the merger

(*ii*) Inability to realize the potential economies

(*iii*) Inadequate or defective planning

In 2006, Bharti Retail and Walmart Stores had joined hands promising to create thousands of direct jobs in India. Seven years later, the two former partners are retrenching employees and the Indian company is preparing to shutt some unviable Easyday stores, as they restructure their operations following a split two months ago.

Some of the actions that can be taken to overcome these problems and to avoid failure of mergers are given below:

1. A firm with poor growth prospects should merge with another firm in high growth area
2. A firm faced with unstable sales and profits can merge with the one having more stable sales and profits
3. A firm with limited technological capability should merge with another having strong R and D base
4. A firm with weak marketing system may merge with another having strong marketing capability.

Strategic Issues in Mergers

The basic issues involved in a merger are as follows:

1. **Synergistic Effects:** First of all, consider the synergistic effects of the proposed merger. For this purpose, the strategic advantages and distinctive competencies of the merging firms have to be analysed. These must be complementary and there should be a match between the objectives/strategic interests of the partners.
2. **Financial Issues:** The valuation of business/shares of the merging firm, sources of finance for the merger, taxation implications of the merger are the main financial issues.

Valuation of business is a comprehensive process and depends on several factors such as tangible and intangible assets, firm's industry profile and growth prospects, stock market price, quality of top management, etc. Owned funds and borrowed funds and new issues are the sources of finance for a merger.

3. **Managerial Issues:** A merger is usually followed by changes in top management. A well-entrenched management may attempt to foil the merger when it feels insecure, other-wise, professional management can be adopted easily.
4. **Legal Issues:** In India, mergers are regulated under the Companies Act and the Competition Act. Under the Income Tax Act, accumulated losses can be carried forward and unabsorbed depreciation of the merged company can be written off after merger.

6.4.4 Acquisition or Takeover Strategy

When one company acquires majority or full ownership and control of another company, it is called acquisition or takeover. If this is done through mutual agreement between the two companies, it is **friendly takeover**. When the company is acquired against its wishes, it is **hostile takeover.**

The terms merger and acquisition are often used together as M & A. However, there are some differences between the two. Merger does not necessarily involve acquisition. For example, two or more firms owned by a business house may be merged together. It is also not essential that an acquired firm is merged with the acquiring firm. For example, Sterlite is operating as a stand-alone company even after its acquisition by Balco.

After liberalisation and globalistation began in 1991, there has been a rapid increase in takeovers in India.

Acquisitions in India

- Tata Steel acquired Corus Steel and Jaguar Land Rover Brand cars of U.K.
- Aditya Birla Group acquired Novelis
- Bharti Airtel acquired Zain of South Africa for $ 10.7 billion
- Amtek Auto Group acquired Germany's Neumayer Takfor Group and the British company JL French Castings
- HDFC Mutual Fund acquired Zurich MF and Stanley MF
- Ahmedabad-based Torrent Pharma's acquisition of debt-laden Elder Pharma's domestic branded formulation business may have given Torrent access to high-growth segments including women's healthcare, nutraceuticals and pain management, but analysts are concerned over the huge debt Torrent itself would have taken on to fund the ₹ 2,000-crore deal.

  Due to this acquisition, Torrent is likely to accrue a debt of ₹ 2,600 crore by 2014-15, analysts said. Post-acquisition, Sudhir Mehta, Torrent Group chairman, had said the transaction was a strategic fit; it would strengthen Torrent's core prescription-based business. "The acquisition benefits could be leveraged over three-five years, but in the medium-term, Torrent would have immediate cost-push concerns, which would outweigh the synergy benefits,"

- Fiat of Italy acquired 41 per cent stake in Chrysler of USA at a cost of $ 4.35 billion. Fiat will dip into Chrysler's cash pile to finance a new range of models in the hope of boosting annual sales to 6 million vehicles and to increase the proportion of profitable premium cars it sells from its sporty. Alfa Romeo and Maserate ranges.
- Essar Group acquired Zisosteels of Africa for $ 7.5 million.
- I Gate the outsourcing services firm acquired Patni Computer Systems for ₹ 7441 crore in 2012.
- The world's largest dairy products maker, Group Lactalis SA (Lactalis), has acquired Hyderabad-based Tirumala Milk Products in a deal estimated to be around $250–300 million. The transaction is likely to give Lactalis, which develops well-known international brands including President, Galbani and Paramalat, a foothold in India. Tirumala is the second-largest private dairy company in South India with a processing capacity of 1.66 million litres per day across 7 plants.

Advantages of Acquisitions

(*i*) Acquisition of an existing firm's products and facilities provides a quick entry into the target market

(*ii*) When the acquired and the acquiring firms are in the same business, there can be substantial economies of scale

(*iii*) By acquiring a supplier/distributor, a firm can reduce its dependence on others for supply of material/distribution of finished product.

(*iv*) Acquisition of a firm having complementary facilities/competence can provide benefits of synergy.

(*v*) Acquisition of a rival helps to reduce competition and increase market share.

Limitations of Acquisitions

1. Huge funds at a short notice are needed for acquisition.
2. The interests of minority shareholders may not be taken care of in an acquisition.
3. Takeovers encourage oligopoly and monopoly in the industry. There they have to face legal hurdles.
4. It is difficult to integrate the culture and managerial practices of the two firms.
5. There may be hidden liabilities.

In an audacious $ 19 billion deal that would mark the next step in the Internet revolution, Facebook has decided to buy WhatsApp, the SMS-killing messaging service that links groups of people through their mobile numbers by working through their data plans. India's huge market is one of the key factors at the heart of the deal.

The deal is poised to help the social networking giant steal a lead in two of its hottest bets–India and mobile Internet. India is set to see an explosive growth in the use of mobile Internet as hundreds of millions of users graduate from voice calls to using their handsets to surf the Net through smartphones or cheaper feature phones enabled for dedicated applications like Facebook or messenger apps.

Mumbai-based drugmaker Lupin has announced that it will acquire Netherlands-based injectibles company Nanomi BV in an attempt to expand its business in patented products. Lupin didn't reveal the valuation of the deal.

Defence Strategies

There are several defence strategies which companies may employ against hostile takeover attempts. Important strategies are the following.

Pacman Defence: Under this strategy the target company attempts to raid the predator. This would be more effective if the target company is larger in size than the predator.

Swallowing Poison Pill: This strategy attempts to make the takeover target less attractive by measures such as issue of convertible debentures. As this strategy can prove to be very dangerous to the target company itself, it is also known as Scorched Earth Policy.

Disposing of Crown Jewels: This strategy, by disposing of the most valuable assets, also aims at making the target less attractive to the predator in a bid to discourage any takeover move. Such a strategy may find favour with the target company if it is possible to sell the crown jewel to an associate company.

Management Buy-Out: Under this strategy the target company raises funds from the market by issue of bonds. The high gearing also makes the company less attractive.

Operation Gray or White Knight: The target company launches a counter-takeover attack on the predator offering a higher bid to the target company than the other raider.

Golden Parachutes: This strategy involves providing protection to the company directors through such measures as extravagant termination packages which would make it unattractive for raiders to replace them.

Table 6.2: SEBI's Takeover Code

1.	An acquirer who acquires 5 per cent or more shares in any listed company, he must inform the stock exchange concerned within two days from the date of acquisition or date of agreement for acquisition.
2.	The company concerned must inform the stock exchange concerned within 7 days if a single entity acquires shares with voting rights of 10 per cent or more in it along with facts having impact on the share price movement.
3.	Upon acquiring shares carrying voting rights of 20 per cent or more, the acquirer must make an open offer to buy not less than 20 per cent shares from the remaining shareholders at the same price or at the highest quoted price during the preceding six months.
4.	The acquirer will deposit 10 per cent of the purchase consideration in a bank account to be kept under the custody of a third party to be appointed by the concerned stock exchange.

Issues and Steps in Acquisition Process

1. **Defining the Objectives:** First of all the acquirer company must identity the strategic reason (s) behind the acquisition. The objective should be value creation and synergy rather than asset creation. It may be to gain entry into a market, to improve competitive position, to gain market leadership, to achieve economies of scale or to acquire technology. For example, Hindustan Unilever acquired Kwality, Milkfood and Dollops ice cream brands to expand its food business. Acquisition of TOMCO enabled HUL to consolidate its market power in soaps and detergents. The acquisition must fit with the company's mission and strategy.

2. **Constituting the Task Force:** A team consisting of experts is set up because acquisition requires a variety of skills. The main functions of this team are: to identify the target firm, to conduct due diligence, to make acquisition bid and to complete the formalities involved in the acquisition.
3. **Identifying the Target Firm:** In order to identify the firm to be acquired the following considerations are kept in view:
   (*a*) The synergy between the two firms
   (*b*) The savings, improvements, etc that can flow from it
   (*c*) The volume of these savings and improvement
4. **Conducting Due Diligence:** The acquiring firm has to pay for the tangible and intangible assets of the acquired firm. It is necessary to determine the reasonable price of these assets. All aspects (strengths and weaknesses) of the target firm must be considered in such assessment. Earning potential, market position, condition of assets, quality of management, human resources, are some of the main considerations.
5. **Making Acquisition Bid:** Once the due diligence is complete and found satisfactory the bid for acquisition is made in either of the two ways:
   (*a*) making the initial offer—in case this offer is not acceptable, further negotiations take place until the mutually agreed price is settled
   (*b*) by acquiring controlling votes from institutional and other shareholders, wage a successful battle for replacing the present management
   A friendly takeover is better than a hostile takeover.
6. **Acquiring the Target Firm:** The target firm is taken over when the acquisition attempt is successful either through mutual agreement or hostile manner. The acquiring company may or may not replace the acquired company's board of directors.
7. **Post-Acquisition Action:** An acquisition can be successful only when the acquired firm is well integrated with the acquiring firm. Ghosal[9] has given some guidelines for successful management of an acquisition (Table 6.3).

Table 6.3: Post-Acquisition

	Phase I: Cleaning up and building the foundation	Phase II: Strategic and organisational revitalisation	Phase III: Integration of people and operations
1.	Change in top management	Vision, values and guiding principles	Functional integration
2.	Protection of existing management at the next level	Management development	Systems integration
3.	Financial reporting system	Workforce rationalisation	Strategic investment and market expansion
4.	Functional discipline	Structural reorganisation	Two-way flow of people at different levels
5.	Debottlenecking capacity	Skills upgrading	
6.	Morale building	Continuous involvement of top management	

9 Sumantra Ghosal, "Integrating Acquisitions," ***The Economic Times* (*CD*)**, January 1, 1999, p. 2

6.5 STABILITY STRATEGIES

Stability does not mean remaining stable over longtime period or keeping the *status* quo. Rather, stability strategy means incremental improvement in performance through marginal changes in one or more businesses. It refers to maintaining the present course. It is a slow and steady race. A company pursuing stability strategy keeps on serving the same markets with the present product, using the existing technology. Stability means sustaining moderate growth rather than 'doing nothing'. Generally, small and medium-sized organisations follow stability strategy. Large firms may also adopt this strategy in the short run when they are satisfied with their current performance.

Examples of Stability Strategy

- Steel Authority of India Limited (SAIL) adopted stability strategy due to over – capacity in steel sector. It has, instead, concentrated on increasing operational efficiency. Many other companies in public sector have been forced to adopt stability strategy owing to government's policy of reducing budgetary support and cutting the role of public sector.
- A copier machine company tried to improve its company and product image through better customer service.

Advantages of Stability Strategy

Stability strategy has several advantages and is adopted for many reasons:

(*i*) Stability is basically a defensive strategy. It involves less risk and less investment

(*ii*) It involves less changes and therefore employees feel comfortable. Organizations which are slow to change prefer stability

(*iii*) Stability is suitable in a stable and predictable environment.

(*iv*) Stability may be adopted when expansion is perceived as being threatening.

(*v*) After a period of rapid expansion, stability may be adopted for consolidation.

(*vi*) When there is scope for incremental improvement of performance in the present line of business, stability may be used to take complete advantage of the situation.

(*vii*) Managers having limited ambitions may be satisfied with current performance.

(*viii*) When competitive advantage of a firm lies in the present business and market, it may pursue stability.

The firm may seek to protect its existing strengths, *e.g.,* technical expertise, patent right, etc.

Limitations of Stability Strategy

(*i*) The company may lose significant opportunities for growth created by changes in technology, government policies and other environmental changes.

(*ii*) The market share and competitive position of the company may decline due to expansion by rival firms.

(*iii*) Stability strategy may create inaction and demoralise the staff.

Types of Stability Strategy

1. **No-change Strategy:** In this variant of stability strategy, the firm does nothing new. The firm does not find it worthwhile to alter its business definition due to absence of opportunities and threats in the external environment. Many small-scale firms operating in a small niche market and offering products or services through a time tested technology depend on no-change strategy. Thus, no change strategy is an incremental growth strategy.
2. **Profit Strategy:** No firm can continue with a no-change strategy indefinitely. Business environment changes over time, and a firm has to change. It may be faced with short-term threats like economic recession, industry downturn, competitive pressure, government attitude, etc. The firm lies low and attempts to sustain its profitability until the crisis is over. For example, a firm may sell off its prime office in a commercial centre and shift to a suburb.
3. **Pause or Proceed-with-Caution Strategy:** Firms which have had rapid expansion and want to consolidate before moving ahead adopt this strategy. Firms that wish to test the ground before moving ahead with a full-fledged corporate strategy may also pursue pause. Thus, like the profit strategy pause is a temporary strategy. But profit strategy is a forced choice while pause is a deliberate move. For example, Hindustan Unilever started selling in later half of 2000 a few thousand pairs of shoes in cities to judge the market reaction. Later on it began exporting shoes through Ponds Exports.

6.6 RETRENCHMENT STRATEGIES

Retrenchment strategy is adopted when an organisation substantially reduces the scope of its activities. It involves partial or total withdrawal from one or more businesses which are no longer profitable. For example, Raymonds sold off its unprofitable cement business. A firm may reduce the number of products and markets it serves to reduce costs and to improve profitability. Thus, retrenchment strategy is the opposite of growth strategy.

Decline may occur due to both internal and external reasons. Ineffective top management, faulty strategies, strong resistance to change, inappropriate organization design, high costs, unproductive new products, excess assets are the internal reasons. External reasons include demand saturation, unfavourable government policies, changes in customer needs and preferences, emergence of substitute products, new business models, new technologies, etc.

There are several symptoms which indicate the need for retrenchment strategy. Declining profitability, falling cash flows, dwindling sales turnover, loss of credibility, etc. are such symptoms. Several industries in India show these symptoms of decline. Cotton textiles, jute, coalmining, manual typewriters, teleprinters, steam engines are some examples. Many firms in India have downsized or sold themselves out due to reduction in import duties, stiff competition from multinationals, rising costs of inputs, etc.,

Shekhar Bajaj-promoted Bajaj Electricals is getting rid of loss-making projects and being selective about choosing new ones in an effort to put its past behind and rediscover itself as a leaner and more effective entity. The company is mainly involved in three businesses—consumer appliances, lightings and EPC.

The reason for the poor show on bourses is the EPC business, which has been a drag for the company: it wiped out 53% of the total operating profit in FY13 and 66% in the first half FY14. Cost overruns and execution delays in the EPC business have resulted in the poor performance. But now the company is trying to set things in order. "We have become very selective about the projects we choose and will take the ones only with high margins. We have also set up a new ERP system and a new team for the EPC business and our focus will only be on execution," said Bajaj.

As the older projects are closed and newer ones are reorganised, there will be a steady rise in the company's overall operating margins. "We believe, given the changes in the company's processes, Bajaj Electricals' EPC segment will soon turn profitable. Bajaj Electricals' new projects are running ahead of schedule and are profitable with margins at 8%," said Vikas Manthri and Satish Kothari, mid-cap analysts with ICICI Securities recommending the stock with a 40% upside from the current levels. However, there are two other business potentials—consumer durables and lighting. Its consumer durables business, which provides more than half its sales, is growing at a 25% CAGR over the last three years, and its lighting business, which accounts for one-fourth of its sales, is growing at a 17% CAGR. Operating margins for these are around 8%.

The company has also started brand building and spent about ₹ 26 crore in the first half of FY14 on advertising and will be spending another ₹ 45-50 crore in the second half, which will help it improve its margins.

Reasons for Retrenchment Strategy

(*i*) The firm wants to exit from a particular product/service, business or market due to continuing losses and bleak future.

(*ii*) Reallocation of resources from unprofitable to profitable businesses can ensure viability and stability of the firm

(*iii*) The firm's environment is threatening.

(*iv*) The management is under pressure to improve performance and other strategies are not succeeding

6.5.1 Turnaround Strategy

Turnaround means reversing a negative trend or converting an unprofitable or sick business into a profitable (healthy) one. The major danger signs which indicate the need for turnaround strategy are as follows:

(*i*) Continuous losses

(*ii*) Negative cash flows

(*iii*) Declining market share

(*iv*) Deterioration of physical facilities

(*v*) Overstaffing, high employee turnover

(*vi*) Non-competitive products or services

(*vii*) Mismanagement

(*viii*) Increasing debt.

Managing Turnaround

Before deciding to turnaround a firm, it is necessary to decide whether the business is worth saving. When the going concern value of the firm is more than its liquidated value, it is worthwhile to turn it around. Otherwise divestment or liquidation is better. After it is found that the business is worth sarving, its current operating health is analysed. This involves a detailed analysis of its strengths and weaknesses. The third step is to choose the turnaround strategy—strategic or operating. Strategic turnaround involves change in corporate strategy while operating turnaround involves increasing revenues, reducing costs and assets and so on.

Firstsource Makes a 'Perfect Turnaround'

Firstsource, one of India's top three business process outsourcing companies, has been through hell and back. Investors, bondholders, lenders and even its employees had given up on the company in 2011: its stock had crashed to a mere ₹10 in 2011 from ₹70 in 2008, the company was grappling with rising debt, and facing an outstanding FCCB payment. It had no earnings to get out of this mess.

It was when Rajesh Subramaniam, who had resigned from Firstsource in 2008, was asked to come back and rescue the ship. In August 2012, Subramaniam was appointed the managing director and CEO, and since then, he has scripted an almost perfect turnaround story. Subramaniam helped the company repay debt and FCCB, consolidated facilities, broke operational silos, realigned sales functions, renegotiated unvaible client agreements, and rationalise cost. This included realigning the processes, rationalising employee structure and renegotiating with all the clients.

Using the cash from preference allotment to promoters and other internal accruals, the company was able to pay back $237 million, or ₹1,300 crore, FCCB in 2012. Then the company undertook various restructuring exercises: it weeded out non-profitable customers—mostly Indian clients with low margins—and identified areas of growth, especially the healthcare industry in the US. Under the new leadership, Firstsource's profit after tax more than doubled to ₹146 crore in FY13 from ₹62 crore a year ago, and the stock has more than trebled to ₹24 at present from its low of ₹8 in 2011. The debt has also halved to ₹1,000 crore.

Finolex Inds on a Roll after Renewing its Focus on Pipe Business

Two years of stagnation and margin erosion forced India's top PVC pipes and fittings maker, Finolex Industries, to reinvent itself to stage a comeback.

The company not only recovered its profits in FY13 to FY10 levels, but further doubled them in the April-December' 13 period. Its market capitalisation has nearly tripled over the past one year, signailing that things are on the mend.

The company's problems in the past emanated from its huge exposure to the commodity PVC business, which it entered as part of a backward integration course. But now there is a renewed focus on pipes, which was its main forte. Simultaneously, Finolex is trying to improve margins in the pipes business, where it enjoys a strong brand value.

The decision to reduce its foreign exchange exposure and to hedge, after seeing the impact on its earnings in the past, has also helped. "We used to take 360 days credit from overseas suppliers in the past, which was unhedged, exposing us to great foreign exchange volatility. We cut that to 90 days now, while hedging 70% of our exposure, so we won't have any volatility in earnings," Saurabh Dhanorkar, its managing directors, said.

The company is also set to exploit the potential in PVC fittings, which is a fast growing, high-margin business with limited competition. Finolex generates over ₹300 crore of cash annually and will become debt-free in three years. The demand for PVC pipes in India appears to be rising, especially due to the vast unirrigated agricultural land and usage in construction for plumbing and sewerage. And to tap more markets, Finolex has already set up a network of 15,000 dealers.

Through all these measures, Finolex is on course to report a steady improvement in its margins even if the topline remains flattish as its current PVC resin sales get converted to more value-added pipes. However, lower capital expenditure and higher margins will result in a marked improvement in return on investment, which could signal a good long-term investment.

The strategy chosen for turnaround is implemented through action plans. These plans depend on the firm's health, nature of industry, competitive position of the firm, etc. Three major action plans involved in turnaround are as follows:

1. **Change in Top Management:** In case the present top management team lacks the qualities for turnaround, it should be replaced by a new one. An entrepreneurial and strategy oriented team may be needed for high growth strategic turnaround. On the Other hand, an experienced and hard nosed CEO maybe required for major cost cutting, stream-lining operations and improving the organization's culture.
2. **Strategic Turnaround:** A firm having a strong operating health but loss of strategic position requires strategic turnaround. Increase in market share, exit from unprofitable line of business, focus on market niche or defensible product/market segment are the alternatives available for strategic turnaround.
3. **Operating Turnaround:** A firm which has maintained its strategic position but has poor operating health requires operating turnaround. Cost cutting, revenue generation, asset reduction and combination of these are the alternatives. It is necessary to improve cash flows through inventory reduction, collecting receivables, reducing wastages, selling off surplus assets, retrenching excess staff and focusing on high margin products.

Mirchandani[10] has identified three ways of managing turnaround:

(*i*) The existing chief executive and management team handles the entire turnaround strategy, with the advisory support of an external consultant. This method can be successful if the chief executive still enjoys credibility with the banks and financial institutions and a qualified consultant is available. This method is rarely used.

(*ii*) The existing management team withdrawns temporarily and an executive consultant or turnaround expert is appointed by the banks and financial institutions. This method is rarely used in India.

(*iii*) The existing chief executive and top management team is replaced or the sick firm is merged with a healthy firm. This is the most widely used method of turnaround.

10 G. A. Mirchandani, "Turning a Business Around", **Business India**, March 7-20, 1988, pp.110–11

Table 6.4 : Elements of Turnaround Strategy

Ten comparable Indian companies, in five groups of two each, were selected for a study. In each group, one company seemed to have been more successful while the other less successful, in adopting the turnaround strategy. Based on a set of ten elements that contribute to turnaround, the case studies of these ten companies were analysed. First, it is important to note what these ten elements are:

1.	Changes in the top management
2.	Initial credibility-building actions
3.	Neutralising external pressures
4.	Initial control
5.	Identifying quick payoff activities
6.	Quick cost reductions
7.	Revenue generation
8.	Asset liquidation for generating cash
9.	Mobilisation of the organisation
10.	Better internal coordination

The comparative analysis of the actions taken by the more successful companies and the less successful companies revealed that no significant difference was there as far as the first three elements were considered. The crucial difference lay in the way the companies attempted a turnaround on the basis of initial control of operation by the new management, quick cost reductions through various means, mobilising the organisation for improving motivation and morale, and better internal coordination.

Source: Pradip N.Khandwalla, '10 Elements in Turnaround'. ***Business World,*** June 7–20, 1989, pp. 18-19.

Regulatory Issues in Turnaround

Any Indian company which wants to turnaround must first be declared as a sick company under the Sick Industrial Companies Act, 2003. The National Company Law Tribunal or NCLT (earlier the Board for Industrial and Financial Reconstruction or BIFR) is entrusted with the revival and rehabilitation of sick companies.

Whenever the accumulated losses at the end of a financial year exceed 50% of the peak net worth attained during the preceding five years the company has to report its sickness. After receiving the report, the NCLT prepares a rehabilitation scheme, decides on the need for change of management or amalgamation with other companies and other appropriate measures.

HCL Insys Reboots to Revive

In yet another attempt to revive itself, HCL Infosystems is scaling down its computer business and venturing into distribution of consumer durables like TVs, fridges, washing machines and kitchen appliances. The rejig is needed to save the company. A fluctuating currency, a stagnant and shifty hardware market, and wafer-thin margins have made the computer business, on both the manufacturing and the distribution side, unattractive. As a result, HCL following on the lines of home-grown rival Wipro, is exiting manufacturing. They have tried other businesses like security without success in an attempt to derisk from hardware manufacturing.

The company plans to use its existing manufacturing facilities as repair factories for computers and mobile handsets. The consumer durables push should reduce concentration. HCL has tied up with several manufacturers of consumer durables, including Braum, DeLonghi, JBL, Hamilton Beach and Whirlpool. It is also in talks with other manufacturers to distribute durables in rural areas. "Consumer durables distribution has largely been an urban story," says Bhattacharya, chief strategy officer. "Our reach goes to remote and rural areas."

HCL has about 1,000 distributors, covering 80,000 retail outlets in 9,000 cities, towns and villages. Another issue for HCL has been government projects, where an award of a contract can take two years and payment delays normal. This is another area where HCL will reduce focus. The company's new strategy has two planks: beef up distribution, and increase services, where operating margins average 15-20%. Services is currently a ₹800 crore business for HCL, which expects to be ₹2,500 crore in three to four years. Lastly, HCL has some smaller businesses like learning (creating digital education content for schools) and customer care (after-sales services to Nokia and Blackberry).

Retrenchment strategy often involves reduction in the number of employees. This is a very sensitive issue because the hire and fire policy is not allowed in India. No clear-cut exit policy has yet been formulated due to its social and political implications. Even the voluntary retirement schemes (VRS) adopted by some companies have not been successful. Government of India created a National Renewal Fund (NRF) to provide for a social safety net to compensate, retrain and redeploy the retrenched workers.

Turnaround Cases in India	
• Arvind Mills	• Binny Mills
• Bata India	• Calico Mills
• Scooters India	• Firestone
• Bharat Heavy Electricals LIMITED (BHEL)	• Metal Box
• GKW	• Hindustan Cables

The package for revival of a sick company may include any one or more of the following measures:

(*a*) A change in top management

(*b*) Technology upgradation and modernisation

(*c*) Tax exemption or tax rebate

(*d*) Infusion of additional capital

(*e*) Soft loans or rescheduling loans

(*f*) Writing off the interest burden

(*g*) restructure

The turnaround towards profitability at Mahindra & Mahindra's Korean subsidiary Ssangyong Motor Company is now within reach. Company is inching towards break-even as consistent growth in volumes has helped the company post a record 21.3% growth in revenues for 2013 at ₹20,203 crore or 3.4 trillion won. The company posted a marginal net loss of ₹13.93 crore or 2.4 billion South Korean won, while the operational loss has come down by a tenth at ₹51.66 crore versus ₹569.46 crore of operational loss or 98.1 billion South Korean won registered in 2012.

The company said this performance was achieved based on stable labour management relations and the successful launch of new products that helped restore customer confidence. This is the strongest sales performance of the company in a decade and this is despite the difficult business environment.

The sales growth at Ssangyong which enabled the company overtake Renault Samsung as the fourth largest passenger vehicle maker in South Korea in 2013 has seen its operating losses reduce significantly in the last three years, thereby making the financial structure of the company stronger than before. In the domestic market, sales of models like the Korando Turismo increased, which helped the company grow volumes by 34.1% compared to 2012.

6.6.2 Corporate Restructuring

The term restructuring is used in different ways e.g. business restructuring, organisational restructuring, financial restructuring, etc. **Corporate or business level restructuring** refers to change in the company's portfolio of business to improve its probitability. **Organisational restructuring** means changes in the organisation structure such as delayering, downsizing, redesigning managerial positions and changing reporting relationships. **Financial restructuring** implies changes in equity holdings, debt servicing schedule, altering debt equity ratio, etc.

Restructuring may be done to turnaround a sick unit, to prevent a unit becoming sick, to improve efficiency, to facilitate growth and expansion, etc.

Forms of Corporate Restructuring

- Joint venture
- Merger and acquisition
- Portfolio restructuring by selling some business to sharpen business focus and to ensure better utilisation of resources
- Split or spin off a division as separate company
- Divestiture—sale of a division to reduce loss
- Buyback of shares
- Management buyout
- Rescheduling loss
- Conversion of debt into equity

Corporate restructuring may involve exiting some business or acquiring others. The rationale behind such restructuring lies in the thinking of top management, and changes in business environment. Over time, managerial opinions about the company and the industry undergo changes. A company may divest a line of business which its management considers a sunset industry. Similarly, it may enter into an industry considered the sunrise industry. Economic liberalisation, globalisation and other environmental changes are another reason for corporate restructuring. Organisations restructure to realign with the new environment. Since 1991, for example, several companies in India have restructured themselves. Economic reforms such as removal of industrial licensing opened up banking, insurance, infrastructure and several other sectors to private sector and foreign companies. As a result, there have been changes in shareholding pattern, mergers and acquisitions, etc. Large business houses diversified into newly opened sectors. Many companies restructured to face global competition while others divested non-core businesses. Cost reduction, quality improvement, product differentiation, niche marketing have been adopted to remain competitive.

Some cases of corporate restructuring in India are given below:

- Larsen and Toubro (L&T), a highly diversified company, began restructuring in 1993. It decided to focus on its core businesses, namely, engineering, construction and information technology. Therefore, the company divested its non-core businesses such as shipping, shoe manufacturing, cement, glass and milk processing equipment.
- In 1992 the Tata Group decided to reduce the number of companies from 107 operating in 25 businesses to 30 operating in 12 businesses. On the recommendations of its consultant, McKinsey a&Co, it sold out Lakme, Tata Oil Mills, Goodlass Nerolac and several other firms. The restructuring strategy of the Tata Group is characterised by focus on core areas, changing group ethos across companies and emphasis on knowledge-based businesses.
- Hindustan Unilever Limited (HUL) formulated a comprehensive transformation plan to restructure and manage change. The plan (called Project Millennium) aimed at transformation from a diversified conglomerate to a configuration of empowered virtual firms, each built around a single product line. In order to focus on its core business, HUL sold off non-core businesses such as tea and chemicals. It also restructured its brand portfolio.
- In 1997 the TTK Group formulated a ten-year restructuring plan. It aimed at focussing on its core sectors and reducing the number of companies from 52 to 8.
- Infosys will separate its new generation business into a subsidiary, freeing it to focus on large outsourcing contracts, its traditional area of strength, while maintaining interest in an area which could be the future growth engine. This is part of the ongoing, restructuring since the return of the founder Narayana Murthy. The Products, Platforms and Solutions (PPS) unit was set up in 2011 with the aim of getting at least one-third of the company's revenues through intellectual property based software products, platforms and solutions by 2020. However, the initiative which was a key part of Infosys 3.0 strategy failed

  Being part of a services organisation made it difficult to reach out to clients and sell products. A subsidiary is formed to help PPS operate with more independence, and to bring in greater clarity on its strategy and direction,
- Reliance Communication is undergoing a new round of restructuring, aimed at separating the mobile phone major's growing GSM business from the lagging CDMA operations, which could even be sold off at a later stage to pare debt.

  The fresh restructuring not only intends to split the two technologies, but also create circle specific managements to carry through more regional focused strategies and plans.
- PepsiCo India has restructured its senior management team to make the reporting structure more functional. The heads of the three operations—foods, company-owned bottling and franchisee bottling—will report directly to Shivakumar. All unit heads will report to the central functional heads, with food and beverages clubbed as an integrated entity.

6.6.3 Divestment Strategy

Under the divestment strategy, the organisation sells a part of its business or a major division that cannot be turned around. Divestment is also known as **divestiture** or cutback. It is different from disinvestment wherein the government equity in a public sector enterprise is sold off. For example, Government of India diluted its shareholding in Maruti Udyog, in favour of Suzuki Motors.

Divestment may be done for both economic and non-economic reasons. Economic reasons include inadequate market share, poor returns on investment, lack of growth potential, technological change that requires huge investment beyond the capacity of the organisation, etc. Non-economic reason means that business which is not core and is divested during business restructuring.

Divestment may be done in two ways. **First**, a major division of the company may be off as an independent company. **Second**, the division may be sold off. The decision to divest spinned is painful because it amounts to admitting a failure. Moreover the top management team has an emotional attachment with the unit to be divested.

Reasons for Divestment

(*i*) Persistent negative cash flows from a unit that creates financial pressure on the company as a whole.

(*ii*) Inability of the company to face increasing competition in a particular business.

(*iii*) The company is unable to carry out the technological upgradation necessary for the unit's survival.

(*iv*) The project is unviable and its sale proceeds can generate better return in some other business.

(*v*) A business acquired earlier proves to be a mismatch and cannot be integrated into the company.

(*vi*) Divestment is a part of the merger scheme wherein an unprofitable division is not to be merged.

Divestment In India

Divestment has become a popular strategy in India due to pressures for restructuring and streamlining in the area of economic liberalisation and globalisation. Many family business houses diversified into unrelated businesses during the licence raj when growth opportunities were limited. Since 1991 they are divesting to focus on their core competencies. Some cases of divestment are as follows:

- The Tata Group divested its non-core businesses. It sold off Tata Oil Mills and Lakme to Hindustan Unilever and pharmaceutical units to Wockhardt.
- Hindustan Unilever divested its marine food business which for it is a non-core business. The company also sold its sea food processing plant in Andhra Pradesh.
- The TTK Group divested its clock making, ball pens and ink, toys, chemicals and card-board businesses.
- Sony India believes that the decision to sell off the Vaio brand and laptop business and hive off the TV business into a separate entity will allow operations in the television and mobile phone segments in each market to become more dynamic and adapt swiftly to local needs.

6.6.4 Liquidation Strategy

Liquidation means closing down the entire company and selling of its assets. It is an extreme strategy and is adopted as a matter of last resort. Liquidation is a difficult and undesirable strategy. It causes loss of employment and, therefore, trade unions oppose liquidation.

Investors, lenders and suppliers may suffer a financial loss. Government, therefore, may not allow liquidation. Moreover, it is difficult to find buyers who are willing to pay reasonable amount. The promoters and top management lose their reputation. Even through liquidation is unpleasant, it may be a good strategy if the company's real estate can bring in more money than the returns of doing business. Liquidation may also be an appropriate strategic alternative under the following circumstances:

(*i*) When the business has no future and direction.

(*ii*) When the accumulated losses are huge and the business cannot be revived.

(*iii*) When the liquidation value is higher than the discounted present value of future earnings.

Liquidation Strategy in India

Under the Companies Act 1956, liquidation is known as 'winding up'. The Act provides for a liquidator who carries out the winding up. When the affairs of a company are fully wound up, the company is dissolved. On dissolution the company's name is struck off the Register of the companies. Under the Act, warming up may take place in three ways:

(*i*) Voluntary winding up

(*ii*) Voluntary winding up under the supervision of the court.

(*iii*) Compulsory winding up under an order of the court.

6.7 COMBINATION STRATEGIES

Combination strategies are also known as mixed or hybrid strategies. These are a mixture of stability, expansion and retrenchment strategies. Combination strategies may be adopted in a simultaneous manner (at the same time in different businesses) or in a sequential manner (at different times in the same business). A multi-business organisation may find that some of its businesses require growth while others have to remain stable or need to be retrenched. On the other hand, a single business firm may follow the stability strategy during difficult situation and may expand when the environment is favourable.

Combination Strategies in India

- ITC Ltd. is a diversified conglomerate operating in tobacco products, paper boards, FMCG, agribusiness, readymade garments and IT. It diversified into hotels in 1975 and agri-business in 1990. It adopted a turnaround strategy for the paper business (Triveni Tissues) and divested its financial services business.

Under the combination strategy a company adopts any one of the following:

1. Stability and growth strategies.
2. Stability and retrenchment strategies.
3. Growth and retrenchment strategies.
4. Growth, retrenchment and stability strategies.

Reasons for Combination Strategy

The basic reason for adopting combination strategy is that a single strategy is not appropriate for all the businesses of a diversified conglomerate. This is so due to the following reasons:

(*i*) **Varying Life Cycles:** Different products of a company may be at different stages in their life cycles. Products in the introduction or growth stage require expansion whereas those in the maturity stage need stability. Retrenchment may be needed for products at the declining stage.

(*ii*) **Business Cycle:** Business cycles may have varying impact on different businesses. These may create recession in some business and growth opportunities in others.

(*iii*) **Too Much Expansion:** A business house might have expanded in several unrelated businesses in the past. Now it may like to concentrate on its core business. It may divest non-core business and expand its core businesses. Tatas, Birlas and other conglomerate business houses have adopted a combination of stability, growth and retrenchment strategies over the years for their different businesses.

GUIDELINES FOR SITUATIONS WHEN PARTICULAR STRATEGIES ARE MOST EFFECTIVE

Forward Integration

- When an organisation's present distributors are especially expensive, or unreliable, a or incapable of meeting the firm's distribution needs.
- When the availability of quality distributors is so limited as to offer a competitive advantage to those firms that integrate forward.
- When an organisation competes in an industry that is growing and is expected to continue to grow markedly; this is a factor because forward integration reduces an organisation's ability to diversify if its basic industry falters.
- When an organisation has both the capital and human resources needed to manage the new business of distributing its own products.
- When the advantages of stable production are particularly high; this is a consideration because an organisation can increase the predictability of the demand for its output through forward integration.
- When present distributors or retailers have high profit margins; this situation suggests that a company could profitably distribute its own products and price them more competitively by integrating forward.

Backward Integration

- When an organisation's present suppliers are especially expensive, or unreliable, or incapable of meeting the firm's needs for parts, components, assemblies, or raw materials.
- When the number of suppliers is few and the number of competitors is many.
- When an organisation competes in an industry that is growing rapidly; this is a factor becasue integrative-type strategies (forward, backward, and horizontal) reduce an organisation's ability to diversify in a declining industry.
- When an organisation has both the capital and human resources needed to manage the new business of supplying its own raw materials.
- When the advantages of stable prices are particularly important; this is a factor because an organisation can stabilize the cost of its raw materials and the associated price of its products through backward integration.

- When present suppliers have high profit margins, which suggests that the business of supplying products or services in the given industry is a worthwhile venture.
- When an organisation needs to acquire a needed resource quickly.

Horizontal Integration

- When an organisation can gain monopolistic characteristics in a particular area or region without being challenged by the federal government for "tending substantially" to reduce competition.
- When an organisation competes in a growing industry.
- When increased economies of scale provide major competitive advantages.
- When an organisation has both the capital and human talent needed to successfully manage an expanded organisation.
- When competitors are faltering due to a lack of managerial expertise or a need for particular resources which your organisation possesses; note that horizontal integration would not be appropriate if competitors are doing poorly because overall industry sales are declining.

Market Penetration

- When current markets are not saturated with your particular product or service.
- When the usage rate of present customers could be significantly increased.
- When the market shares of major competitors have been declining while total indusrty sales have been increasing.
- When the correlation between dollar sales and dollar marketing expenditures has historically been high.
- When increased economies of scale provide major competitive advantages.

Market Development

- When new channels of distribution are available that are reliable, inexpensive, and of good quality.
- When an organisation is very successful at what it does.
- When new untapped or unsaturated markets exist.
- When an organisation has the needed capital and human resources to manage expanded operations.
- When an organisation has excess production capacity.
- When an organisation's basic industry is rapidly becoming global in scope.

Product Development

- When an organisation has successful products that are in the maturity stage of the product life cycle; the idea here is to attract satisfied customers to try new (improved) products as a result of their positive experience with the organisation's present products or services.

- When an organisation competes in an industry that is characterized by rapid technological developments.
- When major competitors offer better quality products at comparable prices.
- When an organisation competes in a high-growth industry.
- When an organisation has especially strong research and development capabilities.

Concentric Diversification

- When an organisation competes in a no-growth or a slow-growth industry.
- When adding new, but related, products would significantly enhance the sales of current products.
- When new, but related, products could be offered at highly competitive prices.
- When new, but related, products have seasonal sales levels that counterbalance an organisation's existing peaks and valleys.
- When an organisation's products are currently in the decline stage of the product life cycle.
- When an organisation has a strong management team.

Conglomerate Diversification

- When an organisation's basic industry is experiencing declining annual sales and profits.
- When an organisation has the capital and managerial talent needed to compete successfully in a new industry.
- When the organisation has the opportunity to purchase an unrelated business that is an attractive investment opportunity.
- When there exists financial synergy between the acquired and acquiring firm: note that a key difference between concentric and conglomerate diversification is that the former should be based on some commonality in markets, products, or technology; whereas, the latter should be based on profit considerations.
- When existing markets for an orgnisation's present products are saturated.
- When anti-trust action could be charged against an organisation that has historically concentrated on a single industry.

Horizontal Diversification

- When revenues derived from an organisation's current products or services would significantly increase by adding the new, unrelated products.
- When an organisation competes in a highly competitive and/or a no-growth industry, as indicated by low industry profit margins and returns.
- When an organisation's present channels of distribution can be used to market the new products to current customers.
- When the new products have countercyclical sales patterns compared to an organisation's present products.

Joint Venture

- When a privately owned organisation is forming a joint venture with a publicly owned organisation; there are some advantages of being privately held, such as close ownership; there are some advantages of being publicly held, such as access to stock issuances as a source of capital. Sometimes, the unique advantages of being privately and publicly held can be synergistically combined in a joint venture.
- When a domestic organisation is forming a joint venture with a foreign company; joint venture can provide a domestic company with the opportunity for obtaining local management in a foreign country, thereby reducing risks such as expropriation and harassment by host country officials.
- When the distinctive competencies of two or more firms complement each other especially well.
- When some project is potentially very profitable, but requires overwhelming resources and risks; the Alaskan pipeline is an example.
- When two or more smaller firms have trouble competing with a large firm.
- When there exists a need to introduce a new technology quickly.

Retrenchment

- When an organisation has a clearly distinctive competence, but has failed to meet its objectives and goals consistently over time.
- When an organisation is one of the weakest competitors in a given industry.
- When an organisation is plagued by inefficiency, low profitability, poor employee morale, and pressure from stockholders to improve performance.
- When an organisation has failed to capitalize on external opportunities, minimize external threats, take advantage of internal strengths, and overcome internal weaknesses over time; that is, when the organisation's strategic managers have failed (and possibly been replaced by more competent individuals).
- When an organisation has grown so large so quickly that major internal reorganisation is needed.

Divestiture

- When an organisation has pursued a retrenchment strategy and it failed to accomplish needed improvements.
- When a division needs more resources to be competitive than the company can provide.
- When a division is responsible for an organisation's overall poor performance.
- When a division is a misfit with the rest of an organisation; this can result from radically different markets, customers, managers, employees, values, or needs.
- When a large amount of cash is needed quickly and cannot be reasonably obtained from other sources.
- When government anti-trust action threatens an organisation.

Liquidation

- When an organisation has pursued both a retrenchment strategy and a divestiture strategy and neither has been successful.
- When an organisation's only alternative is bankruptcy; liquidation represents an ordely and planned means of obtaining the greatest possible cash for an organisation's assets. A company can legally declare bankruptcy first and then liquidate various divisions to raise needed capital.
- When the stockholders of a firm can minimize their losses by selling the organisation's assets.

Source: F.R. David, "How Do We Choose Among Alternative Growth Strategies?" **Managerial Planning** 33, No. 4 (January-February 1985): 14-17, 22.

SUMMARY

Concentration Growth Strategies: (*i*) Market penetration (*ii*) Market development (*iii*) Product development.

Integration Strategies: (*i*) Horizontal integration (*ii*) Vertical integration – backward and forward.

Diversification: (*i*) Concentric or related (*ii*) Conglomerate or unrelated.

Cooperation Strategies: (*i*) Strategic alliance (*ii*) Joint venture (*iii*) Mergers – horizontal, vertical, concentric, conglomerate (*iv*) Acquisitions or takeovers.

Stability Strategies: (*i*) No charge (*ii*) Profit strategy (*iii*) Pause or proceed-with-caution.

Retrenchment Strategies: (*i*) Turnaround (*ii*) Restructuring (*iii*) Divestment (*iv*) Liquidation

Combination Strategies: (*i*) Simultaneous combination (*ii*) Sequential combination (*iii*) Simultaneous-cum-sequential combination.

TEST QUESTIONS

1. "A stability strategy is not merely a do-nothing strategy." Discuss.
2. Under what circumstances is 'turnaround strategy' expected to be successful? When is 'divestment strategy' likely to be better than 'turnaround strategy'?
3. When and why is stable growth strategy preferred?
4. Is business expansion and growth an unmixed blessing? What are the limits of growth strategy?
5. "The strategy of growth with foreign collaboration has been quite popular in India in recent times particularly in the automotive industry." Why? Discuss briefly the government's regulatory policy in that context.
6. Why and under what circumstances do executives prefer to adopt the strategy of (*a*) horizontal diversification, and (*b*) vertical integration?

7. Why do companies want to grow? Describe concentration growth strategies.
8. Explain the advantages and disadvantages of growth through concentration.
9. Compare the merits and demerits of horizontal integration and vertical integration.
10. Distinguish between concentric diversification and conglomerate diversification, pointing out their merits and demerits.
11. What are strategic alliances? Why are such alliances formed? Describe various types of strategies alliances.
12. What do you mean by diversification? Explain the merits and demerits of diversification.
13. Why do large organisations adopt diversification strategy? Explain different forms of diversification.
14. Can we predict if a particular strategy will be successful even before it has been implemented? Discuss taking examples of diversification strategy followed by Indian companies.
15. What are the specific reasons that may underlie conglomerate diversification strategy?
16. Identify and discuss the factors to be considered for undertaking a strategic alliance with another organisation. Compare and contrast two cases of successful and unsuccessful alliance.
17. In view of Joint Venture route of growth for an organisation, discuss the salient factors that must be considered before finalizing a JV partner. Compare and contrast two cases of successful and unsuccessful Joint Ventures.
18. What is joint venture strategy? Explain the strategic issues and problems involved in joint ventures.
19. Explain various types of joint ventures and their advantages.
20. What is a merger? Describe different types of mergers. Why do mergers fail?
21. Explain the advantages and disadvantages of mergers. How can failure of a merger be avoided? Discuss the strategic issues involved in a merger.
22. Distinguish between:
    (*a*) Organic growth and Acquisitive growth.
    (*b*) Horizontal integration and Vertical integration.
    (*c*) Joint venture and Merger.
    (*d*) Merger and Acquisition.
    (*e*) Turnaround and Restructuring.
    (*f*) Divestment and Liquidation.
23. What is acquisition strategy? Describe the advantages and limitations of this strategy.
24. What are the steps in the process of acquiring a firm? Explain the significance of post-acquisition action.
25. What is stability strategy? Explain its types.
26. Discuss the advantages and limitations of stability strategy.

27. What is retrenchment strategy? Why companies opt for retrenchment?
28. What is turnaround strategy? Describe the major action plans involved in a turnaround.
29. How is a turnaround managed? Explain the regulatory issues involved in turnaround.
30. What is corporate restructuring? Explain with reference to any company in India.
31. What is divestment? Why does a company divest?
32. What is combination strategy? Give reasons for its use.
33. Differentiate between growth through concentric and conglomerate diversification strategies.
34. What is a strategic alliance? What are the reasons for forming strategic alliances?
35. What is joint venture strategy? Explain the issues and problems involved in joint ventures.
36. Discuss the types of strategies that the business firms consider for strategic decision-making and show them in a hierarchical order.
37. What is corporate restructuring and what are its common forms? Also discuss the short and long term outcomes associated with the different restructuring strategies.
38. Differentiate between horizontal and vertical growth strategy. How do these differ from concentric diversification? Give suitable examples.
39. When should a company or business unit outsource a function or activity as against opting for vertical integration? What are the risks involved in outsourcing these activities?
40. When is a company likely to choose related diversification and when is it likely to choose unrelated diversification? Explain the significance of synergies in diversification strategy. What are the pitfalls of diversification strategy?
41. What is corporate restructuring? What motivates firms to do so?
42. What prompts a firm to undertake backward/forward integration? What are various consequences thereof? Discuss.
43. What is liquidation strategy? When should it be used?
44. What do you believe are the advantages the internal growth has over growth through mergers and acquisitions? What particular advantages might mergers and acquisitions have over internal growth?
45. Explain the following statement: "While diversifying into related industries is strategically driven, diversifying into unrelated industries is largely financially driven".
46. What are the motives for diversification? Explain different strategies adopted for diversification bringing out their merits and demerits.
47. What is meant by Corporate Restructuring? What is its importance in strategy implementation? Are Corporate Restructuring and Corporate Reengineering different or are these terms used interchangeably?
48. What is a strategic alliance? What are the reasons for the companies to form strategic alliances?
49. What are different strategic alternatives available to an organisation? Explain the salient features of different alternatives.
50. Describe the alternative strategies for expansion with suitable examples.

51. What is Strategic Advantage Profile? How is it prepared?
52. An organisation wishes to pursue growth strategy: Describe the alternative strategies the organisation can follow to grow.
53. What do you mean by corporate level strategies? Explain with suitable examples.
54. What arguments can you give to support a strategy of diversification into related business?
55. "Mergers involve a complex set of decisions to be made." Explain, suggesting suitable guidelines for effective mergers.
56. A company manufacturing TV sets is considering backward vertical integration in view of the growing competition in the TV market. Discuss the pros and cons of such a strategy.
57. If a company decides to resort to acquisition of a related business, in how many ways can it conduct post-acquisition management of acquired firm? Give suitable example of each case.
58. Discuss the strategic options available to an organisation at the corporate level. Which particular strategic option would you advise the head of an organisation in India's petroleum sector?
59. Why moderately diversified companies outperform more diversified ones?
60. Why do organisations diversify? Give suitable examples of Indian companies to illustrate the difference between related and unrelated diversifications.
61. Why are strategic alliances considered advantageous? Why do they break apart?
62. Put yourself in the position of the CEO of a large electronics company. You have been able to get an opportunity to acquire a small software company which offers new technology that can result in major improvement in the quality and features of your product. You do not see any immediate threats from existing environment that would negatively impact your product line. The acquisition is not likely to cost very much.

    In the light of the above situation answer the following questions:

    (*i*) What might be some reasons due to which you would want to acquire this company?

    (*ii*) Do you see any danger in such acquisition?

    (*iii*) What precautions you must take to improve the chances of success of your acquisition strategy?

CASE STUDY

Size matters. Or does it? That was the dilemma facing Suhas Nair and his team. The issue under discussion was the restructuring of Indian General Insurance Ltd. (IGIL), the largest, state-owned, non-life firm in the country. Nair had a personal stake too. His tenure as Chairman and Managing Director of IGIL was to end in two years. And he was keen on hanging up his boots on a high note. Nair opened the meeting: "Should we merge the four subsidiaries of IGIL into a single outfit that would gives us the advantage of size?" "Or should we delink them into leaner, autonomous, and agile unit?"

"Just to provide a perspective," said Rajiv Parasnis, Director (Management Services), "consolidation is the global trend. Look at Japan. The top six insurers are in merger-talks." "Out context is different," said Anup Sinha, Director (Personnel). "First, the insurance markets where consolidation is taking place are mature, making it easier to diversify into other financial services, invest in technology, and expand our operations. A merger will also help integrate our business."

"Let us look at the numbers," said Abhinav Saran, Director (Finance), punching some keys on his laptop. "A merger will bring in 85,000 employees under one roof. We will have a total of 80 regional offices, 1,200 divisional offices, and 2,920 branch offices. Out combined free reserves would be ₹6,450 crore, net worth ₹7,360 crore, investment income ₹2,350 crore, and total investment ₹19,000 crore. And all this on a modest equity of ₹375 crore! We can leverage this enormous clout to attract new business. We will also be able to reduce overhead costs. Like the rent outflow, for example. A merger prevents duplications of branches resulting in huge savings. And that is just one example."

"But, Abhinav," chipped in Suresh Talwar, the newly-appointed Director (IT), "a merger will pose problems of integration. This becomes a time-consuming activity for senior managers, overriding their business concerns. True, each of our subsidiaries is financially strong. However, each segment of non-life insurance has different parameters of performance. There is simply no parity. That is why it is best to set up an autonomous unit for each activity of non-life business."

"Talwar has a point", remarked Vijay Santoor, Director (Operations). "A merger downplays all the inherent weaknesses in the system. Take, for example, our motor portfolio. It represents over 30 per cent of the total premium. But is a loss-making line in all our subsidiaries mainly because of laxity in underwriting and claims control? Once you spin it off, you ensure discipline. Of course, you need to move of the current pattern of cross-holding among subsidiaries and make each of them truly independent."

"Both approaches have their merits," said Nair. "There is also the growing business of reinsurance. If we decide on a break-up, it makes sense to convert IGIL from a holding company to a national reinsurer. It we merge, we may be able to live up to our corporate vision of being among the world's majors in non-life by 2015. Still, given the right focus, there is no reason why some of our sectoral businesses cannot reach a global scale.

Questions

(*i*) What are the threats being faced by Indian General Insurance Ltd. (IGIL)?

(*ii*) What are its traditional strengths? What 'business definition' should it follow while capitalising on its traditional strengths?

(*iii*) Would you suggest restructuring of IGIL? Why or why not?

(*iv*) What strategies should IGIL follow to retain its market leadership?

7

CHAPTER

BUSINESS LEVEL STRATEGIES

CHAPTER OUTLINE

Corporate level strategies provide the broad direction and lay down the broad framework within which business level strategies operate. Each individual business requires its own strategy because competition and other relevant forces are different in different businesses.

For example, if the corporate strategy of a firm is expansion or growth, business level strategies state how growth is to be achieved. Corporate level strategies are concerned with the industries and markets in which a company operates and competes. On the other hand, business level strategies seek to develop a competitive advantage in the individual businesses in the portfolio of a company. The purpose of corporate level strategies is to allocate and transfer resources and skills so as to create synergies between the different businesses. The purpose of business level strategies is to enhance competitive advantage through effective use of these resources, skills and synergies.

7.1. CONCEPT OF BUSINESS LEVEL STRATEGIES

Business level strategies refer to the strategic actions taken by a company for each of its businesses. Their aim is to gain and sustain competitive advantage by providing value to the customer. The company makes use of its competencies to develop and expand its strategic or competitive advantage. Business level strategies are concerned with:

(*i*) positioning the business against competitors;

(*ii*) anticipating changes in demand and other factors and adjusting to provide for them; and

(*iii*) influencing the nature of competition through strategic action.

According to Michael Porter[1], two main forces, namely, the industry structure and the positioning of a firm in the industry, determine the choice of a competitive strategy.

1. **Industry Structure:** Every industry has a unique structure which is determined by the competitive forces. These forces include the threat of new entrants, the threat of substitute products/services, the bargaining power of buyers, the bargaining power of suppliers, and the rivalry among the existing competitors. There forces shape competition in an industry and determine the long-term profitability of firms in that industry.

2. **Positioning of Firm in Industry:** The overall approach adopted by a firm towards competing with its rivals is known as its positioning. This approach aims at gaining a sustainable competitive advantage. It is based on the following variables:

   (*a*) *Competitive Advantage:* A firm can gain a competitive advantage either through lower cost or though differentiation.

   In lower cost positioning, a firm offers mass-produced products and distributes them through mass-marketing. In differentiation approach, the firm offers higher-priced products to an identified group of customers. The products/services are differentiated in some way from the rival ones.

   (*b*) *Competitive Scope:* The breadth of a firm's target within its industry is called competitive scope. It refers to the range of products, distribution channels, types of buyers and the geographic areas served. A firm can either adopt a broad target approach or a narrow target approach. Under the former it offers a wide range of products to several customer groups through several distribution channels in different geographical areas. In the latter case, it offers a limited range of products to a few customer groups in a narrow geographical area.

7.2 GENERIC BUSINESS STRATEGIES

Combination of competitive advantage and competitive scope yields a matrix (Fig. 7.1) consisting of various business strategies. Porter had classified them into the following generic business strategies:

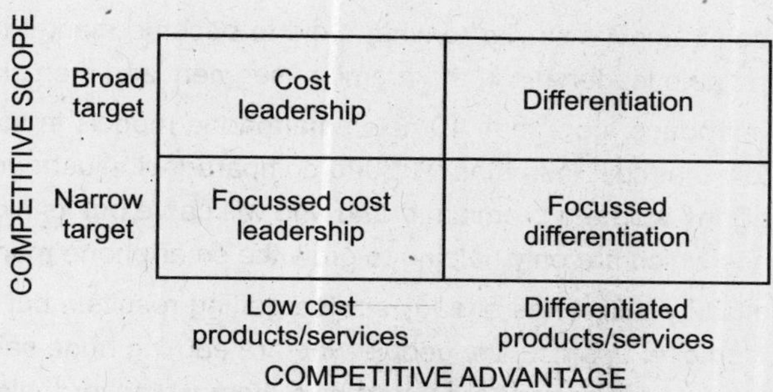

Fig. 7.1. Porter's Generic Business Strategies

1. Michael E. Porter, Competitive Strategy: Techniques for Analysing Industries and Competitors, 1980.

1. Cost leadership (lower cost and broad target)
2. Differentiation (differentiation and broad target)
3. Focus (lower cost or differentiation and narrow target)

7.2.1 Cost Leadership Strategy

Cost leadership strategy means offering a product/service of the same quality at a lower per unit price than the rival firms in a broad target market. When all the firms in an industry offer the product/service at the same price, the cost leader earns higher profit margin than its rivals.

Sources of Cost Leadership

Cost structure of a firm depends on how it manages its value chain. Each activity in the value chain involves cost. A firm can achieve cost leadership by minimising the cost of each activity. Some of the **actions which can be taken to become a cost leader are as follows:**

(*i*) Securing economies of large scale operations;

(*ii*) High capacity utilisation through accurate forecasting of demand;

(*iii*) High level of standardisation of products and offering a uniform service package through mass production;

(*iv*) Investment in cost-saving technologies; and

(*v*) Vertical integration – backward and forward – that creates value.

Cost Leadership Strategy of Indian Firms

- Tata Steel has become the lowest cost producer in the world. It has achieved cost leadership by reducing consumption of energy and materials, rationalising workforce (from 78,000 in 1992-93 to 46,000 in 2001–02), increasing labour productivity (from 104 to 206 tonnes), continuous modernisation of plants, captive iron ore mines, finishing steel close to the consumption points which save transportation costs, and economies of scale
- Gujarat Cooperative Milk Marketing Federation (GCMMF), the producer of Amul brand milk and milk products, is the least cost producer. It has achieved cost advantage through chain of milk processing plants and procurement of milk through a network of cooperative societies located across the country, and an efficient distribution network
- Sony's business strategy is similar to what it did to become market leaders in flat panel televisions – first gain leadership in the premium segment and then skim the entry-level. Sony plans to introduce more than 10 new smartphone models in India this year, which will involve a few that cost less than ₹10,000 compared with just one now. "Even in the entry segment Sony will be a premium brand and will carve out its niche as compared to the Indian brands which are only helping to grow the smartphone market,"
- "Our cost optimisation effort has already started getting results... but there is still a lot of fat we need to remove... particularly people who are earning huge salaries... and are not bringing value to the company. We have to give them whatever tools they need to bring value commensurate with their salaries." said The chairman, Mr. Narayna Murthy.

Benefits of Cost Leadership Strategy

(*i*) Cost leadership helps the firm to face competition in the industry.

(*ii*) A low cost firm can secure a large market share.

(*iii*) Cost advantage protects the firm from the adverse effect of downward trend in the industry.

(*iv*) Cost leadership helps the firm to bear the increase in the prices of inputs by powerful suppliers.

(*v*) The low cost firm can better face the threat of cheaper substitutes.

(*vi*) Cost advantage acts as an entry barrier for possible entrants who cannot offer the product/service at the leader's price

Risks of Cost Leadership Strategy

(*i*) Cost advantage does not provide a sustainable competitive advantage. In the long run, competitors can imitate the cost reduction techniques and the cost leader loses its advantage.

(*ii*) Cost leadership is not a market friendly strategy. Too much emphasis on cost reduction may dilute customer focus and value addition.

(*iii*) When the cost leader captures a huge market share, less efficient firms may leave the industry. The scope for product/service may get reduced and market stagnation may adversely affect the cost leader.

(*iv*) Changes in technology may change the ground rules in the industry. New competitors may enter with better technology and the cost leader's old technology may no longer provide a cost advantage.

(*v*) Customers may be willing to pay a higher price for a product/service having unique features. Cost leader may lose such customers. For example, after-sale service is an essential feature for consumer durables.

Conditions Wherein Cost Leadership Strategy is Suitable

Cost leadership strategy is useful in the following conditions:

1. The market for the product/service is characterised by price-based competition, e.g., markets for commodities like sugar, metals, etc.
2. There exist no significant differences in products/services offered by different firms in the industry. In other words, the product/service is highly standardised.
3. The buyers are large and possess a significant bargaining power to negotiate a price reduction from the supplying firm.
4. There is no customer loyalty and customers can easily switch over from one seller to another.

7.2.2 Differentiation Strategy

Differentiation is the business strategy of incorporating special features into the product/service for which the customers are wiling to pay more. The firm gains a competitive advantage when its competitors are not able or willing to offer products/services with these special features. According to Kotler differentiation is "the act of designing a set of meaningful differences to distinguish the company's offerings from competitors' offerings"[2].

A product/service with unique features which are valuable for the target group of customers commands a higher price and creates customer loyalty.

Sources of Differentiation

A firm can differentiate its product/service from rival products/services in several ways:

(*i*) The product/service may contain unique tangible features such as design, shape, size, colour, smell, taste, etc.

(*ii*) Some intangible features such as the firm's reputation or prestige may be built into the product/service.

(*iii*) The product/service may be of superior quality and its performance level is high.

(*iv*) The product/service enables the customer to enjoy higher status or prestige in the society, *e.g.*, Rolex watches, BMW cars, Louis Vuiton luggage, etc.

(*v*) The firm offers the full range of product/service needed by customers.

(*vi*) The firm may offer excellent after-sale service *e.g.* Maruti Suzuki.

Differentiation Strategy of Indian Firms

- Gillette India differentiates its razor blades on the basis of quality – unique three blades razor system that gives superior shave. It has differentiated its shaving gel on the basis of economy – one drop is enough and one tube lasts for months. As a result of such differentiation the firm has gained a large market share.
- Parle Agro differentiates its non-aerated natural fruit-based drink, Frooti, on the basis of packaging. It launched Frooti in tetrapack in 1985. Customers prefer tetrapack as they perceive bottled drinks to be synthetic.
- Bharti Airtel has differentiated itself through better customer service. It ensures that complaints are attended within four working hours. Customers can pay their bills online or by dropping cheques in drop boxes located at convenient places. Such differentiation has helped Bharti Airel to become the biggest mobile telephone services firm in terms of customers.

Benefits of Differentiation Strategy

(*i*) Differentiation creates brand loyalty which acts as a safeguard against competition. It creates a captive market which reduces the impact of competitive rivalry

(*ii*) High brand loyalty created through differentiation discourages new entrants in the market because they find it difficult to compete against such brand loyalty.

2. Philip Kotler, **Marketing Management,** Prentice Hall of India, New Delhi, 2005.

(*iii*) Customers get value for money and do not have alternate suppliers of such a product or service. Therefore, they are not able to put pressure on the firm to reduce prices.

(*iv*) The firm has loyal customers who are not very sensitive to increase in prices. Therefore, the firm can easily absorb increase in prices of inputs by suppliers.

(*v*) The differentiating firm faces negligible threat from substitute products/services.

Risks of Differentiation Strategy

(*i*) It is difficult to sustain differentiation in the long run. Therefore, the first mover advantages of differentiation are limited. New entrants reap the benefits of the market created by the first mover. For example, Hindustan Unilever popularised synthetic detergents as an alternative to washing soaps. Nirma Limited entered the market much later and reaped the benefit of huge detergent market.

(*ii*) When several firms start differentiation, distinctiveness is gradually reduced and ultimately lost. This is happening in some segments of motorcycles and passenger cars.

(*iii*) In a growing market, there is a limit to price premiums. The customers may forgo the additional advantage from a differentiated product/service when they feel it is not worth the higher price.

(*iv*) Differentiation based on something that is not valuable for customers is likely to fail. When unnecessary features are added these may provide little benefit to customers.

(*v*) Differentiation strategy fails when the firm does not properly communicate and popularise the benefits of differentiation.

(*vi*) Too much differentiation may cause a sharp rise in cost and price.

Conditions under which Differentiation Strategy is Useful

Differentiation strategy is suitable in the following conditions:

1. The market size is large enough to accommodate several firms offering standardised and/or differentiated products/services.
2. Customer needs and preferences are diversified so that the market can be divided into distinct segments.
3. The firm can differentiate in such a way that is valued by customers and they are willing to pay higher price.
4. The product/service is of such nature that it is possible to create and sustain brand loyalty.
5. There exists enough scope for increasing the sale of differentiated product/service at a premium price.
6. Competitors cannot easily or quickly copy the differences.

7.2.3 Focus Business Strategy

Focus business strategy is based either on cost leadership or differentiation but caters to a narrow segment of the total market. It terms of the market, therefore, a focus strategy is a niche strategy. Customer groups or niche segments are usually identified on the basis of demographic characteristics (age, gender, income, occupation, etc), geographical areas (rural/urban or northern/southern region) and life style (traditional/modern).

Sources of Achieving Focus

Focus strategy essentially involves identifying and operating in a narrow market segment which is not being served by cost leaders and differentiators. Such a segment requires special attention which is not given by cost leaders and differentiators in their attempt to cover a broad target market. They feel it is not profitable enough to cater to such niches. For example, market for aircraft tyres is very small and most tyre firms neglect this segment. A firm that has the necessary expertise to provide specialised tyres for aircrafts can focus on this segment. Thus, focus can be achieved in the following ways:

(*i*) identifying gaps left by cost leaders and differentiators:

(*ii*) building superior skills to fill these gaps:

(*iii*) achieving lower cost/differentiation in comparison with competitors for securing such niche markets; and

(*iv*) making innovations to add value in the value chain.

Focus Strategy of Indian Firms

- In toothpaste industry, multinationals such as Colgate and Hindustan Unilever dominate the market. Dabur India and Vicco Laboratories have caved out niche market segments by offering toothpastes containing herbal ingredients that protect and clean teeth.
- Hindi film songs dominate the music cassettes industry in India. International and Indian classical music (Indipop) is a niche market in recorded music. Sony Music and Magnasound focus on upper end of this niche market. On the other hand, Times Music and Music Today focus on sophisticated listeners of Indian classical music. Both these firms operate on the basis of differentiation and premium pricing.
- Jewellery market in India has traditionally been dominated by highly-skilled craftsmen and buyers consider it an investment in gold. The Tanishq brand of jewellery by Titan Industries (a Tata Group company) is focussed on buyers who consider jewellery a fashion item. Titan offers a wide range and new designs are introduced frequently on the basis of customer feedback. The company adopts a differentiation strategy.
- Companies such as Page Industries, Asian Paints, GSK Consumer, Pidilite and Nestle which operate in the niche categories have outperformed diversified companies such as HUL, ITC, Dabur, Procter & Gamble and Marico in terms of increase in market capitalisation, sales and after-tax profit. The better performance of these niche companies is attributed to their focus on a single segment brand strength and lower investment in newer categories and products. Brand strength, strong distribution franchise, high market share and capital efficiency provide these niche companies with better pricing power and higher capital efficiency. [**The Economic Times**, 6.1.2014].

- LG Electronics India, the country's largest consumer durables maker, is shifting its focus back to mass product categories such as single-door refrigerators and semiautomatic washing machines, as its move to push only premium products (such as flat-panel television, frost-free and side-by-side refrigerators, front-loading washing machines and split air conditioners) has failed to boost revenues. LG has realised that Indian consumers do not easily shift to latest appliances.

  Several consumers, for example, still prefer to buy a single-door refrigerator since the notion is that it preserves cold better during a power cut due to the presence of ice.

  Similarly, consumers believe a semi-automatic washing machine cleans better and many prefer no-frills microwave oven because Indians use it predominantly for re-heating than cooking.

  "Hence, we have decided to focus on these categories and launch newer models in larger size with premium features and technology to enable consumers to upgrade faster.
- At an investor conference in London in early December, Polman, Chairman of unilever, announced that Unilever will cut 800 marketing jobs, slash its product variant by 30% and focus predominantly on brands with over € 1 billion in sales, all in a bid to save costs. Its Chief Marketing Officer Keith Weed also hinted that the company is now more inclined to favour fewer global advertising concepts over multiple local ideas.
- With the bigger players catering to urban markets. Atul Auto saw opportunity in tier-II and -III cities and built its strategy around them. For instance, it customized its products to meet the expectations of smaller cities and rural areas. The customization included capacity to bear overloading, higher mileage of 35 a litre and a warranty of 24 months against 14-16 months offered by competitors.

  The strategy worked for Atul Auto as sales started trickling in from other states other than Gujarat the western state now contributes 40% to its sales compared with 100% about five years ago. States like Kerala and Assam contribute 7% to its sales now and the company is planning to make inroads into West Bengal and Tamil Nadu.

Benefits of Focus Business Strategy

(*i*) A focused firm is protected from competition to the extent that other firms operating in broader markets are unable or unwilling to serve niche markets.

(*ii*) A focused firm buys in small quantities. Therefore, powerful suppliers may not show much interest. To some extent price increase by suppliers can be passed on to customers due to customer loyalty.

(*iii*) Powerful buyers do not have other options and, therefore, remain loyal to the focused firm.

(*iv*) The competence to serve niche markets acts as an effective entry barrier.

(*v*) The special skills of the focused firm in serving a niche market prevents competition from substitute products.

Risks of Focus Business Strategy

(*i*) In order to serve niche market, a firm has to develop distinctive competencies which is a difficult and time-consuming process.

(*ii*) A focused firm is committed to a narrow market segment. Therefore, its sales volume is small and it does not enjoy economies of scale. As a result its unit cost is high.

(*iii*) Once a firm makes commitment to a niche segment it may face difficulty in moving to other segments of the market.

(*iv*) Niches are temporary and may disappear due to technological and market-related changes. For example, the process of making niche products may become easy due to a new technology. Similarly, changes in needs and preferences of customers may make them shift to lower priced products of cost leaders.

(*v*) Increasing competition in big markets and high profitability in niches may create the interest of cost leaders and differentiators in niche markets. They may pose a threat to the focused firm. For example, by extending its Pepsodent brand of trothpaste priced at ₹10 only, Hindustan Unilever has caused a threat to Balsara which focused on low-priced toothpaste market segment.

(*vi*) Rival firms devise ways to better serve the niche markets and thereby out-focus the focused firm.

Risks for focused firms have increased due to a wider choice of products, greater variety in services, customization of products/services, etc. For example, a large number of car models are available now to suit the buying capacity, tastes and preferences of all types of car buyers in India.

ITC is firming up plans to foray into non-carbonated beverages and dairy business next fiscal to establish itself as one of the largest food companies in the country .

The Kolkata-based tobacco-to-hospitality conglomerate is developing products in categories such as juices, tea and coffee in the non-carbonated beverage space, while its ambitious dairy business rollout will include products such as packaged milk, butter and ghee, to take on category leaders such as Nestle, PepsiCo, Amul, Hindustan Unilever and Dabur.

The company also plans to soon start scientific trials on functional foods – addressing various metabolic disorders such as blood pressure, diabetes and nutritional deficiency.

Market watchers say ITC has carved out its niche in the food space and can give tough competition in the beverage and dairy space to big marketers operating in the space. ITC's food business clocked ₹4,720-crore sales last fiscal, 27% more than the previous year's ₹3,712 crore. ITC has found a differentiated proposition with fairly unique products and customer marketing skills even in highly penetrated categories such as biscuits. Successful examples include a ₹5 pack of instant noodles and unique packaging for Dark Fantasy biscuits. Last fiscal ITC overtook HUL in branded food and beverage sales a decade after it entered the business. ITC plans to position its dairy products and beverages on the health platform. Wal-Mart focusing on the 20 Best Price cash-and-carry stores is the best option for the US giant as the business has proved lucrative and finding partners for retail entry will take time. This will help them attain a critical mass in India in setting up retail business, if they wish to, in future. It will also help them achieve a comfort level in working in the Indian environment.

Walmart got into wholesale business in India by default, because that was the only space foreign retailers were allowed to operate in when it entered the country. India allowed FDI in multi-brand retail space only last year. But, thanks to several tough riders, big supermarket chains such as Walmart and Carrefour have yet to enter the space despite the government making the norms easier since.

The cash-and-carry business, in comparison, comes without any restriction on foreign investment, and offers huge growth potential. Industry officials estimate it will be a $22 billion (about ₹1,36,000 crore) business in India by 2017 and the market leader can eye revenues of about $5 billion (about ₹31,000 crore) then. Business has proved highly lucrative with thousands of mom-and-pop store owners in the country finding-cash and-carry outlets more convenient than local wholesale markets.

Escorts Get Back on Track with a Focus on High-end Products

For about two years, tractor maker Escorts had been struggling with a sliding market share and margin pressure. But the company did a course correction, tweaked a few things around, and is getting back on track.

In order to improve its earnings profile, Escorts is now redefining market share by focusing on higher-priced products and vacating lower-margin ones completely. It is also taking a series of steps to prune cost, align company's parameters with that of the industry and carve out a pan-India presence for itself. It has exited low-margin business of tractors up to 30 HP (horse power) and concentrated on the higher margin segment between 30 HP and 60 HP, and plans to top the 50 HP-plus segment.

The changes are paying off. The margins from the tractor vertical have risen to 10% from 4.5% in the past two years. With better financial, its stock, too, has gained 81% in the past year compared with BSE Auto index's 6%. But the company's real challenges lie in the 40-50 HP segment, which constitutes nearly 50% of industry sales. Historically, Escorts enjoyed a market share of 20% in this segment, but slipped to 16% because of its limited presence in the southern/western markets. Escorts is taking corrective measures to change this situation. It is raising its dealership to 900 from 750 currently, out of which 50% are likely to be in the southern/western region.

Conditions under which Focus Strategy is Suitable

Focus strategy can be useful in the following conditions:

1. The market can be segmented and each segment requires products/services with special features or attributes.
2. The niche market is large enough to be profitable for the focused firm.
3. The nioche market segment is growing.
4. The leading firms in the industry do not consider the niche market segment to be attractive for entry.

5. The focused firm has enough capability to cater to the full potential of the niche market.
6. The focused firm has the expertise to protect its market standing.

Integration of Cost Leadership and Differentiation (Hybrid Strategy)

Firms which have no clear positioning strategy are 'stuck-in-the-middle'. Such firms have no competitive advantage. In order to improve performance, they must adopt either low cost or differentiation or a combination of both the strategies.

Low cost and differentiation are not necessarily mutually exclusive strategies. In some cases, the two strategies can be used simultaneously. New technologies have made it possible to produce differentiated products/services at low cost. For example, firms using Computer Aided Design (CAD), Computer Aided Manufacturing (CAM) and robot technology can produce small batches of a wide variety of products at low cost. This is known as mass customization.

The assumptions that low costs are possible in only large volumes and differentiation is always costly are not always true. Flexible manufacturing systems and mass customization allow low volume production at low costs. Parts, components and sub-assembles are produced on a large scale. These are then used to produce small batches of customized products.

The discussion given above reveals that none of the business strategies can be successful at all times. A firm must align its business strategy with the changing environment. This is called competitive gaming which involves imposing upon the rival the time, place and conditions for competing. For this purpose tactics are formulated.

Niche Vs Diversified Consumer COS Cost Focused Play Pays Off as Larger Peers Trail

Convential wisdom is that it is a better bet to invest in a company with diversified product portfolio. However, the numbers for consumer companies speak otherwise. Companies such as Page Industries, Asian Paints, GSK Consumer, Pidilite and Nestle, which operate in the niche categories, have all outperformed diversified companies such as HUL, ITC, Dabur, Procter & Gamble and Mirico over the longer term. Market capitalisation, sales and profit after tax of all these niche-category companies have grown at faster pace compared to diversifed companies. For instance, the profit after tax, or PAT, of all these niche consumer companies grew four-to-10 fold while that of diversified companies rose by just 1.5-4 times. Thanks to their blistering growth, the market capitalisation of these niche consumer companies surged 5-18 times while for the diversified companies it grew just two-to-five fold.

The outperformance by these niche companies is attributed to their focus on a single segment, brand strength and lower investment in newer categories and products. Brand strength, strong distribution franchises, high market share and capital efficiency provide these niche companies with better pricing power and higher capital efficiency.

–Jwalit Vyas

Table 7.1: Distinctive Features of the Generic Competitive Strategies

Type of Feature	Low-Cost Leadership	Differential	Focus
Strategic target	• A broad cross-section of the market.	• A broad cross-section of the market.	• A narrow market niche where buyer needs and preferences are distinctively different from the rest of the market.
Basis of competitive advantage	• Lower costs than competitors.	• An ability to offer buyers something different from competitors.	• Lower cost in serving the niche or an ability to offer niche buyers something customised to their requirements and tastes
Product line	• A good basic product with few frills (acceptable quality and limited selection)	• Many product variations, wide selection, strong emphasis on the chosen differentiating features.	• Customised to fit the specialized needs of the target segment.
Production emphasis	• A continuous search for cost reduction without sacrificing acceptable quality and essential features.	• Invent ways to create value for buyers.	• Tailor-made for the niche.
Marketing emphasis	• Try to make a virtue out of product features that lead to low cost.	• Build in whatever features buyers are willing to pay for. • Charge a premium price to cover the extra costs of differentiating features.	• Communicate the focuser's unique ability to satisfy the buyer's specialized requirements.
Sustaining the strategy	• Economical prices/ good value. • All elements of strategy aim at contributing to a sustainable cost advantage—the key is to manage costs down, year after year, in every area of the business	• Communicate the points of difference in credible ways. • Stress constant improvement and use innovation to stay ahead of imitative competitors. • Concentrate on a few key differentiating features; use them to create a reputation and brand image.	• Remain totally dedicated to serving the niche better than other competitors; don't blunt the firm's image and effort by entering other segments and adding other product categories to widen market appeal.

Source: Arthur A. Thompson and A.J. Strickland, *op. cit,* p. 104.

7.3 TACTICS

In order to execute business strategies, tactics are needed. A tactic means "a specific, operating plan detailing how a strategy is to be implemented in terms of when and where it is to be put into action. By their nature, tactics are narrower in their scope and shorter in their time horizon than are strategies."[3]

Thus, a tactic may be described as a sub-strategy. Two main tactics – timing (when) and market location or place (where) used in implementing business strategies are described here.

7.3.1 Timing Tactics

Timing tactics deal with when to make competitive moves and at what speed. When to move is as important as what move to make. A good business strategy may fail if it is moved at the wrong time. In other words, timing is a source of competitive advantage. For example, Japanese firms gained competitive advantage by reducing the time involved in product development and processing.

First Mover and Late Movers: The first firm which enters the market with a new product/ service is called the first mover. The firms which enter the industry subsequently are known as late movers. For example, Life Insurance Corporation (LIC) of India is the first mover in India's life insurance market. HDFC Standard Life, Birla Sun Life and ICICI Prudential life are late movers. Similarly, Unit Trust of India (UTI) is the first mover in the mutual funds industry whilel HDFC MF, ICICI Prudential MF, and Reliance MF are late movers.

The first mover enjoys the following **advantages:**

(*i*) The first mover acquires operational efficiency due to experience which serves as an entry barrier to late movers. It can attain cost leadership and become market leader.

(*ii*) Moving first in an industry enables the firm to gain commitment or loyalty from customers, suppliers and distribution channels.

(*iii*) The first mover creates an image of being a pioneer which helps in building reputation.

(*iv*) The first mover sets standards which late movers may find difficult to imitate.

The **disadvantages** of being a first mover are as follows:

(*a*) The first mover has to spend considerable amount of money to create customer awareness and educate people in new products.

(*b*) The first mover faces more risks than late movers.

(*c*) Late movers can imitate technological and marketing skills due to which the first mover may lose advantages.

(*d*) Late movers can enter with better technology causing a threat for the first mover.

(*e*) Late movers can take away market share from the first mover who has to make additional efforts to retain market share and customer loyalty.

---

3. J. D. Hunger and T.L Wheelen, **Strategic Management,** Addison Wesley, Reading Mass, 1991, p. 121.

First Movers in India

- Life Insurance Corporation (LIC) of India is the first mover in India's insurance sector because private insurance firms were not allowed before 1993. It has a vast network of branches to provide speedy and efficient service to customers. It has earned the trust and built credibility to handle savings of people. LIC has been growing at a fast rate but it is facing tough competition.
- Maruti Suzuki (earlier Maruti Udyog) is considered to be the first mover in compact car segment. Despite fierce competition from foreign firms, it has been able to maintain its number one position.
- Hero Motor Corp (earlier Hero Honda Motors) is the first mover in fuel-efficient motorcycle market. It has created a world record of selling more than one million units of its Spelendor brand of motorcycle. It still enjoys the number one position in this segment.
- Unit Trust of India (UTI) is the first mover in mutual funds industry. It has now been relegated to third position, by Reliance Mutual Fund and ICICI Prudential Mutual Fund.

7.3.2 Market Location Tactics

Another set of tactics relates to choice of target market *i.e.* where to compete. On the basis of the role that firms play in the target market (market share), market location tactics may be classified into four types – leader, challenger, follower and niche[4].

1. **Market Leaders:** A market leader is the firm having the largest market share in the relevant product/service market. It leads the industry in terms of technological development, product/service features, price benchmarks, etc. Hindustan Lever in FMCG, Reliance Industries in petrochemicals, Maruti Suzuki in cars are some examples of market leaders in India. In order to acquire and retain market leadership, firms use the following methods:

   (*a*) Expanding the total market by creating new users, new user and more usage.

   (*b*) Defending the market share through position defence, flank defence, counter-offensive defence, mobile defence, and contraction defence.

   (*c*) Expanding the market share by enhancing operational effectiveness through new product development, raising manufacturing efficiency, improving product quality, superior support services and increasing marketing expenditure.

2. **Market Challengers:** A market challenger is the firm that has second or lower ranking in the industry concerned. Bajaj Auto in motorcycles. Ashok Leyland in heavy commercial vehicles, ICICI Prudential MF in mutual funds are some examples of market challengers in India. A market challenger may either challenge the market leader, or follow it. In order to challenge the market leader and capture larger market share, a market challenger may use the following methods:

   (*a*) Frontal attack which involves matching the opponent in terms of the product/service features, pricing, promotion, and distribution.

   (*b*) Flank attack by challenging the opponent's weak or uncovered geographical areas or segments.

   (c) Encirclement attack by making a grand move to capture the opponent's market share through an advertising campaign, an unbeatable product/service offering, or a unique service guarantee.

4. For detailed description, see Philip Kotler, **Marketing Management,** *op. cit.*

(*d*) **Bypass attack** which involves ignoring the opponent and attacking the easier markets through diversification into unrelated products, moving into new geographical areas, or leapfrogging into new technologies.

(*e*) **Guerrilla attack** involves small intermittent attacks to harass or demoralise the opponent through price cuts, price discounts, intensive comparative advertising, etc.

3. **Market Followers:** A market follower is the firm that imitates the market leader without upsetting the competitive power balance in the industry. It avoids direct attack, keeps out of the way of other firms and imitates the innovations made by the market leader. A market follower uses the following:

(*a*) Counterfeiter strategy which involves duplication of the market leader's product and packaging and selling it in the black market.

(*b*) Cloner strategy which involves emulation of the market leader's product, name and packaging.

(*c*) Imitator strategy which involves copying something from the market leader while retaining some other features such as pricing, packaging, etc.

(*d*) Adopter strategy which involves adopting one's own products to those of the market leader and selling them in different markets.

4. **Market Nichers:** A market nicher is a firm that carves out a distinct niche that other firms do not serve or do not find attractive. It may serve a niche market by providing a unique product/service, serving a distinct geographical area or offering a customised product/service. A market nicher may use the following methods:

(*a*) Creating niches *i.e.* identifying or creating niches in an industry.

(*b*) Expanding niches *i.e.* enhancing the coverage of the present niche to include similar market niches or new niches.

(*c*) Protecting niches *i.e.* shielding the niches from attacks by other firms in the industry.

Tyre maker Ceat had a bad run between 2011 and 2013, and was way behind rivals such as MRF Tyres and Apollo Tyres.

Although Ceat's sales were growing in double digits, its earnings were declining, and its profitability was one of the lowest among tyre makers. The company realised that the existing model was not working and it would have to quickly fix a few things. So, Ceat decidd to focus more on the high-margin two-wheeler and SUV segments and cut down on its bus and truck categories.

The strategy worked. Ceat is now the second largest tyre manufacturer in the two-wheeler segment in the country from a lowly fourth two years ago and is also the price leader. Its market share in the SUV category has also doubled in this period.

At the same time, the Mumbai-based company also increased its focus on export markets, where the margins are much higher. Now, exports are around 23% of total sales compared with less than 20% two years ago.

The company also invested in R & D over the past few years, which is paying off. This strong growth in these two profitable product categories – two-wheelers and SUVs – has really improved its earnings. In the first half, the operating margins increased to 13% from 8%, much in line with its peers. While its profit after tax more than trebled in the first half to ₹142 crore.

ABB India's strategy to focus on near-term orders to combat the risk of an uncertain economic scenario is slowly starting to reflect in the company's financials. In order to mitigate pressure emanating from a long-cycle order, especially deferring orders, ABB has adopted a strategy to choose cash over revenue and profit over volume.

ABB India is now relying more on short-term orders, which are usually executed in less than a year. The reason for a change in focus is short term cycle orders do not pose the risk of deferment or cancellation and the customer does a complete homework before awarding these orders. That means a lowering of risk on execution and payment.

Reckitt Benckiser has topped Godrej Consumer and Marico to clinch the third spot in the Indian home and personal care market. Reckitt Benckiser, which has made a fortune selling soap, cleaner and disinfectant brands in the country is now betting big on its healthcare portfolio, including OTC brands and Durex condoms, as disposable income rises and consumers get more health conscious.

The company, however, said its focus on the health portfolio won't affect its established brands in the home and personal care segments.

Analysts say while most companies have been making efforts to reach more than a billion Indians through affordable products in mas segments, RB India is trying to capture the new age and small categories, which can be challenging in the short term.

"Most of Reckitt Benckiser's segments are niche are will take years to have a sizeable business in India. The only large category they are in is soaps, which is getting extremely competitive, and Dettol trails HUL brands Lifebuoy and Lux," an analyst at a foreign brokerage house said.

7.4 BUSINESS STRATEGIES DURING INDUSTRY LIFE CYCLE

Like a product, an industry passes through different stages in its life cycle (Fig. 7.2). These stages and business strategies used in each stage are given below[5]:

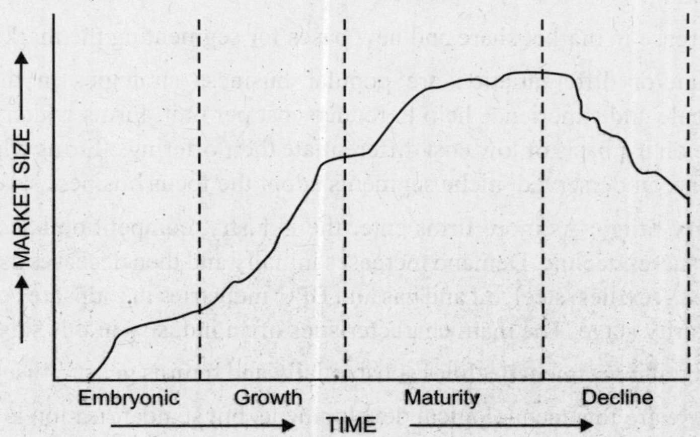

Fig. 7.2. Industry Life-cycle Stages

5. M.A Carpenter and W.G. Sanders, **Strategic Management: A Dynamic Perspective,** Prentice Hall, New Jersey, 2007, pp. 142-144 and C.W.L Hill & G.R. Jones, **Strategic Management: An Integrated Approach** Houghton Miffin, Boston, 2007, pp. 201-204.

1. **Embryonic or Take-off Stage:** In this stage an industry is characterised by the following:
   (*a*) Huge investment is needed while returns are low and uncertain.
   (*b*) Firms are first movers and fast followers which have to generate capital internally or attract outside capital usually from venture capitalists.
   (*c*) Technology is unproven and non-standardised
   (*d*) Demand is being created, customers are hesitant to try out new products/services due to lack of information.
   (*e*) Managerial decision-making is highly risky due to great uncertainty and unproven business models.

   Organic foods, biotech, cyber media and bioinformatics industries in India are in the embryonic stage.

   The main aim of business strategies in this stage is to develop competencies and build market share. In case a firm fails to develop competencies, or attract adequate capital or to build market share, it should exit the industry.

2. **Growth Stage:** An industry enters the growth stage with expanding markets and sophistication of products/services. Technological progress helps to reduce costs and improve quality. Information technology, automobiles, pharma, mobile telephony and retailing are considered to be in growth stage in India. The growth stage of the industry life cycle is characterised by:
   (*a*) Decrease in investment and increase in returns.
   (*b*) Increase in technology and standardisation
   (*c*) Rise in demand due to better informed and discerning customers.
   (*d*) Better business models, more secure business and less risk in managerial decision-making.
   (*e*) Increase in market share and new bases for segmenting the market.

Low cost and/or differentiation are popular business strategies in the growth stage. Economies of scale and experience help to reduce cost per unit. Firms which cannot or do not want to compete on the basis of low cost differentiate their offerings. Firms which build special expertise and serve underserved niche segments adopt the focus business strategy.

3. **Maturity Stage:** As more firms enter the industry, competition becomes intense and market shares decline. Demand increases initially and then deceases as markets become saturated. Textiles, steel, oil and gas and BPO industries in.India are considered to be in the maturity stage. The main characteristics of an industry in this stage are as follows:
   (*a*) Capital investment declines substantially and returns get stabilised at lower levels.
   (*b*) There are few technological developments but standardisation is high.
   (*c*) Demand stabilises and customers are well-informed.
   (*d*) Market shares are well protected.
   (*e*) Business models become well-established.
   (*f*) A few large firms dominate the consolidated industry.

All the three business strategies – cost leadership, differentiation and focus are used in the maturity stage. Firms which have achieved cost advantage in the growth stage adopt cost leadership strategy. Differentiation strategy is used by firms which can segment markets in new ways. Focus firms may sell out where large competitors enter the niche markets.

4. **Decline Stage:** Some industries decline faster than others. Print media, mining, cotton textiles, agriculture and tobacco industries in India are considered to be in the decline stage. Weak firms in these industries become 'sick.' Main characteristics of an industry in the decline stage are as under:

   (*a*) There is no new investment and returns get reduced.

   (*b*) Demand declines and it becomes difficult to attract new customers.

   (*c*) Brand power of products is lost as these become commodities.

   (*d*) Market shares decline.

   (*e*) Technological developments are rare.

Firms using cost leadership stages have an advantage due to absence of product differentiation. Even niche customers shift to cost leaders. Differentiators and focusers sell out and exit the industry.

The conditions and strategies prevailing in the four stages described above are usual. But there can be exceptions. For example, some early entrants in the growth stage may exit while in the decline stage well entrenched focused firms may survive.

7.5 BLUE OCEAN STRATEGY

Until now, we have described competitive strategies. A new strategy called 'blue ocean strategy' claims to make competition irrelevant. Kim and Mauborgne developed the blue ocean strategy on the basis of a study of 150 companies in the USA. These companies created unique customer value by entering uncontested business space. According to Kim and Mauborgne[6], the business universe consists of two distinct kinds of space—red oceans and blue oceans. Red oceans are the known market space consisting of all the existing industries. In this space industry boundaries are well defined and accepted and rules of competition are well-understood. Firms try to capture a greater share of existing demand by outperforming their rivals. As the space gets crowded, competition becomes intense and prospects for profits and growth decline.

Blue space consists of all the industries that do not exist now. They constitute the unknown market space without competition. Firms in this space create rather than fight demand. There exists considerable opportunity for profits and growth. Blue oceans can be created in two ways. **First**, a firm can create completely new industries. For example, Ford Motors replaced horse-drawn carriages with motor cars as a means of personal transport in USA. **Second,** a firm can create a blue ocean within a red ocean by altering the boundaries of an existing industry. This is a more common method of creating blue oceans.

---

6. W. Chan Kim and Renee Mauborgne, **Blue Ocean Strategy: How to Create Uncontested Market Space and Make the Competition Irrelevant,** Harvard Business School Press, Boston, 2005.

Table 7.2: Comparison Between Red Ocean Strategy and Blue Ocean Strategy

Basis of Comparison	Red Ocean Strategy	Blue Ocean Strategy
1. Nature of market space	Compete in the existing market space	Create uncontested market space
2. Approach to competition	Beat the competition	Make the competition irrelevant
3. Approach to demand	Exploit existing demand	Create and capture new demand
4. Value-cost tradeoff	Make the value-cost tradeoff	Break the value-cost tradeoff

Distinct Characteristics of Blue Ocean Strategy

(*i*) Firms in the blue ocean make competition irrelevant by creating superior customer value. For them competition is not a benchmark.

(*ii*) Operators in the blue ocean adopt both low cost and differentiation at the same time. Their cost, price and utility activities are well aligned.

Logic Behind Blue Ocean Strategy

According to Kim and Mauborgne, blue ocean strategy is based on the following logic:

(*i*) Leading-edge technology can in some cases create blue oceans. But in most cases technology innovation is not the cause of blue oceans.

(*ii*) It is not necessary to enter new businesses for creating blue oceans. Firms often create blue oceans usually within their core businesses.

(*iii*) Strategic move rather than firms and industry are the proper units of analysis for blue oceans. Strategic move refers to managerial actions involved in making a business offering that can create a big market.

(*iv*) A blue ocean strategic move can create a lasting brand equity.

Blue ocean strategy is sustainable due to the following reasons:

1. Firms which create blue oceans immediately attract a large number of customers because they add customer value in a unique manner. They achieve low cost due to large scale. They cannot be challenged easily by new entrants which have to build scale and/or change business models.
2. A firm that adds huge customer value quickly earns brand loyalty. Even the most expensive marketing campaigns cannot unseat the creator of a blue ocean. Well-established imitators face a conflict as it may hamper their existing brands.

Action Framework for Blue Ocean Strategy

Kim and Mauborgne have suggested the following framework (Fig. 7.3) for applying the blue ocean strategy.

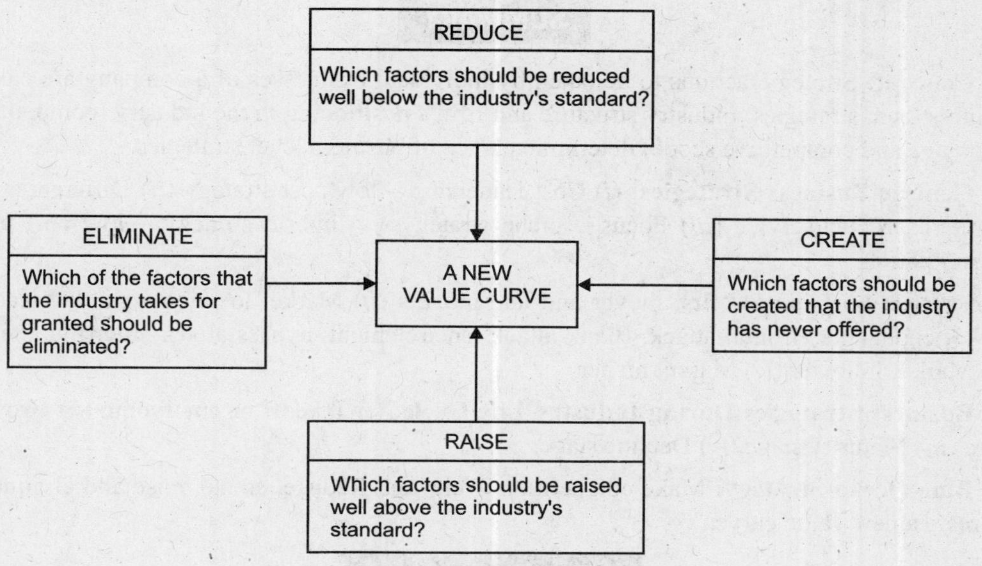

Fig. 7.3. Action Framework for Blue Ocean Strategy

The actions given above may differ from one industry to another. Therefore, a firm that wants to create a blue ocean should decide how it can add more value for customers and for itself on a sustainable basis.

Risks Involved in Blue Ocean Strategy

Certain risks are involved in both formulation and implementation of blue ocean strategy. These risks are summarised in Table 7.3.

Table 7.3: Risks Involved in Blue Ocean Strategy

Activities	Risks Involved
Formulation Stage	
1. Reconstruction of market boundaries	Search risk as many searches may not result in appropriate alternatives
2. Focus on big pictures	Planning risk as it involves creating big pictures of the business, and not just the numbers
3. Reaching beyond existing demand	Scale risk as success depends on large scale of operations
4. Getting the strategic sequence right	Business model risk as a new business model has to be prepared
Implementation Stage	
1. Overcoming key organisational hurdles	Organisational risk as whole organisational processes including structure and culture have to be changed
2. Building implementation into strategy	Management risk as implementation of blue ocean strategy requires altogether a new type of thinking

SUMMARY

Concept: Strategic actions to be taken by individual businesses of a company are called business level strategies. Industry structure and firm's positioning in the industry (competitive advantage and competitive scope) determine choice of business level strategies.

Generic Business Strategies: (*i*) Cost leadership – low cost strategy (*ii*) Differentiation – unique product/service (*iii*) Focus – niche strategy (*iv*) hybrid strategy – low cost cum differentiation.

Tactics: (*i*) Timing – first mover and late movers (*ii*) Market location – market leader, market challenger (frontal attack, Blank attack, encirclement, bypass attack, guerrilla attack) (*iii*) Market follower (*iv*) Market nicher

Business Strategies During Industry Life Cycle: (*i*) Takeoff or embryonic (*ii*) Growth stage (*iii*) Maturity stage (*iv*) Decline stage.

Blue Ocean Strategy: Make competition irrelevant. Reduce, create, raise and eliminate, to create a new value curve.

TEST QUESTIONS

1. What do you mean by business level strategies? Why are these formulated?
2. For each of these business strategies, describe how they are used, under which conditions they are used, and the associated benefits and risks:
   (*a*) Cost leadership
   (*b*) differentiation
   (*c*) focus.
3. Explain Porter's Generic Business Strategies, stating the merits and demerits of each. Which of these is the best option for Indian firms under the present conditions?
4. What is joint venture strategy? Explain the issues and problems involved in joint ventures.
5. "Cost-based strategies are more relevant in developing countries while differentiation strategies are more relevant in developed nations." Comment.
6. "Growth is the most frequently used corporate strategy." Do you agree? Discuss the reasons why an organisation must grow. Under what circumstances may an organisation not consider growth a desirable strategy?
7. A textile company is seriously considering a proposal for diversifying its operations and entering the business of ready-made garments lured by the rapid growth of demand in India and export potential of garments. You are required to advise the company. Discuss the pros and cons of the proposal and give your recommendations.
8. A company producing a number of internationally known brands of malted food (like Bournvita), chocolates and biscuits, has recently decided to diversify into computer software business. Earlier, in 1981, the company ventured into manufacture of apple juice but had to sell off the plant in 1984. During the year 1987, the company's sales were higher by 19% over the previous year. Production of chocolates increased by 14% and of malted food by 22%. The sale of biscuits was also higher although these

are processed by third parties and sold under popular brand names. On the whole, the company had quite satisfactory financial results in 1987. What could then be the possible reason underlying the company's decision to diversify into computer software business? Explain.

9. Why do firms diversify? What are the limitations of diversification strategy?
10. What are the major strategies available to a company that wants to expand and grow fast? Point out the merits and demerits of each of these strategies with suitable examples.
11. It is generally believed that joint ventures abroad by Indian companies have proved successful. To what strategic reasons could this be ascribed? What could be done by a company to make the joint ventures successful?
12. Describe the problems you envisage to encounter in a post-merger situation. How can one mitigate the influence of these? Narrate steps followed by a company which has been able to manage these problems in a satisfactory manner.
13. Distinguish between joint venture and merger.
14. Do you agree with the view that strategic alliance is the shortest route to entry in a foreign market? Discuss. How is strategic alliance different from a joint venture? Elucidate your answer with the help of a foreign firm in beverages business contemplating to enter the Indian market.
15. What are the conditions, risks and benefits of following each of the following strategies:

    (*a*) Cost Leadership;

    (*b*) Differentiation and;

    (*c*) Focus strategies

    Is it possible for a company to follow a cost leadership and differentiation strategy simultaneously? Why or why not?
16. Discuss the generic business strategies, pointing out the merits and demerits of each.
17. Explain the Michael Porter's competitive strategies in detail. Is it possible for a firm to follow cost leadership and differentiation strategies at the same time?
18. State the advantages of Michael. Porter's generic competitive strategies. How can companies pursuing these strategies become "Stuck in the middle"?
19. Examine, how does a firm obtain competitive advantage through distinctive competencies under the resource based view of the firm. What determines the sustainability of a firm's distinctive competencies?
20. Why do successful companies often lose their competitive advantage and fail? How can companies avoid competitive failure and sustain their advantage overtime?
21. What according to Michael Porter determines the level of intensity in industry? What are the benefits and risks of low-cost leadership strategy for an auto company? Is it possible for a company to follow both low-cost leadership strategy and differentiation strategy simultaneously? Why or why not?
22. You have been appointed as a consultant to advise a large business house on strategies to be pursued for various businesses in its portfolio. How will you go about it? Explain your approach with the help of examples.

23. Many corporate parents argue that they search for synergies between the businesses in their portfolio. Do you think this is a realistic aspiration? Give examples from organisations with which you are familiar to support your arguments.
24. Briefly discuss the various offensive tactics used to attack a competitor's position.
25. Explain the various offensive and defensive competitive tactics used by companies to attack competitors or defend its position. Is it possible for a company or business unit to follow a cost leadership strategy and a differentiation strategy simultaneously? Why or why not?
26. Explain the alternate consequences of planned cost reductions for firms competing in an expanding market. What possible suggestions can you offer for reducing costs in the Indian Industry in general?
27. (*a*) What steps would you take to determine why your company is competitively stronger or weaker than key rivals?

    (*b*) When does a low-cost provider strategy prove best? What are the pitfalls of such a strategy.
28. Give a detailed account of Henry Mintzberg's business positioning strategies. Explain how Tata Group is using these strategies in their diverse businesses.
29. "The strategy of a company is intended to maximise its competitive advantage". Explain this statement with suitable examples.
30. "Strategies that target the bottom of the pyramid in emerging economies must be exclusively of a cost leadership type." Discuss. Also discuss whether differentiation-based strategies are superior to cost-based strategies.
31. When does a differentiation strategy work best? What are the pitfalls of such a strategy?

CASE STUDY

In mid-October, at the Annual General Meeting (AGM) of Reliance Industries Ltd. (RIL), Chairman Mukesh Ambani talked about five "fundamental strategic shifts" that were underway at his petrochemicals and refining Goliath. RIL will now pursue (global) acquisition for global size and scale. That is the first major shift. The second big departure from the part is Ambani's willingness to accept partnerships primarily joint ventures as a way of life. The other changes involve relying on agriculture and rural sectors for growth, focusing on research and innovation, and getting a global footprint in a bid to be recognized as a true Indian multinational.

A couple of those shift became more evident last fortnight. The head of RIL's global oil business let on at an investment summit that acquisitions of oil and gas assets, worth up to 1.5 billion dollars, were on the anvil. Around the same time, RIL signed an initial agreement with the state-run gas transporter GAIL (India) Ltd. to jointly set up petrochemicals units in foreign markets. The shift towards JVs became more apparent when reports surfaced that RIL and Kuwait Petroleum were in talks to set up refining and petrochemicals units in Kuwait. The shifts have begun. Time will tell how they change the paradigms at RIL.

Questions:

(*i*) As a strategy professional, how do you look at these shifts?

(*ii*) What has been the experience, in general, with mergers/acquisitions and joint ventures?

8 CHAPTER
STRATEGIC ANALYSIS AND CHOICE OF STRATEGY

CHAPTER OUTLINE

Once strategic alternatives (corporate level strategies and business level strategies) are identified, a firm has to choose the strategic alternative(s) it will adopt.

8.1. CONCEPT OF STRATEGIC CHOICE

Strategic choice involves the selection of one or more strategies that an organisation will use to achieve its objectives. According to Glueck and Jauch, "Strategic choice is the decision to select from among the alternative grand strategies considered, the strategy which will best meet the enterprise objectives. The decision involves focussing on a few alternatives, considering the selection factors, evaluating the alternatives against these criteria, and making the actual choice."[1]

---

1. William F. Glueck and Laurence R. Jauch, **Business Policy and Strategic Management,** McGraw Hill, New York, 1984, p. 270.

Strategic choice involves considerable analysis and a large number of objective and subjective factors influence it. The choice is called strategic because it involves long-term commitment and determines the future of the organisation. Strategic choice involves risk because the organisation is taking a leap into the unknown. Therefore, an organisation must have contingent strategies to face the unforeseen situations.

8.2. STEPS IN THE PROCESS OF STRATEGIC CHOICE

Choice of strategy is essentially a decision-making process. This process consists of four major steps as shown in Fig. 8.1.

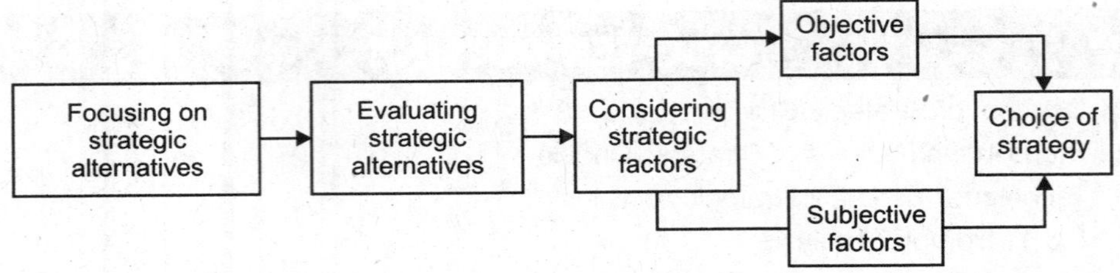

Fig. 8.1. The Process of Strategic Choice

The manner in which each step in the strategic choice process is undertaken may differ from organisation to organisation. Therefore, the choice process may be simple for some organisations and rigorous for others.

1. **Focusing on Strategic Alternatives:** First of all the various alternative strategies from which choice will be made are identified. It is neither possible nor worthwhile to consider all possible alternatives. Therefore, in practice strategists focus on only those alternatives which are relevant and feasible. Considering a few alternatives, however, involves the risk of overlooking some promising alternatives. In order to resolve this dilemma, an organisation formulates some broad guidelines in the form of investment required, types of industry or market, etc. For example, Reliance Industries ignores projects which involve an investment of less then ₹ 1000 crore. Similarly, Tata Group considers only those industries in which it can have either number one or number two position. Gap analysis is helpful in focusing on strategic alternatives.

   Gap Analysis[2]: A firm makes strategic choice to achieve its objectives or desired performance in a future time period, say five years. The difference between present performance and desired performance is known as the gap. If the gap can be filled through the present strategies, the firm may continue with these strategies. Otherwise it must adopt alternative strategies.

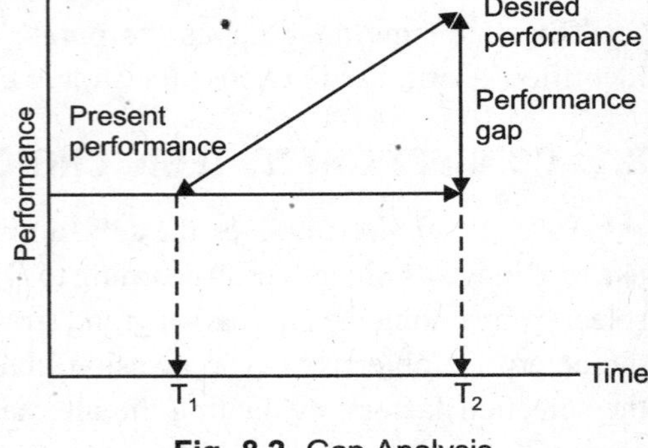

Fig. 8.2. Gap Analysis

2 W.F. Glueck and L.R. Jauch, **Business Policy and Strategic Management,** McGraw Hill, New York, 1984, p 271.

The size of the gap and the time available to fill it determine the focus on strategic alternatives. For example, when the gap is narrow and adequate time is available to fill it, stability strategy may be a feasible alternative. But in case the gap is wide due to environmental opportunities, expansion strategy is likely to be a better alternative. If the gap is large due to poor performance in the past or future, retrenchment may be the appropriate alternative. When the gap is due to multiple reasons, combination strategy can be considered.

2. **Evaluating Strategic Alternatives:** Once the few feasible alternatives are identified, these are thoroughly analysed and compared with one another. Strategic analysis helps to answer questions such as: which industries to enter or exit, which businesses to acquire or divest which products and markets to retain or grow or divest. Each alternative is evaluated in terms of its capability to help the firm achieve its objectives. The pros and cons of each alternative are analysed. Various techniques used in strategic analysis are explained in section 8.3.

3. **Considering Decision Factors:** The criteria used in the evaluation of strategic alternatives consists of several objective and subjective factors. These factors are known decision factors. Objective factors, e.g., market share, are rational. On the other hand, subjective factors, e.g., perception of top executives are based on personal judgment and preferences of strategy makers. These objective and subjective factors that influence choice of strategy are described in section 8.4.

4. **Choosing from among the Strategic Alternatives:** The evaluation of strategic alternatives reveals the most suitable alternative(s) under the present situation. Choice of strategy is, therefore, the last step. The firm may choose one or more alternatives for implementation. Contingency strategies are also decided to meet unforeseen circumstances. Contingency strategies are described in section 8.5. A description of the strategies and the conditions under which these would operate is prepared for implementing the chosen alternative(s). Such a description or blueprint is known as the strategic plan which is explained in section 8.6.

While choosing the acceptable strategy, strategy makers may raise the following questions:

(*a*) Does the strategy fit the values, philosophy, and preferences of top management?

(*b*) Is the strategy consistent with environmental opportunities and threats?

(*c*) Is the strategy in tune with the objectives, strengths and weaknesses of the firm?

(*d*) Does the strategy involve acceptable degree of risk?

(*e*) Is the strategy consistent with other strategies of the company?

(*f*) Does the company have adequate resources to implement the strategy?

(*g*) Is the strategy acceptable to the major stakeholders of the firm?

It may not always be possible to select the best strategy due to lack of information, time, knowledge, etc. Therefore, a firm may have to go for an acceptable or reasonably good strategy.

8.3. TECHNIQUES USED FOR STRATEGIC ANALYSIS

Strategic analysis can be undertaken at two levels — corporate level and business level. At the corporate level, different businesses in the portfolio of a company are analysed. Such analysis is needed in case of only a diversified company. At the business level, the focus of strategic analysis is on individual business. Such analysis reveals the industries and markets in which the company should compete. Corporate level strategic analysis helps to decide in which direction to proceed (stability, growth, retrenchment, or combination thereof). On the other hand, business level strategic analysis helps to decide how to proceed (low cost, differentiation or focus) in the chosen direction.

Some of the major techniques used in strategic analysis are described below:

8.3.1. Portfolio Analysis

In a multi-business firm, there are several businesses which have varying future prospects. Similarly, a single business firm may have several products in its portfolio. Portfolio analysis is a set of techniques that help strategy makers to take strategic decisions concerning individual businesses or products in the firm's portfolio. Portfolio analysis helps an organisation in balancing its investments in different products, businesses or industries in terms of cash flows, product development, risks, etc. Portfolio analysis is also known as corporate portfolio analysis, business portfolio analysis or product portfolio analysis.

Portfolio analysis was initially developed and applied in investment management, wherein portfolio refers to a mix of securities with varying risks and returns. It was introduced in strategic management during the 1960s. Since then several portfolio analysis techniques have been developed. BCG growth-share matrix, GE nine-cell matrix, product-market evolution matrix, directional policy matrix, and strategic position and action evaluation matrix are the prominent techniques. Each of them is a two-dimensional technique. One dimension is organisational (internal) variable and another dimension is environmental (external) variable. However, the forms and names of these variables are different in different techniques. These techniques are described below.

BCG Growth Share Matrix

Boston Consulting Group of USA developed the BCG portfolio matrix. This matrix consists of two dimensions — market growth rate and relative market share. Each dimension is divided into two degrees—high and low. [Fig. 8.3].

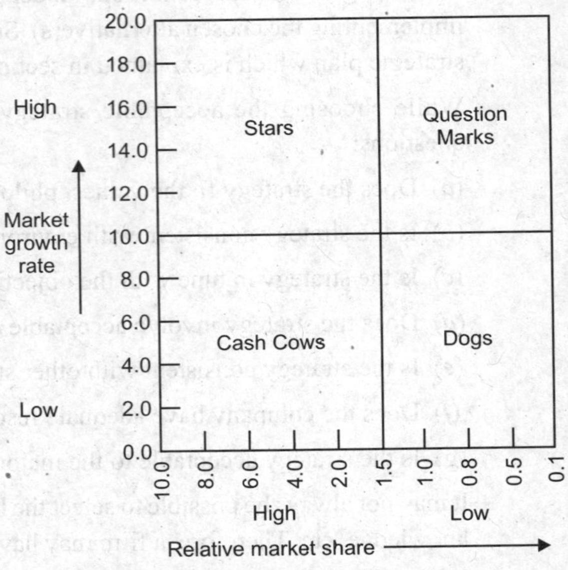

Fig. 8.3. BCG Growth-Share Matrix

In this matrix, the market growth rate on the vertical axis shows the annual growth rate of the market in which the business operates. The relative market share on the horizontal axis indicates the firm's market share in relation to its largest competitor. It is measure of the SBU's strength in the relevant market segment. The matrix is divided into four cells, each representing a different type of business.

The four quadrants are divided on the assumption that 10 per cent of volume growth is the dividing line between high growth and low growth. A relative market share of 1.5 times may separate question marks from stars.

The relative market share is chosen with an assumption that the relative competitive position of a company would be proportional to the rate of cash generation. A firm that has a higher relative market share in comparison to a competitor signifies that it would have higher profit margins and would affect higher cash flows. Selection of rate of growth of industry is based on an assumption that in cases where rate of growth is higher it would lead to expansion of operation of participating companies. High growth rate opens up possibilities of reinvestment in business for further increasing rate of return on investments.

In an industry where growth rates are lower, profitable investments would be scarce and usually the increase in market share would come from the reduction in the market share of a competitor.

1. **Stars:** Businesses with high market share in a high growth market are known as stars. These have the maximum growth and profit opportunities in the firm's portfolio. Therefore, the firm should nurture and develop these businesses in future. In order to maintain its market share, the firm will have to make investment more than its cash inflow. However, some star businesses may be well-established and self-sustaining.
2. **Cash Flows:** Businesses with high market share in a low growth market are called cash cows. These businesses are needed to generate cash for the firm's needs but do not deserve much investment. Cash cows are of two types—strong and weak. Strong cash cows were stars in the near past and generate substantial cash surplus. Weak cash cows have been stars in remote past but generate comparatively less cash surplus. Colgate toothpaste, Lux soap, etc. are examples of cash cows. Companies try to avoid these cash cows becoming dogs. For example, Nestle repositioned, its Milkmaid as an item for preparing quick desserts. The surplus cash generated in cash cows is needed for investment in stars in order to maintain competitive position.
3. **Question Marks:** Businesses with low market share in a growing market are known as question marks. It is questionable whether the firm can exploit the growing market potential. Two alternative strategies are available for such businesses:

   (*a*) making additional investment to convert them into stars, or

   (*b*) divesting them in case costs of improving them exceed the returns on them.
4. **Dogs:** Businesses with low market share in low growth market are called dogs. The firm has weak competitive position and profit potential is low due to low growth potential in

the market. Such businesses should be divested particularly when these do not generate positive cash flows.

Advantages: BCG matrix is a useful technique for evaluating strategic alternatives. It makes two valuable contributions for choosing corporate level strategies.

(*i*) It helps in deciding the role of particular business, for example' cash cows may support stars in the initial stage.

(*ii*) It facilitates integration of different businesses into the overall corporate strategy. BCG model suggests that in a balanced business portfolio cash cows and stars should contribute highest share of total sales while there should be a few question marks and very few dogs with positive cash flows.

Limitations: BCG matrix suffers from some limitations:

(*i*) The four-cell matrix does not represent the true nature of businesses. Some businesses are neither high nor low but in the medium category in terms of market share.

(*ii*) The matrix does not take into consideration some important dimensions such as market size, competitive advantage, stage of product/market evolution, strategic posture of businesses, capital requirement, etc.

(*iii*) Factors other than market share and market growth influence profitability in the long run. For example, in several industries a firm with low market share earns high profits and sometimes outperforms bigger rivals. Similarly, a high market share business in low growth market may fail to generate adequate cash surplus due to stiff competition and low profit margin.

(*iv*) Market share and market growth alone are not true measures of the success of a business. Other considerations such as synergistic effect on other businesses may require that a business is retained.

(*v*) According to BCG matrix, any new business with low market share initially due to long gestation period is a dog. But the business may have huge potential to stay in the business portfolio.

(*vi*) There is no direct proportional relation between relative market share and cost savings. Firms with low market share and focus on a market niche can have low operational cost.

Table 8.1: Strategic Positioning as per BCG Growth Share Matrix

Quadrant	Market Share	Profitability	Investment	Cash flow
Stars	Hold or Increase	High	High	Zero or Negative
Question Marks	Increase or Harvest/Divest	Zero or Negative	Very High	Large Negative
Cash Cows	Hold	High	Low	Large Positive
Dogs	Harvest or Divest	Zero or Negative	Disinvest	Small Positive

(*vii*) The BCG analysis is made on the basic assumption that profits depend on growth rate and market share, however, the attractiveness of an industry may not be reflected in its growth rate. Research shows that dogs can turn to cash cows with better management.

(*viii*) It is quite difficult to determine the market share as it is dependent on the definition of business and the market. In complex business situations, where market interdependence is significant, assessing correct market share may be quite difficult.

(*ix*) The synergy created due to the experience curve is neglected. Synergies can be created between dogs and question marks and star SBUs, leading to higher corporate profits.

(*x*) The human factor that can effectively or ineffectively manage the cash flow has not been considered in the matrix. Thus strategic options may not be practical at all in some situations.

(*xi*) It is recommended that if products are regrouped as per the manufacturing processes to account for economies of scale, it would be a better representation.

(*xii*) There is a widespread resentment in the use of words like dogs, cows, etc. and terms used in GE model, like build, hold, harvest have been found to have better appeal.

(*xiii*) A research study[3] reveals that the tags star, cash cow, question mark and dog attached to different businesses are psychologically undesirable. The study suggests that build, hold and harvest are better as these indicate a more clear strategic focus.

GE Nine-Cell Matrix

The General Electric Company (GEC) of USA developed a nine-cell matrix[4] with the help of McKinsey & Company of USA. GE matrix is superior to BCG matrix in two ways:

(*i*) The GE matrix considers more factors in assessing the industry attractiveness and business strength than the BCG matrix.

(*ii*) The GE matrix contains three degrees (high, medium and low) while the BCG matrix contains only two degrees (high and low) of each dimension.

The GE matrix like the BCG matrix is a two-dimensional grid.

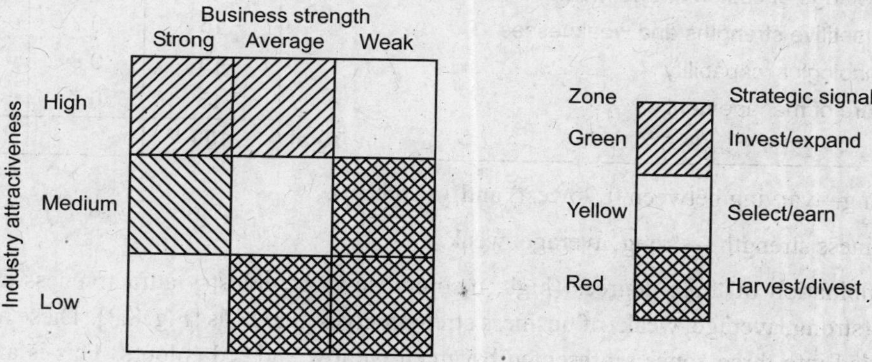

Fig. 8.4. GE Nine-Cell Matrix

3 Anil K. Gupta and V. Govindarajan, "Build, Hold, Harvest: Converting Strategic Intentions into Reality", **Journal of Business Strategy,** March 1984, pp. 34-47.

4 Gerald M. Allen, "Diagramming GE's Planning for What's WATT", in R.J. Allio and M.W. Pennington (eds.), **Corporate Planning—Techniques and Applications,** AMACOM, New York, 1979.

The vertical axis represents industry attractiveness while the horizontal axis represents business strength/competitive position.

Industry Attractiveness: This is a weighted composite rating of eight factors. These factors and their quantitative measurement is given in Table 8.2.

Table 8.2: Measurement of Industry Attractiveness

Industry Attractiveness Factors	Weight ×	Rating =	Score
1. Market size	15	0.8	12.0
2. Growth rate	25	1.0	25.0
3. Industry profit margin	20	0.7	14.0
4. Intensity of competition	20	0.8	16.0
5. Economies of scale	10	0.5	5.0
6. Technology	10	0.6	6.0
7. Environmental factors (seasonality, cyclicality, social, legal and human factors)	Non-restrictive		
Total	100		78.0

Various factors given above vary from one industry to another depending on its nature.

Business Strength/Competitive Position: This is the weighted composite rating of seven factors. These factors and their quantitative measurement are given in Table 8.3.

Table 8.3: Measurement of Business Strength

Business Strength Factors	Weight	Rating	Score
1. Relative market share	15	0.8	12.0
2. Profit margins	10	0.6	6.0
3. Ability to compete	20	0.8	16.0
4. Knowledge of customer and market	15	0.5	7.5
5. Competitive strengths and weaknesses	15	0.7	10.5
6. Technological capability	10	0.8	6.0
7. Calibre of management	15	0.7	10.5
Total	100		70.5

Rating—varying between 0 (lowest) and 1 (highest).

Business strength—strong, average, weak.

Combination of three degrees (high, medium, low) of industry attractiveness and three degrees (strong, average, weak) of business strength gives nine cells [Fig. 8.3]. These nine cells are divided into three zones represented by green, yellow and red colours. This is analogous to traffic signals—green for 'go ahead', yellow for 'wait and see', and red for 'stop'. For this reason, **GE** matrix is also known as the **stop light strategy model.** The strategies to be adopted for these zones are as follows:

Invest/Expand: The strategy for business in green zone is to grow and build, *i.e.,* expansion strategies. In the cell on the extreme left-hand corner, both industry attractiveness and business strength are high. This is the ideal situation for investment and growth. But this situation cannot continue for long due to the entry of other firms. The other two cells in the green zone are more realistic. In the high attractiveness and average strength cell, a firm must build strength to grow. In the medium attractiveness and strong strength cell, the firm can achieve competitive advantage to restrict entry of new firms.

Select/Earn: Hold and maintain (stability and consolidation) strategy is recommended for businesses in the yellow zone. As both industry attractiveness and business strength are high or medium, there is opportunity for selective earning. The cell with medium attractiveness and average strength needs hold strategy. The third cell with high attractiveness provides scope for both continued earning and improving strength. In the cell with low attractiveness and strong growth the firm may go for vertical integration or diversification depending on the nature of the industry.

Harvest/Divest: In case of businesses in the red zone, harvesting or divesting is recommended. Harvesting is suitable in case of cells with low attractiveness and average strength, and medium attractiveness with weak strength. Harvesting is gradual withdrawal as the focus initially is to reduce costs of R&D, advertising, etc., so as to earn profit in the short-term. Immediate divestment is needed in case of the cell in the low attractiveness and weak strength.

Advantages: The GE nine-cell matrix is a powerful analytical tool that incorporates a large variety of strategic variables. It can help a diversified company to identify feasible strategic alternatives and to allocate resources among them. It can lead to better strategic decisions through a more perceptive understanding of multiple businesses.

Limitations: The GE matrix provides only broad strategic prescriptions rather than specific business strategies. Problems arise in measuring variables such as growth rate of a business.

Product/Market Evolution Matrix

Hofer and Schendel[5] suggest that the GE matrix does not depict the positions of businesses that are about to emerge as winners as the product is in the take-off stage. To overcome this weakness, they have developed a fifteen-cell matrix consisting of two dimensions—product/market evolution and competitive position. This matrix is given in Fig. 8.5.

Stage of Product/Market Evolution	Competitive Position		
Development		A	
Growth	B		C
Shakeout		D	
Maturity Suturation	E		
Decline			F

Fig. 8.5 Product/Market Evolution Matrix

5. Charles W. Hofer and Dan Schendel, **Strategy Formulation: Analytical Concepts,** West Publishing, St. Paul, Minnesota, 1978.

The future of various businesses can be decided with the help of this matrix. Business *A* appears to be a developing winner, business *B* may be classified as a potential winner, business *C* can be developed into future winner by improving its competitiveness, business *D* may be called an established winner, business *E* may be a cash cow, business *F* may be a dog.

Directional Policy Matrix

The Shell Chemicals (UK) developed the Directional Policy Matrix (DPM) which consists of two dimensions—business sector prospects and company's competitive capabilities. There are three degrees in each dimension. The combination of two dimensions with three degrees in each gives nine cells as depicted in Fig. 8.6. Each cell shows the type of strategy which a firm may adopt[6].

Competitive Capabilities \ Business Sector Prospects	Unattractive	Average	Attractive
Weak	Divestment	Phased withdrawal	Double or quit
Average	Phased withdrawal	Custodial	Try harder
Strong	Cash generation	Growth	Market lendership

Fig. 8.6. Directional Policy Matrix

1. **Divestment:** A business with weak capability and unattractive business prospects usually incurs losses at present and is likely to incur losses in future too. Therefore, such a business should be divested and the resources released from it should be invested in some other business.
2. **Phased Withdrawal:** Businesses falling in cell 2 and cell 4 should be divested in phases because these businesses are not likely to earn as much as other businesses in the portfolio.
3. **Double or Quit:** The business with weak capability and high prospects may be strengthened by investing more resources so as to take advantage of attractive business prospects. Alternatively, such business may be divested when it is not possible to invest more resources in it.
4. **Custodial:** The business with average capability and average business prospects also has two alternatives. The firm may either bear with the situation or it may divest such business to concentrate on other business.
5. **Try Harder:** The business with attractive business prospects and average capability needs to be strengthened through additional resources so as to take advantage of attractive business prospects.
6. **Cash Generation:** The business with strong capability but unattractive business prospects may be used to generate cash. No further investment is needed due to unattractive business prospects.

---

6. David E. Hussey, "Portfolio Analysis: Practical Experience with the Directional Policy Matrix", **Long Range Planning**, August, 1978.

7. **Market Leadership:** The business with strong capability and attractive business prospects may be converted into a market leader by investing more resources and through innovation.

Strategic Position and Action Evaluation (SPACE) Matrix

Strategic position and action evaluation is a four-dimensional model. These four dimensions are: firm's competitive advantage, firm's financial strength, industry strength, and environmental stability[7]. Competitive advantage and financial strength are internal dimensions. Industry strength and environmental stability are external dimensions. The purpose of SPACE matrix is to determine the organisation's strategic posture in the industry. The factors considered in assessing these four dimensions are given in Table 8.4.

Table 8.4: Space Factors

Competitive Advantage (CA)	Industry Strength (IS)
• Market share • Quality of product/service • Product life cycle • Product replacement cycle • Customer loyalty • Capacity utilisation • Technical know-how • Vertical integration	• Profit potential • Growth potential • Financial stability • Resource utilisation • Capital intensity • Ease of entry into market • Productivity
Financial Strength (FS)	**Environmental Stability (ES)**
• Return on investment • Leverage • Liquidity • Capital needed and available • Cash flow position • Ease of exit from the market • Risk involved in the business	• Technological changes • Rate of inflation • Variations in demand • Price range of competing products • Competitive pressure • Price elasticity of demand • Entry barriers

Each SPACE factor is measured in degrees ranging from 0 (most unfavourable) to 5 (most favourable). SPACE diagram is shown in Fig. 8.7.

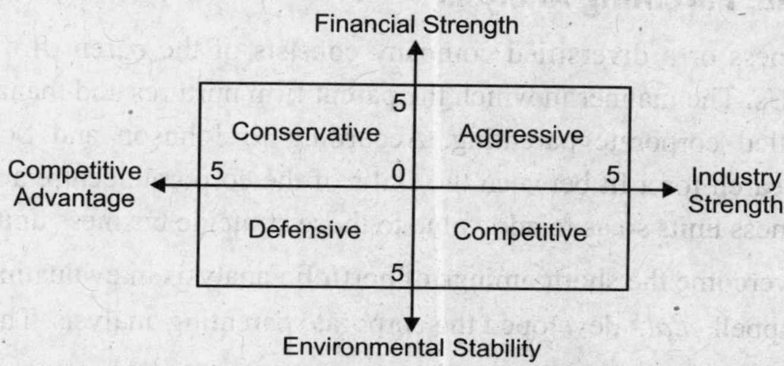

Fig. 8.7. SPACE Diagram and Strategic Postures

7. A.J. Rowe *et.al.*, **Strategic Management and Business Policy—Methodological Approach,** Addison–Wesley, Reading MA; 1988.

The four strategic postures or options are explained below:

1. **Conservative Posture:** A business with financial strength but having very limited competitive advantage requires conservative posture. The industry in which the firm operates is not attractive but environment is relatively stable. The conservative posture leads to stability strategy and conglomerate diversification.
2. **Aggressive Posture:** A business with competitive advantage and good financial strength can adopt aggressive posture. The firm operates in an attractive industry and stable environment. The aggressive posture leads to concentric expansion, vertical integration and concentric diversification.
3. **Defensive Posture:** A business lacking both competitive advantage and financial strength has to adopt a defensive posture. The firm operates in an unattractive industry and in an unstable environment. The defensive posture leads to divestment, liquidation and other forms of retrenchment.
4. **Competitive Posture:** A firm with competitive advantage but having limited financial strength should adopt competitive posture. It operates in an attractive industry but in an unstable environment. The competitive posture leads to concentric merger, conglomerate merger, and turnaround.

Evaluation of Portfolio Analysis

Portfolio analysis is a valuable technique for multi-business/multi-product firms. It is helpful in rational allocation of resources among different businesses. More resources are invested in businesses wherein returns are likely to be high. Portfolio analysis also helps in better understanding of multiple businesses.

Portfolio analysis, however, suffers from some **limitations. First,** the various dimensions used in the construction of a portfolio matrix are not precisely defined. For example, different strategists may interpret business prospects differently and, therefore, may take different strategic actions. This is so because the dimensions or factors in a portfolio matrix are qualitative in nature.

8.3.2. Corporate Parenting Analysis

A multi-business or a diversified company consists of the parent firm (corporate head-quarters) and SBUs. The manner in which the parent firm nurtures and manages the individual businesses is called corporate parenting. According to Johnson and Scholes, "Corporate parenting is the search for a fit between the skills of the corporate centre and the strategies of the strategic business units so as to add value to those strategic business units."[8]

In order to overcome the shortcomings of portfolio analysis in evaluating various strategic alternatives, Campbell *et.al.*[9] developed the corporate parenting analysis. This technique views

---

8. Gerry Johnson and Kevan Scholes, **Exploring Corporate Strategy: Text and Cases,** Prentice Hall, New Jersey, 2002, p. 290.
9. A. Campbell, M. Gould and M. Alexander, **Corporate Level Strategy: Creating Value in the Multibusiness Company,** John Wiley & Sons, New York, 1994.

the company in its totality and focuses on the value created from the relationship between the parent firm and individual businesses. There are four ways in which the parent firm can create value for strategic business units:

1. **Stand-Alone Influence:** The parent views each SBU as a separate profit centre. The SBUs are monitored and controlled through performance targets. Strategic decisions such as appointing key executives and approving major capital expenditures are taken to create value.
2. **Linking Influence:** Value is created through better cooperation and synergy.
3. **Central Functions and Services:** The parent provides administrative and managerial services to SBUs to create value.
4. **Corporate Development:** Value is created through portfolio management.

These value creations occur when there is a fit between the parent's skills and characteristics of SBUs. Corporate parenting analysis seeks to evaluate this fit. While doing so, a diversified company must find the right answers to the following questions:

(*i*) What businesses should it own and why?

(*ii*) What organisation structure, management processes, and philosophy will foster superior performance for its individual businesses?

Once the strategic fit is ensured, the following steps are taken in the search for appropriate corporate strategy.

(*a*) Examine each business in terms of its critical success factors (CSFs).

(*b*) Evaluate each business in terms of those areas in which performance can be improved.

(*c*) Analyse how can the parent firm improve performance in these areas.

On the basis of the foregoing analysis, a corporate parenting-fit matrix can be prepared as shown in Fig. 8.8.

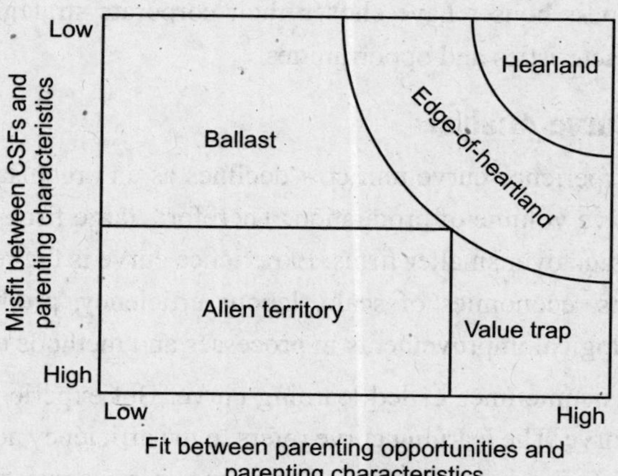

Fig. 8.8. Parenting-fit matrix

The matrix given above has two dimensions—positive effects in the form of fit between parent characteristics and SBUs and negative effects in the form of misfit between CSFs and parent characteristics. On the basis of these two dimensions, businesses can be classified into the following categories:

1. **Heartland Businesses:** These businesses have very high fit with the parent firm. Expansion strategies are suitable for such businesses due to opportunities for nurturing them.
2. **Edge-of-Heartland Businesses:** Some parenting characteristics fit with these businesses but others do not. In case the parent can devote time and money to develop these businesses, expansion strategies are useful.
3. **Ballast Businesses:** These businesses fit well with the parent but there are few opportunities for improvement. These are just like cash cows of BCG matrix. Retrenchment strategies are suitable when the sale proceeds exceed the value of future cash flows from them.
4. **Alien Territory Businesses:** There is a misfit between these businesses and the parent characteristics. These are usually the outcome of misplaced diversification. These businesses should be retrenched.
5. **Value-Trap Businesses:** These businesses fit well with the parenting opportunities. But parent lacks understanding of their critical success factors. Retrenchment is adopted for such businesses.

In corporate parenting, the corporate headquarters attempts to create synergy among business units by allocating resources, transferring critical skills, and coordinating their activities. It enables the headquarters to focus on core competencies and create value by establishing a fit between needs, opportunities, resources and capabilities.

Corporate parenting analysis offers new insights for evaluation of strategic alternatives. Therefore, several business houses have chosen their corporate strategies on the basis of fit between parenting characteristics and opportunities.

8.3.3. Experience Curve Analysis

According to the experience curve unit cost declines as an organisation gains experience in terms of the cumulative volume of production. Therefore, large firms in an industry have a competitive cost advantage over smaller firms. Experience curve is the result of several factors such as learning effects, economies of scale, labour efficiency, product redesign, product standardisation, technological improvements in processes and methods of production[10].

Experience curve is sometimes called learning curve. But experience curve is a broader concept than learning curve. The learning curve refers to the efficiency achieved by labour over a period of time by performing repetitive work. Experience curve consists of many factors other than efficiency of labour.

10. David A. Aker, **Strategic Market Management,** John Wiley & Sons, New York, 1988, pp. 162-163.

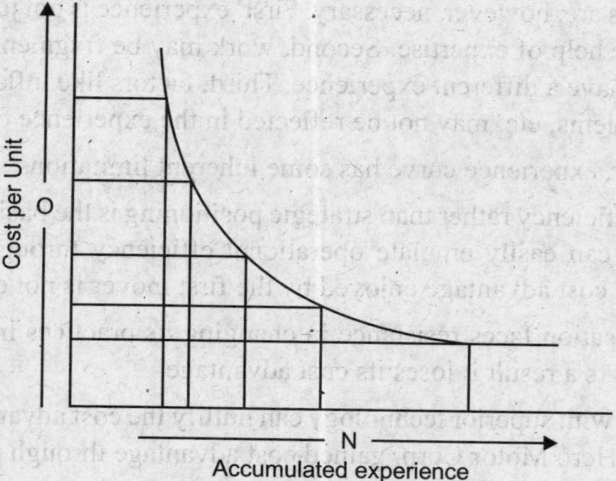

Fig. 8.9. Experience Curve

Experience curve can be used to gain competitive advantage and create an entry barrier against new entrants.

Firms which are first movers in an industry and become market leaders enjoy a competitive edge. Their cost leadership strategy acts as an entry barrier. For example, till the 1990s, Bajaj Auto was the market leader in the scooter market. New entrants such as Scooters India, Andhra Scooters, Gujarat Scooters and Punjab Scooters could not succeed in competition and exited. Kinetic Honda and LML Ltd. also did not do well.

Experience, however, indicates that many new entrants to an industry have outperformed their well established rivals. For example, Hero Cycles outperformed Hind Cycles, TI Cycles Atlas Cycles, Avon Cycles and Sen Raleigh'. Similarly, in the motorcycle segment, Hero Honda (now Hero Motor Corp.) outperformed the earliest entrants such as Escorts and Enfield India. In the car market, Maruti Suzuki outperformed old rivals like Premier Automobiles and Hindustan Motors.

We have seen the effect of experience curve in electronics, computers, television and several other industries where costs and prices have declined with growing production and sales volumes.

The experience curve effect can be used to benefit only if the demand is elastic. If demand is inelastic, the fall in price will not lead to proportionate rise in demand, and hence the experience curve effect cannot be used beneficially in such circumstances.

Experience curve may lead companies to work only efficiently and not effectively. There may be a general reluctance to go for introspection and do fundamental rethinking of technology, business process, etc. and the likelihood of doing right things in different ways is considerably reduced.

The experience curve effect arises due to:

(*a*) improvements in productivity of labour due to accumulated experience;

(*b*) saving of time due to specialisation;

(*c*) reduction in scrap, etc. through value engineering;

(*b*) production of more units without extra investment due to product line balancing.

Certain precautions are, however, necessary. First' experience is not just passage of time but reducing costs with the help of expertise. Second, work may be fragmented and specialisation in each fragment may have a different experience. Third, factors like inflation, business cycles, industrial relation problems, etc. may not be reflected in the experience curve.

As an entry barrier, experience curve has some inherent limitations:

(*i*) Operational efficiency rather than strategic positioning is the basis of experience curve. New entrants can easily emulate operational efficiency through benchmarking, etc. Therefore, the cost advantage enjoyed by the first mover is not everlasting.

(*ii*) An old organisation faces resistance in changing its practices in line with changes in environment. As a result it loses its cost advantage.

(*iii*) A new entrant with superior technology can nullify the cost advantage of early entrants. For example, Hero Motor Corp. gained cost advantage through new technology.

(*iv*) When more than one strong company uses experience curve to build their strategies, industry growth may suffer. As all firms compete on the same basis, weaker ones will exit.

8.3.4. Life Cycle Analysis

According to the life cycle concept, products, markets, businesses and industries pass through various stages in their life cycles. Life cycle analysis offers a useful framework to determine the stage at which each of these exists. On the basis of such diagnosis, appropriate strategic alternative can be selected. For example, expansion may be the right strategic alternative for businesses which are in the introduction and growth stages. Businesses in the maturity stage may be used to generate cash while those in the decline stage may be retrenched. Such strategic choices on the basis of life cycle model help in developing a balanced, portfolio of businesses. However, there can be reverse trends in some products, markets, businesses and industries. For example, old fashion again came in vogue.

8.3.5. Profit Impact of Market Strategy (PIMS)

Strategic Planning Institute (USA) carried out a study[11] called, PIMS to identify the main variables which influence profitability. The study identified the key variables as: market share, product quality and a few others. They study revealed that a firm's profitability (pretax return on investment) rises with its relative market share in the served market. [Fig. 8.10]

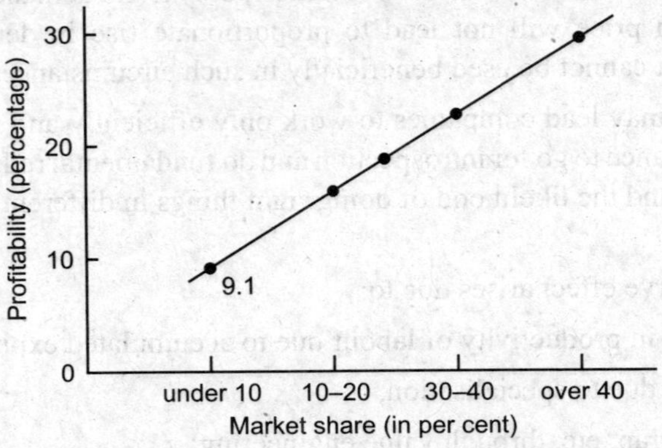

Fig. 8.10. Market share-profitability relationship

11 Strategic Planning Institute, **The PIMS Programme,** Cambridge MA, 1974.

Fig. 8.10 shows a linear relationship between market share and profitability. As per one report, "The average ROI for business with under 10 per cent market share was about per cent. On the average, a difference of 10 percentage points in market share is accompanied by a difference of about five points in pretax ROI".[12] According to the PIMS study businesses with market shares above 40 per cent earn an average ROI of 30 per cent, or three times that of those with market shares under 10 per cent".[13]

On the basis of these findings, several companies expanded their market shares to increase their profitability. The linear relationship between market share and profitability occurs under the following conditions:

(*i*) When increase in market share leads to lower unit costs due to economies of large scale

(*ii*) When the firm sells superior quality products at a premium price which is more than the cost of higher quality.

Beyond a certain level, however, the costs of increasing market share may be too high and the threats from prospective competitors may be high. It is, therefore, necessary to decide the optimum level of market share. The optimum market share is the level at which ROI is the highest. Up to this level the most appropriate strategy is expansion in the same product line. Beyond this level, diversification may be a more appropriate strategy.

8.4. FACTORS INFLUENCING STRATEGIC CHOICE

Various factors that influence choice of strategy may be classified into two broad categories—objective factors, and subjective factors.

1. **Objective Factors:** The strategic intent and the SWOT analysis of an organisation are the main objective factors in strategic choice. The strategic intent defines what an organisation should do and why. Every organisation attempts to choose strategies that will help it in achieving its strategic intent. SWOT analysis is helpful in strategy formulation in the following ways:

   (*a*) It provides a logical framework for systematic assessment of different issues involved in strategic choice.

   (*b*) It provides a summary of relevant factors in the external and internal environment. These can form possible combinations of opportunities and threats in the environment, and strengths and weaknesses of the organisation.

   (*i*) great opportunities and high strengths,

   (*ii*) great opportunities and low strengths,

   (*iii*) great threats and high strengths, and

   (*iv*) great threats and low strengths.

   Each combination requires a different strategy.

---

12. Robert D. Buzzell, Bradley T. Gale, and Ralph G.M. Sultan, "Market Share—A Key to Profitability" **Harvard Business Review,** Jan.-Feb., 1975, pp. 97-106.
13. Robert D. Buzzell and Bradley T. Gale, **The PIMS** Principles: Linking Strategy to performance.

(*c*) Sometimes a business situation may involve both opportunities and threats. Similarly, a firm may have both strength and weakness in some situation. In such situations, the strategy makers can visualise the firm's overall position with the help of SWOT analysis.

2. **Subjective Factors:** Strategic choice is not completely a rational and analytical process due to many reasons. **First,** there are constraints of time, information and competence in searching for the best or most rational alternative. Therefore, the strategists choose the acceptable alternative. **Second,** strategists are human beings and personal factors influence strategic choice. **Third,** power and politics are an integral part of organisational functioning. **Fourth,** in strategic choice several qualitative factors are involved. Their interpretation is likely to be personalised. **Fifth,** strategic choice is mainly the responsibility of top management. The attitudes and preferences of top executives inevitably influence strategic choice. That is why a company's strategies may change due to changes in its top management teams. **Lastly,** when objective factors fail to lead to a clear-cut choice subjective factors dictate the choice.

The major subjective factors involved in strategic choice are given below:

(*i*) **Past Strategies:** While choosing strategic actions, the strategists begin with the past or existing strategies. Therefore, alternatives arising out of past strategic actions are more likely to be chosen. Moreover, past strategies have created commitment in terms of resources and personnel. Strategists prefer to avoid alternatives that make the existing resources and personnel redundant. They may be forced to go for these alternatives due to imminent threat from environmental changes.

(*ii*) **Preferences and Aspirations of Decision-Makers:** Promoters and top executives have certain ambitions and preferences. These key decision-makers use the organisation as a means for satisfying personal ambitions and dreams. For example, Reliance Industries adopted rapid growth strategy due to the ambition of its founder, Dhirubhai Ambani, to make it the biggest private sector company in India.

(*iii*) **Value System of Top Management:** The personal philosophy of the founder and other strategists influences how strategic alternatives are explored and evaluated. For example, the Bajaj Group did not consider the liquor business due to the staunch belief of its founder Jamnalal Bajaj in Gandhian ideology.

(*iv*) **Attitudes Towards Risk:** Strategic choice depends on the risk-taking attitudes of those who make this choice. Different strategic alternatives involve different degrees of risk. Generally, the risk involved is high when the strategy involves huge investment, uncertain environment and long gestation period. Strategic decisions involve a tradeoff between risk and returns. Strategists who are willing to take high risk may adopt an aggressive or proactive approach to strategy making. For example, ITC, Reliance, Bharti Group, Adani Enterprises have opted for rapid extension. On the other hand, Bajaj Group and Sarabhai Group have adopted 'stick-to-the, knitting' strategy that involves relatively less risk.

(*v*) **Internal Power Politics:** Strategy formulation is partly a political process. Every organisation is a coalition of several groups and each group puts pulls and pushes depending on its internal power relationship. For example, a dominant chief executive may dictate choice in one company while in another company where the chief executive is weak, a clique makes the choice. For example, Ratan Tata faced considerable problems in dislodging the powerful chief executives chosen by J.R.D. Tata. In family business houses, power struggle between family members affects strategic choice. For example, Rahul Bajaj did not like his son, Rajiv's strategic decision to divest the scooter business. In case of public sector enterprises, politicians and bureaucrats affect strategic choice. Similarly, the parent company exercises a political influence on strategic choice by its subsidiaries.

(*vi*) **Timing Considerations:** Time element influences strategic choice in following ways[14]:

(*a*) When a company has limited time to make a strategic choice, strategists tend to be defensive and assign more weightage to negative information.

(*b*) Strategists make a strategic choice when they reasonably believe that all possible alternatives have been considered and no other feasible or attractive alternative is likely to emerge in the near future. A short-run strategic choice may be made as a stop-gap arrangement before choosing a long-term strategy. For example, a company may choose stability before it is prepared for diversification.

(*c*) A company also considers the timing of competitor action in strategic choice. When it expects that a particular strategy would elicit an aggressive reaction from rivals, the company will choose such strategy only when it can counteract.

8.5. CONTINGENCY STRATEGIES

While making strategic choice, some assumptions are made. When there is a change in the assumed conditions, the chosen strategies have to be modified. Therefore, contingency strategies are formulated in advance to face the unforeseen situations. The need for contingency strategies is more in those firms which operate in a turbulent environment. Telecommunications, IT, insurance, power, FMCG, oil and gas, air transportation are some of the industries which operate in a turbulent environment. Therefore, firms in these industries have to formulate contingency strategies to respond quickly and rationally to environmental uncertainties. In addition to environmental uncertainties, crises (emergencies or disasters) also require contingency strategies. War, civil disturbance, factory fire, natural catastrophe such as tsunami, an epidemic, IT system failure are some examples of such crises. For example, Haldia Petrochemicals project of Reliance Industries faced a natural disaster in Gujarat. In order to minimise the loss due to such disasters and to put back the project in place after the disaster, a firm needs sound crisis management including recovery strategies. Favourable events such as an unexpected opportunity due to a sudden shift in government policy or a technological

14. Peter Wright, "The Harassed Decision-Maker", **Journal of Applied Psychology,** 59(5), 1974, pp. 555-561.

breakthrough may also require contingency strategies. For example, Bharati Enterprises became the largest telecommunication company because it was the first to take advantage of opening up of the telecommunications industry to private sector in 1994.

The basic purpose of contingency strategies is to help a firm deal successfully with unexpected events. These strategies reduce the uncertainty and time delays in responding to an emergency. A contingency strategy may also boost the confidence and morale of management as the company is prepared to deal with sudden developments.

Contingency strategies, however, involve some problems and weaknesses. **First,** when a contingency strategy is revealed before it is adopted as an alternative, it may create fear and uncertainty in the company. For example, a contingency strategy to reduce the volume of operations in case of market recession may affect employee morale and efficiency. **Second,** a downward contingency strategy (lower sales volume or market share or profit) may create pessimistic or negative attitudes among managers. **Third,** the time and effort spent on contingency strategy will go waste in case the original strategy does not need modification.

The main **issues** involved in a contingency strategy are as follows:

1. **The Events:** Contingency strategy is formulated to deal with events which can cause a serious damage to the organisation, unless these are dealt with speed and logic. As all contingencies cannot be covered, the strategists must identify few contingencies that can have a major impact in terms of competitive position, cash flows, profitability, employee morale, etc.
2. **Trigger Points:** The signals that give warming of the event may be specified in the contingency strategy. But in some cases the event itself (*e.g.*, fire) is the trigger point. In other cases, the contingency strategy should indicate at what point the alternative strategy is to be put into action.
3. **Details:** The details of a contingency strategy may vary from one situation to another. In a critical situation, the strategy may be elaborate specifying the actions to be taken in case of the emergency. In another situation wherein response time is less, the strategy may be just an idea in the strategist's mind about how to respond.
4. **Number:** Another issue that needs to be decided is how many contingency strategies to formulate at a time. Too many strategies involve considerable managerial time and efforts and may create confusion. The focus should, therefore, be on critical rather than on merely troublesome events.

8.6. STRATEGIC PLAN

On the basis of its strategic choice, a company prepares a strategic plan. A strategic or corporate plan is a document indicating the manner in which the company proposes to put its chosen strategies into action. This document may run into several pages or may be a brief plan of three to five pages depending on the nature and size of the company. When the strategic management process is highly formal and structured, the strategic plan document is likely to be quite lengthy and comprehensive. Otherwise, the plan document tends to be short.

A comprehensive strategic plan document may contain the following details:

1. A clear statement of the company's strategic intent covering its vision, mission, business definition and objectives.
2. Results of environmental appraisal indicating major opportunities, threats and critical success factors.
3. Results of organisational appraisal, indicating major strengths, weaknesses, and core competencies.
4. Strategies chosen and the assumptions on which these are based.
5. Contingent strategies to be adopted under different conditions.
6. Time horizon of the strategic plan.
7. Amount and type of resources needed for implementing the plan and how these resources will be raised.
8. Strategic budget for allocation of resources among different businesses.
9. Schedule for implementation of the plan.
10. Changes to be made in organisational structure, systems, processes and top management team.
11. Functional strategies and the mode of their implementation.
12. Measures to be used to evaluate performance and to judge the success of strategy implementation.

The time horizon of a strategic plan may vary from company to company. In public sector enterprises, five year time horizon is more common due to the country's five year plan. Private sector companies and multinational corporations prepare strategic plan for periods ranging between three and ten years. National Thermal Power Corporation (NTPC) adopted a 15 year (2002-2017) corporate plan. Larsen & Toubro (L&T) formulated a five year strategic plan (called Lakshya) to achieve global competitiveness. Indian subsidiaries of foreign multinationals draw their strategic plans on the basis of guidelines issued by the parent firms. Family business houses such as Tatas, Aditya Birla Group, Reliance, etc. draft strategic plans to provide strategic direction to different companies within the group.

The strategic document informs the different stakeholders what the company stands for and what it plans to do in the given time period.

SUMMARY

Concept of Strategic Choice: The process of choosing one or more strategies to achieve corporate objectives. It is an analytical and complex process.

Steps in Strategic Choice: (*i*) Focus on strategic alternatives—Gap analysis (*ii*) Evaluate strategic alternatives (*iii*) Consider decision factors (*iv*) Choose.

Techniques of Strategic Analysis: Portfolio analysis—(*a*) BCG Matrix (stars, cash cows, question marks, dogs) (*b*) GE Nine-Cell Matrix (industry characteristics, business strength; Green Zone—invest/expand, yellow zone—select/earn, red zone—harvest (divest) (*c*) Product Market Evolution Matrix (competitive position and stage of product/market evolution—A, B, C, D, E, F cells (*d*) Directional Policy Matrix + (Business sector prospects and competitive capabilities—divestment, phased withdrawal, double or quit, custodial, try harder, cash generation, growth and market leadership) (*e*) Strategic Position and Action Evaluation (SPACE—Competitive advantage, financial strength, industry strength, environmental stability—conservative, aggressive, defensive and competitive).

Corporate Parenting Analysis—(*i*) Stand-alone influence (*ii*) Linking influence (*iii*) Central functions and services (*iv*) Corporate development—heartland businesses, edge-of-heartland businesses, ballast businesses, alien territory businesses, value trap businesses.

Experience Curve Analysis: Cost declines with accumulation of production, Broader than learning curve.

Life Cycle Analysis: Products, markets, industries and businesses pass through different stages in their life cycles. Different strategies are needed in different stages.

Profit Impact of Market Strategy: Profitability and market share.

Factors Influencing Strategic Choice: (1) Objective factors—Strategic intent and SWOT analysis (2) Subjective factors—past strategies, personal preferences and aspirations, values of top executives, attitudes towards risk, internal power politics, timing.

Contingency Strategies: Help to meet emergencies/crises; may create fear and uncertainty, involve time and efforts; Events to be caused, trigger points, details and number are the main issues in contingency strategies.

Strategic Plan: A long-term plan for the company as a whole indicating what the company stands for and proposes to do in future, helps to implement corporate level and business level strategies.

TEST QUESTIONS

1. Describe the manner in which the process of strategic choice works.
2. Describe some of the important techniques for strategic analysis and discuss their limitations in the Indian context. What is meant by strategic choice?
3. Describe the strategies that can be pursued by firms operating in competitive environment. What specific options would you recommend for the following?

   (*a*) traditional textile firms

   (*b*) fertiliser units in public sector?
4. Why is the choice of strategy often influenced by past strategy? Explain how managerial attitudes towards risk determine the choice of strategy.

5. Critically examine the GE Nine-Cell matrix used for strategic choice.
6. Explain Product/Market Evolution Matrix.
7. Describe the SPACE technique of strategic analysis.
8. What is Corporate parenting Analysis? Explain its role in strategic choice.
9. What is BCG's Growth Share Matrix? Explain how the portfolio matrix is helpful in strategy formulation?
10. "Experience Curve phenomenon is irrelevant in the fast changing world of the late nineties." Discuss and point out the case of a company in India which thrives on its innovativeness as against a company which relies on its cost competitiveness.
11. "Growth Share Matrix and Directional Policy Matrix are at best only display matrices and cannot be used to identify the action oriented plan for companies." Critically examine the statement and discuss the shortcomings of Growth Share Matrix.
12. "Boston Consulting Groups' recommendations are too simplistic". Comment on the statement. Can this limitation be overcome by suitable modifications?
13. Do you think that Directional Policy Matrix is a distinct improvement over the Product Portfolio Matrix? Elucidate your answer with the help of appropriate examples. Critically examine the procedure of assigning rating to different parameters such as market quality, feedstock, hardware, etc.
14. What is Life Cycle Analysis?
15. Discuss Profit Impact of Market Strategy?
16. Explain the factors that influence choice of strategies.
17. What are contingency strategies? Why are these formulated? Explain the key issues involved in contingency strategies.
18. What is a strategic plan? Describe its main contents and utility.
19. What do you understand by corporate parenting? Explain the various parenting strategies adopted by corporations.
20. Assume the role of an entrepreneur who has a burning desire to get into the pizza business. What value-adding activity would you focus on to build your own source of competitive advantage? How will you compete with the sit-down restaurants as the firms that focus on home delivery?
21. "If the first mover advantage was to last for ever, no new firm would appear in the list of major players in the industry." Elucidate.
22. How and why does the past strategy influence the choice of current strategy? Also discuss the nature of time constraints in the choice of strategy.
23. How are TOWS Matrix, SPACE Matrix, BCG Matrix, IE Matrix and Grand Strategy Matrix similar and how are they different?
24. Explain BCG growth share matrix and GE Nine-cell matrix for portfolio analysis of organisations. Also explain the differences between them.

25. Explain the Shell's Directional Policy Matrix as a business portfolio analysis technique. Is it different from GE's Strategic Business Planning Grid?
26. What is Portfolio Analysis? What is the contribution of BCG matrix in the evaluation of strategic alternatives? Under what situations divestment strategy should be adopted?
27. Examine the utility of BCG Matrix for a multi-product company. Under what circumstances should a company resort to (i) diversification; and (ii) retrenchment?
28. Discuss briefly the various stages of corporate development.
29. What is meant by Portfolio Analysis? Discuss BCG growth share matrix and GE business screen analysis for conducting Portfolio Analysis with the help of a hypothetical company. Also discuss international portfolio analysis.
30. What do you understand by corporate parenting? List the steps of developing a corporate parenting strategy.
31. Discuss the difficulties faced in strategy formulation. Outline the role of leadership in strategy formulation.
32. Discuss the alternative approaches for formulating corporate strategy. What factors should the top management keep in mind in implementing strategy?
33. (*a*) Why does the need for developing contingency strategies arise?

    (*b*) What should be the contents of a strategic plan for a medium-sized company?
34. Describe some of the important techniques for strategic analysis in a firm. Discuss their limitations in the Indian context.
35. How can government priorities significantly affect the strategic choice made by an Indian company? Explain with two examples.
36. Write notes on:

    (*i*) GE's Stoplight Strategy Model.

    (*ii*) Product/Market Evolution Matrix.

    (*iii*) Strategic Business Planning Grid.

    (*iv*) Corporate Fit Matrix
37. Explain briefly SPACE as an extension of two-dimensional models of portfolio analysis, pointing out its pros and cons.
38. Describe GE's nine-cell matrix. Place various product groups of a large FMCG company in the various cells of this matrix and suggest the strategy that it should adopt with respect to each product group.
39. Discuss any two tools of product portfolio analysis. Which tool should be used in a recession-prone climate? Give suitable examples.
40. What is a resource-based view in strategy? How does it differ from classical view of strategy? In which school of strategy will you classify the views of Richard Rumelt and why?

41. What is 'Value Denials'. Give some examples of value denials.

42. "Portfolio models such as the BCG matrix are a poor guide to making diversification decisions. The firm must instead pay attention to its core competencies when considering diversification". Discuss.

43. Explain BCG Matrix. What is the logic of this model? What are the model's limitations and weaknesses?

CASE STUDY

Last year, Ajay Oswal became the CEO of the 50-year-old family-managed textiles company, Oswal Cotton Industries Ltd, at the age of 30. His heart was now pumping to the thrill of a turnaround.

"Still relishing the number?" asked the CFO, Sadashiv Godbole, referring to OCIL's Quarter 1 results for 2008, which showed a Rs. 2.5 crore profit against a Rs. 21 crore loss for the same quarter of 2007. "We're back in business," said Godbole, sinking into the upholstery.

Godbole was a 20-year OCIL veteran and he had signed up Ajai's father Prem Chand Oswal, who'd started the firm in 1958, in Ludhiana, to make cotton textiles. Cotton sheets, shirtings, cambric and mazril were the products that the firm produced and marketed during the early years, and it seemed like only yesterday that the firm went public—before getting into synthetic fibre and also steel.

By the late 1990s, the OCIL tapestry, once richly interwoven with natural, synthetic and silver threads, had started fraying. First, the polyester division became a drag, and then, steel as competitive dynamics started changing.

By 2006, OCIL had got to what then seemed like a point of no return. Debt had-mounted to a staggering Rs. 1,300 crore, almost equivalent to the group turnover. Financial institutions threatened to pull the plug on the company, and the pink papers went to town with obituaries on OCIL.

The diversification was unnatural to start with, said critics. In his time, Prem Chand Oswal, a cotton loyalist himself, used to respond philosophically, arguing that so long as people were discerning of what was natural and what was man-made, and the business was not deceiving anyone, there was no cause for worry.

But Ajay Oswal had only hard options left. Painful as it was, he had to restructure the group. The uncompetitive polyester division was sold off to the Bansal group for Rs. 810 crore. Financial institutions got a chunk of preference shares. At the end of it all, OCIL came out lean, and still weak with the residual debt of Rs. 730 crore.

In spite of all that, young Oswal had defied the impending bankrupty, and managed to haul OCIL out of the red. "Ask Vishwanath to see me," Oswal told his secretary. Godbole knew what was coming—three way brainstorming session with Vishwanath Pradhan, the Group Marketing Head."

"Terrific results", began Pradhan, on entering the office "To be frank, I did not expect our cost-saving efforts to show results so soon."

Oswal could see that this top executive had been excited by OCIL's showing. But he was keen on knowing what his **best minds ought of OCIL's future.** "We all know that this recovery was due to three factors : the staff optimisation drive, coupled with aggressive technology implementation in the plants; the performance of our textiles division, which was mainly due to the 25 per cent slump in cotton prices; and the successful diversification of the filament division into lucrative thermoplastic and engineering grade nylon. My question is : where do we go from here?"

Cost-cutting couldn't be a perpetual strategy, nor could expect cotton prices to remain low forever. Pradhan spoke: "I think it's time we decided what OCIL is. 1 don't think we can continue being a textiles-nylon-steel player, and compete with the market leaders."

"Be direct", said Godbole.

"I'm talking about steel," said Pradhan, "We'll never be a steel major, so why are we making steel?"

"You must be joking", interjected Godbole. "Our debt is off the danger mark, and if only you'd read the balance sheet carefully, you'd have noticed that the steel division was our productivity topper. Besides, we'll never fetch a half-decent price for it".

Pradhan responded: "I still think we should stick with cloth fibre and cloth, that's it, but integrate the business either backward or forward. Backward routes are blocked by heavy competition in polyester—it's a scale-of-operations game. That leaves cotton farming, which could be complicated. But forward? Shouldn't we redouble our efforts in getting closer to the consumer? It's almost an axiom now. The link closest to the consumer sits on the fattest margins."

"What's wrong with OCIL as a consumer brand?" asked Oswal.

"Nothing, it's just that textiles aren't what people talk about any more, even if we have product distinction. They talk about Fashion Weeks and all that, and those are the actual brands young people have in mind. Value addition has moved forward, from cloth to the design-that's where we should be headed as well."

"We're a high-volume industrial group", said Godbole, "not a boutique for the urban elite."

"Well", retorted Pradhan, "I meant a mass-market initiative. The market's cotton versus synthetic balance affects our bottomline directly, and we have a big stake in tomorrow's clothing trends—we should be out there, shaping them. Cotton's a winner,, so long as consumers turn discerning and see clothing as a means of communication rather than a shield against the elements."

"We have no control over that", said Godbole.

Oswal looked unmoved by either of them. ''Now let me suggest something," said the CEO, "I understand you guys are keen on some radical strategies. But let's realise that we're barely out of the woods yet".

Godbole and Pradhan recognised the tone of voice the young chief had spoken with. Some soul-speak was on its way. "I think we should begin with the basics," Oswal began, leaving his seat and walking up the window overlooking the beautiful garden. "First of all, we should infuse some much-wanted capital into the textiles and filament divisions. Let's replace old looms. On the front-end, let's go after exports, big time. We mustn't miss the 2010 world trade opportunity, and the natural versus synthetic trends are clearer in the high-margin western markets. Cotton wins",.

"Great", muttered Pradhan, turning to Godbole. ''Now if only we had that much required capital to infuse."

"I think we have", smiled back Godbole. "We have been current for the last one-and-a-half years with all our financiers. I have it covered."

"Setting the priorities is the first task. I have just spelt out a survival strategy. Something we must do. But what we need next is a clincher. Something that will tell our shareholders that OCIL is on the path of growth. I Suggest we break up now and reassemble on Monday with an imaginative plan on everybody's mind."

Questions

(*i*) Examine the various emerging opportunities before OCIL.

(*ii*) Should OCIL go in for forward integration? Why or why not?

(*iii*) Should it dump its steel business? Why or why not?

(*iv*) Would you advise OCIL to define its strategic intent? Why or why not?

PART – IV

STRATEGY IMPLEMENTATION AND CONTROL

9 CHAPTER KEY ISSUES IN STRATEGY IMPLEMENTATION

CHAPTER OUTLINE

Excellent strategies by themselves cannot lead to action and to the attainment of strategic intent. Strategies have to be implemented effectively for the realisation of objectives. Firms which are able to implement strategies in an effective manner emerge winners against those which fail to execute their strategies effectively. Thus, strategy implementation is as important as strategy formulation. A study[1] revealed that 70 per cent of CEOs failed not because of bad strategy but because of bad execution.

There are, however, differences between strategy formulation and strategy implementation. While strategy formulation prescribes what actions are to be taken to reach the strategic intent, strategy implementation describes "who, where, when and how the actions" are to be taken. **Second,** strategy implementation is an ongoing process whereas strategy formulation is an intermittent exercise. **Third,** responsibility for strategy formulation rests mainly at top level management while managers at all levels are involved in strategy implementation. **Fourth,** strategy formulation is more a *thinking* (intellectually or analysis-oriented) exercise whereas strategy implementation is mainly a *doing* (action-oriented) job. **Fifth,** strategy formulation is primarily an entrepreneurial activity that involves strategic decisions. On the other hand, strategy

1. Ram, Charan and G. Colvin, "Why CEOs Fail", **Fortune Magazine,** June 21, 1999.

implementation is mainly an administrative task which involves operational decisions. **Lastly,** strategy formulation requires conceptual and analytical skills whereas strategy implementation needs administrative skills.

9.1. CONCEPT AND NATURE OF STRATEGY IMPLEMENTATION

According to William Glueck, "Strategy implementation is the assignment or reassignment of corporate and SBU leaders to match the strategy. The leaders will communicate the strategy to the employees. Implementation also involves the development of functional policies, the organisation structure and climate to support the strategy that helps to achieve the organisational objectives."

In the words of Harvey, "Implementation involves actually executing the strategic game plan. This includes setting policies, designing the organisation structure, and developing a corporate culture to enable the attainment of organisational objectives."

Thus, strategy implementation is the process of creating the necessary structure, systems, processes, resources, policies and plans, culture, etc and integrating them to provide a framework within which strategies can be successfully put into action.

Strategy implementation may be defined as the process of putting a chosen strategy into action so as to move towards the achievement of strategic objectives. The essential characteristics of strategy implementation are as follows:

1. **Action-Orientation:** Strategy implementation inevitably involves managerial actions. Managers use knowledge, skills and managerial techniques for putting strategies into action. The intellectual and theoretical content of strategy formulation is converted into practical or operational shape through strategy implementation.
2. **Integrated Process:** The different phases of strategy implementation are not stand-alone tasks. They are inter retated and form an interconnected network. Strategic plan is the hub of this network. Therefore, strategy implementation should be undertaken with a holistic view. Various phases of strategy implementation process move forward simultaneously on several fronts.
3. **Comprehensive:** Strategy implementation comprises practically every aspect of an organisation. It includes a wide range of functions and activities. All functional areas — finance, marketing, production/operations, human resources — are involved in the implementation of corporate strategies.
4. **Variety of Skills:** Due to its comprehensive nature, strategy implementation requires a wide variety of skills, knowledge, and attitudes. Ability to communicate and explain strategies, ability to allocate resources judiciously, ability to design effective structure and systems, ability to develop right functional strategies, right leadership styles, appropriate culture are some of these skills.
5. **Widespread Involvement:** Strategy implementation requires involvement of managers at all levels of authority. Middle managers must properly understand the strategies and they must get them executed through managers at the operating level.

Strategy implementation requires:

(*i*) An organisation structure that is necessary to put the strategy into action. The organisation must possess the skills needed to execute the strategy successfully.

(*ii*) Adequate resources to carry out the tasks involved in strategy implementation.

(*iii*) Administrative systems and processes.

(*iv*) Corporate culture supportive to strategy.

(*v*) Strategic leadership that can obtain commitment to strategy and its accomplishment.

9.2. INTERDEPENDENCE BETWEEN FORMULATION AND IMPLEMENTATION OF STRATEGY

Strategy formulation and implementation are closely interrelated. There are two types of linkages between these two phases of strategic management [Fig. 9.1].

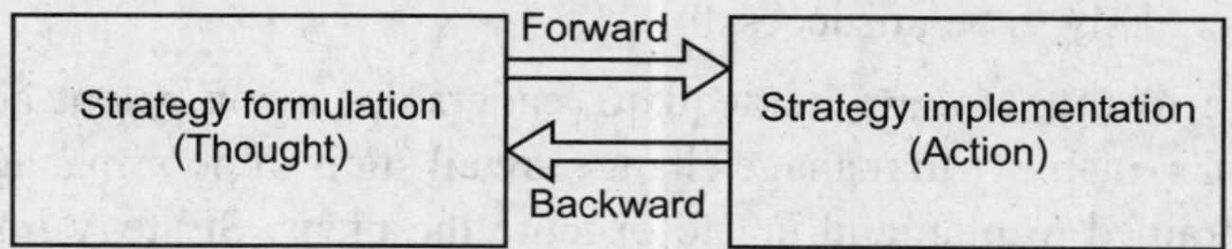

Fig. 9.1. Two-Way Linkage between Strategy Formulation and Implementation

Forward Linkage: Formulation of strategies indicates the changes required for their implementation. For example, new or modified strategies may require changes in organisational structure and/or leaderships style. Strategy formulation, therefore, provides the direction for strategy implementation. In this sense, formulation of strategies has forward linkage with their implementation.

Backward Linkage: Past strategic actions influence the choice of future strategies. An organisation tends to prefer those strategies which can be implemented with present structure, processes and resources. Moreover, the feedback from the implementation of strategies serves as a guide in strategy formulation.

The two-way linkage between strategy formulation and strategy implementation shows that these two stages in the process of strategic management operate in an iterative manner. The dynamic interconnection between them keeps on changing with the emerging conditions.

Sometimes, a new strategy may require refocus by the organisation in terms of products, markets, technology, etc. Strategy implementation requires a 'fit' between strategy, and structure, processes, systems, culture and functional strategies.

9.3. BARRIERS TO STRATEGY IMPLEMENTATION

Strategy implementation (doing) is much move difficult than strategy formulation (thinking). Most strategies fail not because they are not well formulated but because they are not effectively implemented. That is why it is said that "a reasonably good strategy implemented effectively is better than an excellent strategy implemented poorly".

The main factors causing unsuccessful implementation of strategy are as follows:

1. **Vague or Poor Strategy:** In some cases, the chosen strategy cannot be implemented because it is vague or defective. You might have heard the story of rats and the cat. In order to escape from a sudden attack by the cat, rats decided in their meeting to bell the cat. Whenever the cat comes, rats shall hear the bell's sound and escape before they are attacked. But they could not find answer to the question "who will bell the cat".

Therefore, the organisation's capability to implement must be considered while making strategic choice.

2. **Lack of Commitment:** When the employees are not fully committed to the chosen strategy, it cannot be implemented successfully. Lack of employee commitment may be caused by several factors. **First,** employees may feel that the new strategy is not practical and the earlier one was better. **Second,** strategists may have assumed that employees will willingly accept the new strategy. **Third,** most people focus on smooth and efficient conduct of current operations.
3. **Resistance to Change:** A new or modified strategy usually requires major changes in the organisation. In case the changes are resisted by the employees, implementation of strategies is likely to be unsuccessful.
4. **Ineffective Management:** Inadequate leadership, incompetent administration, ill-defined tasks, inability to manage change are all signs of poor management. Managers are often trained to plan and not to execute the plans. Strategy implementation is a time-consuming process and requires the involvement of all. Top managers often lack the patience and aptitude needed for execution of strategies. The pressure to show short-term results may hamper strategy implementation.
5. **Poor Communication:** Strategies need to be communicated and explained so that those who are to implement understand and accept them. Poor or inadequate information sharing, unclear responsibilities, poor comprehension of roles are the major hurdles in successful implementation.
6. **Power Politics:** Internal and external factors may work against the organisation's power structure. These factors or elements may have vested interests in making strategies unsuccessful.

In order to overcome barriers to strategy implementation and to make it effective, the following steps may be taken:

(*i*) Clear guidelines may be laid down for implementing strategies. These guidelines can specify the major issues/elements in the implementation process. Otherwise managers act as per their wishes and abilities and implementation becomes an unsystematic and uneven process.

(*ii*) Management must manage change effectively. Changes in culture, leadership style and employee behaviour are much moue difficult to carry out than structural changes. Optimum implementation requires effective management of the change process.

Three tourists are on a safari in Africa. While they are walking along in a nature reserve, a ferocious lion suddenly jumps out of the bush in front of them. It is hungry and sees an opportunity to make an easy kill. It roars loudly, showing its fangs. Its intentions are clear: it wants to feast on one of the unlucky tourists.

The first tourist, terrified and overcome by fear, turns white, stops dead in his tracks, and is unable to move. The second tourist, after a moment of reflection, starts to remove all his unnecessary equipment and clothing and begins to stretch out. Meanwhile, the third tourist stands there with his hands in his pockets, calmly assessing the situation. After a couple of moments pass, the first tourist looks at the second and yells hysterically, "You're crazy! There is absolutely nothing you can do to run away from this lion!" The second tourist turns to him and says, "You are right. But it's not the lion that I have to outrun. It's you that I must outrun." A few seconds later, the third tourist reaches into his pocket, pulls out a lighter, flicks it on, and scares away the lion.

What's the lesson of this story? The three tourists represent the different reactions companies tend to have. The first tourist, of course, is the one that is completely caught off guard and is unable to adjust, finding himself in the most vulnerable position. He has no plan of escape, just as many companies lack the flexibility to deal with unexpected market developments. The second tourist is a little better, but his strategy is that of mere survival. His approach is that as long as he is not the one caught by the lion, he will be okay. The way he feverishly throws off his clothes and equipment is symbolic of companies blindly slashing expenses just to stay afloat.

In contrast, the third tourist personifies the perspective of unconventional wisdom. When companies dare to continuously ask the 'what if?' questions, they no longer have to accept the undesirable consequences of a seemingly threatening situation. Instead, they can look for creative alternatives that may be very simple, even trivial, in hindsight. Just like the third tourist, who puts himself in full control of the confrontation with the lion by the simple, unexpected step of igniting a lighter. So ask yourself this: Do you have something in your back pocket? Put slightly differently, does your business have the flexibility to adapt to unforeseen developments, and to turn adversity into opportunity?

9.4. ACTIVATING STRATEGIES

Strategy formulation involves a small group of top executives while strategy implementation requires involvement of people at all levels in the organisation. Therefore, it is necessary to activate strategy so that it does not remain confined in the minds of strategy makers. Activation means the process of stimulation and operationalisation. It consists of the following steps:

1. **Institutionalisation of Strategy:** The institutionalisation of strategy involves its communication to and acceptance by those responsible for its implementation.

   (*a*) **Communication of strategy:** The chosen strategy needs to be communicated in such a manner that it appeals to and gets support from members of the organisation. A written document may be prepared. Such document may contain:

   (*i*) the context in which the strategy has been formulated, *i.e.,* the strategic intent and SWOT analysis;

   (*ii*) how the strategy will contribute to the realisation of objectives;

   (*iii*) changes required in the structure, processes, systems, culture, etc., of the organisation; and

   (*iv*) the expectations from executives at different levels in the organisation. Oral interactions among personel at all levels can be used to supplement the written communication.

   (*b*) **Acceptance of strategy:** Mere communication of the context and content of strategy is not enough. Willing acceptance of the strategy by organisational members is necessary. They must have commitment and positive attitudes towards the strategy.

Managers at lower levels often resist a strategy that requires a major break from the existing practices. For example, trade unions oppose restructuring, divestment and modernisation due to the fear of loss of jobs. Effective implementation of a strategy is impossible without its acceptance.

2. **Formulation of Action Plans:** Derivative or action plans are formulated for strategy implementation. These plans are derived from the strategic plan and specify the actions to be taken to operationalise the strategic plan. The action plans must specify the following:
   (*a*) The actions to be taken for implementation.
   (*b*) The manner in which action plans help in achieving the objectives.
   (*c*) The time points at which the actions are to be taken.
   (*d*) The people who will perform these activities.
   (*e*) The support needed to perform the activities.

The relationship between strategy and action plans is shown in Fig. 9.2.

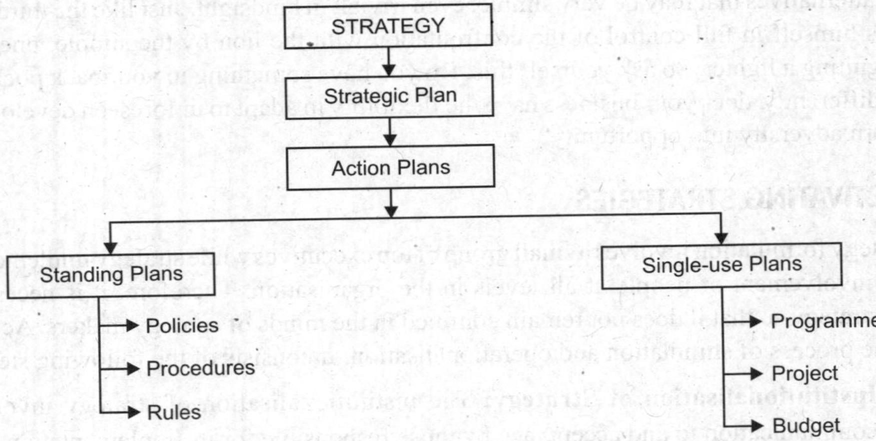

Fig. 9.2. Action Plans

Action plans are classified into two broad categories – standing and single use. Standing plans are relevant for a longtime period. These guide actions during recurring situations. On the other hand, single use or ad hoc plans are one shot actions and are time bound. For example, a budget is valid usually for one year. A brief description of action plans is given below:

(*i*) **Policies:** Policies are broad guidelines for decision-making. These are very useful in strategy implementation. "Employees will be promoted on the basis of their performance irrespective of age or seniority " is an example of policy.

(*ii*) **Procedure:** A procedure is a sequence of steps to be taken to implement a policy. To implement the 'performance based promotion policy', a procedure for assessing performance of every employee is needed. Procedures are established for all activities of a recurring nature such as procurement of raw materials, execution of customers' orders, taking disciplinary action, etc.

(*iii*) **Rules:** Rules are the prescribed mode of conduct in given situations. These clarify what is to be done or not done. 'No smoking in the factory' is an example of rules. Rules are needed in several situations to guide employee behaviour. A rule does not allow any discretion or deviation from the prescribed conduct.

(*iv*) **Programme:** A programme is a comprehensive plan that outlines

(*a*) what is to be done?

(*b*) when it is to be done?

(*c*) who is to do it?

(*d*) how it is to be done?

(*a*) how much money is to be spent?

Programme may relate to developing a new product, modernisnig the factory, training of employees, etc.

(*v*) **Project:** A project is a time-bound and cost-bound plan. It follows a predetermined pattern and is expected to be completed within a given time period and budget. Setting up a new plant is an example of a project.

(*vi*) **Budget:** A budget sets out the funds to be spent or revenue to be earned during a given time period, usually one year.

3. **Translation of General Objectives into Specific Objectives:** Organisational objectives established in the hierarchy of strategic intent are too general and broad to be meaningful for lower level executives. These need to be transformed into specific and time-bound targets for different units of the organisation. For example, growth as an organisational objective has to be specified into how much growth and in what time period. The specific objectives must be measurable and specify the time limits for achievement. The process of management by objectives (MBO) is very helpful in defining objectives for different units and individuals in the organisation. Under MBO key result areas of performance are identified, subordinates' objectives are set, resources are matched with the objectives, and performance is measured against the set objectives.

9.5. MANAGING CHANGE

Organisations function in a dynamic and turbulent external environment. They have to continually adjust themselves to environmental changes. They must be internally fit to respond quickly and effectively to changes in the external environment. Implementation of corporate and business level strategies often requires changes in the organisation. Effective management of organisational change is, therefore, a part of strategy implementation. Managers act as change-agents. They identify the need for change, prepare the organisation for implementing the change, take steps to overcome resistance to change and ensure that planned changes are taking place as desired.

Management of change involves innovation and learning. Innovation means new ways of doing things and learning refers to avoiding the repetition of mistakes. Change is a complex and broad area. Key issues relevant to strategy implementation are quite significant — the degree of change, the timing of change, and the areas of change.

(*a*) **Degree of change:** On the basis of degree, changes may be radical or incremental. Changes in top management team, and redesigning the organisation structure are examples of radical change. Improvement in quality, reformulation of sales policy, training programmes to improve employee attitudes are examples of incremental change.

(*b*) **Timing of change:** On the basis of timing, change can be either reactive or proactive. When change is carried out as a reaction to some crisis or environmental event it is reactive change. On the other hand, proactive change is planned in anticipation of some opportunity or threat. Setting up a joint venture and flattening the organisational hierarchy are examples of proactive change.

(*c*) **Areas of change:** Change may be made in products/services, jobs, organisation structure, leadership styles, technology and employee behaviour.

9.6. RESOURCE MOBILISATION AND ALLOCATION

In order to implement a strategy the organisation must have adequate financial and human resources. The procurement of these resources is known as **resource mobilisation.** The volume and type of resources to be mobilised depend on the nature and type of strategy. For example, expansion strategy requires more resources than stability strategy. An organisation can mobilise resources by owning or leasing. Less critical resources can be outsourced whereas critical resources are owned. The quality and utilisation of resources determine the success in strategy implementation.

The mobilised resources need to be allocated judiciously among different units and functions of the organisation. **Resource allocation** involves commitment and risk which depend on the time required to recover the cost of resources. Resource allocation is both a one-time and continuous process. Whenever a new project is undertaken, it requires allocation of resources. An ongoing enterprise requires continuous allocation of resources for its day-to-day activities. While allocating resources, both the needs of various units and expected returns should be considered.

9.6.1. Importance of Resource Allocation

An organisation's ability to acquire adequate resources to support strategic initiatives and steer them to various units has a major impact on strategy implementation. Shortage of resources, delays actions and slows down execution of strategy. At the same time, too much funding causes wastage and reduces financial performance. Therefore, resource allocation is a critical aspect in strategy implementation, particularly in case of major shifts in product/market scope. For example, when the strategy is expansion in one line, withdrawal from another and stability in the rest of the products, then greater resources will have to flow to the first and lesser to the second and the third. Similarly, if the strategy is to develop competitive edge through product development, greater resources will have to be committed to R&D.

Resource allocation is a powerful means of communicating the strategic priorities of the organisation as it gives the signals to all concerned. Resource allocation decisions should be taken judiciously because using a formula approach (*i.e.* allocating funds as a percentage of sales or profits) may be inappropriate and counter-productive. Care should be taken to see that the resources are not allocated or withdrawn because of easy availability or paucity. For example, cutting down R&D budget in view of sudden fall of profitability should be avoided as such expenditure may be most critical for developing future competitive advantage.

9.6.2. Approaches to Resource Allocation

1. **Top-down approach:** In this approach, resources are allocated through a process of segregation down to the operating levels. The Board of Directors, the Managing Director or members of top management typically decide the requirements of each sub-unit and distribute resources accordingly.
2. **Bottom-up approach:** In this approach, resources are distributed through a process of aggregation from the operating level. The operating levels work out the requirements of each sub-unit and the resources are allocated accordingly.
3. **Strategic budgeting:** This approach is a mix of the above two approaches, and involves an interactive form of decision-making between different levels of management.

9.6.3. Strategic Budgeting

Budget is the main instrument for resource allocation. Budgeting may be based on either of the three approaches. Under the top-down approach, the top management distributes resources as per the requirements of different units in the organisation. In the bottom-up approach resources are allocated after aggregating needs from the operating level upwards. The entrepreneurial mode of strategy implementation makes use of the top-down approach whereas the bottom-up approach is adopted in the participative mode of strategy implementation. Under the combined approach, there is iterative interaction among different levels of management. This approach to budgeting is called strategic budgeting.

Strategic budgeting is the process of determining the objectives, defining the performance and results expected from different units and allocating the resources needed to achieve the expected results. It is an iterative process that requires the involvement of people throughout the organisation. The strategic budgeting process consists of the following steps [Fig. 9.3].

1. **Preparation of Position Papers:** First of all, position papers on external environment, resources and constraints of the organisation, past performance, future targets, etc are prepared. These papers are presented to the top management.

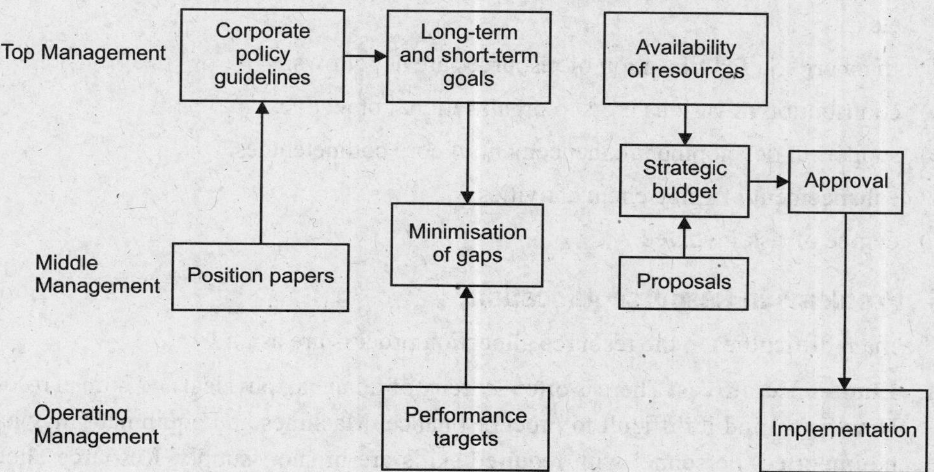

Fig. 9.3. Strategic Budgeting Process

2. **Formulation of Corporate Policy:** On the basis of position papers, top management formulates corporate policy guidelines.
3. **Deciding Goals:** Top management also lays down long-term and short-term goals.
4. **Fixing Performance Targets:** Operating managers prepare operational plans and performance targets on the basis of long-term and short-term goals set by the top management.
5. **Preparation of Strategic Budget:** The resource availability and proposals are reconciled in the form of strategic budget.
6. **Approval and Sanction:** The top management approves the strategic budget and sanctions it for implementation.

In the process of resource allocation through budgeting, it is necessary to align resources to strategy. A strategy lays down priorities which guide the managers in resource allocation among competing claims. Resources are often scarce and need to be invested in the most deserving projects.

9.6.4. Factors Influencing Resource Allocation

1. **Organisational Objectives:** The objectives at corporate, SBU and operational levels exercise maximum influence on the pattern of resource allocation.
2. **Strategy Makers' Preferences:** The preferences of the most influential strategists determine how corporate resources are allocated. Managers at SBU and functional levels often present their demands in accordance with these preferences.
3. **Power Politics:** Employees usually judge the importance and power of SBUs and departments on the basis of resources they get. More powerful or influential heads are often able to get more resources for their units.
4. **External Factors:** Government, shareholders, lenders and other stakeholders influence resource allocation. For example, government regulations may require additional investment in labour welfare and social security, pollution control, energy conservation, etc.

The main criteria for allocation of resources are as follows:

(*a*) contribution of various units to organisational objectives.

(*b*) support to development/enhancement of core competencies.

(*c*) enhancement of value chain activities.

(*d*) degree of risk involved.

9.6.5. Problems in Resource Allocation

The main difficulties in the resource allocation process are as under:

1. **Limited Resources:** There is often scarcity of financial, physical and human resources. New firms find it difficult to procure finance. Machines and equipment may have to be imported. Personnel with required skills are in short supply. Resource allocation becomes difficult when an organisation has limited resources.

2. **Overstated Demands:** Every SBU, division or department tries to get maximum possible resources. It overstates its needs in the hope that its claim will not be met in full. Amount of resources obtained is considered as a symbol of power.
3. **Past Allocation:** Different units in the organisation usually quote previous year's allocation as the basis of their current claims. They often resist cut in resource allocation. Units with good performance in the past claim a major share of available resources.
4. **Imitating Competitors:** While allocating resources, a company may imitate its competitors. It may follow a different strategy but may fail to change its resource allocation.

9.7. PROCEDURAL IMPLEMENTATION

Procedural implementation of strategy refers to completing all the legal and administrative formalities prescribed by the Central and State governments. These regulations and guidelines may differ from industry to industry. Some major regulations for business firms in India are given below:

1. **Formation of a Company:** The Companies Act, 2013 regulates the formation of companies. Registration or incorporation of a company involves formalities that result in the issue of a certificate of incorporation. A public company is also required to obtain a certificate of commencement of business. Integration, diversification, joint venture, takeover and other corporate strategies may involve information of a separate company. The prescribed formalities have to be completed for this purpose.
2. **Licensing Requirements:** An industrial licence may be needed for some industries such as tabucco, liquor, etc., atomic energy, defence equipment, etc. In order to get a licence a company has to apply in the prescribed form to the Secretariat for Industrial Approval (SIA). Once a project is approved, a letter of intent is issued. After fulfilling the prescribed requirements an industrial licence can be obtained.
3. **Foreign Collaboration Procedure:** Expansion/diversification in high-technology industries and international joint ventures may require foreign collaboration and investment. Similarly, an Indian company may need to import foreign technology or technical know-how. Approval of the Foreign Investment Promotion Board (FIPB), Project Approval Board or the Reserve Bank of India may be required in case of foreign equity and technical collaborations.
4. **FEMA Requirements:** Under the Foreign Exchange Management Act (FEMA), permission of the Reserve Bank of India is needed by foreign companies and foreign shareholding in excess of the prescribed limits.
5. **Import-Export Formalities:** In case of imports of raw materials and capital goods, permission under the Foreign Trade Development and Regulation Act (FTDRA) 1992 is needed in the prescribed cases. Similar permission may be necessary for certain exports.
6. **Securities and Exchange Board of India (SEBI) Requirements:** Companies wanting to raise capital through public issue of securities are required to get their prospectuses vetted by SEBI. For raising funds abroad through Global Depository Receipts (GDRs) and American Depository Receipts (ADRs), RBI's approval may be needed.

7. **Trade Marks and Patents Requirements:** Companies wanting to protect their intellectual property in the form of trade marks, patents and copyrights are required to follow the formalities prescribed under the Trade Marks Act, the Patents Act and the Copyrights Act.
8. **Pollution Control Regulations:** There are several Central and State laws for the prevention and control of pollution. A 'no objection' certificate from the Pollution Control Board must be obtained in case of pollution industries.
9. **Labour Legislation Requirements:** Firms are required to observe the provisions of various labour laws concerning wages, bonus, working conditions, social security, trade unions, industrial relations, etc, etc.
10. **Consumer Protection Requirements:** Laws which are designed to protect the interests of consumers (e.g., the Consumer Protections Act 1986) are another set of formalities.
11. **Incentives and Benefits:** Certain incentives and benefits are offered by the Central and State governments to specified industries. Loans at concessional rate of interest, tax holidays and tax concessions, subsidies, etc are examples of these incentives and benefits. Business firms which want to avail of these incentives and benefits are required to fulfil the prescribed formalities.

The procedures and formalities given above have a significant implication for strategy formulation and implementation. Preparation of vision and mission statements, objective setting, strategic choice, and implementation of strategies must take these into account.

Regulations increase the time and costs involved in strategy implementation. Since 1991 Government of India has drastically reduced and simplified the regulatory framework for business and industry. Still India ranks low when it comes to starting and operating business. All organisations must be aware of the regulatory framework that affects formulation and implementation of strategies. Different companies react to regulations in different ways. Some of them conform (submission) to the prescribed regulations. Others criticise, lobby and pressurise against (confrontation) regulations. Still others explore opportunities in the regulatory framework. Large business houses maintain a close liaison with government agencies (collaboration) to get quick approvals, sanctions, permissions and statutory benefits.

Regulatory framework keeps on changing from time to time. Therefore, strategists must not only follow the existing framework but anticipate changes in it and be prepared to face these changes.

9.8. PROJECT IMPLEMENTATION

A project has been defined as "a one-shot, time-bound, goal-oriented major undertaking, requiring the commitment of varied skills and resources".[2] A project is characterised by the following features:

(*i*) Each project is unique and non-repetitive.

(*ii*) Every project is time-bound.

(*iii*) It involves investment of funds and other resources.

(*iv*) It has a specific objective.

2. Project Management Institute, **Project Management Journal,** USA, August 1984.

(v) It consists of several interdependent tasks.

(vi) The completion of a project at the right time and the right cost is necessary or critical for the realisation of organisational objectives.

The nature, number and size of projects depends upon the corporate strategy. For example, diversification may lead to a large scale project involving investment of thousands of crore of rupees while stability may require modernisation of plant with much lesser investment.

The application of knowledge, skills and techniques to the formulation, implementation and evaluation of projects is known as **project management.** It is the key mode of strategy implementation. Successful implementation of strategy requires that the organisation undertakes the right projects and executes them in line with the underlying strategy. This is possible when project management is aligned with corporate strategy.

Fig. 9.4 shows the process of strategy implementation through project management. Strategy provides the basis for setting objectives/targets of projects. Management of projects leads to certain outcomes or results which in turn lead to execution of strategy. Effectiveness of strategy implementation depends largely on success in project management. In a project-oriented organisation there is close linkage between project management process and strategy implementation.

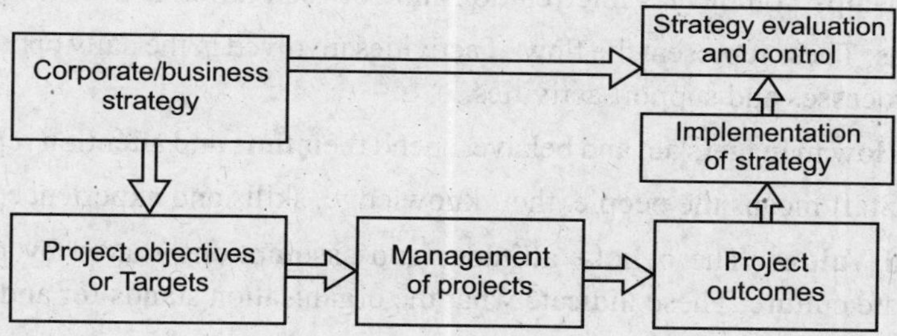

Fig. 9.4. Strategy Implementation Through Project Management

The project management process consists of the following steps:

1. **Conception Phase:** An organisation may undertake a new project to implement its growth strategy. Several competing projects may emerge at this stage. These projects are arranged in order of priority on the basis of a set criteria.

2. **Definition Phase:** A specific project is selected from the various projects arranged in order of priority. Detailed feasibility reports are prepared before making the final choice.

3. **Planning Phase:** The plan document of a project identifies activities, their sequence, cost estimates, time schedules, resources required and degree of risk involved. A formal plan document is useful in obtaining funds from lenders and also in the execution of the project. Necessary clearances are obtained from various authorities, a project team is constituted and procedures are drawn for project implementation.

4. **Execution Phase:** This is the action phase of project management process. During this phase various activities such as acquisition of land, construction of factory premises, procurement and installation of plant and machinery etc., are undertaken. In other words, the project plan is put into action.

5. **Controlling Phase:** This phase involves monitoring and regulating the cost, time, resource use and risk in the execution of the project.
6. **Clean-up Phase:** Once the project is completed, the project team and infrastructure are disbanded. The project is handed over to those who will run or operate it. This is thus a closing phase.

9.9. MCKINSEY'S 7-S FRAMEWORK

McKinsey's 7-S framework highlights the interconnection between seven factors and their role in successful implementation of strategy. When the seven variables are properly aligned, strategy implementation becomes easy. Therefore, strategists must achieve a good fit among the seven variables by making appropriate alterations from time to time.

The 7-S framework developed by McKinsey & Co., world's biggest consultancy firm, consists of the following seven variables:

1. **Strategy:** Strategy means a set of decisions and actions aimed at gaining a sustainable competitive advantage. It is the broad framework to reach organisational goals.
2. **Structure:** The organisation structure is a network of authority responsibility relationships. It indicates interrelationship between different units of the organisation.
3. **Systems:** These represent the flow of activities involved in the daily operations, including core processes and support activities.
4. **Style:** How managers act and behave, spend their time and attention represent the style.
5. **Staff:** Staff means the people, their knowledge, skills and experience.
6. **Shared Values:** The beliefs, attitudes and assumptions shared by people represent corporate culture. These indicate what the organisation stands for and believes in.
7. **Skills:** These refer to the organisation's capabilities and competencies.

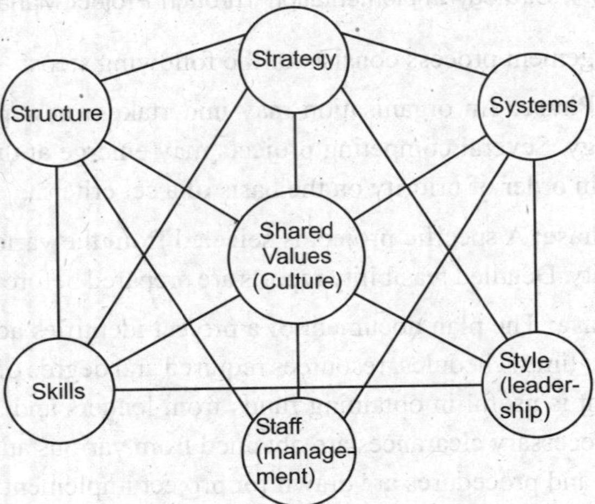

Fig. 9.5. The 7-S Framework.

The hard elements–strategy, structure and systems– are visible and management has some control on them. But the soft elements–shared values, style and skills– are difficult to describe and management has little control on them. The successful implementation of strategy requires proper alignment of all the seven elements.

SUMMARY

Nature: (*i*) action-oriented (*ii*) integrated (*iii*) comprehensive (*iv*) variety of skills required (*v*) involves people at all levels.

Interdependence Between Formulation and Implementation: (*i*) backward linkage (*ii*) forward linkage.

Barriers: (*i*) vague strategy (*ii*) lack of commitment (*iii*) resistance to change (*iv*) ineffective management (*v*) poor communication (*vi*) power politics

Activating Strategies: (*i*) Institutionalisation of strategy, communication and acceptance of strategy (*ii*) Formulation of action plans – (*a*) policies, procedures, rules (*b*) programme, project and budget (*iii*) Translation of general objectives into specific objectives.

Managing Change: (*i*) degree of change, (*ii*) timing of change (*iii*) areas of change.

Resource Mobilisation: Procurement of necessary resources.

Resource Allocation: Distribution of available resources among different projects. It involves commitment and risk.

(1) Strategic budgeting – (*a*) preparing position papers (*b*) formulating corporate policy (*c*) deciding goals (*d*) preparing strategic budget (*e*) approval and sanction.

(2) Factors influencing resource allocation – (*a*) organisational goals (*b*) strategists' preferences (*c*) power politics (*d*) external factors.

(3) Problems in resource allocation – (*a*) limited resources (*b*) overstated demands (*c*) past allocation (*d*) imitating competitors

Procedural Implementation: (*i*) company formation (*ii*) licensing (*iii*) foreign collaboration (*iv*) FEMA (*v*) imports exports (*vi*) SEBI (*vii*) Trade Marks and patents (*viii*) pollution control (*ix*) labour legislation (*x*) consumer protection (*xi*) incentives and subsidies.

Project Implementation: (*i*) conception (*ii*) definition (*iii*) planning (*iv*) execution (*v*) controlling (*vi*) clean-up phase.

TEST QUESTIONS

1. Explain the concept and nature of strategy implementation.
2. Discuss the differences between strategy formulation and strategy implementation.
3. Discuss the nature of the interrelationship that exists between the formulation and implementation of strategies. Provide examples of such an interrelationship.
4. Discuss *three* most important elements of implementation of strategy. What type of organisation structure would you recommend for a firm which is in (*i*) Pharmaceuticals business, (*ii*) Services sector?

5. Explain backward and forward linkages between strategy formulation and strategy implementation, giving appropriate examples.
6. Discuss the barriers to effective implementation of strategy. How will you overcome these barriers?
7. What is meant by 'activating strategies'? Explain the steps involved in it.
8. Distinguish between resource mobilisation and resource allocation. Describe the factors influencing resource allocation.
9. What is strategic budgeting? Explain the steps in the strategic budgeting process.
10. Explain the problems that arise in resource allocation.
11. What is procedural implementation? Discuss the major procedural formalities faced by business firms in India.
12. What is a project? Explain the role of project management in strategy implementation.
13. Explain the steps involved in the management of a project.
14. Write notes on:
    (*a*) Management of change.
    (*b*) Translation of general objectives into specific objectives.
15. Bring out, with the help of examples, the nature of interrelationship between the formulation and implementation of strategies.
16. "Decisions bearing an allocation of resources have vital significance in the process of strategy implementation." Elucidate.
17. "If top management devotes more effort to assessing the strategic feasibility of projects in its allocated role than it does to the task of multiplying resources effectiveness, its value added will be modest indeed." Discuss with a real life example.
18. What is strategy drift? Explain methods used to diagnose and fight it.
19. Describe various types of offensive and defensive tactics with suitable examples.
20. "Excellent execution of a strategy is the best test of managerial excellence." Discuss.
21. Critically examine any two offensive strategies to secure competitive advantage.
22. How can a company use defensive strategies to protect its market position?
23. "When to make a strategic move is often as crucial as what move to make." Discuss

CASE STUDY

Elegance Products Incorporation (EPI) is a medium-sized American company promoted and headed by three sisters— Bobby, Monica and Sweety— who are the daughters of a successful pharmaceutical company owner of Indian origin, Pradeep Sethi. Through continuous efforts since 1988 when he came to the United States in search of a good job, Pradeep has made remarkable progress in his business in California. EPI also looked to be a promising venture by three sisters in its initial operations. Within two years of founding in 1995, EPI was able to register $150 million sales mark on the strength of its **original product** alone. With the introduction of a **new range** of EPI products, the Sethi sisters predicted they would **easily**

triple that figure in 1999. Instead, they have come to the verge of bankruptcy. What went wrong? Industry analysts say that the Sethis' catastrophic failure was due to a fatal lack of strategic planning by these budding entrepreneurs.

The story had started happily enough. Pradeep Sethi bought United States **marketing rights** to an Israeli hair-removal product called 'E-lady'. E-lady works by somewhat **comfortably** pulling hairs out by their roots; this offers women who shave their legs an opportunity to **throw away** their razors – and to stop nicking themselves. Pradeep gave the E-lady marketing rights and initial investment money to his three daughters. The sisters established **Elegance Products Inc.** in California with Bobby as President, Monica as head of East Coast Operations, and Sweety as head of advertising. In July 1995, the Sethis launched 'E-lady' in some of the **country's most prestigious department stores.** Things went better than they had imagined. Within **five months,** E-lady was the **top-selling** department store item of any kind.

However, Beauty Products Inc. **(BPI),** a leading manufacturer of shaving products which had originally rejected the offer to purchase the rights to 'E-lady', soon posed a serious **challenge** to the Sethis. It introduced a product called **'Silky'** that would do the same job as 'E-lady' but would be **available in more stores** and **for less money.** To meet this challenge, the Sethis came up with a plan: They would market a **deluxe edition** of the original E-lady, packaged with **luxury accessories** to be sold only at very high prices in department stores located in posh areas. Then in about six months, they would start selling the original E-lady model, with **no deluxe** packaging or accessories, at sharply discounted prices in same mass-market stores that Beauty had targeted. This way, they could maintain the **high profit margins** they got from posh areas segment while competing in the mass market with Beauty Products Inc.

Meanwhile, the Sethis decided it was time to start capitalising on the now familiar EPI name. They introduced **E-Sauna,** a facial sauna, and **E-Ped,** a foot whirlpool massager, as well as a **brush with retractable** bristles, a tooth whitener, and about 25 additional beauty-aid products, all to be sold in department stores located in posh areas.

When the Sethis had first announced plans to move the original E-lady to the mass market, **many of the dealers** in the **posh area stores** had been **angry.** They worried that the strategy would adversely **affect E-lady's prestige** in the well-to-do class of customers and thus reduce the sales in their stores. Despite these fears, EPI products **sales** at these department stores were very **high** during the 1997 Christmas season – traditionally the peak sales time for personal grooming appliances, and these dealers were no longer unhappy.

During 1998, E-lady seemed to be selling faster and smoother for the good of Sethis than they or the industry analysts had ever anticipated. That year, EPI products recorded a sale of $ 250 million. However, with the onset of 1999, the **Sethis' glittering** new company began **to fall apart** quickly. Profits from EPI product sales could not keep pace with the **pace** at which the **Sethis were investing** money to keep **their company growing.** By the end of 1999, the Sethi sisters decided to close their company.

Industry analysts, who had once been impressed with the Sethis' success, began to conduct a **critical analysis** of EPI products. It was found that the sales of second-generation products such as **E-Sauna** had declined sharply after the initial rush. Analysts said that the Sethis should have expected this since none of these products was as original a concept – or considered by many women to be as necessary – as the E-lady. EPI **was too new** a company to expect that the 'E' prefix alone could sell just any product, they said. Analysts also called the Sethis' **advertising strategy unsophisticated** and not worthy of a company of EPI's size. Instead of advertising all the EPI products together, some analysts said the **products should have been advertised separately,** and the **benefits of each** product for potential customers should have been emphasized.

Also, the Sethis' original strategy to outwit Beauty, which had been hailed by many as brilliant as long as it succeeded, was a drastic mistake, analysts added. Customers were bound to understand the simple fact that **they could buy essentially the same product sold in posh area** department stores for **less money in mass-market** stores. All this decreased the EPI profit margins and lowered its image.

By the end of 1999, the Sethis had employed some **professional managers** and consulted strategy experts to try to pull EPI out of its **sorry state** of affairs, but many analysts predicted it was **too late to turn** the company around. Hence, the decision **to close the** company.

Questions

1. In considering the general environment within which EPI did business, how do you think social values affected E-lady sales, and how should these have been taken into account in planning future sales strategies?
2. How significant is the role of competitive forces in determining the fate of EPI? What major competitive advantage did BIP's 'Silky' have over E-lady? What major advantage did E-lady have?
3. Write a mission statement for EPI products which you think should have helped the Sethi sisters to clarify their strategy and avoid closure of their company. Give reasons in support of your viewpoint.
4. As a SBU of EPI, E-lady should be characterised as which of the following – a star? a cash cow? Give reasons.
5. Do you think the Sethis engaged in sound strategic planning? In sound tactical planning? Why or why not?

Chapter

STRUCTURAL ISSUES IN IMPLEMENTATION

CHAPTER OUTLINE

Structural implementation involves two major issues—design of a suitable organisational structure, and development of appropriate organisational systems.

10.1. CONCEPT OF ORGANISATIONAL STRUCTURE

An organisation structure is the framework of authority-responsibility relationships among different job positions. It is a formal arrangement of tasks and sub-tasks which are needed to execute strategies. An organisation structure has two broad dimensions:

1. **Vertical Dimension:** The vertical dimension is characterised by:
   (*a*) specialisation of tasks
   (*b*) hierarchy of authority or chain of command consisting of several levels
   (*c*) formal reporting relationships
   (*d*) grouping of individuals into departments
   (*e*) upward and downward communication through the scalar chain
   (*f*) rules and regulations
   (*g*) centralised decision-making
   (*h*) focus on efficiency

The vertical structure is designed to enable superiors to exercise control over the work of subordinates. Vertical structures are known as **tall structures.** Such structures are appropriate for companies which produce standardised products/services on a large scale with the help of mass production systems and well-established technologies.

2. **Horizontal Dimension:** The horizontal dimension is characterised by:
   (*a*) sharing of tasks
   (*b*) sharing of information
   (*c*) decentralised decision-making
   (*d*) focus on learning
   (*e*) few rules and regulations

The horizontal dimension is designed to ensure cooperation and coordination among employees working at the same level of authority.

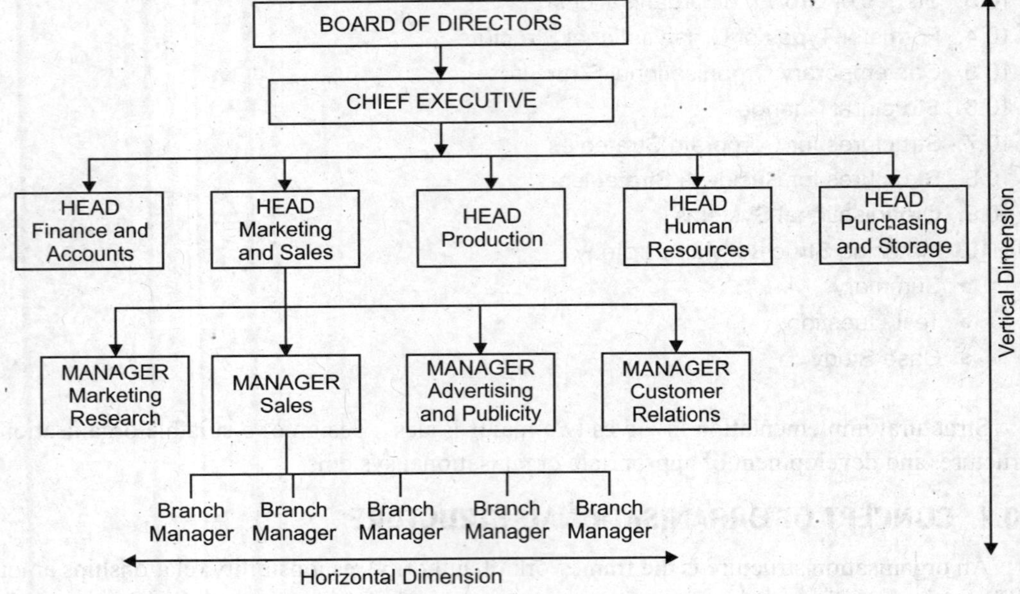

Fig. 10.1. Vertical and Horizontal Structures

Horizontal structures are also known as **flat structures.** Such structures are more appropriate for companies making differentiated products/services in batches and with advanced technologies for niche markets. Medium-sized manufacturing and service enterprises and non-profit organisations which offer specific social services are examples of these organisations.

The vertical and horizontal dimensions exist side by side despite their contradictory features.

PepsiCo India has made sweeping changes in its senior leadership structure, part of the beverage and snacks maker's push to become more aggressive in the market as it battles Coca-Cola in soft drinks and ITC and Parle in foods. The new hierarchy clubs beverages and foods into an integrated entity, with functions of marketing, operations, HR, finance, legal, corporate affairs and R&D being brought together under common heads, Three chief operating officers heading foods, company-owned bottling and franchisee bottling, respectively, will report directly to D. Shivkumar, the CEO.

The structure makes the organisation more reponsive, quicker on decision-making and more competitive.

Internally, the structure is changing from a business unit based organisation to an integrated 'power of one' function—a strategy led by global chairman Indra Nooyi. Key global markets such as Russia and China follow this model.

Besides taking on competition, the company is battling growth slowing across foods and beverages, fluctuating weather conditions that make market behaviour unpredictable and consumers turning to healthier foods and drinks. The parent firm announced last year that it would invest ₹33,000 crore in India by 2020 as it looks to the country to pick up the slack as sales slow elsewhere.

10.2. INTERRELATIONSHIP BETWEEN STRATEGY AND STRUCTURE

There is close interdependence between strategy and structure. This interdependence is both forward are backward (Fig. 10.2)

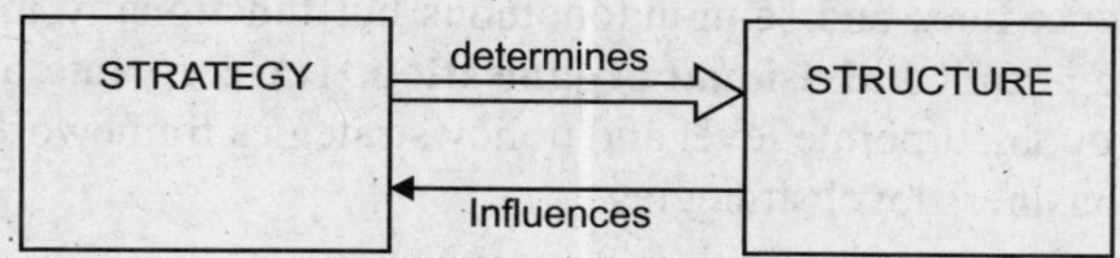

Fig. 10.2. Strategy-Structure Interrelationship

1. **Forward Relationship:** Effective implementation of strategy requires a suitable organisational structure. According to Chandler[1] "Structure follows strategy." Growth strategy requires a different structure then stability strategy. Organisational structure is not an end itself but a means for strategy implementation. Therefore, an organisation's structure should be such that it enables effective implementation of the chosen strategy. When there is a significant change in strategy the structure has to be redesigned. Changes in corporate strategy create new administrative problems which cannot be handled without a new organisational structure.
2. **Backward Relationship:** Structure also influences strategy. Structural considerations affect the implementation of present strategy and the formulation of future strategies.

Thus, there is a two-way reciprocal relationship between strategy and structure. Structural implementation is in fact an ongoing process of matching the structure of an organisation with its strategy. Whenever there is a mismatch between the two, changes in structure have to be made. Otherwise strategy implementation becomes difficult and performance suffers. In the words of Canon, "The experience of McKinsey supports the view that neither strategy nor structure can be determined independently of the other. If structure cannot stand alone without strategy, it is equally true that strategy can rarely succeed without an appropriate structure"[2].

1. Alfred D. Chandler, **Strategy and Structure,** MIT Press, Cambridge MA, 1962
2. Warren M. Canon, "Organisation Design: Shaping Structure to Strategy," **McKinsey Quartely**, Summer, 1972.

People working in an organisation must know how their actions interrelate to support and execute the strategy. Without a structural framework, confusion, chaos and duplication of efforts arise at various levels.

10.3. STAGES OF GROWTH OF ORGANISATIONS

Like products, organisations have a life cycle. The life cycle of an organisation consists of the following stages:

Stage I: In the first stage an organisation is a small-scale enterprise. It is managed and controlled by the owner. Its objectives, operations and management are simple. It usually adopts expansion strategy. It is characterised by centralised decision making and single product line with focus on production. This type of organisation is called **entrepreneurial organisation.**

Stage II: The organisation grows in size and the scope of its operations widens. It adopts functional specialisation with finance, marketing, operations and personnel departments. The chief executive takes critical decisions and departmental heads are responsible for managing various departments. The focus is on efficiency through coordination between different functional areas. This type of structure is known as **functional organisation.**

Stage III: During this stage an organisation is characterised by large size widely scatted operations, multiproduct lines and semi-autonomous but functionally independent divisions. This type of structure is called **divisional organisation**. The corporate headquarters provides strategy direction through corporate level and policy strategies framework. Different divisions formulate their own business level strategies.

The stages given above overlap. Moreover all organisations may not pass through every stage of growth. But several companies in India (*e.g.* Reliance Industries, Aditya Birla Group, Infosys Technologies) started with an entrepreneurial structure. Over the years they expanded and adopted functional structure. After diversifying into related and unrelated areas they became conglomerates with matrix structure.

In order to decide whether the existing structure does or does not require change, two tests can be applied. **First,** proper implementation of strategy requires that certain functions are performed. Therefore, the structure must ensure that these functions are performed without duplication of activities. **Second,** a function's contribution to strategy should be basis for its placement in the organisational hierarchy . Critical key functions should be centralised while the support functions should be subordinated or decentralised.

10.3.1. Cannon's Stages of Development Model

Cannon's model consists of five stages of development.

Stage I: *The Entrepreneurial Stage*: This stage represents the small business, generally operated by the owner-manager. The market of the firm is limited to a specific geographical area.

Stage II: When the company grows in its size, the owner-manager cannot perform increased volume of managerial functions. Therefore, the owner-manager hires an accountant, sales representatives and functional managers. A functional form of organisation structure will be adopted. But the problems of functional structure will come to the surface with the further increase in the company's operations. These problems include: delay in getting approval for new products and other innovations. These problems may push the company to the next stage.

Table 10.1: Summary of Cannon's Stages of Development

Characteristics	Entrepreneurial I	Functional Development II	Decentralisation III	Staff Proliferation IV	Recentralisation V
Strategic decisions	Made mostly by the top person	Made more and more by other managers	May have loss of control	Corporate staff assists in decisions	Corporate management makes decisions
Organisation structure	Informal Operations	Specialisation based on functions	To cope with problems of functionalisation	Corporate staff assists chief executive	Similar to Stage 1
Communication and climate	From leader down. Informal communication	Internal communication is important, is difficult	By industry or product division	Conservatism may result in slower communications	
Control system	Minimal need for coordination and control	Concerned with everyday situations	Problems with control	May be problems between line and staff	Tightening of control
1. J. Thomas Cannon, *Op.cit.*, pp. 525-528., p. 302.					

Stage III: Organisation will be restructured either based on product or geographic or customers. Control may become difficult when each division develops its own view of product quality, pricing, etc.

Stage IV: To regain control of the organisation, management may employ additional human resources to assist top management.

Stage V: This stage involves increasing involvement of top management in strategic decision-making. This move to recentralisation may be a part of a cutback and turnaround strategy.

10.3.2. Thain's Stages of Corporate Development Model

Thain proposed a different conceptualisation of organisational stages of development. Table 10.2 presents Thain's model. It identifies three stages of organisational development with different factors relevant to top management in each stage.

Stage I: Stage of Thain is similar to Cannon's entrepreneurial stage. The manager maintains absolute ownership and control. The company's strengths, weaknesses, and performance are shaped by the owner-manager's personality, ability and style. The increase in the size of the business forces the owner to appoint managers for different functions.

Stage II: In this stage, there is the existence of a management team built around one business and selling primarily to one market. The company in this stage specialises in one product and concentrates in one area. These characteristics may threaten the survival of the firm consequent upon changes in consumer preferences or ability to buy. Companies try to overcome this danger by diversifying the activities.

Stages III: The firms in this stage are conglomerately diversified with multiple operating units controlled by corporate office. Companies in this stage can often operate independently of outside resources. But the organisation adopts a bureaucratic structure to manage and control a large size and diversified business.

Table 10.2: Thain's Key Management Factors by Stage of Development

Key Factor	Stage I	Stage II	Stage III
1. Size up major problems.	Survival and growth, dealing with short-term operating problems.	Growth, rationalization, and expansion of resources, providing for adequate attention to product problems.	Trusteeship in management and investment and control of large increasing and diversified resources, Also important to diagnose and act on problems at division level.
2. Objectives.	Personal and subjective.	Profits and meeting functionally oriented budgets and performance targets.	ROI, profits, earnings per share.
3. Strategy.	Implicit and personal; exploitation of immediate opportunities seen by owner-manager.	Functionally oriented moves restricted to "one-product" scope; exploitation of one basic product or service field.	Growth and product diversification; exploitation of general business opportunities.
4. Organization, major characteristic of structure.	One-unit "one-man show".	One-unit functionally specialized group.	Multi-unit general staff office and decentralized operating divisions.
5. (*a*) Measurement and control.	Personal, subjective, control based on simple accounting system and daily communication and observation.	Control grows beyond one man, assessment of functional operations necessary, structured control systems evolve	Complex formal system geared to comparative assessment of performance measures, indicating problems and opportunities and assessing management ability of division managers.
(*b*) Key performance indicators.	Personal criteria, relationships with owner, operating efficiency, ability to solve operating problems.	Functional and internal criteria such as sales, performance compared to budget, size of empire, status in group, personal relationships, etc.	More impersonal application of comparisons such as profits, ROI, P/E ratio, sales, market share, productivity, product leadership, personnel development, employee attitudes, public responsibility.

6. Reward punishment system	Informal, personal, subjective; used to maintain control and divide small pool of resources to provide personal incentives for key performers	More structured usually based to a greater extent on agreed policies as opposed to personal opinion and relationships.	Allotment by "due process" of a wide variety of different rewards and punishments on a formal and systematic basis. Company-wide policies usually apply to many different classes of managers and workers with few major exceptions for individual cases.

Source: D.H. Thain, "Stages of Corporate Development," **Business Quarterly,** Winter 1969.

10.4. FORMS OR TYPES OF ORGANISATIONAL STRUCTURE

The main types of organisational structures are given below:

1. **Entrepreneurial Structure:** The entrepreneurial structure is the most elementary and the simplest type of organisational structure. This structure is suitable for an organisation that is owned and managed by one person. Such an organisation is typically a single product/service firm that serves a local market. The owner-manager makes both strategic and operational decisions.

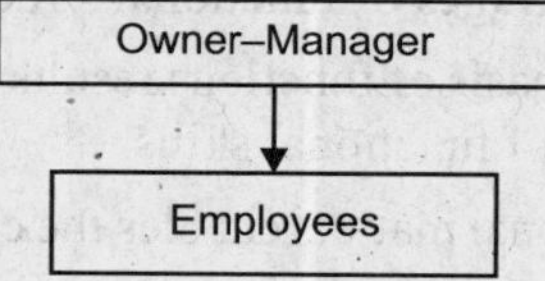

Fig. 10.3. The Entrepreneurial Structure

The entrepreneurial structure offers the following **advantages:**

(*i*) It is very simple.

(*ii*) Decision-making is quick due to centralisation of power in one person

(*iii*) It can make timely response to environmental changes, *i.e.*, it is flexible.

(*iv*) It ensures centralised control over the entire business

The entrepreneurial structure suffers from the following **disadvantages:**

(*i*) The owner-manager is overburdened.

(*ii*) Preoccupation with operational matters may lead to overlooking strategic issues.

(*iii*) There is very little scope for growth of business.

(*iv*) Employees feel insecure.

2. **Functional Structure:** The expansion into the same line of business necessitates specialisation of tasks and delegation of authority to heads of different functional areas. Grouping of activities on the basis of functions performed for strategy implementation creates functional structure. For example, production, marketing, finance and personnel are the basic functions in a manufacturing organisation. A basic function may be further

divided into sub-functions. For example, marketing department may be sub-divided into marketing research, advertising and publicity, sales, and customer service. The process of functional differentiation may continue through successive levels in the hierarchy. In addition to the basic functions, secondary functions such as public relations, legal, etc. are provided.

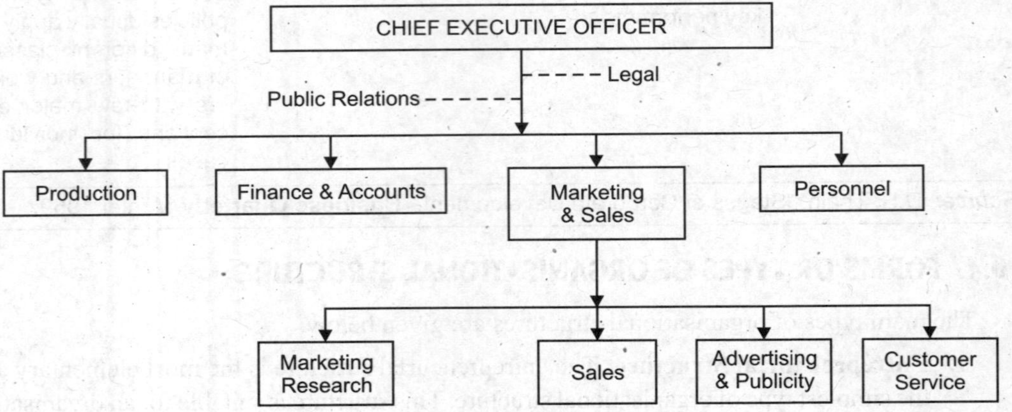

Fig. 10.4. The Functional Structure

Functional structure is suitable for medium-sized firms having limited number of products. The main **advantages** of functional structure are as follows:

(*i*) Specialisation on the basis of functions results in efficient distribution of work and maximum utilisation of functional skills.

(*ii*) Delegation of operational matters enables the chief executive officer to concentrate on strategic issues.

(*iii*) Structure can be linked to strategy by designing key activities as functional departments.

(*iv*) It permits centralised control of strategic results.

(*v*) There is minimum duplication of facilities.

(*vi*) Specialisation increases operational efficiency.

(*vii*) Coordination within functional areas becomes easy.

(*viii*) Focussed concentration on functional tasks can develop core competencies.

The functional structure suffers from the following **disadvantages:**

(*i*) There is difficulty in maintaining cooperation and coordination among different functional departments.

(*ii*) Narrow specialisation may lead to neglect of overall goals of the organisation.

(*iii*) Conflicts may arise among functional and advisory staff.

(*iv*) Decisions that require involvement of two or more functional areas may get delayed.

(*v*) There is lack of quick response to environmental changes. Innovation and creativity may get stifled.

(*vi*) No single department can be held responsible for sales revenue and profits.

(*vii*) Development of managers with cross-functionl experience not possible.

Functional structure is suitable for single business firms which compete on the basis of technical specialisation in a relative stable environment.

3. **Divisional Structure:** When a company expands into new products and/or geographic areas, the functional structure proves unsuitable. Firms which diversify into related and unrelated businesses tend to adopt the divisional structure.

Under the divisional structure the organisation is divided into several semi-autonomous divisions on the basis of product lines, or types of customers or geographic areas. Each division is self-contained in terms of manufacturing and marketing facilities. Each division is headed by a divisional manager who is responsible for efficient and profitable working of the division. All divisional managers report to the Chief Executive.

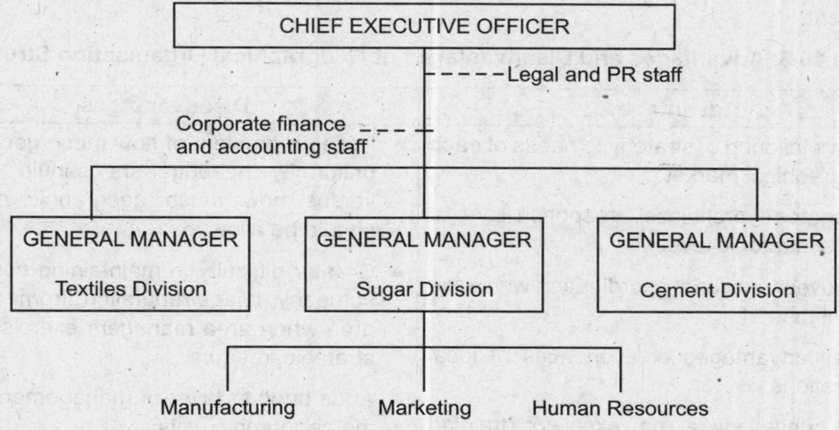

Fig. 10.5. Divisional Structure

Multi-product organisations have product divisions. Each product line requires different manufacturing and marketing knowledge and skills. For example, ITC has six product divisions: Tobacco Products, Paper and Paperboard,Food and Beverages, Hotel and Tourism, Ready-to-Wear Garments, Personal Care.

Territorial or geographic divisionalisation is adopted by banks, insurance and transportation companies. For example' Life Insurance Corporation of India (LIC) has divided the country into five zones—Northern, Southern, Eastern, Western and Central. Indian Railways has also adopted territorial divisionalisation.

Divisional structure offers the following **advantages:**

(*i*) Adequate attention can be paid to problems specific to each product line/territory.

(*ii*) There is sufficient autonomy to each division for efficient management.

(*iii*) Each division can respond quickly to environmental changes.

(*iv*) Top management can focus on strategic matters.

(*v*) There is scope for expansion and growth of business.

(*vi*) Coordination among functional areas like product design, manufacturing, marketing is etc is effective.

(*vii*) Each division can be held responsible for performance.

(*viii*) Development of general management talent is possible.

Divisional structure suffers from some **disadvantages:**

(*i*) Operating costs increase due to duplication of facilities.

(*ii*) Cooperation and coordination among various divisions become difficult. There may be unhealthy competition among divisions.

(*iii*) Policies pursued by different divisions may be inconsistent. Inconsistency may also arise from sharing of authority between corporate and divisional levels.

(*iv*) Problems may arise in the allocation of resources among divisions. Inter-division conflicts may arise on sharing of resources, allocation of common overheads, etc.

Divisional structure is appropriate for multibusiness firms operating in a dynamic environment.

Table 10.3: Advantages and Disadvantages of Geographical Organisation Structure

Advantages	Disadvantages
• Allows tailoring of strategy to needs of each geographical market. • Delegates profit/loss responsibility to lowest strategic level. • Improves functional coordination within the target market. • Takes advantages of economies of local operations. • Area units make an excellent training ground for higher level general managers. • Clarifies profit/loss accountability. • Results in good functional coordination.	• Poses a problem of how much geographic uniformity headquarters should impose versus how much geographic diversity should be allowed. • Greater difficulty in maintaining consistent company image/reputation from area to area when area managers exercise much strategic freedom. • Adds another layer of management to run the geographic units. • Can result in duplication of staff services at headquarters and regional levels, creating a relative cost disadvantage. • Result in duplication of equipment and personnel. • Encourages dysfunctional competition for resources. • Results in loss of specialisation. • Emphasises regional rather than company goals.

10.5. CONTEMPORARY ORGANISATIONAL STRUCTURES

Some of the relatively new types of organisational structures are given below:

1. **SBU Structure:** Top management may face difficulty in exercising strategic control over divisions due to increasing size and diversity. SBU structure is designed to solve this problem. A strategic business unit **(SBu)** is distinct part of the business serving specific product markets and having identified competitors. Each SBU consists of a few divisions. Several information technology firms in India such as Infosys, HCL, Wipro and TCS have adopted the SBU structure.

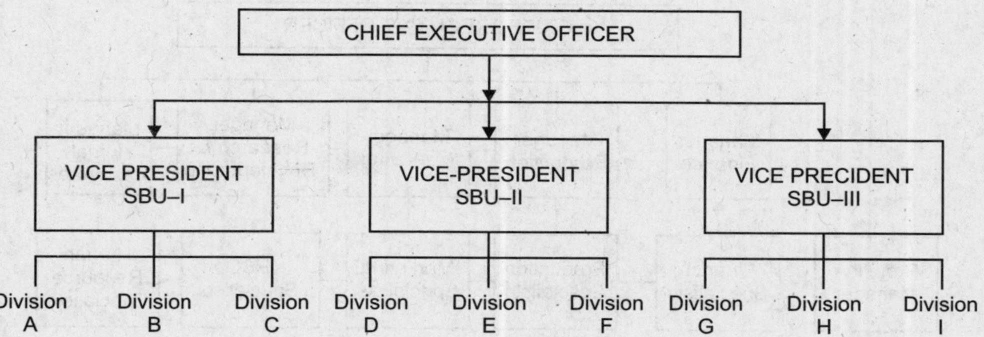

Fig. 10.6. SBU Structure

The main **advantages** of SBU structure are as follows:

(*i*) Each SBU head can be held accountable for ultimate results and operates as a stand-alone profit centre.

(*ii*) Coordination between all divisions within an SBU becomes easier. There is greater decentralisation of authority.

(*iii*) SBU structure facilitates strategic control over a large and diverse organisation.

(*iv*) There is considerable scope for growth and expansion of business.

(*v*) Individual SBUs can react quickly to changes in environment.

Some of the **disadvantages** of SBU structure are given below:

(*i*) It is quite difficult to clearly define the autonomy and responsibility of various SBU heads and to achieve synergies across SBUs.

(*ii*) The hierarchy increases due to addition of one more level between corporate management and divisional management.

(*iii*) In a large and diversified company, effective handling of several SBUs may not be easy.

(*iv*) It may lead to costly duplication of staff and facilities.

(*v*) There may be rivalry among SBUs for corporate resources.

(*vi*) Top level managers may lose touch with business level situations

2. **Matrix Structure:** Matrix structure is a two-dimensional structure. It is a combination of pure project structure and functional structure. This type of structure is created by deputing functional specialists to work on special projects/products. These specialists from different functional areas form a group or team and report to the team leader (project manager). Once the project is completed, they go back to their respective departments.

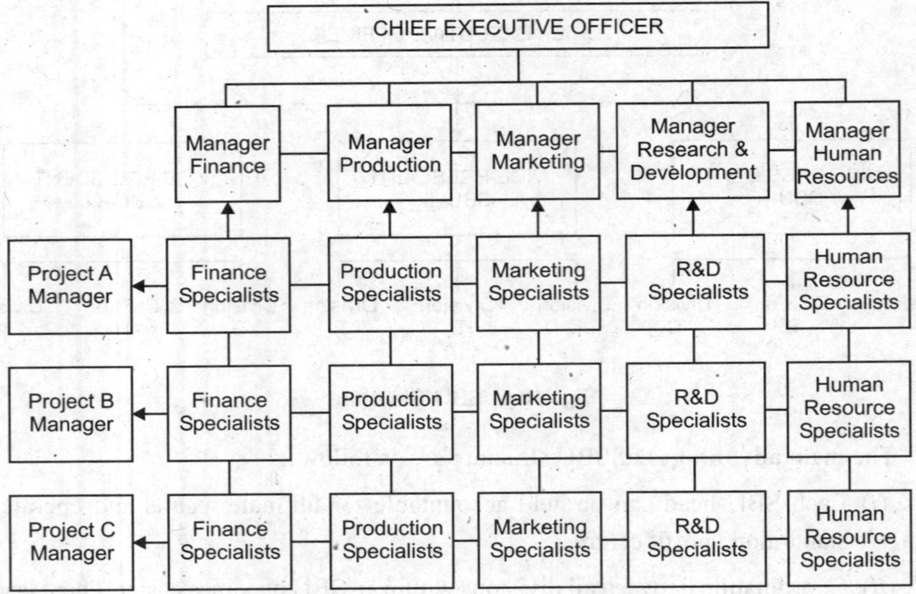

Fig. 10.7. Matrix Structure

Matrix structure offers the following **advantages:**

(*i*) Matrix structure permits specialists to be assigned where their talent is required.

(*ii*) It fosters creativity through pooling of diverse skills without duplication.

(*iii*) It provides good exposure to functional specialists in general management. Functional managers can gain hand on experience.

(*iv*) It allows sharing of resources which helps to reduce costs.

Matrix structure was evolved to overcome the limitations of traditional organisation structures. It is useful wherever dual focus is required—need for high information processing and pressure for sharing resources. Matrix structure, however, suffers from some **disadvantages:**

1. It violates unity of command. Dual accountability may create confusion and conflict. Each functional specialist has two bosses—his administrative head and his project manager.
2. A high level of vertical and horizontal integration is required due to shared authority.
3. Problems in communication and control may arise due to shared authority.
4. The organisation may fail to respond quickly due to complexity
5. Timely decision-making may become difficult.

Matrix organisational structure is appropriate when:

(*i*) management attention must be focused on two or more key issues (technical issues, consumer needs, functional efficiency).

(*ii*) large amounts of diverse information need to be processed.

(*iii*) problem-solving is complex (environmental uncertainty, interdependence among organisational units, complex products or technology).

(*iv*) economies of scale require the sharing of human resource expertise to achieve high performance.

3. **Network Structure:** Network structure has been developed to cope with increasing volatility of environment. "Virtual corporation is a temporary network of independent companies—suppliers, customers, even erstwhile rivals linked by information technology to share skills, costs, and access to one another's markets. It has neither central office nor organisation chart; it has no hierarchy, no vertical integration".[3] In other words, virtual organisation is a temporary alliance between two or more organisations that come together to undertake a specified venture. Several virtual organisations have been created in telecommunication and other knowledge-based industries in India.

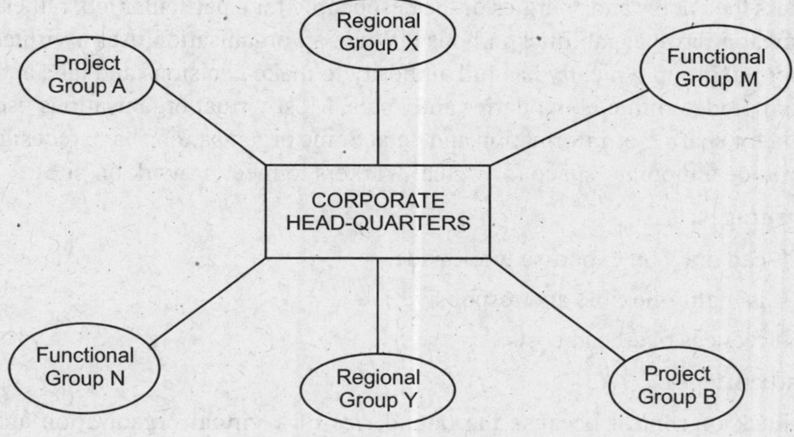

Fig. 10.8. Network Structure

As shown in Fig. 10.8 network structure is composed of several groups or teams which are linked through cob web = like structure. This structure is non-hierarchical and highly decentralised. The core group is responsible for coordination between the semi-autonomous groups to which specialised functions are outsourced. The network structure is most appropriate for organisations which require strong innovation skills and high degree of flexibility so as to respond quickly to fast-changing environment.

The main **advantages** of network structure are as follows:

(*i*) There is high degree of adaptability to changes in environment.

(*ii*) The firm can concentrate on its core competencies.

(*iii*) The structure can be modified to meet changing business needs.

(*iv*) Synergy can be achieved by combining complementary skills of different groups in the network.

The network structure suffers from the following **disadvantages:**

(*i*) There may be conflicts among several semi-autonomous groups.

(*ii*) Coordination and control may become difficult due to several partners.

3. "The Virtual Corporation", **Business Week,** Feb, 8, 1993, pp.98-100.

(*iii*) As most tasks are performed by others, there are risks of overspecialisation.

(*iv*) Duplication of facilities and resources may result in high costs.

4. **Virtual Organisation:** This is an extension of the network structure. In this approach, independent organisations form temporary alliances to exploit specific opportunities, and then disband when their objectives are met. The term virtual means in effect but not actually so. The virtual organisation consists of a network of independent companies—suppliers, customers or even competitors—linked together to share skills, costs, markets and rewards. The members of a virtual organisation pool and share the knowledge and expertise of each other. The virtual organisation will have few full-time employees or may temporarily hire outside specialists to complete a specific project, such as a new software application. These people do not become a part of the organisation, but join together as a separate entity for a specific purpose. Sometimes companies use a virtual approach to harness the talents and energies of the best people for a particular job, rather than trying to develop those capabilities in house. When an organisation uses a virtual approach, the virtual group typically has full authority to make decisions and take actions within certain predetermined boundaries and goals. Most virtual organisations use electronic media for sharing of information and data. Some organisations have redesigned offices to provide temporary space for virtual workers to meet or work on-site.

Advantages:

1. It can draw on expertise worldwide.
2. It is highly flexible and responsive.
3. It reduces overhead costs.

Disadvantages:

1. Lack of control because the boundaries of a virtual organisation are weak and ambiguous.
2. Virtual teams place new demands on managers, who have to work with new people, new ideas and new problems.
3. Virtual organisation poses communication difficulties, and managers may lose motivation.

10.6. STRUCTURAL CHANGE

The basic question in relating structure to strategy is: which structure best meets the requirements of a strategy. Whenever there is a change in strategy, changes are needed in the structure. The external environment also affects the structure. For example, an organisation operating in a volatile environment requires a more flexible structure (*e.g.* matrix structure) than the one operating in a stable environment (*e.g.* functional structure).

Whenever the existing organisation structure does not adequately meet the needs of the chosen strategy, changes must be made in the structure. Some of the developments that may create the need for structural change are as follows:

1. Rapid growth in size of the enterprise.
2. Diversification into related and unrelated businesses.
3. Growing competition and other environmental changes.

4. Shift from centralised family management by professionals.
5. Changes in organisational climate and culture.
6. Formulation of new strategies.

Structural changes are of several types. Changing the organisation structure in line with changes in strategies and environment is called **reorganisation**. On the other hand, radical redesign of business processes so as to reduce cost and improve quality, service and speed is known as **reengineering.** Reducing the number of levels in the hierarchy so as to improve communication and control is called **delayering.**

10.6.1 Strategic Change

Once an organisation adopts a particular strategy, it tends to adhere to it. But strategic change may become necessary due to major change in environment or organisational capabilities. Strategic change can be a continuum varying from no variation in strategy to a complete and radical change in the project procedure, organisational mission, objectives and organisational structure. Samuel C. Certo and Paul Peter[4] divide strategic change into five discrete stages. They are stable strategy, routine strategy change, limited strategy change, radical strategy change and organisational redirection. [Table 10.4]

Table 10.4: Levels of Strategic Change

Strategic Change	Industry	Organisation	Products	Market Appeal
Stable Strategy	Same	Same	Same	Same
Routine Strategy Change	Same	Same	Same	new
Limited Strategy Change	Same	Same	new	new
Radical Strategy Change	Same	new	Same	new
Organisational Redirection	new	new	new	new

Source: Samuel C. Certo and J. Paul Peter, *op. cit*, p. 113.

1. **Stable Strategy:** Stable strategy is continuation of stability in all aspects of the business. Therefore, mostly, it requires continuation of strategy from the previous planning period. It requires running of the business and performing the same tasks with the same skills. Successful implementation of stability strategy requires monitoring the activities to ensure that the objectives are achieved. The learning from previous experience (experience curve effects) will help to achieve the objectives effectively.
2. **Routine Strategy Change:** In the routine strategy change, a firm seeks to attract customers, by making normal, predicted adjustments in the methods. The strategy changes include: changing advertising appeals, update packaging, using different pricing tactics, change the distributors. For example, the strategy of price reduction will enhance the demand for the product. Hence, the strategist should coordinate the activities of marketing department and production department to increase production, capacities of distribution channels and distributors. This strategy does not require major efforts and major changes for its successful implementation.

---

4. **The Strategic Management Process,** Richard D. **Irwin,** Chicago, 1993, p.5

3. **Limited Strategy Change:** This strategy involves offering new products to new markets within the same general products class. Hence, the managers have to perform many new activities, such as designing the new products, procurement of new kinds of inputs, new machinery, producing new products, arranging new market intermediaries (if necessary), new market channels and the like.
4. **Radical Strategy Change:** This strategy involves a major shift for the firm. The radical strategy change is necessary when the firm adopts the strategies like mergers and acquisitions in the same basic industry. These strategies create complex problems in integrating the two firms into one firm. These complex problems include: restructuring the organisation, organisational change, change in orgnisational culture, change in the positions of key personnel, change in the distributors and distributing channels etc.
5. **Organisational Redirection:** This strategy involves mergers and acquisitions of firms in different industries. The magnitude of strategic change depends on the degree of variation of the nature of industries and the degree of centralisation of the new firm. Another form of organisational redirection involves when a firm leaves one industry and enters new one. For example, a firm enters the hot drinks industry by leaving the soft drinks industry.

10.7 STRUCTURE FOR CORPORATE STRATEGIES

Different strategies at the corporate level require different organisational structures. Some examples are given below:

1. **Structures for Integration Strategies:** Horizontal integration extends the value chain and increases commitment to adjacent businesses. In order to accommodate the adjacent businesses, a geographical or product structure may be created. In case of vertical integration (backward and forward), divisions may be created in the organisation.
2. **Structures for Diversification Strategies:** In the strategy of concentric or related diversification, linkage among functions and departments is needed to ensure synergy. Strategic business units (SBUs) structure may be created to implement related diversification. In case of conglomerate or unrelated diversification, divisional structure may be used so as to grant more autonomy to divisional heads for managing unrelated businesses. In both the cases, legal, public relations, finance and HRM functions are centralised at the corporate headquarters.
3. **Structures for Cooperative Strategies:** Strategic alliances, joint ventures, mergers and acquisitions are examples of cooperative strategies. Network structure is the appropriate organisational framework for implementing these strategies.

   Corporate strategies like stability, retrenchment, etc. require little changes in organisational structure.

10.8 STRUCTURES FOR BUSINESS STRATEGIES

As stated earlier, cost leadership, differentiation and focus are the main business level strategies. Each of these strategies requires a different organisation structure.

Under **cost leadership strategy** a company sells on mass scale to minimise costs. It needs a strong centralised authority and strict control to check costs. Employees perform routine tasks as per standard operating procedures and under close supervision. Centralisation of decision-making authority and high degree of functional specialisation are needed to maximise efficiency. Therefore, a **mechanistic structure** is appropriate for cost leadership strategy.

Differentiation strategy requires a more flexible and leaning structure cross-functional work teams, horizontal coordination, low job specialisation, employees performing a wide range of tasks are main features of such an organisation. Decentralised decision-making and employee empowerment are necessary so as to foster creativity and innovation in differentiating products/services and to facilitate quick response to environmental changes. Thus, an **organic structure** is suitable for differentiation strategy.

The **focus strategy** involves emphasis either on cost or differentiation. Therefore, organisation structures used for generic cost leadership and differentiation may be used. In case of cost leadership-cum-differentiation strategy, focus on both marketing and R & D is necessary. The structure must contain features of both **mechanistic and organic structures.**

10.8 ORGANISATIONAL SYSTEMS

Organisational systems are operating mechanisms through which different elements of an organisation interact. These systems are created to perform the tasks for implementation of strategies. Organisational systems also help to bind together the various components of the organisation. The major systems are described below.

1. **Information Systems:** In order to perform their tasks effectively and to relate (coordinate) their work to that of others, managers need information. Every organisation designs a system for collecting, screening, processing, storing and disseminating the required information. Such a system is called management information system (MIS). Its basic objective is to provide the right information, in the right form, and at the right time. MIS plays a vital role in improving decision-making, planning, coordination and control. It also enhances the efficiency of other systems and processes in the organisation. Information needs vary from one level of management to another. (Table 10.5)

Table 10.5: Information Needs at Different Managerial Levels

Level of Management	Information Needs
1. Top Level	Information needed for strategic decision making and strategic control.
2. Middle Level	Information for operational planning and control
3. Lower level	Information for transaction processing, response, etc.

Information Technology (IT) had led to the development of Computerised Information System and other advancements in MIS.

Information needs depend on the nature and type of strategy. An organisation pursuing the stability **strategy requires** a transaction processing system and a mainframe computer which can support many users in time-sharing mode. It is designed to ensure efficient performance of clearly defined, routine and repetitive tasks. On the other hand, under the growth strategy, an organisation requires considerable information about external environment. Its information system has to be more flexible, using microprocessor and decision support system. (Table 10.6)

Table 10.6: Generic Strategies and Key Dimensions of Computerised Information System

	Generic Strategies		
	Stability	**Retrenchment**	**Growth**
Key dimensions	Rigid policy stance	———	Flexible policy stance
	Mainframe computer	———	Microprocessor
	Transaction processing systems	———	Decision support systems

Source: J.C. Camillus and A. L. Lederer, "Corporate Strategy and the Design of Computerised Information System", **Sloan Management Review,** Spring 1985, pp. 35-42.

Management information system can help an organisation gain competitive advantage through business strategies of cost leadership and differentiation. An organisation can achieve a major edge over its competitors by developing unique product/service and capabilities through information technology.

Information systems and information technology play a strategic role in the following ways:

(*i*) Substantially reduce costs through business process reengineering so that the company becomes a cost leader.

(*ii*) Differentiate the company's products/services from those of its competitors or reduce the differentiation advantage of competitors by introducing new features.

(*iii*) Developing unique products/services or to develop unique markets/market niches.

(*iv*) Expanding the company's capacity to produce goods/services or diversifying into new products or services.

(*v*) Creating alliances with suppliers, customers, competitors, consultants, etc.

Thus, information technology and information system can change the way an organisation competes and does business.

2. **Control System:** A control system is needed to monitor behaviour and performance of people and to ensure that strategies are being implemented in accordance with predetermined plans. The control process consists of the following steps:

(*i*) *Setting Performance Standards*: First of all, standards are established in the form of desired results. These serve as the criteria against which actual results are to be measured. Standards should be reasonable, feasible and challenging. It is also necessary to decide how much deviations from the standards will be allowed. Performance standards are set on the basis of the company's objectives and strategies.

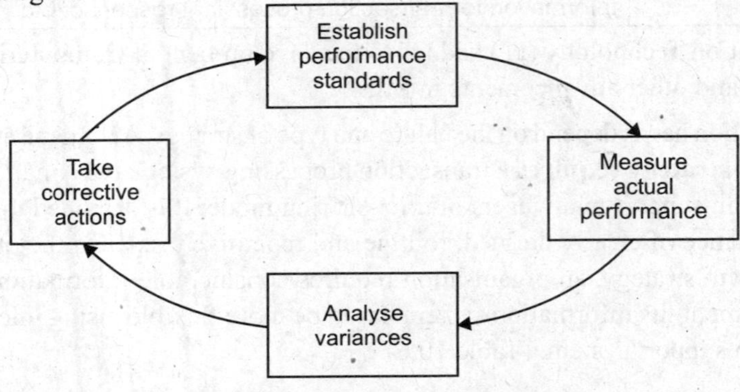

Fig. 10.9. The control process.

(ii) *Measuring Actual Performance*: The actual performance is measured against the standards on an ongoing basis. This helps in detecting and correcting deviations quickly.

(iii) *Analysing Variances*: Differences between standard and actual performance are called variances. When actual performance exceeds standard performance, the variance is positive and may require no action. Excess of standard performance over actual performance is a negative variance. When such variance is unaccountable, it is analysed to identify the causes which may be internal or external.

(iv) *Taking Corrective Action*: Appropriate actions are taken to prevent undesirable variances. Corrective actions will depend on the causes of variance. For example, steps may be taken to improve performance. Alternatively, performance standards may be revised or reset.

An organisation's control system will depend upon its corporate and business strategies. Traditional, rigid and formal controls (*e.g.* budgets, cost standards, etc) may be adequate for stability, concentration and cost leadership strategies. But diversification, cooperation and differentiation strategies require informal, flexible and long-term controls.

As organisations are becoming more organic through delayering, flat hierarchies cross-functional teams and networking, the is need to move from mechanistic controls to organic controls. But shift from traditional contoral systems (*e.g.* profit centres, responsibility accounting, budgeting and cost controls) to modern control system is difficult as a change in the mindset is needed.

3. **Development System:** In this fast changing business world, training and development of personnel is essential. It is necessary to determine the needs, methods, duration and types of training. People may be trained both on the job and off the job. The frequency of training has increased due to rapid advancement in technology and changes in strategies. People at all levels need training. Suitable trainers both from within and outside the organisation are employed to impart training. Large firms have set up their own training centres for this purpose. Companies diversifying into related and unrelated areas and those going global need highly trained and experienced managers, technicians, etc.

   The importance of training and development has increased due to the knowledge economy. Continuous and life-long learning are needed to avoid the mismatch between jobs and jobholders. Attitudinal and behavioural training are as important as structural training.

4. **Appraisal System:** A system is needed for continuous and unbiased evaluation of employee performance. Such an appraisal system provides the information for deciding incentives, promotion, training and development. Various methods used in appraisal are classified broadly into two categories: traditional methods and modern methods. Traditional methods are largely trait based while modern methods are result based. In designing an appraisal system, decisions are taken regarding objectives, frequency and methods of appraisal. Moreover, the roles of line managers and human resource department in appraisal should be specified.

5. **Reward System:** Employee rewards are usually linked to their performance. Such linkage helps to control the behaviour of employees. There is, thus, a close relationship between appraisal system, reward system and control system.

The reward system helps in strategy implementation by reinforcing desirable behaviour. Rewards are given in several forms *e.g.* salary increase, bonus, stock options, perquisites, promotion, etc. In a strategic reward system the focus is on alignment between rewards and corporate strategy so as to secure desired behaviour and achievement. For example, firms pursuing stability strategies focus on improving efficiency in current operations. On the contrary, firms pursuing expansion strategies stress long-term improvement in performance. Team-based rewards and group incentives are more appropriate in case of diversification and internationalization strategies.

Thus, strategies and structures influence the design and administration of reward systems. In case of small and entrepreneurial firms, the owner-manager has a direct contact with employees.

Therefore, the reward system can be informal. But in case of professionally managed and large firms, a formal reward system is necessary. The relative mix of monetary and non-monetary rewards will also differ from one organisation to another. In non-profit organisations and organisations which provide opportunities for creative pursuits, there may be less focus on monetary incentives. Large and growing organisations provide enough opportunities for career advancement and personal growth.

10.10 MATCHING STRUCTURE WITH STRATEGY

The steps that can be taken to match organisation structure with the strategy are given below[5]:

1. **Identify Key Activities:** The functions and tasks essential for execution of strategy are pinpointed. For example, strict cost control is a key task in case of cost leadership strategy.
2. **Understanding Interrelationship Among Activities:** The strategic relationship among the critical, supportive and routine activities should be analysed. Activities may be related through the flow of material, production process, types of customers served etc. Geographical location may help in grouping or regrouping of activities during organisation redesigning.
3. **Grouping Activities into Units:** The critical activities should be used as the main building blocks in structuring the organisation. The role and power of key groups should be duly recognized. Adequate resources should be allocated to critical activities. The managers in charge of such activities should be given influential position.
4. **Deciding Degree of Authority:** Strategies are implemented by managers at different levels. Enough authority should be delegated to them. But activities and organisational units with a crucial role in strategy implementation process should not be subordinate to routine and non-key activities. Revenue-producing and result producing activities should not be subordinate to internal support or staff functions.
5. **Coordination Among Units:** Coordination among different organisational units is essential to ensure that these do not work at cross purposes but supplement efforts of one another.

5. La Rne T. Hosmer, **Strategic Management: Text and Cases on Business Policy,** Prentice Hall, New Jersey, 1982.

Table 10.7: Criteria for Deciding Appropriateness of Organisational Structure

1. Is the structure compatible with the corporate profile and the corporate strategy?
2. At the corporate level, is the structure compatible with the firm's business units?
3. Are there too few or too many hierarchical levels at either the corporate or business unit level?
4. Does the structure promote coordination among its parts?
5. Does the structure allow for appropriate centralisation or decentralisation of authority
6. Does the structure permit the appropriate grouping of activities.
Source: Peter Wright, Charles D. Pringle and Mark J. Kroll, **Strategic Management,** Allyn & Bacon, Boston, 1992.

SUMMARY

Concept of Structure: A framework consisting of vertical and horizontal authority relationships deliberately created by the management to ensure smooth functioning and achievement of its objectives.

Interrelationship Between Strategy and Structure: Forward and backward linkages.

Stages of Growth: (*i*) entrepreneurial (*ii*) functional (*iii*) divisional (*iv*) matrix.

Forms or Types of Structures: (*i*) Entrepreneurial – owner-manager (*ii*) functional (*iii*) divisional (*iv*) SBU structure (*v*) matrix (*vi*) network structure

Structures for Corporate Strategies: (*i*) product or geographical structure for integration strategy (*ii*) SBU structure for diversification (*iii*) network structure for joint ventures, mergers and acquisitions.

Structures for Business Strategies: (*i*) a mechanistic structure for cost leadership (*ii*) organic structure for differentiation (*iii*) a combined structure for focus strategy.

Organisational Systems: (*i*) Information system (*ii*) Control system (*iii*) Development system (*iv*) Appraisal system (*v*) Reward system.

Matching Structure with Strategy: (*i*) identify key activities (*ii*) understand interrelationships among them (*iii*) group activities into units (*iv*) delegate authority (*v*) coordinate units.

TEST QUESTIONS

1. "Structure follows strategy." Discuss with the help of suitable examples and explain the linkage between strategy and structure.
2. Explain the various types of organisation structures that a large and diversified firm can adopt.
3. Explain the essential features of implementation of a strategy. Describe the role of organisation structure in ensuring the success of a strategy.
4. Is it true that MNCs have a preference for having a lateral organisation structure? Describe the conditions under which this is the ideal form of organisation structure. What has been the experience of Indian companies in this context?

5. "Strategy governs structure." In the light of this statement, explain the role of structure in the implementation of strategy.
6. "An appropriate organisation structure is one of the prerequisites of effective implementation of strategy." Discuss the nature of interaction between strategy and structure of organisations in the light of the above statement.
7. Mention four important components of strategy-structure sequence given by Alfred Chandler.
8. "Strategy determines structure." Do you agree? Explain structural issues in implementation of strategy, giving suitable examples.
9. "Implementation of strategy requires a right organisational structure." In the light of this statement, examine the inter-relationship between the strategy and the structure.
10. "Team-based organisational structures are superior to functional, multidivisional and matrix structures." Critically evaluate the statement.
11. Do you agree with the view that structure follows strategy? Give reasons for your answer. What is the role of Board of Directors and top management in the implementation and review of a strategy?
12. In strategy implementation structure follows strategy. How?
13. "An appropriate organisational structure is one of the prerequisites for effective implementation of strategy." Discuss the nature of interaction between strategy and structure in the light of this statement.
14. To what extent do organisation structures both facilitate and spring from strategies? Explain.
15. "Different types of strategies require different structures." Discuss.
16. Why do large diversified companies adopt the divisional structure? In what respects is the divisional structure superior to the functional structure?

CASE STUDY

In the mid-1980s Arvid Mills – the 70 year old textile mill at Ahmedabad—was struggling for a marketplace. But within a decade, an Arvind mill has not only survived but has become one of the darlings of the stock exchanges. Presently it is the third largest denim producer in the world.

Six of Arvind's garment brands are market leaders in their respective segments in India. From a manufacturing focus, the company has achieved a marketing orientation setting up exclusive showrooms and commanding premium brand equity. This growth strategy and emerging environment just like Ranbaxy's Arvind too is a fascinating story of successful application of the concepts of strategic management in the hard world characterised by global competition.

In 1986 Indian Textile industry was dominated by mills with obsolete and old machinery producing quality unacceptable in international market. The main reason for this state of affairs was largely the protected domestic market and government policies discouraging modernization.

Imports of capital goods was controlled by rigid licensing and high import tariffs. The domestic textile machinery industry quoted long delivery periods (of more than three years). The cost of money for modernisation was also very high. As against this domestic environment there was remarkable advancement in the development of sophisticated, electronically controlled textile machinery overseas, which ensured consistent and good quality product with minimum labour inputs. In such an environment, Indian textile units could not hope to compete with in the international markets. Another major trend was the change in the technological structure of the industry. Spinning and weaving, traditionally carried out under one roof, became two different split operations bringing the integrated plants under a cloud of viability. Spinning the capital-intensive apart was still under automatic mills but the labour-textile companies were increasingly outsourcing intensive component.

The economic environment for the textile industry was equally depressing. Ten countries accounted for two-third of textile exports and the leading ten market consumed 80 per cent of the world trade in the industry. Textile was the largest net exporter (value of ₹29,000) crores comprising 33 per cent of India's exports. India also had the largest area in the world under cotton cultivation (24 per cent) but figured amongst the lowest in terms of yield output is 122 per cent of global production.

The long strikes in Mumbai textile units had crippled this industry and resulted in large-scale sickness. Powerlooms emerged as a major competitive force. High wage structure, low productivity and surplus labour in composite textile mills made them non-viable in most product categories in the domestic markets. The government's emphasis remained towards job preservation without consideration of the emerging economics.

On the positive side (for Arvind Mills), textiles was a global industry in which many firms sold in many nations. For instance, Dominion Textiles produced denim fabrics in Canada, U.S.A, and Tunisia and marketed them in USA and EC and Mitsubishi purchased denim globally, manufactured jeans in China, and marketed them in Japan. For an Indian textile company, obviously there existed a huge market opportunity.

The combination of the highly negative technological and economic environment and the existence of a global opportunity in the textile industry called for a bold and innovative approach for survival and growth. Arvind Mills examined the textile industry environment in relation to government policy through Porter's five forces framework, viz.

rivalry amongst existing units;

new entrants;

barriers to new entry;

How powerful are suppliers; and

Government policy-how it affects these five.

From the analysis it became clear to the company strategists that there was intense rivalry both in the lower as well as in the upper end of the market. In the lower segment, powerlooms were a formidable force, and at the upper and were five composite mills and many spinning mills set up as 100 per cent EOUs.

The macro economy of the country in 1986 gave two clear signals, (*i*) Mounting deficit in budget and therefore, pressure on indirect taxes to continue. One could not expect major reliefs on excise, taxes or other government controlled inputs like power, coal, freight, and so, on. The inflationary pressure on prices would continue and (*ii*) Balance of payments position of the country was extremely difficult and was expected to remain difficult. Therefore (*i*) rupee would continue to depreciate, and (*ii*) government's policy would always be favourable to exporters.

Consequently, an idea in the government was forming that India would have to be a part of global economy, and the currency cannot be kept up artificially for long. It was also relevant for the company to examine the competitive advantage of the textile industry in international markets. The most commonly stated advantages of the Indian textile industry were: (*i*) low cost of domestically produced cotton; (*ii*) low cost of labour, and (*iii*) weak currency.

However, experience at Arvind Mills showed that the domestic price of cotton rises as restrictions on export of cotton are relaxed and the advantage of labour cost is nullified by their low productivity and the need to use sophisticated automation for quality products, especially in international markets.

Therefore, the above advantages were considered only as fleeting advantages. Arvind's strategy was not based on these advantages. Instead, the real competitive advantages of Indian textile industry lay in the availability of technical personnel, trained work force, specialized research institutions in textiles, skill and knowledge base to absorb new technology and improve product quality.

The emergence of sophisticated buyers demanding quality,

The favourable conditions in capital market conducive to innovation and large investments, and

The existence in India of well developed textile related supporting industries.

With this background on competitive environment, the strategic options for Arvind Mills were evolved.

The main considerations while evolving the strategic options were;

(*i*) The product selected should involve high technology content and be capital-intensive so that entry barrier for competitors was high.

(*ii*) The product segment should be relatively less dependent on fashion changes.

(*iii*) The focus should shift to international trade in textile and garments from purely domestic orientation.

(*iv*) Within the domestic market, the focus should be only on specialty products of Arvind and readymade garments where the powerloom sector cannot compete.

Based on these considerations, Arvind Mills articulated its corporate mission to achieve global dominance in select business built around the core competencies, through continuous products and technical innovation, customer orientation and a focus on cost effectiveness. It also selected product market segment – Denim, cotton quality fabric, specially products, yarn, and garments. To implement its strategy it faced several challenges in financial strategy, human resources, and work culture and government policies and reformulated its strategies in these areas. In formulating financial strategies, the company dropped its age-old strategy of relying on internal cash accruals and retained earnings and emphasized on equity financing through capital market. It also obtained finance from ICICI and International Finance Corporation. On human resources front the company inducted professional managers, not necessarily from textile industry.

To improve the work culture the company carried out new expansions at new locations with fresh personnel who could be trained in a conducive work culture right from the beginning. On government policies the company analysed various government policies and incentive schemes and took advantage of them. It also brought about changes in structure of the company by interlinking various offices, focussed on just-in-time delivery by setting up warehouses across the globe. It also resorted to innovation and new competencies development both on process and product sides. On human resources development front, the delayerisation and flattening of the management structure was carried out to enable employees get early substantive responsibility.

The company's results are as follows:

(Sales: Unit lack, size: ₹Crore)

Brand	1996-97	Actuals	1997-98	Targets
	Sales	Size	Sales	Size
Arrow	4.0	40	5.0	50
Lee	1.5	20	2.25	30
Newport	20.0	60	30.0	100
Flying Machine	3.0	20	35.0	30
Ruf & Tuf	32.0	65	6.5	170
Excalibut	nil	nil	4.6	25

The financial results of the company after implementation of strategy were:

	Y/E 1987	Y/E 1992	Y/E 1995	Y/E 1996
Sales	113.00	238.00	568.00	755.00
Profit after tax	0.78	20.00	106.00	113.86
New Worth	33.00	88.00	1026.00	1095.00
EPS	1.95	14.70	10.65	11.40
Export earnings	3.40	2.00	193.00	310.00
Export as % of Sales	3.00	22.00	34.00	41.00

The above financial data is only of Arvind. Mills. If the performance of its associate companies is included, then the export earning would be above ₹500 crores on a turnover of ₹750 crores in 1994-95.

With WTO and its policies the company is likely to face stiff competition in the future.

Questions:

(*i*) Make a SWOT analysis of Arvind Mills bringing out clearly its strengths and weaknesses, opportunities and threats.

(*ii*) Prepare the strategic advantage profile (SAP) for Arvind Mills.

(*iii*) On the basis of SWOT and SAP, propose the strategic alternatives before Arvind Mills and compare the alternatives you propose with those identified in the case.

(*iv*) Analyse critically the aspect of strategy implementation described in the case. Do you propose any change in these aspects? If yes, what are these changes and why do you propose them?

CHAPTER 11

BEHAVIOURAL ISSUES IN STRATEGY IMPLEMENTATION

CHAPTER OUTLINE

Behavioural implementation is concerned with the behaviour of strategists. The individuals and groups who actually implement the company's strategies must behave properly to ensure achievement of the desired objectives. Leadership style, corporate culture, corporate governance, personal values and ethics, social responsibility, politics and power are the key behavioural issues involved in strategy implementation.

11.1 CORPORATE CULTURE

Every company has a culture which exercises considerable influence on the behaviour of its managers and employees. According to O'Reilly, "organisational culture is the set of assumptions, beliefs, values and norms that are shared by an organisation's members."[1]

Beliefs are the assumptions about reality. These are derived from and reinforced by experience. Values are the ideals that are considered desirable and worth striving for. Norms are the expected standards of behaviour. Assumptions, beliefs, values and thought processes are abstract and intangible elements of culture. The tangible and visible elements of culture include physical settings, artefacts, dresses, ceremonies, stories, slogans, etc. The corporate culture in an organisation is manifested in[2]:

- Shared things (*e.g.* the way people dress)
- Shared sayings (*e.g.* let's get down to work)

---

1. Charles O'Reilly, "Corporate Culture and Commitment: Motivation and Control in Organisations," **California Management Review,** Summer, 1989, pp. 9-25.
2. V. Sathe, **Culture and Related Corporate Realities** Richard D. Irwin, Homewood, Illinois, 1985, p. 18.

- Shared actions (*e.g.* service-oriented approach)
- Shared feelings (*e.g.* hard work is rewarded here)

On the basis of these characteristics, an organisation's culture may be strong or weak. When these characteristics are widely and deeply shared, the culture is considered strong. It is weak in case these are not shared widely and deeply. A company that conducts its business according to a clear and explicit set of principles and values has a strong culture. In a weak culture, there are several sub–cultures, environment is politicized, bureaucracy is high and people do not look outside for best practices.

11.1.1 Impact of Culture

Corporate culture provides the framework within which the behaviour of people takes place. It influences strategy implementation in several ways:

1. **Decision-Making:** Culture affects the way managers take decisions about the company's relationship with its environment and strategy.
2. **Resistance to Change:** A strong culture facilitates smooth implementation of strategy by reducing resistance to change.
3. **Communication and Control:** Strong corporate culture facilitates communication and control in the organisation.
4. **Cooperation and Commitment:** In a strong culture, members of the organisation have a high sense of identity, and a high degree of loyalty and commitment.
5. **Innovation:** Organisations with a strong culture are relatively creative and entrepreneurial.
6. **Work Ethics:** Culture determines the ethical standards of an organisation and its members. In a healthy culture employees consider 'work as worship' and work hard.
7. **Motivation Level:** Culture determines the attitudes of people to their jobs and life. In achievement-oriented culture, people are self-motivated.

Thus, corporate culture can be either a strength or a weakness depending upon whether it is healthy or unhealthy. A strong culture is essential for success in strategy implementation. In order to build a strong culture there must be.

- a genuine concern for the well-being of all stakeholders;
- a founder or leader who establishes high values;
- a sincere commitment to run the organisation in accordance with these values.

Table 11.1: Relationship between Strategic Management and Organisational Culture

An Organisation's Culture					
Values and Beliefs	*Language and Metaphors*	*Rites Rituals, and Ceremonies*	*Symbols*	*Heroes and Heroines*	*Myths, Stories, Legends, and Sagas*

Strategy Formulation	*Strategy Implementation*	*Strategy Evaluation*
Is our mission compatible with our culture? Do our external stakeholders understand our culture? Do our managers and employees understand our culture and our strategy? Do our strategies capitalize on our culture? Are our objectives reasonable considering our culture? Which heroes and heroines will actively support our strategies? Culture?	Are our management policies and objectives consistent with our culture? Are our marketing and financial policies consistent with our culture? Is our organisational structure compatible with our altere Is our resource allocation process consistent with our culture? What culture products could be used to reinforce our new strategies?	Is our performance evaluation system consistent with our culture? Is the timing of our evaluation procedures consistent with our culture? Are our evaluative criteria consistent with our values and beliefs? Do we effectively monitor changes in our strategy and culture? Are proposed corrective actions appropriate considering our culture?

Source: Fred R. David, **Concepts of Strategic Management,** Merrill Pubblishing Company, Toronto, 1989, p.83.

11.1.2 Relating Culture to Strategy

Corporate culture can be a source of sustainable competitive advantage when there is a proper fit between corporate strategy and corporate culture. It contributes to competitive advantage by widening the strategic options, facilitating interaction and assisting information processing. A strong culture enables the management to predict employee reactions to strategic options thereby minimising the unintended consequences Corporate culture determines managerial behaviour which in turn influences implementation of strategy. Therefore, corporate leaders must create an appropriate fit between strategy and culture. In creating such a fit, strategists can adopt any of the following approaches[3]:

1. **Ignore Corporate Culture:** When it is almost impossible to change the culture, strategists may ignore it while implementing a strategy. Culture is built over a long time period and cannot be changed overnight. Cultural change is a slow and time-consuming process. Overnight changes in culture may create trauma for members of the organisation.
2. **Adapt Strategy Implementation to Suit Culture:** An easier alternative is to change strategy implementation to suit the corporate culture. Strategists have some flexibility in case of organisation structure, systems and processes. These variables may be modified to meet the requirements of corporate culture. However, each specific situation in the organisation may require an innovative solution. However changing strategy midway

3. H. Schwartz and S.M Davis, " Matching Corporate Culture and Business Strategy", in G.A Steiner, John B. Miner and E.R. Gray (eds.), **Management Policy and Strategy,** Macmillan,, New York, 1982, pp. 475-93.

is not desirable. Therefore, culture should be considered while making strategic choice. In case it is not possible to change the culture, it may become necessary to abandon the strategy.

4. **Change the Culture to Suit the Strategy:** The most difficult alternative is to change the corporate culture so as to fit with the strategy. Cultural change is no doubt a slow and time-consuming process. But it may become necessary in some situations. For example, in the post-liberalisation era, family business houses in India went through cultural transition so as to succeed against global competition. Strong assertive leadership, making strategic tasks explicit, enhancing managerial ability to imbibe changes, etc. are required for cultural change.

   The important thing is not the destination but the process by which you align an organisation. From the board room to the shopfloor, everybody needs to be listening to the same signs of the future. Then the organisation is able to respond to change in competence, in technology, in consumer demand, in business environment. Businesses fail, not because they do the wrong thing or because they do the right thing poorly but because they fail to see and understand the change in the theory of business. There have been fundamental changes in the theory of business over the last few years. Big is no longer secure and competitive. It could lead to bureaucracy and lethargy and make a business vulnerable. That's why there is so much changes in the Fortune 500 companies.

11.1.3 Cultural Barriers to Strategy Implementation

Culture acts as a barrier to strategy implementation when it does not match the organisation's strategy. For example, an organisation with low-performing culture finds it very difficult to implement a strategy that requires high performing culture.

1. **Low-Performing Culture:** Rigid rules and policies, resistance to change, centralised decision-making are the main characteristics of a low-performing culture. Organisations which operate for long in a stable environment and captive markets tend to become complacent. When they have to change their strategies due to significant changes in environment, they face cultural barrier. For example, telecommunications and automobile firms operated in a competition-free market before 1985. They became complacent about product quality and delivery schedule. After economic liberalization they suffered badly due to low-performing culture.

   Culture in any organisation doesn't change easily. It is formed over a number of years from the actions and behaviour of management and employees.

   If you reward behaviour that justifies shortcuts, recognise and promote people who use whatever means to get the outcome the management wants, and this happens over decades, it gets ingrained in the DNA of the organisation.

   Investing money in upgrading facilities, paying top-notch consultants to develop changes management strategies cannot substitute for a few "teachable moments" that leaders within the organisation can create, when they choose to join hands with scientists and operators at the lowest rungs.

2. **Cultural Diversity:** When two or more companies join together, cultural diversity becomes a barrier in strategy implementation. In case of a strategic alliance and joint

venture, differences in the cultures of the partners create problems in objective setting and in choosing the methods of achieving objectives. Since liberalization and globalization, takeovers and mergers have become very common. When the cultures of the acquirer and acquired differ significantly, integration becomes difficult. For example, several high-level managers left Madura Coats when it was acquired by the Birla Group. They resigned due to the fear that they would not be able to adjust with the new management culture.

The problem of cultural diversity also occurs when a company goes global. The company's domestic culture does not suit the host country's culture. For example, family business houses in India treat employees as family members and offer lifetime employment. But when they do business abroad, they have to adopt the policy of term employment.

11.1.4 Developing Sound Corporate Culture

In this era of cut throat competition and global business, companies need a high-performing culture. The following guidelines[4] are helpful in developing such culture:

(*i*) Preserve core ideologies while allowing for change.

(*ii*) Stimulate progress through challenging objectives, purposeful evaluation, and continuous self-improvement.

(*iii*) Encourage experimentation and accept mistakes.

(*iv*) Accept paradox while rejecting 'either or thinking'.

(*v*) Create alignment by translating core values into goals, strategies, and practices.

(*vi*) Grow new managers internally by promotion from within.

Cyrus Mistry Calls for Openness, Synergy Among Tata Group Cos

Calling for a culture of openness and pooling of resources across companies, Tata Group chairman Cyrus Mistry has asked firms of the conglomerate to focus on innovation and remain agile to succeed in an uncertain and volatile environment. In a year-end letter to employees, Mistry, who has completed a year at the helm of the group, said that after realising the distinctiveness of every Tata enterprise, "each needs to be viewed in a manner that is appreciative of its uniqueness".

Exhorting the employees to carry forward the legacy of the group's founder Jamsetji Tata, Mistry said the year gone by has witnessed a business environment that has continued to be volatile and uncertain. "This is a time for us to re-look at some of our strategies, recalibrate our business models, fine-tune our execution capabilities and invest in our future," he said. "To succeed in an uncertain and volatile environment, it is critical that our businesses evaluate alternate scenarios of the future while crafting our strategies. Our organisations will need to embrace agility, powered by teams with the aptitude and capability for continual learning," Mistry said. Calling for more synergy among the over 100 operating companiesof the group, Mistry said: "As a group we must also continue to seek opportunities for our companies to pool resources to co-create shared value. There is so much that collaboration between our companies can offer, be it in areas like innovation, management of technology, or identifying the emerging needs and wants of consumers."

4. James C. Collins and Jerry I. Porras, **Built to Last: Successful Habits of Visionary Companies,** Harper Business, New York, 1994.

Highlighting factors that will influence on how successful the group will be in achieving its goals, he said: "Principal among these will be our ability to foster a culture of openness across the Tata Group, and develop a performance-oriented framework that values each colleague's contribution as well as cultural fit with the group. This requires significant investment in people development and in encouraging diversity in the workplace."

Cultural Differences Cause Labour Unrest

The 'Japanese Way' focuses on continuous improvement and cost reduction. It is the reason that Japan has emerged as the lowest cost manufacturer of cars in the world. Japanese companies facing intense global competition and the pressure to reduce costs, have little choice but to exploit the workforce. According to the old order, a Japanese worker was ensured lifetime employment and was expected to be loyal to his employer by putting in long hours. Complaining was seen as dishonourable and there was little notion of any life beyond work. It is only now, reacting to the crises at the workplace, the government is implementing a new 'work-life balance charter.'

This tradition is, however, giving way and the younger generation do not subscribe to warped notions of loyalty and sacrificing oneself for the employer. "Youngsters aspire for a better life, and are beginning to think and act differently.

The problem manifests in terms of rising number of contract workers almost a third of the total workforce, and unpaid overtime. Leave requests are disregarded and even toilet breaks are frowned upon. The typical Indian worker with high family attachments and responsibilities expect leave of absence when necessary. This is unlike Japanese workers who display their love for family by immersing themselves at work for the family's sake. Indian workers want to be with family to mourn and to celebrate. Japanese managers do not understand these cultral differences. Indian managers do not provide the right feedback to their Japanese bosses about brewing workers' unrest. They go into meetings merely to nod their heads. As a result labour unrest has occurred in Maruti Suzuki, Honda, Toyota (all Japanese companies) in India.

11.2 STRATEGIC LEADERSHIP

Leadership is the process of influencing others to strive willingly and enthusiastically towards the achievement of organisational objectives. Strategic leadership is the process of transforming an organisation through its people into a unique position. Strategic leaders are mainly at the top level of the organisation. They manage the process of strategic management. They are the chief architect of corporate strategy and mobilise people for strategy implementation. Bill Gates (Microsoft), Akio Morita (Sony), Jack Welch (General Electric), Narayana Murthy (Infosys), J.R.D. Tata (Tata Group), Azim Premji (Wipro) are some examples of strategic leaders.

The main characteristics of strategic leadership are as follows:

(*i*) Strategic leadership is visionary and keeps the mission in sight. Its focus is on effective ness rather than on efficiency.

(*ii*) Strategic leadership is transformational not transactional. Strategic leaders recognise the need for change, and create a vision to guide the change effectively, execute the change.

(*iii*) Strategic leadership has an external rather than internal focus. It helps the organisation to be in tune with its environment.

(*iv*) Strategic leadership inspires people to work together for achieving the purpose and the mission.

Role of Leadership in Strategy Implementation

Strategic leadership plays a vital role in strategy implementation by performing the following tasks:

1. **Initiating Change:** Growing organisations require change. Strategic leaders act as change agents. They overcome resistance to change by showing concern for people and taking them into confidence.
2. **Providing Strategic Direction:** Strategic leaders provide a sense of direction in terms of envisioned future and core ideology. The envisioned future is concerned with the future shape of the organisation. The core ideology guides members of the organisation. Strategic leaders are visionary and clarify strategic intent.
3. **Shaping Corporate Culture:** Corporate culture defines an organisation and differentiates it from other organisations. Strategy is implemented by people and culture shapes behaviours of people. Strategic leaders build and sustain a supportive culture.
4. **Reconciling Conflicting Interests:** An organisation consists of several interest groups. Their interests are often at conflict. There exist conflicts between management and labour, between departments, etc. These conflicts create problems in strategy implementation. Strategic leaders integrate different interests by creating commitment to common interest.
5. **Setting Ethical Practices:** It is necessary that members of the organisation behave ethically during strategy implementation. Strategic leaders establish ethical standards and practices to guide behaviours.
6. **Developing Motivation System:** The pursuit of strategy by itself does not meet all the needs of organisational members. Therefore, individuals and groups involved in strategy implementation must be properly motivated. Strategic leaders develop a sound motivation system to meet their needs and to optimise performance.
7. **Establishing Effective Controls:** Both financial and non-financial controls are required to ensure effective implementation of strategy. Strategic lenders establish appropriate controls to monitor and control progress towards strategic success.

Matching Leadership Style and Strategy

Leadership style means the behaviour pattern of leaders. Broadly, various leadership styles can be classified into three categories. **First** is the authoritarian or autocratic style under which the leader takes unilateral decisions and asks the people to implement them. **Second** is the participative or democratic style wherein the leader decides and acts in association with the subordinates. **Third** is the combination of first two styles. It may be called nurturing or paternalistic style under which the leader is both directive and participative.

Effective strategy implementation requires that leaders adopt a style that matches the requirements of strategy. For example, unilateral methods of implementation may be better for transformational change *e.g.* changing culture or redesigning organisation structure, systems and processes, whereas participative methods may be adopted to implement environmental changes.

In industries like information technology, pharmaceuticals, etc well qualified technical and other professionals are employed. High degree of participation and empowerment are needed to manage them. Growth strategy may require participative leadership. Paternalistic leadership may be appropriate in case of stability strategy. On the other hand, authoritarian leadership may be adopted for retrenchment strategy.

Since economic liberalisation and globalization, several family business groups in India have shifted from family management to professional management. Professional management requires drastic changes in leadership styles. For example, chief executive officers in Dabur, Ranbaxy and some other groups are professionals rather than family members. They adopt team approach and apply modern management techniques. Competitive rather then connections with the family serve as the basis of career advancement. Professional management is more responsive to society and strategic decision-making is not guided by the sole motive of profit maximisation. Change is accepted and implemented quickly as several Indian firms are globalising rapidly.

Developing Strategic Leaders

Leadership development is essential for survival and success of an organisation in the long run. Therefore, several companies have established in-house facilities for developing future leaders. Many business schools are offering training programmes for leadership development. For example, Harvard Business School, Indian School of Business (Hyderabad), Indian Institute of Management (Ahmedabad) run Advanced Management Programmes for would-be CEOs. The need for developing transformational leaders has increased due to several reasons.

- Rapid growth of economies
- Growing resignations by CEOs to become entrepreneurs
- Globalisation of firms
- Increasing competition
- Fast changes in technology
- More stringent norms of corporate governance.

Development of strategic leaders is primarily the responsibility of founders, board of directors and chief executives. The key issues involved in leadership development are given below:

1. **Selection of Future Leaders:** Choosing future leaders is a strategic decision as the future of the company depends on these leaders. In professionally managed companies managers with proven talent and potential are chosen and groomed for top positions. The Tata Group created the Tata Administrative Service (TAS) in 1950 for this purpose. Wipro started the Wipro Leaders Programme in 1988. Under it, about 30-50 managers are chosen each year to be groomed for top positions. These must have seven qualities: vision, high energy, aggressive commitment, self-confidence, commitment to excellence, team building, sense of ownership. In many family-owned groups such as Reliance, Bajaj, etc. family members who have gone through the grind are appointed to top positions.

2. **Career Planning and Development:** Formal career planning and development for future leaders are becoming increasingly necessary. Tatas, Infosys, Wipro, Hindustan Unilever and many other companies have set up their own leadership training institutes. In several firms, would-be leaders are appointed as executive assistants to the chairpersons to provide critical inputs and to assist in strategic decision-making. Indian Institutes of Management, Administrative Staff College of India and some other institutions offer courses in strategic management. In family-owned groups the chief executive may informally train and groom the future chief executives.
3. **Succession Planning:** Several family owned-companies have faced tussles and even court cases between heirs. Considerable behind-the-scene manoeuvres take place for filling up chief executive positions in public sector enterprises. There may be a clash of interests among family heirs and professional managers in some family-owned firms. Therefore, succession planning is necessary to fill top executive positions whenever the vacancy arises due to death, disability and retirement.

Table 11.2: Leadership Road map

1. Determine the best leadership style for your organisation.
2. Identify current and potential leaders within or outside the company.
3. Identify leadership gaps.
4. Develop succession plans for critical roles
5. Develop career planning goals for potential leaders
6. Develop a skill road map for future leaders.

11.3 CORPORATE GOVERNANCE

Corporate governance refers to the system by which companies are governed. It involves relationships amongst the company's board of directors, its management and various stakeholders. It involves maintaining a balance between economic and social goals, individual and common goals by aligning the interests of individuals, companies and society. Accountability of the board of directors and the management to shareholders, transparency in working and disclosures, fairness in dealings and integrity are the main pillars of good governance. Both voluntary and statutory mechanisms have been created to ensure good governance in India. The Companies Act 2013; the Securities Contract (Regulations)Act 1956, the Securities and Exchange Board of India Act 1992 are the main statutory regulations. Clause 49 of the listing agreement states the corporate governance practices which all listed companies must follow.

Organisational mechanisms which help to ensure good governance are as follows:

(*a*) an independent and effective board of directors;

(*b*) commitment to a code of governance;

(*c*) sound internal control system;

(*d*) transparency through disclosure of information concerning the company's financial and operational performance;

(*e*) proper risk management procedures;

(*f*) a sound whistleblower policy;

(*g*) fair executive compensation policy

(*h*) an effective external audit system.

Role of Corporate Governance in Strategic Management

1. **Corporate Governance and Strategic Intent:** The strategic intent of an oragnisation comprises its vision, mission, business definition, business model and objectives. The vision and mission must reflect the aspirations and intentions of all the stakeholders and not only those of shareholders. There must be a consensus amongst the stakeholders on the business definition, business model and objectives of the company. Various mechanisms of corporate governance help the stakeholders in arriving at such a consensus. Thus, corporate governance plays an important role in each element of strategic intent.
2. **Corporate Governance and Strategy Formulation:** Top management must keep in mind the interests and goals of different stakeholders in making the strategic choice. Some strategies help in achieving high returns for shareholders. Other strategies are chosen to ensure long-term growth, corporate image and decision-making authority of managers. Both-long term and short-term goals must be kept in mind while formulating corporate level and business level strategies.
3. **Corporate Governance and Strategy Implementation:** The success of an organisation depends as much on effective implementation of strategy as on strategy formulation. Strategy implementation is the job of managers. Shareholders and board of directors usually do not intervene in the job. Corporate governance mechanisms help to ensure that-managers do not deviate from the company's strategic intent while implementing the strategies.
4. **Corporate Governance and Strategy Evaluation:** Board of directors and shareholders play a major role in strategic evaluation and control. They have to ensure that the corporate objectives are achieved. Board of directors sets up operational and strategic controls to monitor and evaluate performance. Corporate disclosures and other mechanisms of corporate governance enable the shareholders to judge whether the company is on the right track.

11.4 VALUES AND BUSINESS ETHICS

Values are convictions of what an individual or group considers desirable. An individual imbibes personal values from parents, teachers, elders, etc. These values are adapted and refined as the individual gains new knowledge and experience. The values of an organisation are developed by its founder and chief executive. For example, the values of the Tata group have been derived from the ideals of J. N. Tata, the founder of the group.

Honesty, transparency, reliability, trustworthiness and fairness are the core values of the Tata Group. The core values or moral principles constitute the ideology of an organisation. The values and beliefs give a common sense of purpose across all Tata companies. They define the spirit of the group. Core ideology consisting of enduring tenets is not compromised for financial gain or short term results. The group does not change its values and beliefs as these bind, guide and govern its business.

Business ethics refers to the values and beliefs as applied to business activities. It is a set of moral principles about desirable conduct in business.

Role of Values and Ethics in Strategic Management

Personal values and business ethics play a vital role in strategic management process. These

(*i*) shape the corporate culture of the organisation;

(*ii*) govern the way politics and power are used in the organisation;

(*iii*) determine the way in which members of the organisation perceive situations and problems;

(*iv*) influence organisational values and the means used to achieve these goals;

(*v*) affect the degree to which change is accepted/resisted;

(*vi*) affect the degree of risk taken; etc.

Values of organisational members particularly those of strategists, exercise major impact on strategy formulation and implementation. For example, a service-minded chief executive may lead the organisation to focus on delighting customers. Similarly, a owner-manager with a benign attitude towards labour may offer welfare facilities beyond what labour laws require.

Sometimes, strategists face an ethical dilemma when they are under tremendous pressure to compromise with their values to meet the situational needs. Their personal values and performance often affect formulation and implementation of strategies. Strategists are custodians of considerable economic power and wealth. They determine by their decisions and actions the destinies of corporations. Therefore, strategists must inculcate high moral values and beliefs and apply them in strategic decision-making. For example, some strategists may prefer cost minimisation through mass production whereas others may give priority to product differentiation and quality. Divergent values of strategists in the same organisation can be a source of conflict in strategy formulation and implementation.

Problems arise in strategy implementation when there is divergence of values of the organisation and those of its managers. In such a situation, it becomes necessary to modify the values of individuals to match the organisation's core values. Strategists should develop a code of conduct (do's and dont's) to guide executives in strategy implementation. The strategists can reconcile personal values, business ethics and corporate strategy by modifying personal values, matching divergent values and inculcating the right set of values.

Economic liberalisation and globalization have created pressure on business enterprises to be more value driven. Global firms are strengthening their systems and processes to detect and prevent frauds. But unethical practices continue to occur in global giants such as Ranbaxy Laboratories, Adidas, etc.

Business ethics can be a source of competitive advantage. Ethical organisations outperform those considered unethical. Companies which are perceived ethical are in a better position to:

- attract global investment;
- attract and retain talent;

- differentiate themselves in the marketplace;
- earn reputation or goodwill;
- develop strong brand loyalty; and
- build long-term relationship with suppliers and dealers.

Inculcating Values and Ethics

Like culture, values and ethics are enduring and it is very difficult to change them. Thompson and Strickland[5] have suggested the following actions for inculcating moral values and ethics in organisations:

(*i*) Considering values and ethics in recruitment and selection to ensure compatibility of the character traits of potential employees to the ethical system of the organisation.

(*ii*) Incorporating the statement of values and code of ethics into employee training and educational programmes.

(*iii*) Example-setting by top management in terms of actions and behaviours that reinforce the values.

(*iv*) Communication of the values and code of ethics through wide publicity and explanation of compliance procedures.

(*v*) Constant monitoring of compliance by superior staff and top management.

(*vi*) Consistent nurturing of values within the organisation through their integration into policies, practices and actions.

(*vii*) Paying special attention to those parts of the organisation that are susceptible to ethically-sensitive activities such as purchase and procurement, dealing with government and other external agencies.

Thus, systematic changes in the organisation and judicious use of power and politics are needed to inculcate values and ethics.

11.5 CORPORATE SOCIAL RESPONSIBILITY (CSR)

Corporate social responsibility means a corporation's obligations to keep social interest n mind while taking decisions and actions.

Business firms and business leaders all over the world are showing increasing concern for social problems and issues. Business organisations function within society and social issues exercise an impact on their operations and performance. At the same time the decisions and actions of the business organisation have far reaching impact on different sections of society. Some of factors which have led to growing concern for corporate social responsibility in India are as follows:

(*i*) The well-established tradition of charity and philanthropy in family owned business houses in India.

(*ii*) Market pressures on Indian companies to adhere to global standards and practices of CSR.

---

5. A.A. Thompson Jr. and A. J. Strickland III **Strategic Management: Concepts and Cases** Richard D. Irwin, Illiois, 1995,. pp. 299-300.

(*iii*) Pressures from non-government organisations (NGOs) and civil society groups.

(*iv*) Wide ranging regulations concerning consumers, workers and weaker sections of society.

(*v*) The urge to improve corporate image and develop cordial relationships with shareholders, employees, customers and local community.

(*vi*) Strong tradition of religious benevolence.

In India, public health and eduction, poverty alleviation, rural development, community welfare and environmental pollution are the major areas of CSR. Major CSR initiatives in a company are primarily the responsibility of its top management consisting of board of directors and chief executive officer. They decide what social activities the company should undertake, how much to do and how to incorporate social interest in the decision-making process.

A company can operationalise social responsibility through the following measures:

1. **Top Management Commitment:** An organisation can incorporate CSR into its strategic decision-making with commitment of its top management. In leading organisations formal mechanisms such as a CSR committee, CSR manager, etc. have been created by top management.
2. **Policy Formulation for CSR:** An organisation functions on the basis of a set of established values, precedents, policies and programmes. CSR policies can be formulated at the corporate level as well as at functional level. Corporate level policy lays down guidelines concerning what and how much social programmes the organisation will undertake. In functional areas, a company may, for example, decide that its advertising will be fully ethical or its product will be safe and healthy for users.
3. **Institutionalising CSR:** In order to implement its CSR policies, CSR is injected into the decision-making process. Managers at all levels are asked to incorporate social considerations in their decisions and actions.
4. **Monitoring Social Performance:** The performance of managers is evaluated in terms of both economic results and social achievements. Rewards are decided accordingly. Several companies in India (*e.g.* Tata Steel, ITC, Infosys, Dr. Reddy's Laboratories have adopted the systems of social audit and social support. Social audit is a systematic assessment of and reporting the social impact of an organisation's activities.

   Corporate social responsibility initiatives undertaken by companies raveal their values and should ideally be part of the employee value proposition. Managers today should look at employee engagement in CSR as a "strategic imperative." They should understand that a company's CSR involvement constitutes a legitimate, compelling and increasingly important way not just to attract business but also to draw and retain good employees.

   A recent survey conducted by Shine. com reveals that the young Indian workforce prefers working for organisations that exhibit good corporate citizenship. The survey reveals that the core value of a company can be a part of the "employee value proposition".

Role of CSR in Strategic Management

Leading organisations treat CSR as a strategic issue rather than an ad hoc or once-in-a-while charity or just legal compliance. They have incorporated CSR in their strategic management process.

(*i*) **CSR and Strategic Intent:** While deciding its vision, mission, business definition, business model and objectives, an organisation must incorporate the social viewpoint. Its strategic intent must reflect its concerns for the society. The role of the organisation in society must be clear from its vision and mission statements. Its objectives must indicate both economic and social goals.

(*ii*) **CSR and SWOT Analysis:** The strategists can identify the social problems and issues that need attention through appraisal of social environment. Organisational appraisal will indicate the organisation's capabilities for tackling social problems. Environmental appraisal reveals what the company **might do.** Organisational appraisal shows what it **can do.** CSR indicates what it **ought to do**.

According to the new Companies Act, from April 1, every company with a net worth of at least ₹ 500 crore, or annual revenues of above ₹ 1,000 crore or a net profit of more than ₹ 5 crore will have to spend at least 2% of its average net profits for the past three years on corporate social responsibility (CSR) activities.

Result: an additional ₹ 22,000 crore will flow into sectors such as education, healthcare, women and child welfare, etc. and companies and non-government organisations (NGOs) will need qualified people at all levels to manage the much larger social sector projects that this humongous sum will generate.

"This spending will also have a multiplier effect and generate many indirect jobs as well but we don't have any estimate on numbers or sectors," said Parul Soni executive director and practice leader, development advisory services, EY, which has done extensive studies on the subject.

(*iii*) **CSR and Strategic Choice:** Corporate and business strategies must be chosen to address not only economic issues but social issues too. CSR must be considered in strategy formulation.

(*iv*) **CSR and Strategy Implementation:** Social considerations need to be kept in mind while allocating resources and assigning duties and responsibility. In order to discharge CSR, an organisation might need to develop policies and procedures. Mechanisms are needed for formulation and implementation of social projects. Strategists have to set an example in promoting social responsiveness.

Thus, CSR needs to be aligned with each and every phase of strategic management process.

11.6 ORGANISATIONAL POLITICS AND POWER

An organisation consists of individuals and groups. Members of the organisation have their opinions, prejudices, preferences and expectations. Therefore, politics and power are inevitable features of organisations.

Power means the ability to influence others. Managers derive their power from their ability to reward and penalise, their official positions, their expertise, and their charisma. They compete for few top positions which results in jockeying for power. Struggle for material rewards, promotions, prestige, etc. leads to politics in organisations.

Strategic Use of Power and Politics

The power relationships in an organisation emerge from various influential groups. These groups form coalitions to support or oppose certain strategies. In strategy implementation, management must understand and manage coalitions to avoid their dysfunctions and to win their commitment.

Power and politics can have both negative and positive consequences. When used as means for domination, manipulation and subjugation to serve narrow personal interests, power and politics lead to conflict and disharmony in the organisation. As means of change and innovation, power and politics can help resolve conflicts, create collaboration, build consensus, manage coalitions and develop commitment to organisation's mission. Therefore, strategists must know when to use power and politics to achieve results and when to shun power and politics to maintain harmony.

Power and politics affect strategic management process. Formation of groups and coalitions influence the strategic intent or direction of the organisation. The priority of corporate objectives and the choice of strategy are also influenced by political considerations.

Politics and power are more important in strategy implementation than in strategy formulation. Implementation of strategy involves consensus building conflict resolution, balancing diverse interests and managing coalitions. For example, resource allocation is a natural-cum-political process. Organisation structure results in distribution of authority (official power) and use of politics and power affects corporate culture. In order to make strategic changes, strategists must use politics and power in a judicious manner. For this purpose, strategists must:

(*i*) recognise that politics and power are inevitable in every organisation.

(*ii*) understand working of the organisation's power structure – which individuals and groups wield real power and cannot be disregarded.

(*iii*) be alert to political signals emerging from different parts of the organisation.

(*iv*) know when to push through decisions and actions by selective use of power and politics and when to build consensus and manage coalitions.

(*v*) gather support for acceptable proposals and let the unacceptable ideas die a natural death.

(*vi*) reward loyalty and commitment and penalise negative attitudes and behaviour.

(*vii*) be open and honest in checking unprincipled politics and practise principled politics.

(*viii*) clearly define job roles, authority rules and procedures to minimise favouritism, nepotism unfairness and other forms of dysfunctional politics

(*ix*) set standards of behaviour so as to discourage dysfunctional politics at all levels.

(*x*) use objective criteria in rewarding and penalising people.

SUMMARY

Corporate Culture: (*i*) The set of assumptions, beliefs, values and norms shared by people in an organisaiton is its culture. (*ii*) Corporate culture influences decision-making, resistance to change, cooperation and commitment, communication and control, innovation, work ethics and motivation level. (*iii*) While trying to relate culture to strategy, strategists can ignore culture or adapt strategy to culture, adapt culture to strategy. (*iv*) Low performing culture and cultural diversity act as barriers to strategy implementation. (*v*) Therefore, it is necessary to create a high performing culture.

Strategic Leadership: (*i*) Strategic leadership is the ability to transform an organisation. (*ii*) It initiates change, provides strategic direction, shapes corporate culture, reconciles conflicting interests, sets ethical standards, develops motivation system, establishes control. (*iii*) Leadership styles and strategy implementation must match. (*iv*) Development of strategic leaders involves selection, career planning and succession planning.

Corporate Governance: (*i*) It is the process of managing and controlling an organisation in the best interests of its stakeholders (*ii*) Corporate governance is important in defining the strategic intent, strategy formulation, strategy implementation, and strategic evaluation and control.

Values and Ethics: (*i*) Values are convictions about desirable conduct. Ethics is a set of values (*ii*) Personal values and business ethics shape corporate culture, determine use of politics and power, affect power perceptions, influence attitudes towards change and risk. (*iii*) In order to inculcate moral values and ethics, strategists must set an example by their conduct, reward desirable behaviour, and penalise undesirable behaviour.

Corporate Social Responsibility: (*i*) CSR are the obligations towards society (*ii*) There is growing concern for CSR due to external and internal pressures. (*iii*) In order to operationalise CSR, top management commitment, CSR policies, monitoring social performance are required. (*iv*) CSR plays a vital role in all stages of strategic management process.

Organisational Politics and Power: (*i*) Politics is jockeying for power, prestige, rewards and other benefits. Power is the ability to influence others. (*ii*) Strategic use of power and politics helps in both formulation and implementation of strategies. (*iii*) Strategists must know when to use 'hard' approach and when to adopt 'soff' approach in carrying out strategic changes and in securing successful execution of strategies.

TEST QUESTIONS

1. What do you mean by social considerations in strategic management? Is it necessary for every company to be responsible to society?
2. Should the management be concerned with social responsibilities? Why? What are the constraints in this respect?
3. How do social considerations influence strategy formulation and implementation? Explain with relevant examples.
4. Why is it strategically important for organisaitons to behave in a socially responsible manner?
5. "The quality of leadership is a vital element in the implementation of strategy" Explain.
6. "There is a strong body of opinion against social responsibilities of business." Expound the statement and critically examine the viewpoints of Friedman and Hayek in that connection.

7. "Business belongs to society in as much as the society belongs to business." Comment on this statement. How would you prove that business and industry have grown in the wake of socio-economic transition from traditionalism to modernity?
8. "Questions of social responsibility are perhaps the thorniest of all issues faced in defining a company mission". Comment. Do Indian companies adopt strategic management techniques to conduct business in a socially responsible manner? Support your answer with appropriate Indian illustrations.
9. "A company must behave and function as a responsible member of the society just like any individual. It cannot shun moral values nor can it ignore actual compulsions." Discuss the more important dimensions of corporate social responsibilities to elucidate the statement.
10. A top manager in a professionally-managed company surmised, "I believe in being responsible only to my boss and board of directors. Social responsibility is not my responsibility, rather theirs." Do you agree or disagree with this view? Give reasons.
11. "The issue of social responsibility of business merits consideration in all phases of strategic management." Explain this statement and bring out the relationship between social responsibility and corporate governance.
12. Why is it strategically important for corporations to behave in a socially responsible manner? How can Balanced Scorecard be used to evaluate the effectiveness of corporate strategy?
13. Explain the social and ethical responsibilities of strategic decision-makers.
14. What is the relationship between corporate governance and social responsibility?
15. Define corporate culture. Explain the role of corporate culture in strategy implementation.
16. "Politics and power can be both functional and dysfunctional for strategic management". Explain.
17. Why should corporates be concerned with social responsibilities? Describe the constraints involved in this respect.
18. What is the relationship between corporate governance and social responsibility? Take the case of an Indian company and illustrate.
19. How can the culture of an organisation be changed?
20. Define Corporate Governance. What are the various responsibilities of the Board of Directors and the constitution of Board of Directors in India? How can Board of Directors promote Ethical Behaviour in the conduct of business?
21. Why is understanding of national cultures important in strategic management?
22. Who are the stakeholders in the organisation? How do these stakeholder groups influence organisations?
23. Define leadership and its importance in managing the corporate culture. How is the corporate culture and strategy compatibility assessed? How does an organisation manage diverse cultures after an acquisition?
24. What are stakeholders? List primary stakeholder groups of a company.
25. "Social considerations in strategic management comprise such issues as ecological impact, consumer protection, human development and social justice." Elucidate

26. "The social aspects of strategic management are best understood if business enterprises are recognized as an integral part of the social system". In the light of this statement, discuss the role of corporate social responsibility in strategic management.
27. "The quality of strategic plans and their implementation depend on the quality of leadership at all levels". Discuss.
28. Discuss strategic leadership and discuss the benchmarks which separate success from failure in leadership.
29. "The issue of social responsibility of business merits consideration in all phases of strategic management". Explain this statement and bring out the relationship between social responsibility and corporate governance.
30. "Indian organisations are not at all concerned about corporate governance". Do you agree? Give reasons.
31. Behavioural implementation deals with those aspects of strategy implementation that have an impact on the behaviour of the strategists in implementing chosen strategies". Discuss the major issues involved.
32. "A major task in strategy implementation is to create consistency among the business values and ethics and the proposed strategy". Throw light on this statement with respect to.
    (*a*) inculcating the right set of values
    (*b*) reconciling divergent values
    (*c*) modifying values to create consistency.

CASE STUDY

"There is the world of car industry, and then there is Toyota. Since 2000 the output of the global industry has risen by about 3 m (3 million) vehicles to some 60 m (60 million): of that increase, half come from Toyota alone." Toyota has enjoyed a dramatic growth spurt around and globe, and it is on the verge of making more cars abroad than at home. As of March 2007, Toyota marked vehicles in more than 170 countries and employed approximately 299,400 people worldwide. In addition to its part manufacturing and vehicle assembly facilities in Japan, Toyota has 52 manufacturing companies in 26 nations and regions.

Toyota's strong corporate culture is the "glue" that holds these far-flung "operations together and makes them part of a single entity." "Spend some time with Toyota people and... you realize there is something different about them. The rest of the car industry raves about engines, gearboxes, acceleration, fuel economy, handling, ride quality and sexy design. Toytoa's people talk about 'The Toyota Way' and about customers." Toyota's customer focus is legendary. Jim Press, head of the company's North America sales, says, "[t]he Toyota culture is inside all of us. Toyota is a customer's company...Everything is done to make...[the customer's] life better."

Toyota's culture, labeled "*The Toyota Way*," has five distinct components: *kaizen, genchi genbutslu,* challenge, teamwork, and respect. Kaizen refers to the process of continuous improvement, and it is as much a frame of mind as it is a business process. Genchi genbutsu focuses on going to the source of a problem, finding the facts, and building consensus through arguments that are well supported. Challenge encourages Toyota employees to view problems as a way to help them improve their performance rather than as something undesirable. Teamwork puts the company's interest before those of any individual, and promotes sharing knowledge with other employees. Toyota's employees exhibit respect for other people and their skills and special knowledge.

Toyota's culture has served the company very well for may years. Indeed, competitors as marvel at that culture and its ongoing success. As one General Motors planner observed privately," …the only way to stop Toyota would be the business equivalent of germ warfare, finding a 'poison pill' or 'social virus' that could be infiltrated into the company to destroy its culture."

Over the year. "Toyota has adapted well to changes facing the automotive industry by establishing sound processes and procedures. It has made continuous change and improvements as suggested by employees as many of the suggestions have been implemented. It has built its success with products that are made according to the all embracing 'Toyota Way.' In fact, so confident is Toytoa of its quality and reliability record, that it allows rival companies to visit its factories all over the world."

Recently, however, some chinks seem to be developing in the armour of the company's vaunted culture. An internal Toyota study compared its products against those of its competitors—component by component, car by car—and found Toyota's products to be superior in just over half of hundreds of components and vehicle systems. Toyota judged such quality performance to be unacceptably mediocre. In reference to the U.S. market, some business analysts say the company's rapid growth is one cause of its growing quality-conrtol problems. For example, in 2005 " Toyota recalled 2.38 million vehicles in the U.S. more than 2.26 million vehicles it sold—a sign that indicates Toyota is troubled not only by manufacturing problems but also by design flaws."

Toyota CEO Kastsuaki Watanabe "thinks Toyota is losing its competitive edge as it expands around the world. He frets that quality, the foundation of its U.S success, is slipping. He grouses that Toyota's factories and engineering practices aren't efficient enough. Within the company, he has even questioned a core tenet of Toyota's corporate culture – Kaizen, the relentless focus on incremental improvement." Tetsuo Agata, one of Toyota's manufacturin experts, point out that the company needs to depart from its history of steady, incremental improvement and develop radical new ways of manufacturing vehicle components more economically. Watanable also argues that "The Toyota Way" of the future needs to embreace *kakushin*-revolutionary change in Toyota's design of factories and cars. Watanabe wants Toyota to reduce by half the number of components that it uses in a typical vehicle, and to create new fast and flexible plants for assembling these simplified cars.

How will Toyota's global organisational culture change as the company embraces *kakushin*?

Questions

(*a*) Describe Toyota's culture from the perspectives of espoused values and enacted values.

(*b*) Using the perspective of the functions of organisational culture, explain the impact of "The Toyota Way."

(*c*) Using the perspective of the effects of organisational culture, explain the impact of "The Toyota Way."

(*d*) What challenges does Toyota face as it embarks on transforming its global organisational culture from *kaizen* to *kakushin*?

CHAPTER 12

FUNCTIONAL ISSUES IN STRATEGY IMPLEMENTATION

CHAPTER OUTLINE

Corporate level and business level strategies are implemented through functional strategies. On the basis of functional strategies, functional policies and plans are formulated in different areas such as finance, marketing, production, human resources, etc.

12.1 FUNCTIONAL STRATEGIES

Functional strategies are designed to achieve objectives in different functional areas. They are concerned with the following:

(*i*) allocation of resources among different operations within a specific functional area;

(*ii*) effective utilisation of resources allocated to various functional areas; and

(*iii*) integration of activities in each functional area (*e.g.* market research, promotion, sales, distribution, etc. within the marketing area).

Functional strategies are derived from business strategies (in case of a multibusiness firm) or corporate strategies (in case of a single business firm). For example, ITC is a multibusiness company operating in tobacco products, hotels and hospitality, paper and paperboards, food and beverages, readymade garments, etc. Suppose, ITC adopts the cost leadership business strategy for its foods and beverages business. All the functional areas in that business (marketing, finance, operations, human resources, etc.) must contribute to cost reduction and low cost structure. Similarly, if differentiation business strategy is adopted in paper and paperboards business, then all functional areas should contribute to differentiation in terms of quality and innovation.

Strategic implementation requires that strategies at functional, business and corporate levels are properly aligned. Such alignment or congruence is known as **vertical fit**. Similar alignment or congruence is needed among different functional strategies. Such alignment or congruence is called **horizontal fit**. Vertical and horizontal fits provide the benefit of synergy which means the whole is greater then the sum of its parts (*i.e.* two plus two make five). In other words, alignment among strategies at the three levels helps to achieve organisational effectiveness.

Table 12.1. Difference Between Functional and Business Strategies.

	Functional Strategy	Business Strategy
Time Horizon	Functional strategies focus on short-term goals (one year)	Business strategies focus on the firm's longterm competitive posture (3 to 5 years).
Nature of Direction	Functional Strategies provide more specific direction to functional managers	Business strategies provide general direction.
Level of Management	Functional strategy is the responsibility of the operating managers of the functional area.	Business strategy is the responsibility of the head of the business unit.
Approval	Functional strategies are approved through negotiation between business unit managers and operating managers of the functional area.	Business strategies are approved through negotiation between corporate managers and business unit managers.
Purpose	To help implementation of business strategies	To help implementation of corporate strategies

Functional strategies are implemented through functional policies and plans. When the policies and plans in different functional areas are put into operation, they bring results leading to execution of business strategies and corporate strategies.

12.2 FUNCTIONAL POLICIES AND PLANS

Effective implementation of strategies is essential for the success of strategic management. Proper strategy implementation requires sound functional policies and plans. The number of functional areas in which policies and plans are prepared depends on the nature and size of the organisation. In a small organisation, only a few functional policies and plans are needed. But in a large organisation, a large number of functional policies and plans are prepared.

A functional policy is a broad guideline indicating the criteria that a functional manager should use in making decisions in his functional area. A functional plan is a list of activities to be performed during the plan period. Functional policies and plans are prepared by various functional heads within the framework of guidelines provided by higher authorities. These guidelines are developed to ensure that functional policies and plans are in tune with business and corporate strategies. Functional policies and plans help strategy implementation in the following ways:

(*i*) Top management can ensure that strategic decisions are implemented by all parts of the organisation.

(*ii*) Functional policies and plans specify how things are to be done and limit direction for managerial action. Therefore, functional managers can make decisions more quickly.

(*iii*) Functional managers can handle similar situations in different functional areas in a consistent manner.

(*iv*) Coordination among different functions is ensured.

(*v*) Functional policies and plans serve as the bases for controlling activities in different functional areas.

Functional policies and plans can be judged on the basis of the following criteria:

(*a*) Functional policies and plans should cover all the functional areas critical for strategy implementation.

(*b*) These should be desired behaviour and practices.

(*c*) These should be clear and precise.

(*d*) These must be consistent with one another.

(*e*) These should be workable in existing and expected situations.

12.3 FINANCIAL POLICIES AND PLANS

Financial policies and plans are concerned with raising, usage and management of funds for business operations. The three aspects are interrelated and interdependent. For example, the company's ability to raise funds will influence the amount of funds and their usage. Policies and plans are formulated to ensure that strategies are implemented effectively.

1. **Sources of Funds:** Policies and plans concerning sources of funds determine how and from where funds will be raised for strategy implementation. Funds are needed for both long term and short term. There are two broad sources of funds – equity and debt. Equity shares, preference shares and retained earnings provide equity funds. Debentures and borrowings are sources of debt. Policies and plans concerning sources of funds relate to capital structure, procurement of funds, and relationships with lenders.

   Companies differ in their approach to sources of funds. Some of them depend primarily on internal financing while others rely more on external borrowings. In other words, debt equity ratios vary from one company to another. Indian companies raised funds from Indian sources before 1991. Since liberalization, many of them raise funds through American Depository Receipts (ADRs), Global Depository Receipts (GDRs), Foreign institutional Investors (FIIs), foreign private equity funds, foreign venture capitalists and other foreign sources.

   Companies take into account several factors while deciding their capital mix. Purpose of financing, period of financing, cost of funds, financial leverage, desire to retain control are such factors. Companies like Hindustan Unilever, Bajaj Auto, EIH Limited depend mainly on internal financing. On the other hand, Tata Group and Reliance Industries prefer external funding for acquisitions and green field projects.

2. **Usage of Funds:** Judicious use of funds is essential for strategy implementation. A company can allocate funds between fixed assets and current assets depending on its needs. **Investment in fixed assets** (called fixed capital) may be (*a*) to acquire new fixed

assets for expansion and growth, and (*b*) to replace the existing fixed assets. Investment in fixed assets has long term implications because these assets generate benefits over the long period. These benefits or returns must be more than the cost of capital. In order to optimise investment in fixed assets, a company can take the following steps:

(*i*) *Choice of appropriate technology* – The latest or fully automated technology may involve huge investment resulting in high interest cost. Cost minimisation as well as technical factors should be considered in choosing technology.

(*ii*) *Proper mix of various fixed assets* – Assets critical for project implementation need be given priority over the supporting assets. For example, township can be developed after the project starts generating profits. During the execution of project houses for employees working on the project can be taken on rent.

(*iii*) *Efficient project implementation* – Efficient project implementation helps to reduce investment. Reliance Industries is known for implementing large projects without time and cost overruns.

Investment in current assets is known as working capital. Volume of operations, type of technology, manufacturing cycle, seasonal and cyclical fluctuations, etc. are some of such factors. Some of the steps that can be taken to minimise investment in working capital without affecting operations are as follows:

(*a*) maintain inventory at proper level

(*b*) rationalise credit policy so as to match debtors and trade creditors

(*c*) keep cash and bank balance at right-levels by investing surplus funds.

3. **Management of Funds:** Sound funds management plays an important role in strategy implementation through conservation and optimum utilisation of funds. In the management of funds, policies and plans are developed for accounting and budgeting credit and risk management, cost reduction and control, tax planning, etc. Stringent cost control helps to improve a company's financial health. Sound cash management is no longer merely timely collection of receivables and disbursement of payment. Companies now outsource cash management to banks to ensure more effective management of cash flows and to earn higher interest. Risks arising from technology and environment require more robust internal audit and control systems.

Management of earnings is a critical decision. Dividend policy decision involves allocation of earnings between dividend distribution and reinvestment in business. Company's future needs for funds, expectations of shareholders, legal constraints, etc. influence dividend policy. Some companies reinvest a major portion of their earnings while others distribute most of the earnings in the form of dividends. Firms pursuing expansion/growth strategies are likely to prefer reinvestment of earnings.

Sometimes, the priorities of top management may be in conflict with those of shareholders and lenders. Strategists must resolve this conflict and develop a consensus on financial policies and plans.

Table 12.2: Differing Priorities of Management and Shareholders and the Probable Areas of Conflict

Financial Policy area	Management priorities	Shareholder's priorities	Probable area of conflict
1. Sources of funds	– Retained earnings – Long-term debt – New common stock	– Debt – Retained earning – New common stock	– Extent of use of these resources in financing growth
2. Usage of funds (investment proposals)	– Internal rate of return on the basis of past performance	– External as well as internal investment opportunity rates including competing business organisations of comparable risk	– Cut-off rate of acceptable investment opportunities and amounts committed to perpetuate existing investment
3. Management of funds	– Measuring financial performance on the basis of anticipated changes in specific cash flows in the foreseeable future-amount, certainty and timing	– Anticipated changes in share values as measured by trends in earnings per share and dividends	– Ranking of investment alternatives, depreciation policy, stock option, acquisition, mergers, etc.
	– Acceptable risk on the basis of preserving the individual corporate entity and management goals.	– Acceptable risk on the basis of a portfolio of investment over several companies	– Diversification of product and markets; debt-equity proportions

Source: D.B. Ekpenyong: "Strategic Financial Planning for Emergencies" in **The Chartered Accountant**, March. 1989, p. 799,

12.4 MARKETING POLICIES AND PLANS.

Companies are increasingly recognising that the key to success lies in satisfying needs and wants of customers more efficiently and effectively than competitors. In the area of marketing, policies and plans are formulated and implemented with respect to four major elements – product, pricing, distribution, promotion.

1. **Product Decisions:** Product refers to the goods and services that a firm offers to its target markets. The organisation may offer a single product or several products. A group of closely related products is known as a product line. For example, textiles is a product line consisting of suitings, shirtings, sarees, dress materials, suits, etc. All the products offered by an organisation is called product mix. For example, Hindustan Unilever offers personal care products, soaps and detergents, foods and beverages, etc. The major policy decisions about products are as follows:

   (*a*) *Product Mix*: The business definition determines the product mix. Product mix decision has two aspects: (*i*) the number of product lines called breadth of product mix, and (*ii*) total number of products in product line known as length of product mix While deciding the product mix, an organisation seeks three objectives—stability in sales volume, increasing sales growth, and improving profitability over time. A firm may delete unprofitable products and add new products in its product mix.

(*b*) *Product Features*: An organisation's strategy determines product characteristics. New and better features like size, shape colour, taste, smell, etc. may be added under competitive strategy. Product innovations and customization have become necessary due to global competition. In order to achieve growth, quality and variety are stressed. For example, the product policy of Reliance Industries is to offer high fashion fabrics of new varieties and design.

(*c*) *Product Positioning*: Every organisation attempts to offer its product/service in such a manner that customers perceive it to be different from competitive products. Product differentiation may be achieved through product features (performance, durability, reliability, style, design, etc,) and services offered with the product (delivery, installation, warranty, credit, customer training, etc.)

(*d*) *Branding*: Attaching a brand name to a product helps customers to identify it and differentiate it from rival products. Policy decisions are made regarding the type of brand and brand extension. An organisation may use family brand or individual brand. For example, products offered by the Tata Group carry the prefix 'Tata'. On the other hand, Hindustan Unilever uses individual branding *e.g.* Lux, Lifebuoy, Pears, Annapurna, etc. It also has the policy of brand extension, *e.g.* Lifebuoy, Lifebuoy Plus Lifebuoy Gold, etc.

(*e*) *Packaging*: In the area of packaging, policy decisions specify the types of packaging materials, level of packaging, etc. Packaging materials depend on the nature and types of product, cost of materials, etc. Packaging may be done at three levels – primary (*e.g.* tube of Colgate tooth paste), secondary (*e.g.* a carton of one dozen tubes) and shipping (*e.g.* a box of ten cartons).

2. **Pricing:** Price means the money that customers pay in exchange for goods and services. Price is important both for the seller and the buyer. For a buyer price is the value assigned to need satisfaction. For the seller, price determines the return on efforts. Therefore, the price should be beneficial to both. Several factors such as cost of production, competitor's price. Government regulations, etc. influence price of a product or service.

   Companies use price as a competitive tool. For example, Nirma could compete with Hindustan Unilever due to its low price policy. Tata Motors launched their small car Nano with a basic price tag of ₹ 1 lac. Budget Airlines such as Go Air, Spice Jet captured the market through low airfares. Budget hotels and telecommunications firms use low price to gain competitive advantage.

   Price is also used to segment the market. For example, Hindustan Unilever sells low priced soaps (*e.g.* Lifebuoys) and high-priced soaps (*e.g.* Dove, Pears).

3. **Distribution:** Policies and Plans concerning distribution involve decisions such as channels to be used, transportation, inventory management, customer order processing, etc. A product may be distributed directly to consumers or indirectly through middlemen. Internet, company owned retail stores (*e.g.* Bata), door-to-door selling, mail order selling,

vending machines are forms of direct marketing. Agents, wholesalers and retailers are employed in case of indirect marketing. Per unit cost of distribution, control over distribution and flexibility are the main criteria used to evaluate alternative channels of distribution. While selecting the most suitable channel characteristics of the product, the market, the company, etc. are kept in view. An efficient and effective distribution system is essential for the success of marketing strategies in a competitive environment. Companies are paying increasing attention to supply-chain management and customer-relationship management to gain a competitive advantage. Firms such as ITC, Hindustan Unilever, Dabur, Amul have an advantage due to their countrywide distribution network. In courier service, airlines, railways, etc. logistics is highly important. For example, Blue Dart pays special attention to logistics infrastructure to ensure timely and safe delivery. As a result, it has become South Asia's largest integrated air express and package distribution company. Pizza Hut has gained through its '30 minutes delivery' promise.

Havells' company's lighting fixtures, cables, and switchgears are sold through 4,000 distributors and 100,000 outlets. Its consumer appliances are available through 2,000 retail outlets, and its plan is to increase distribution by 10-12% each year.

Havells also plans to open more of its own 'Galaxy' branded franchisee retail stores. "By the end of March, we will have 250 outlets. We typically open 50-60 stores each year, but the plan is to open at least 75 stores in 2014-15. We hope to have 400 stores in two years."

ITC plans to shake up distribution of fast-moving consumer goods by rolling out its entire range of packaged food and personal care products through lakhs of paan shops across India, taking advantage of relationships it has built up with pannwalahs over the years through the cigarette business.

The strategy is in sharp contrast with that of rivals, which mostly sell confectionery, snacks and at best sachets of shampoos and detergent through panan shops. ITC, on the other hand, even plans to sell its premium cookies and cream biscuits through them. It will offer Sunfeast biscuits, Yippee instant noodles, Vivel soaps, Mangaldeep agarbattis Dark Fantasy Choco Fills and Choco Meltz biscuits, Delishus cookies and Engage deodorants through these outlets, known to the trade as the paan-plus channel.

4. **Promotion:** Promotion consists of activities designed to inform and persuade customers to buy product/services. Policies and plans relating to promotion involve two basic issues – promotion mix, and promotion budget.

   (*a*) *Promotion Mix:* Advertising, personal selling, sales promotion and publicity are the main elements of promotion mix. The relative mix of these elements differ among companies and over time. The nature of product/industry is major determinant of promotion mix. Fast moving consume Goods (FMCG) firms are the biggest advertisers on television, radio and other, media. In order to market brand India' as a tourist destination, Government of India launched a promotional campaign at the world Economic Forum (Davos), World Travel Market (London), print and electronic media.

Several companies such as Colgate, Nokia, Britannia, Hindustan Unilever are using promotion as a source of strategic advantage. Firms struggle to make their presence felt in a highly crowded and competitive market, due to plethora of advertising campaigns. Unique and innovative approaches to promotion have become necessary in such a scenario.

For example, Eureka Forbes uses door-to-door selling and demonstrations at exhibitions as sales promotion tools. LG Electronics adopted the unique selling proposition of health to promote its consumer durable brands through the slogan 'Life is Good'.

There is growing need to harmonise and integrate marketing policies and plans relating to product, price, distribution and promotion due to environmental changes. Increasing competition by both existing and new players, declining profit margins, global quality standards, rising aspirations of customers are some of the major changes in environment. Decisions about any of the four elements of marketing mix must be taken keeping in mind their impact on the other elements.

12.5 PRODUCTION/OPERATIONS POLICIES AND PLANS

Production or operations function is concerned with the transformation of inputs into outputs. Materials, equipment, information and talent are main inputs, which are converted into goods and services. The main objectives are to produce the required quantity and quality at the right time and at the lowest possible cost. Policies and plans are formulated with respect to production system, operations planning and control, research and development and modernisation.

1. **Production System:** The production system involves decisions relating to location, layout, capacity, work system, degree of automation, product/service design, degree of vertical integration, etc. These decisions are critical because they have long-term impact on the organisation's ability to implement strategies. For example, Reliance Industries achieved remarkable expansion through vertical integration. Production system is equally important for service organisations. For example, Make my Trip. com. customises its holiday packages to meet the unique needs and wants of its clients.

   A major decision in designing and developing the production system is the **make or buy decision.** The major considerations involved in this decision are as under:

   (*a*) cost of making vs. cost of buying

   (*b*) how critical the item is for the organisation

   (*c*) need to ensure regular supply

   (*d*) organisation's financial and managerial capabilities

   (*e*) government policy *e.g.* reservation of some items for production in the small scale sector.

   For those items which are to be bought, the organisation has to decide the criteria for selection of vendors and the number of vendors. Maruti Suzuki could achieve cost and quality advantages due to its vendor development policy.

2. **Operations Planning and Control:** The twin objectives of operations planning and control are optimum utilisation of resources and efficient management of day-to-day operations. Aggregate production planning, materials supply, cost and quality of output, inventory management, repair and maintenance of plant and machinery are the key issues in operations planning and control. Ancilarisation, focussed differentiation, high quality are some of the policies which companies use to achieve competitive advantage in operations management.

3. **Research and Development (R & D):** Activities undertaken to introduce new products, to improve existing products, to absorb new technology, etc. are the domain of R & D. Policy decisions in the area of R & D relate to R & D spending, and type of R & D activities. The resources allocation for R & D depends on nature of the organisation, type of R & D activities to be taken, nature of industry, etc. Firms operating in pharma and such other industries where rapid changes in product are necessary spend more on, R & D. For example, Ranbaxy Laboratories spends about five per cent of its revenues on R & D while Tata Steel spends about 0.5 per cent on R & D. Similarly, fundamental research requires more funds than applied research. Firms which get technology from their parent companies abroad can afford to spend less on R & D. For example, Hindustan Unilever regularly gets new technology from its parent company Unilever.

   Foreign multinationals are increasing setting up their R & D facilities in India due to low cost engineering and technical skills. Several companies have used R & D as a source of competitive advantage. R & D helps in the implementation of product development and diversification strategies. Firms which do not have their R & D centres collaborate with research agencies.

4. **Modernisation:** The modernisation strategy involves upgradation of plant and machinery so as to reduce cost per unit and to improve product quality. The organisation gains a competitive advantage by serving customers better. Tata Steel became the lowest cost steel producer using its modernisation programme.

12.6 HUMAN RESOURCE POLICIES AND PLANS

It is the people who formulate and implement strategies. In the post-liberalisation era human resource management has undergone significant changes. Companies are now aligning their human resource policies and plans with their corporate and business strategies. They are outsourcing operational or administrative tasks in human resource management so as to focus on strategic aspects. For example, Hindustan Unilever outsources routine human resource functions form Accenture. Involvement of top management in HR, setting up training and development centres, alignment of performance appraisal systems with business goals, etc. are some of the initiatives companies have undertaken in the area of human resource management.

Human resource policies and plans are needed is respect of procurement, development, appraisal, rewards and industrial relations.

1. **Procurement:** Manpower planning, recruitment and selection are the main activities involved in procurement of the right talent. Job-person fit is essential for efficient working and successful strategy implementation. Firms use multiple sources and techniques to match the new hires with their corporate culture.

2. **Development:** Rapid changes in technology and increasing complexity of jobs require continuous training and development of people. Therefore, companies use both inhouse and outside facilities to train their staff. Hindustan Unilever has built up strategic competence through its management development system.

3. **Appraisal:** Performance evaluation systems have become more transparent. The foucs is now more on grooming people for higher responsibilities. Continuous monitoring is replacing the traditional once-a-year appraisal. There is a closer link between performance and rewards.

   Hindustan Unilever, for the third year in a row, is the most preferred employer across all sectors for the 2014 graduating batch of B-school students, according to the Campus Track Business School survey 2013, conducted by Nielsen. The FMCG major also retained the 'Dream Employer' status for the fifth consecutive year and continued to be the top company considered for application by B-school students.

   "The experience of leading large teams, taking independent decisions early in career, job rotations and diversity of experiences, including international assignment, provide the best foundation for the brightest mind to be groomed for leadership".

4. **Retention:** Retaining talent has emerged as a major challenge owing to high attrition rates specially in information technology sector. HCL Technologies adopted the 'employee first' policy to engage and retain high quality employees.

5. **Industrial Relations:** Policies and plans concerning industrial relations are developed to secure mutual understanding and cooperation between management and worker, to avoid industrial conflicts, to increase productivity and to overcome resistance to change. Companies use several mechanisms such as grievance redressal system, suggestion scheme, joint consultation, worker participation in management, collective bargaining, open door policy, etc. to develop and maintain cordial relations with workers and their unions. Economic liberalisation and globalisation have led to a paradigm shift in approach to industrial relations. Improvement in working conditions, better pay scales, involvement of families in company programes, better training and career advancement opportunities, medical and other welfare facilities are some of the features of industrial relations system. The number and frequency of strikes and lockouts have significantly declined due to 'Firm and fair' approach of employers.

   Looking to "regain" its bellwether status amidst efforts to instill confidence among its workforce, software services major Infosys is reaching out to its US-based employees as it seeks to actively involve them in developing the company's business strategy and shape up its "collective thinking".

12.7 INTEGRATION OF FUNCTIONAL POLICIES AND PLANS

Various functional policies and plans described above are inter related and interdependent. Therefore, their proper integration is necessary for effective implementation of business and corporate strategies. According to Glucck, the main considerations that should be kept in mind in the integration of functional policies and plans are as follows[1]:

1. **Internal Consistency:** Various functional policies and plans must be internally consistent so that they operate in the same direction. Otherwise these may work at cross-purposes leading to sub-optimisation in strategy implementation. For example, rapid expansion strategy requires increase in plant capacity which in turn needs considerable funds, aggressive marketing and availability of qualified employees.

---

1. William F. Glueck and L.R. Jauch, **Business Policy and Strategic Management,** McGraw Hill, New York, 1984, pp 360-362.

2. **Relevance to Development of Organisational Capability:** Integration of functional policies and plans should focus on developing organisational capabilities needed for strategy implementation. Synergistic effects occur across functional areas and core competence emerges as a result of deploying resources in the areas wherein the organisation wants to build up strategic advantages. For example, a company which wishes to become a market leader would have to offer best quality products at competitive prices through an efficient distribution network supported by aggressive promotion policy. Policies and plans in other functional areas must supplement these marketing policies. Liberal approach to sources, usage and management of funds will be necessary to build high-volume and low-cost production capacity. Human resource policies will have to focus on attraction, retention and motivation of employees so as to ensure high productivity.
3. **Making Trade-off Decisions:** During the integration of functional policies and plans, an organisation has to make trade-off decisions due to the inherent nature of the functional areas. For example, production-orientation may require large-volume production with less product variety. On the other hand, marketing-orientation involves low volume and more product variety. In order to gain something the organisation has to lose something. In such a situation, the organisation should ensure that what it gains is more than what it has to sacrifice.
4. **Intensity of Linkages:** While deciding the degree of coordination between different functional areas, the intensity of linkages existing between these areas must be considered. For example, the product differentiation strategy requires close contact between R & D, product development and production functions. Similarly, a strategy based on low cost, mass consumption items needs a high degree of coordination between production and marketing functions. The intensity of linkages is not constant but varies with changes in strategy from time to time.
5. **Timing of implementation:** Policies and plans in different functional areas should be implemented at the appropriate time so that they reinforce one another. For example, a company facing shortage of funds would have to postpone costly R & D activities. Likewise, a company entering into high-tech sector will have to ensure availability of well-trained engineers and technicians.

12.7.1 Mechanisms for Integration of Functional Policies and Plans

Daft[2] has suggested the following mechanisms that can be used to integrate policies and plans in different functional areas:

1. **Direct Contact:** Direct personal interaction in performing related functions is the most effective method of integrating functional plans. A special liaison manager may be assigned the responsibility of ensuring cooperation and coordination among functional areas. At the macro level Krishi Vikas Kendras create direct contact between research institutions and farmers for transfer of new agricultural technology. In order to ensure regular contact between engineering, product development, operations and marketing departments these may be located physically close to one another *e.g* on the same floor.

2. R.L. Daft, **Organisation Theory and Design,** Thompson Learning, Ohio, 2004, pp. 91-94.

2. **Information System:** In case of large and geographically dispersed organisations, information systems can be used to ensure coordination among functional areas. For example, Max Healthcare, (a hospital information system) wide area network is used to connect healthcare facilities at different locations. This realtime system makes patient records available to doctors, nurses, lab technicians and pharmacists. This system facilitates integration among out patient, nursing pathology and radiology functions.
3. **Task Forces:** A task force is an ad hoc unit created to perform a specific task. It consists of members from different functional areas involved in the task. Task forces are widely used in defence organisations, government ministries and other types of organisations. The task forces are called committees. The task assigned to a committee is defined in its 'terms of reference'. Cross-functional composition of the committee helps in maintaining communication and coordination among different functional departments.
4. **Teams:** A team is a permanent task force constituted to achieve a high degree of coordination over a long time period. For example, project teams are created to implement large-scale projects such as change management, organisation development, total quality management, etc.
5. **Full-Time Integrator:** A full-time position or department may be created to achieve cross functional coordination. In matrix organisation structure, project managers act as full-time coordinators. These managers formulate and implement projects by integrating efforts from different functional areas. They may also collaborate with suppliers, contractors, clients, etc. to achieve the objectives.

SUMMARY

Functional Strategies: These are concerned with allocation and use of resources so as to achieve objectives in various functional areas. Functional strategies are derived from business level and corporate level strategies.

Functional Policies and Plans: These are broad guidelines for decision-making at the functional level. These are formulated to execute functional strategies.

Financial Policies and Plans: These relate to sources of funds, usage of funds, and management of funds.

Marketing Policies and Plans: These are concerned with decisions relating to product, price, distribution and promotion.

Production/Operations Policies and Plans: These relate to production system, operations planning and control, R & D, modernisation, etc.

Human Resource Policies and Plans: Procurement, development, appraisal and retention of talent and industrial relations are covered in these policies and plans.

Integration of Functional Policies and Plans: Internal consistency, relevance to development of organisational capability, trade-off decisions, intensity of linkages, timing of implementation are the main considerations in integrating functional plans.

Direct contact, information system, task forces, teams and full-time integrator are the mechanisms used for integration.

TEST QUESTIONS

1. "Strategy implementation involves integration of policies and plans of various functional areas." Discuss.
2. Discuss the nature and scope of financial strategies that should be of concern to a business organisation aiming at growth and expansion.
3. "The level and standard of maintenance of physical facilities, plant and equipment result partly from the personal preferences of key executives and partly reflect a calculated decision." Discuss, in the light of the statement, the significance of preventive maintenance and scheduled replacement of equipments in a manufacturing concern.
4. Explain the problems encountered in implementation of functional plans.
5. "Plant location is one of the critical decisions that can influence the very viability of project." Discuss.
6. State the major considerations that govern make or buy decisions.
7. What is 'backward tapering capacity' as a policy in deciding the size of a plant? Under what conditions is it desirable?
8. "Determination of optimum inventory size involves a balancing of opposite costs." Explain
9. "Non-cost factors are as much relevant in deciding plant location as cost difference". Elucidate.
10. "The level and standard of maintenance of physical facilities depend on personal preferences of key executives and cost considerations." Explain.
11. Discuss the policy issues involved in vendor selection.
12. Discuss the basis considerations to be kept in view while formulating the product mix policy.
13. In a competitive market how should a company make its product distinctive if its product line happens to be: (*a*) bicycles, (*b*) scooters, (*c*) colour TV, (*d*) readymade garments, and (*e*) sewing machines?
14. "Prices at which competitors offer similar products always have a bearing on the pricing policy of a firm." Do you agree, Give, reasons.
15. Explain the nature of and rationale behind Nirma marketing mix strategy.
16. In a three star hotel in Delhi, the occupancy rate has declined to 50 per cent. The management is considering use of appropriate sales appeals and media to overcome the problem. Advise the management.
17. "A major task of management is to ensure that capital necessary to execute the company strategy is available at a reasonable cost." Explain
18. Explain the main issues involved in human resource strategy and their role in strategy implementation.
19. Describe the considerations for functional strategy implementation for marketing, finance, HR and operations managements.

CASE STUDY

The year 1993-94 wasn't kind to Hindustan Ciba Geigy. The ₹ 447-crore drug multinational has had a run of bad luck that would have given any management sleepless nights. Its main manufacturing unit in Goa was facing a prolonged lockout with no immediate end in sight. The erratic monsoon led to a sharp drop in the demand for agrochemicals, its largest business. And its pharma division had been squirming under the grip of price control.

So it wasn't surprising that when the company's top management team talked about results for the year to March 1994, it was unable to hide a note of pride.

Despite the adverse business conditions, Hindustan Ciba Geigy posted a 12 per cent growth in sales income, from ₹ 391.8 crore to ₹ 439.5 crore. It upped dividend from 25 per cent to 28 per cent, and was able to raise exports by 75 per cent, from ₹ 12.7 crore to ₹ 22.4 crore. Yet, there a was profit squeeze. Net profit for 1993-94, at ₹ 14.8 crore, was only marginally higher than the previous year's ₹ 14.2 crore.

The disappointing bottomline had prompted managing director Richard Hartland to take the offensive. Other Swiss multinationals operating in India, especially in areas such as chemical and pharmaceuticals, tended to be conservative and cautious. At Hindustan Ciba Geigy, the contrast couldn't be more glaring.

In quick succession over a year or two, the company set in motion plans to reorient its business activities to fit in with its revised business strategy: to concentrate on its core businesses of speciality chemicals and pharmaceuticals, and gradually promote India as a manufacturing base for Ciba worldwide. The first step was taken when the company wound up operations at Bhandup, Bombay, with an amicable voluntary retirement scheme, and sold off the property.

Hindustan Ciba also brought in Ciba Vision to begin operations in India. A division of Ciba worldwide, with global sales of $700 million, Ciba Vision began manufacturing optical and ophthalmological products, including contact lenses.

Next, it set up a joint venture with the Korean company Chong Kun Dang for a $ 30 million project to manufacture Rifampicin, a bulk drug used in anti-TB formulations. Anti-TB formulations were the pharma division's second most important product (after anti-rheumatics, inculding market leader Voveran).

Finally, Hindustan Ciba decided to sell off its oral hygiene unit, manufacturing Cibaca toothpaste, and toothbrushes to Colgate Palmolive for ₹130 crore. This division, which contributed about 13 per cent of the company's sales, was one of the better performens, but the decision was not as surprising as it seemed. "We had taken a decision to get out of the business, and the best time to sell was when a business was successful, "said Hartland.

The details had not been worked out, but the company was planning to deploy the funds from the sale in its core business, which it wanted to expand. Besides the officially stated aim of a more strategic deployment of resources, industry sources believed that the reason behind the decision was the company's unwillingness to increase marketing and advertising expenditures to levels needed to take on the might of Hindustan Lever and Colgate Palmolive in the highly competitive consumer oral care market.

Toothpaste was the only product of Hindustan Ciba falling in the category of branded consumer goods, and clearly did not fit in with the rest of the company's product line-up. This consisted of agro-chemicals, which accounted for 29 per cent of the turnover, pharmaceuticals (24 per cent), additives, polymers, pigments and composites (APPC, 23 per cent), and dyestuffs and speciality chemicals (11 per cent).

In 1993-94, it was the two smaller division that emerged as stars. The APPC division producing a range of speciality chemcials for use in plastics, synthetic fibres, paints and high-tech applications, grew by a breathtaking 43 per cent, earning over ₹100 crore for the first time.

According to Satish Kalra, head of the division, growth was fuelled by the success of the company's market seeding programme for anti-oxidants. The division was planning to commission a 800 tonne per annum plant for anti-oxidants by the end of next year, and had already begun importing and marketing the products in order to ensure sales volumes once the plant began production. In addition, user industries such as white goods and automobiles had emerged from recession, and demand had been on the rise.

The second star performer had been the dyestuffs and chemicals division, which chalked up exports of about ₹ 20 crore. This division, manufacturing dyestuffs and speciality chemicals of the leather industry, was on the verge of beginning commercial production of Tinopal CBX, a new generation detergent whitener. The division had also finalised plans to set up a joint marketing project with the German company, Stockhausen, to manufacture leather chemicals.

According to S. Rajagopalan, head of the division: "Stockhausen had a worldwide arrangement with Ciba: it would set up a manufacturing base in our facilities, and we would jointly market the products." However in 1994-95, even the pharma division brought a note of cheer. For the first time, the division contributed positively to the company's bottomline, and with new drug policy expected to come into force, it hoped to improve performance.

Already, the division was working overtime to reduce costs and cut expenditure to make the best of the controlled regime. Over a period of a few years, the division had cut its staff strength from 1,480 to 480. Said N.N. Borkar, general manager: "At present over 80 per cent of our products were covered by the Drug Price Control Order. We are gradually trying to move to a situation where 30 per cent of our products will be outside the DPCO." As part of this strategy, the division was gearing up to launch Estraderm, a transdermal patch used by women during menopause.

The agrochemicals division, too, was working on plans to launch new products. Hardest hit by the lockout in Goa, as well as by erratic monsoons in certain parts of the country in 1993-94, the division was soon to launch three new insecticides; Curacron, Polytrin C and Miral, While the first two were to be targeted for cotton crop protection, the third was largely to be used in rice crop protection. In agrochemicals, Hindustan Ciba was among the top three in the industry.

But presently, general manager N.N. Apte's major concern was with the weather. "The next two months will decide the market condition for the current year," he said. Whether the rain gods are kind to him or not, Hindustan Ciba's difficult times were for from over. The main reason for concern, naturally, was the shut-down at the Santa Monica works in Goa. The unit was running into its eight month of closure, with no signs of an early settlement.

As an industry observer said, "Though Hindustan Ciba had managed to retain market share and maintain supplies of its products, it was taking a heavy toll on profitability." The company had managed to maintain supplies though methods such as using executives to run the plant, outsourcing and (in some cases) even importing. As a result, the company's import bill had jumped from ₹ 20 crore to ₹ 36 crore.

With the Bhandup plant in Bombay having been sold off, the Santa Monica works had assumed crucial importance. Except for the consumer health (oral hygiene) division, each of the other divisions had production bases at Santa Monica.

The Bhandup plan was sold to Great Eastern Shipping for ₹43 crore, with the intention of shifting the main base of operations to the Santa Monica works in Goa. The long closure of the Goa unit had also put a spanner in the company's plans to use this unit as a base from which to export to its parent company.

As Hartland put it, "We haven't been able to realise some of our plans for exports." Hence, the aim of establishing India as a major supply base for its Basle-based parent had received a setback. The deadlock with the company's union began at the end of 1992, when the internal union called in Bombay-based R.J. Mehta as external advisor to negotiate a new wage settlement. This led to a series of confrontations, resulting in an indefinite lockout.

One of the major factors behind the company's ability to withstand a shutdown of this magnitude had been that over the past few years, it had been engaged in a major internal restructuring programme to increase efficiency and reduce costs. "We had picked up many of the bad habits that go with a protected environment," said Hartland, who initiated a cultural and an organisational restructuring during his five-year tenure.

According to Apte: "The aim was that we should function as a flotilla of small, swift ships, rather than as an unwieldy supertanker." Besides splitting the company into self-contained divisions, various initiatives for flattening the hierarchical structure and the bureaucracy has been put into motion. In conducting this exercise, the Indian subsidiary had drawn extensively on the systems and structures of its parent company.

Hartland, however, felt that there was still a long way to go: "It takes time to change established attitudes and practices." Clearly, the man who preferred to tighten his belt and take a beating on profits rather than compromise on the grounds of principle, was the driving force behind Hindustan Ciba's new aggressiveness. If he steered the company in line with the newly charted course, Hindustan Ciba Geigy could look forward to maintaining its pre-eminent position even in a competitive environment.

Questions

1. How do you assess the performance of HCG? Support your answer with reasons.
2. What is the revised strategy of the company? What steps does the company propose to take in order to achieve its strategic goal?
3. In the consumer healthcare market HCG has been known for a long time for tis "Cibaca" toothpaste and toothbrushes. Will the divestment of its oral hygiene unit not affect adversely its image or popularity in the market?
4. Which divisions of the company are the star performers? What steps have been taken or are being proposed for further improvement in their performance.

PART – V

Strategy Evaluation and Control

CHAPTER

EVALUATION AND CONTROL OF STRATEGY

CHAPTER OUTLINE

Strategic evaluation and control is the final phase of strategic management process.

13.1 CONCEPT AND NATURE OF STRATEGIC EVALUATION AND CONTROL

Strategic evaluation and control may be defined as the process of determining the effectiveness of the chosen strategy in achieving the organisation's objectives and taking corrective actions wherever necessary.

The key features of strategic evaluation and control are as follows:

(*i*) Strategic evaluation and control has two major aspects – judging the effectiveness of strategy in terms of its results, and taking necessary corrective actions. These two aspects (evaluative and corrective) are intertwined.

(*ii*) Strategic evaluation and control is an ongoing process.

(*iii*) The basic purpose of strategic evaluation and control is to evaluate the success of strategy formulation and implementation in achieving organisational objectives.

(*iv*) Strategic evaluation and control helps to keep the organisation on the right track. Without this mechanism, strategists cannot find out whether or not strategy is producing the desired results.

13.2 NEED FOR AND IMPORTANCE OF STRATEGIC EVALUATION AND CONTROL

The process of strategic management is incomplete without evaluation and control. Strategic evaluation and control plays a vital role in strategic management. It provides the following benefits:

1. **Verification of Strategic Choice:** Strategic evaluation and control provides a check on the validity of strategic choice. Strategy is formulated in the context of a specific situation. Changes in environment occur over time. As an ongoing process, strategic evaluation and control reveals whether the chosen strategy continues to be valid or relevant over time.
2. **Congruence between Strategy and Decisions:** In order to implement the chosen strategy, managers make several decisions. Strategic evaluation and control helps to judge whether these decisions are consistent with the requirements of the strategy. It puts a pressure on managers to exercise their discretion carefully.
3. **Assessment of Progress:** Strategy is not an end in itself. It is rather a means for achieving organisational objectives. Evaluation and control of strategy indicates the progress made by the organisation towards its objectives. Progress should be measured both during and after strategy implementation so that remedial actions can be taken as early as possible.
4. **Linkage between Performance and Rewards:** Strategic evaluation and control measures performance which is the objective basis for rewarding employees. Performance based rewards helps to motivate, retain and attract talent.
5. **Feedback for Future Planning:** Evaluation and control of strategy provide valuable inputs for strategic planning in future. The information and experience gained through it help strategists in making appropriate changes in strategy, and necessary improvements in strategy implementation.
6. **Overcoming Resistance to Change:** Control process helps in introducing planned change in the organisation. Strategists can use the control system to ensure continuing attention to strategic initiatives and to communicate new strategic agenda. They can develop beliefs, attitudes and values to ensure desired behaviour. Discussion and debate about strategic moves can be encouraged.
7. **Functional Coordination:** Strategy implemention involves several key tasks. A task is a set of interrelated functions. Individuals perform different functions. It is necessary to coordinate functions performed by individual managers and groups other wise they may work at cross purposes. They may pursue goals which are not consistent with divisional and organisational objectives. Strategic evaluation and control helps to create and sustain coordination among different functions.

13.3 PARTICIPANTS IN STRATEGIC EVALUATION AND CONTROL

Strategic evaluation and control is a part of strategic management process. Therefore, all those who are involved in strategy formulation and implementation should participate in strategic evaluation and control, except the consultants and other advisors. Large shareholders and lenders (*e.g.*, financial institutions) are interested in the security of the principal and returns rather than in longterm success of the company. In case of public sector enterprises government participates in strategic evaluation and control through its nominees. Thus, the main participants in the process of strategic evaluation and control are as follows:

1. **Board of Directors:** The board of directors periodically evaluates the overall financial performance and longterm success of the company. However, practices may differ among companies. In some companies, the promoter CEO exercises the real power in strategic evaluation. In case of family owned companies, the head of the family or family council exercises strategic control. In multinational corporations strategic control is exercised by parent firms. The controlling ministries evaluate and control in public sector enterprises.
2. **Chief Executive:** The chief executive is responsible for overall performance of the company. But the chief executive is not involved in the evaluation of day-to-day or routine performance. The role of chief executive in strategic control is limited to broad parameters such as market share, return on investment, earnings per share, etc.
3. **Other Managers:** The heads of SBUs are responsible for overall control of their respective business units. Functional heads exercise control over their functional departments. They are concerned more with operational control and with preparing control reports for higher authorities. For example, the marketing manager attempts to control sales volume, market share, brand loyalty, etc. Financial controller, company secretary and auditors exercise control through financial analysis, budgeting and reporting. Middle level managers may provide information and feedback and take corrective actions as per directions from higher level managers.

13.4 ROLE OF ORGANISATIONAL SYSTEMS IN EVALUATION AND CONTROL

Strategic evaluation and control process operates in the context of various organisational systems used for strategy implementation. The information, planning development, appraisal and reward systems play direct or indirect role in strategic control.

1. **Information System:** The information system provides feedback about the organisation's progress and is, therefore, closely related with the control. It provides the right information at the right time to the right person so that timely corrective action is taken. Computerised information systems generate real time information for evaluation and control. For example, a marketing manager can have instant access to sales and distribution data from the company's branches/offices all over the country. On the basis of such data, corrective actions are taken quickly whenever deviations from key performance indicators occur.
2. **Planning System:** Planning is the basis of control as a plan guides the behaviour and activities in the organisation. Control measures progress or performance towards goals and standards specified in planning. Performance measures are specified in strategically important areas. These measures should relate to the domain of managers who are responsible for exercising control.

3. **Development System:** The development system seeks to enhance organisational capability; to achieve better results. It involves preparing people to perform better in their present and likely future jobs. It is not directly or closely related to evaluation but helps in preventing deviations from strategic measures of performance. The development system helps strategists to initiate and implement corrective action.
4. **Appraisal System:** Appraisal System involves systematic evaluation of an individual's performance on the job and potential for development. It indicates how people are performing. This feedback serves as the basis for rewards and corrective actions.
5. **Reward System:** Performance based rewards motivate employees to work towards the achievement of organisational objectives. Reward system, therefore, helps to avoid or minimise deviations.

13.5 BARRIERS TO EVALUATION AND CONTROL

The main barriers to the strategic evaluation and control process are as follows:

1. **Resistance to Evaluation:** The evaluation process faces the psychological barrier of accepting own mistakes. Top management formulates strategy and also exercises strategic control. It may put the blame on operating management for mistakes in strategy formulation by finding faults in strategy implemention. Such a self-serving approach is likely to worsen the situation by developing corrective actions. Top executives must adopt an objective attitude to avoid this tendency. They must be willing to admit their mistakes and ready to lose face for the benefit of the organisation. Open communication among the participants in the evaluation process also helps to overcome resistance to evaluation and control.
2. **Problems in Measurement:** Several problems arise in the measurement of actual performance or results. The information system may fail to provide valid and timely information. Objectives and performance cannot be quantified in many areas. Measurement techniques or criteria used in evaluation may not be fully reliable and valid. Lack of uniformity and objectivity in measurement distorts the control system. Better information system, quantification of objectives, standardised procedures for measurement, and reliable/valid measurement systems help to overcome these difficulties.
3. **Limits of Control:** Strategists find it very difficult to decide the limits of control. Too much controls inhibit initiative and creativity, impede efficient performance and restrict managerial freedom. On the other hand, too little controls, make evaluation ineffective, create problems in coordination, and encourage indiscriminate use of managerial discretion. Managers can overcome this dilemma of too much versus too less control by learning from experience.
4. **Focus on Shortterm:** Quite often managers focus on immediate results and short term achievements. They may ignore longterm impact of strategy. It is tedious to judge longterm implications and immediate assessment is easier and more convenient. In order to overcome this bias the attitude to measurement should be positive. The focus needs to be on finding out the factors that obstruct good performance.

5. **Emphasis on Efficiency:** Efficiency means doing things rightly 'while effectiveness means doing the right things. What constitutes effective performance is not always clear. When wrong parameters are used to measure performance rewards may be given for performance that does not really contribute to organisational objectives. Therefore, the focus should be on effectiveness rather than on efficiency.

13.6 REQUIREMENTS FOR EFFECTIVE EVALUATION AND CONTROL

In order to make evaluation effective, control system should be matched with the requirements of the strategy. For example, under the cost leadership strategy, the control system must provide frequent and comprehensive reports on costs. On the other hand, in case of differentiation strategy, the focus should be on building unique features in the firm's offering. Such a fit between strategy and evaluation helps to make control system effective. Some other requirements of an effective control system are given below:

(*i*) Control should monitor only relevant activities and results

(*ii*) Control system should generate minimum information because too much information creates clutter and confusion.

(*iii*) Both performance evaluation and corrective actions should be done at the most appropriate time.

(*iv*) Control system should focus on exceptional outcomes.

(*v*) There should be a balanced focus on longterm and short term performance.

(*vi*) Those achieving or exceeding performance standards should be properly rewarded.

13.7 CONCEPT AND TYPES OF STRATEGIC CONTROL

Strategic control is the process of judging whether the chosen strategy is progressing in the right direction and producing the desired results and taking corrective actions whenever necessary. In the words of Julian and Scifres, "Strategic control involves the monitoring and evaluating of plans, activities and results with a view towards future action, providing a warning signal through diagnosis of data, and triggering appropriate interventions, be they either tactical adjustment or strategic reorientation."[1] Strategic control is the process of tracking the strategy as it is being implemented, detecting any problem areas and making necessary adjustments.

While formulating strategy, the strategists make several assumptions about external and internal environment of the organisation. There is a time gap between strategy formulation and strategy implementation. During this intervening period the assumptions made during strategy formulation may become invalid or irrelevant. Moreover, strategy implementation by itself is a time consuming process. Therefore, it becomes necessary to continually assess the validity of the strategy and to modify the strategy in view of the changing conditions.

In the process of strategic control, the strategists seek answers to the following questions:

(*i*) Are the premises made during strategy formulation proving to be correct?

(*ii*) Is the strategy guiding the organisation towards its desired objectives?

(*iii*) Is the strategy being implemented properly?

1. S.D. Julian and E. Scifres, "An Interpretative Perspective on the Role of Strategic Control in Triggering Strategic change" **Journal of Business Strategies,** 19(2), 2002 pp. 141–159.

(*iv*) Is there any need for change in the strategy? If yes, what type of change is required?

In this way, strategic central serves as an early warning system.

Strategic controls are of the following types[2]:

1. **Premise Control:** A strategy is based on certain premises or assumptions about the internal and external environment of the organisation. Some of these assumptions are critical and any change in them has a major impact on the strategy.

   The purpose of premise control is to identify the key assumptions, monitor changes in them and assess the impact of these changes on the strategy and its implementation. For example, an organisation may choose its strategy on the assumptions of favorable government policies and a technological breakthrough. Premise control systematically and continually assesses the validity of these assumptions made during formulation of strategy and implementation. Whenever there is a major change in them strategists have to revise the strategy. The corporate planning staff of the company can be assigned the responsibility of identifying, key assumptions and continually checking their validity. The salesforce or marketing research department may be asked to monitor competitors moves and other developments in the market. The trigger points at which a change in strategy is required should be identified. For example, Lafarge of France dropped the idea of setting up a green field project for manufacturing cement in India when it found overcapacity in the industry. It opted for takeover strategy to enter India. Similarly, Tata Motors acquired land to manufacture its Nano Car in West Bengal. But it shifted the factory to Gujarat When the West Bengal government opposed the project.

2. **Implementation Control:** Evaluating whether the plans, projects and programmes developed to implement strategy are actually guiding the organisation towards its predetermined objectives or not is called implementation control. Whenever it is felt that allocation of resources to a project, plan or programme is not yielding the expected benefits, the same is resisted. In this way implementation control may result in strategic rethinking. The purpose is to judge whether the strategy requires change in the context of unfolding events and results of strategy implementation.

   There are two main methods of implementation control – strategic thrusts and review of milestones. Identification and **monitoring of strategic thrusts helps in effective deployment of resources.**

   For example, concept development, product development and test marketing are the main thrusts in introducing a new product. At each of these stages, information is generated. On the basis of such feedback, the company can decide whether to abandon the proposed product or to modify its features to make it acceptable in the market. Milestones can be decided on the basis of critical events, major resource allocations, etc. These milestones may be reviewed in terms of time and cost as and when these are reached. The milestone review can also be conducted when a major environmental change has happened or a major uncertainity is resolved. The aim of **milestone review is** to critically examine the progress in strategy implementation and plan for future contingencies so that the company's objectives are achieved.

2. G. Schreyogg and H. Steinmann, "Strategic Control: A New Prospective," **Academy of Management Review,** 12(1), 1987, pp. 91-103.

3. **Strategic Surveillance:** The purpose of strategic surveillance is to monitor a broad range of events inside and outside the organisation that may influence the results of chosen strategies. These events may either threaten or facilitative the strategies. For example, competitors' new strategies or non acceptance of strategies by a group of employees may threaten the existing strategies. On the other hand, favourable changes in government policies may facilitate implementation of chosen strategies. Thus, strategic surveillance is a sort of internal and external environmental scanning that reveals the hidden information that may be critical for strategy implementation.

Table 13.1: Comparison Between Types of Strategic Control

Basis Characteristics	Premise Control	Implementation Control	Strategic surveillance	Special alert Control
1. Degree of focusing	High	High	Low	High
2. Data acquisition:.				
• Formalisation	Medium	High	Low	High
• Centralisation	Low	Medium	Low	High
3. Use with				
• Environmental factors	Yes	Seldom	Yes	Yes
• Industry factors	Yes	Seldom	Yes	Yes
• Strategy-specific factors	No	Yes	Seldom	Yes
• Firm-specific factors	No	Yes	Seldom	Seldom

Source: G. Schreyagg and H. Steinmann, op. cit;

4. **Special Alert Control:** Sudden and unexpected events occur in business environment. Fall of a government, a technological innovation, entry of a predatory competitor, an industrial disaster, a natural catastrophe are examples of such events. Such crises may threaten the course of a strategy. An organisation can respond quickly and properly if it gets in early signal of sudden and unexpected events. Special alert control is designed to detect such events at an early stage.

13.8 CONCEPT AND PROCESS OF OPERATIONAL CONTROL

Operational control is the process of evaluating the performance of strategic business units, divisions, etc., and their contribution to the achievement of organisational objectives. The results of strategic actions are assessed under operational control. Strategists seek answers to the following questions in operational control:

(*i*) How is the organisation performing?

(*ii*) Are the organisational resourses being utilised properly?

(*ii*) Are the time schedules being adhered to?

(*iv*) What actions are needed to ensure proper utilisation of resources and to achieve organisational objectives?

Table 13.2: Difference Between Strategic Control and Operational Control

Attribute	Strategic Control	Operational Control
1. Basic question	"Are we moving in the right direction?	"How are we performing"
2. Aim	Pro-active, continuous questioning of the basic direction of strategy	Allocation and use of organisational resources
3. Main concern	"Steering" the organisation's future direction	Action control
4. Focus	External environment	Internal organisation
5. Time horizon	Long term	Short term
6. Exercise of control	Exclusively by top management may be through lower-level support	Mainly by executive or middle-level management on the direction of top management budgets, schedules and MBO
7. Main techniques	Environmental scanning, information gathering, questioning and review	Budgets, schedules and MBO

Source: J.A. Pearce III and R.B. Robinson, Jr. Strategic Management: Strategy Formulation and Implementation (3rd edn.), (Homewood, Ill. Richard D. Irwin, 1988), pp. 404-419.

The process of operational control consists of the following elements or steps.

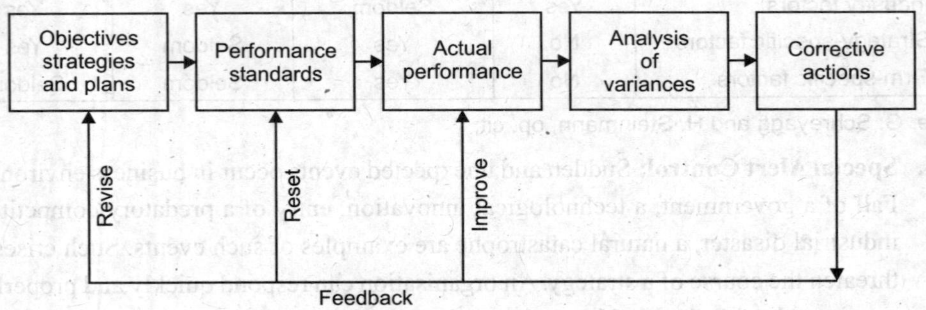

Fig. 13.1. Operational Control Process

These elements are interrelated. Objectives, strategies and plans result in a set of performance standards. Actual performance is measured and compared with the standards. Gap between the two (variance) is analysed to identify the causes. On the basis of feedback, necessary corrective actions are taken which may involve revision of objectives/strategies/plans, adjustment of standards or improvement in actual performance.

1. **Setting Performance Standards:** On the basis of objectives and strategies, standards are set in key areas of performance. For example, cost reduction is the main objective for a company using a cost leadership strategy. Cost standards may be set in production, marketing, finance and other functional areas. These standards represent the desired cost levels which should be reasonable and feasible. A range in terms of minimum and maximum may be prescribed to provide some flexibility.

   Both quantitative (*e.g.*, return on investment, market share, growth rate in sales, net profit, etc., and qualitative (*e.g.,* consistency workability and appropriateness) criteria are used to evaluate performance.

2. **Measuring actual Performance:** The actual results are measured in terms of control standards. Accounting, reporting, information and communication system are used for this purpose. Measurement is difficult in case of managerial performance. It is desirable to measure performance at the right time e.g., at the end of a specific activity or task. Performance should be measured frequently (e.g., every month or quarter) rather than at the end of the financial year.
3. **Analysing Variances:** Comparison of actual performance with the standards reveals gap, if any. When the variance is within tolerate limits, it is considered insignificant and no corrective action is needed. Significant variances are analysed to find out their causes. Variances may be caused by internal or controllable factors (e.g., employee inefficiency) and external or uncontrollable factors (*e.g.*, non-availablity of power, economic slowdown, etc.)
4. **Taking Corrective Actions:** An organisation is not a self-regulating system. Managerial actions are needed to create an equilibrium. Corrective actions may involve.
   (*a*) revision of objectives, strategies and plans in case these are not workable.
   (*b*) resetting performance standard in case these are too high and impractical;
   (*c*) improving performance in case it is not optimum.

Several factors may cause poor performance. Faulty resource allocation, inappropriate organisational structure and systems, defective leadership styles, low performing culture, inconsistent functional plans are some of these factors.

13.9 TECHNIQUES FOR STRATEGIC CONTROL[3]

Strategic evaluation and control involves assessment of the changing environment and their impact on the organisation's strategy. The techniques used for strategic control may be classified into two broad categories on the basis of type of environment. Strategic momentum control is usitable for organisations operating in a relatively stable environment. Strategic leap control is more appropriate for organisations functioning in a relatively turbulent environment.

1. **Strategic Momentum Control:** The techniques in this category are designed to assure that the assumptions on the basis of which strategies were formulated are still valid. The organisation takes steps to maintain its strategic momentum.
   The techniques of strategic momentum control are as under:
   (*a*) *Responsibility Control Centres*: A responsibility centre is assigned the responsibility for a specific area. It is designed on the basis of the measurement of inputs and outputs. There are four types of responsibility centres – revenue expense, profit and investment centres.
   (*b*) *Key Success Factors*: In this technique, the organisation focusses on the factors that contribute to the success of strategies. On the basis of these factors, the strategists can judge whether or not the strategies are leading to the achievement of organisational objectives.

3. Peter Lorange, M.F. Morton and Sumantra Ghoshal, **Strategic Control,** West Publishing, st. Paul Minnesota, 1992.

(*c*) *Generic Strategies*: This technique is based on the assumption that the organisation's strategies are comparable to those of similar organisations. On the basis of such a comparison, the organisation can judge why and how other organisaitons are implementing particular strategies. It can judge align its strategies with them.

4. **Strategic Leap Control:** In a turbulent environment, an organisation has to make strategic leaps. Strategic leap control helps the organisation to identify the strategic changes needed to cope with the changing environment. The techniques used for strategic leap control are as follows:

(*a*) *Strategic issue management*: It involves identification of strategic issues and assessing their impact on the organisation. A strategic issue is any development, either inside or outside the organisation, which is likely to have significant impact on the ability of the organisation to achieve its objectives. Managing strategic issues well in time helps the organisation to avoid the adverse impact of sudden changes in the environment:

The organisation can design contingency plans to shift strategies whenever necessary.

(*b*) *Strategic field analysis*: It means examining the nature and extent of synergies that exist or can be developed between different parts of the organisation. The organisation can move towards its objectives by taking advantage of existing and possible synergies.

(*c*) *Systems modelling*: Under it, the essential features of the organisation and its environment are simulated through computer based models. On the basis of such simulation the organisation can assess the impact of changing environment and can take premptive strategic actions.

(*d*) *Scenarios*: These are perceptions about the environment which the organisation is likely to face in future. Such scenarios enable the organisation to focus its strategies on forthcoming developments.

13.10 HOW TO MAKE STRATEGIC CONTROL EFFECTIVE

Lorange, Morton and Ghoshal make the following recommendations for keeping strategic control creative and viable[4].

(*i*) Use strategic control teams drawn together from various parts of the organisation. Better follow the informal organisation structure and the cross lines of authority to draw individuals with new insights. Composition of the strategic control team should change regularly to assure fresh ideas and avoid stagnation.

(*ii*) Top management must be involved in the interpretation of key success factors and how they are monitored.

(*iii*) Strategic control must focus on bottlenecks in the critical success factors and on changes in the success factors.

(*iv*) Flexibility must be obtained within the strategic control process so that budgets formats, agendas, and other organisational procedures can meet the demands of the particular control context.

4. Peter Lorange, M.F. Morton and Sumantra Ghoshal, **Strategic control,** West Publishing, st. Paul, Minuesota, 1992, p.138.

According to the model[5] given in Fig. 13.2., top managers must ensure consistency between four variables.

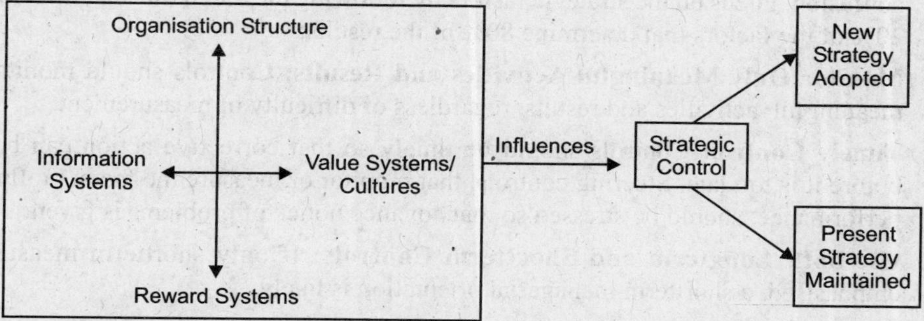

Fig. 13.2. Variables for Strategic Control

Quinn[6] suggests the following steps for effective strategic control.

1. **Create Commitment:** Executives provide broad goals, a proper climate, and resource support. By allowing various groups to develop and present proposals for strategies, mangers are able to build commitment among the groups to support the final strategy.
2. **Maintain Objectivity:** Top Managers should avoid taking a stand on issues too early in the generation and evaluation process. When managers take a position, the generation of new alternatives often ceases and the evaluation of existing alternatives is often biased.
3. **Eliminate Options Two Levels Down:** Managers can maintain their position of neutrality and avoid rejecting proposals by encouraging, discouraging, or killing options through subordinates.
4. **Develop Focus and Consensus:** By controlling membership on committees, managers are able to influence, and if desired, receive the wanted proposals. Properly selected committees can broaden support for and increase commitment to new strategies.
5. **Empower Champions:** Managers are given responsibility for developing new ideas and programmes. As the programme is evaluated and gains support, these individuals tend to become committed to the programme or strategy. Once it is given final approval, these managers are then willing to champion the strategy and guide it through whatever hurdles are necessary to get it operating effectively.
6. **Develop Strategies Incrementally, but not Piecemeal:** It is management's responsibility to make certain that strategies are integrated and appropriate for the environment in which the firm is operating. Strategies may be developed in incremental steps, but they must be made to fit together in a unified, integrated, and cohesive whole.
7. **Recognise Continuing Dynamics:** Strategies do not remain constant and fixed for long periods. Part of the executive's responsibility is to gain consensus and support for the new strategy, but at the same time scope must be maintained to modify or terminate the strategy. Managers should use discretion in making certain that the organisation does not become overcommitted to the new strategy and unwilling to change at some future point.

Some more guidelines are as follows.

5. Samuel C. Certo and Paul Peter, **The Strategic Management Process,** Richard D. Irwin, Chicago, 1993, p.156.
6. J. B. Quinn *Strategies for change* Richard D. Irwin, Homewood, 1980, pp. 126-138.

8. **Minimum Amount of Information:** Control should involve only the minimum amount of information needed to given a reliable picture of events. Too many controls create confusion. Focus on the strategic factors by following the 80/20 rule *i.e.*, monitor those 20% of the factors that determine 80% of the results.
9. **Monitor Only Meaningful Activities and Results:** Controls should monitor only meaningful activities and results, regardless of difficulty of measurement.
10. **Timely Control:** Controls should be timely so that corrective action can be taken before it is too late. Steering controls, that monitor or measure the factors influencing performance, should be stressed so that advance notice of problems is given.
11. **Use both Longterm and Shortterm Controls:** If only shortterm measures are emphasised, a shortterm managerial orientation is likely.
12. **Pinpoint Exceptions:** Controls should aim at pinpointing exceptions; only those activities or results that fall outside a predetermined tolerance range should call for action.
13. **Emphasize Rewards:** Emphasize the reward of meeting or exceeding standards rather than punishment for failing to meet standards.

13.11 RUMELT'S CRITERIA FOR EVALUATION OF STRATEGY

Rumelt[7] has laid down the following tests to judge a strategy.

1. **Consistency:** Corporate strategy must be consistent with the goals for which it is designed. Its different components must be in harmony with one other. Inconsistency in a strategy arises when it is developed in an adhoc or piece meal manner and when it is the outcome of a compromise between opposing power groups. Conflict between organisational objectives and managerial values may also lead to inconsistency in a strategy.
2. **Consonance:** Consonance means a fit between the organisation's mission and environment. "The key to evaluating consonance is an understanding of why the business, as it currently stands, exists at all and how it assumed its current pattern".[8] The business must both match and be adjusted to the changing environment. This is known as the 'generic' aspect of strategy.
3. **Advantage:** Business must compete with other firms that are trying to adapt to the environment. The strategy must provide the firm a competitive advantage. The core competencies in terms of superior skills and superior resources must be exploited through the strategy to give the firm an edge over the competitors.
4. **Feasibility:** Feasibility means the firm's ability to carry out the strategy. The feasibility of strategy can be assessed by asking the following questions:
   (*a*) Does the organisation possess the necessary problem solving abilities and/or competence required by the strategy?
   (*b*) Does the organisation possess the required degree of coordinative and integrative skill to carry out the strategy?

---

7. Richard Rumelt, "The Evaluation of Business Strategy: Theory and Models in Dan Schendel and Charles Hofer (eds.) **Strategic Management: A New view of Business Policy and Planning,** Little, 59 bid Brown, Boston, 1979.
8. Ibid

(c) Does the strategy challenge and motivate key personnel and is it acceptable to those who must lend their support?

Thompson and Stickland[9] have given the following criteria for evaluating strategies of diversified companies:

(i) The longterm prospect of each industry category that the company is and the prospect of the each of the related industries should be evaluated. This is known as 'Industry Attractiveness Test'.

(ii) The competitive position of the business units in the respective industries should be evaluated. This is called 'Test of Competitive Strength'

(iii) The potential competitive advantage that the business units possess with respect to cross-business value chain relationships and strategic compatibility of the units should be evaluated. This is known as the 'Test of Strategic Fit'.

(iv) The company's resource potential should match the resource needs of the business units. This is called the 'Resource Fit Test'.

13.12 TILLES' CRITERIA FOR EVALUATION OF STRATEGY

Seymour Tilles[10] has suggested the following criteria for judging whether an organisation's strategy is right or not

1. **Internal Consistency:** Internal consistency means strategy at different levels are complementary to one another. Functional strategies must support strategies at business and corporate levels. Corporate level strategies must be consistent with the corporate goals. It is difficult to 'maintain consistency in a dynamic company. Many family owned firms pursue strategies of rapid expansion and exclusive family control simultaneously. The criteria of internal consistency is important because it identifies the areas wherein strategic choices will eventually have to be made.

2. **Consistency with the Environment:** The strategy must make sense with respect to the external environment. Consistency with the environment has both a static and a dynamic aspect. In a static sense, it means efficacy with respect to the existing environment. In a dynamic sense, it implies efficacy with respect to the changing environment. Therefore, management must regularly be assessing the relevance to the strategy in the changing environment. Several Indian companies suffered badly due to their failure to fine tune their strategies with liberalisation and globalisation after 1991.

3. **Appropriateness in the Light of Available Resources:** A company's resources represent its capacity to respond to perceived threats and opportunities in the environment. Funds, distinctive competence and physical facilities are the critical resources. Achieving a balance between strategic goals and available resources is one of the most difficult issues in strategy formulation. It is meaningless to pursue a strategy for which the organisation cannot raise the necessary resources.

---

9. Arthur A. Thompson Jr. and A.J. Strickland III, **Strategic Management:** Concepts and Cases Business Publication, Texas, 1994, pp. 319-341.
10. Seymour Tilles, "How to Evaluate Corporate Strategy" **Harvard Business Review,** July-August, 1963 pp. 111-121.

4. **Acceptable Degree of Risk:** Strategy and resources taken together determine the degree of risk which the company is undertaking. Each company must decide for itself how much risk it wants to take. Risk inherent in alternate strategies can be measured by estimating payoffs and their probabilities. Risks also depend on: (*a*) the amount of resources whose continued existence or value is not assured, (*b*) the length of the time periods to which resources are committed, and (*c*) the proportion of resources committed to a single venture. The greater these quantities the greater the risk that is involved. This does not mean the best strategy is the one with the least risk. A high risk strategy often may have high payoff. What is important is the degree of risk must be what the company can undertake.
5. **Appropriate Time-Horizon:** A good strategy is one that results in the accomplishment of strategic objectives within reasonable time period. While choosing an appropriate time-horizon, attention must be paid to the particular organisation and its goals. The organisation must be given enough time to adjust to them. Therefore, large corporations plan far ahead. The time-horizon is also important due to its impact on policymaking. A longer time horizon offers wider choice of tactics. For example, a company that seeks quick growth has to opt for acquisitions and mergers.
6. **Workability:** Quantitative measures of performance are the outcome of both strategy and its execution. The workability or contribution of a strategy to corporate progress can be assessed in terms of: (*a*) the degree of consensus among executives concerning corporate strategy, (*b*) the extent to which major areas of managerial choice are identified in advance, and (*c*) the extent to which resource requirements are determined well in time.

The strategies that satisfy the criteria given above may not guarantee success. But these can be very valuable in giving management both the time and space to maneour.

13.13 STRATEGIC AUDIT

Strategic audit is a comprehensive and systematic evaluation of all facets of the strategic management process. There is no universally accepted method of strategic audit. Both quantitative and qualitative techniques are used for strategic audit. Return on investment, growth in sales volume, market share, etc. are examples of quantitative measures. Samaple questions for qualitative assessment are given in Table 13.3.

Table 13.3: How to Conduct a Strategic Audit

A strategic audit is conducted in three phases: diagnosis to identify how, where and in what priority in-depth analysis need to be made; focused analysis; and generation and testing of recommendations. Objectivity and the ability to ask critical, probing questions are key requirements for conducting a strategic audit.

Phase One: Diagnosis

1. Review key document such as:
   (*a*) Strategic plan
   (*b*) Business or operational plans
   (*c*) Organisational arrangements
   (*d*) Major policies governing matters such as resources allocation and performance measurement.

2. Review financial, market, and operational performance against benchmarks and industry norms to identify key variances and emerging trends.
3. Gain an understanding of:
   (*a*) Principal roles, responsibilities, and reporting relationships
   (*b*) Decision-making process and major decision made
   (*c*) Resources, including physical facilities, capital, management, and technology
   (*d*) Interrelationships between functional staff member and business or operating units
4. Identify strategic implications of strategy for organisation structure, behaviour patterns, systems, and processes—define interrelationships and linkage to strategy.
5. Determine internal and external perspectives.
   (*a*) Survey the attitudes and perceptions of senior and middle managers and other key employees to assess the extent to which they are consistent with the strategic direction of the firm. One way to accomplish this task is through carefully focused interview and/or questionnaires to ask employees to identify and make trade-offs among the objectives and variables they consider most important.
   (*b*) Interview a carefully selected sample of customers and prospective customers and other key external sources to understand their view of the company.
6. Identify aspects of the strategy that are working well. Formulate hypotheses regarding problems and opportunities for improvement based on the findings above. Define how and in what order to pursue each.

Phase Two: Focused Analysis

1. Test the hypotheses concerning problem and opportunities for improvement through analysis of specific issues. Identify interrelationships and dependencies among components of the strategic system.
2. Formulate conclusions as to weaknesses in strategy formulation, implementation deficiencies, or interactions between the two.

Phase Three: Recommendations

1. Develop alternative solutions to problems and ways of capitalizing on opportunities. Test these alternatives in light of their resource requirements, risks, rewards, priorities, and other applicable measures.
2. Develop specific recommendations to produce an integrated, measurable, and time phased action plan to improve strategic results.

Source: A.J. Prager and M.B. Shea, "The Strategic Audit, "in the Strategic Management Handbook, ed. K.J. Albert (New York: McGraw-Hill, 1983), pp. 8-14.

Table 13.4: Sample Questions for Qualitative Organisational Measurement

- Are financial policies with respect to investment, dividends, and financing consistent with the opportunities likely to be available?
- Has the company defined the market segments in which it intends to operate specifically with respect to both product lines and market segments? Has it clearly defined the key capabilities it needs to succeed?
- Does the company have a viable plan for developing a significant and defensible superiority over competitors based on these capabilities?

- Will the business segments in which the company operates provide adequate opportunities for achieving corporate objectives? Do they appear attractive enough to draw an excessive amount of investment to the market from potential competitors? Is the company providing adequately for developing attractive new investment opportunities?
- Are the management, financial, technical, and other resources of the company really adequate to justify an expectation of maintaining superiority over competitors in key capabilities?
- Does the company have operations in which it cannot reasonable expect to outperform competitors? If so, can managers expect these operations to generate adequate returns on invested capital? Is there any justification for investing further in such operations, even just to maintain them?
- Has the company selected business segments that can reinforce each other by contributing jointly to the development of key capabilities? Do competitors combine operations in ways that given them superiority in the key resource areas? Can the company's scope of operations be revised to improve its chances against competitors?
- To the extent that operations are diversified, has the company recognised and provided for the special management and control system this requires?

Source: Milton Lauenstein, "Keeping Your Corporate Strategy on Track, "Journal of Business Strategy 2, No. 1 (Summer 1981), p. 64.

13.14 TECHNIQUES FOR OPERATIONAL CONTROL

The focus of operational control is on the allocation and use of organisational resources. Several techniques are used to judge financial and non-financial performance of an organisation. Some of these techniques are given below:

1. **Activity-Based Costing:** Traditional costing does not reveal cause effect relationship in cost involved and in value created by an activity. Cooper and Kaplan[11] developed activity based costing to overcome this problem. Activity based costing is a system of assigning costs to activities involved in producing products/services. Cost centres are created and overheads are assigned to these centres. For example, production scheduling, machine set up, materials buying and materials management may be treated as cost centres in a manufacturing organisation. The cost of these activities/centres are assigned to relevant product/services. Thus, directs and indirect costs are assigned to activities (not to cost centres) such as processing an order, attending to a customer complaint, setting up a machine, etc.

   Activity-based costing offers several **advantages:** (*i*) It helps in allocating resources to those activities that create more value (*ii*) It helps in understanding the behaviour of overhead costs and their relationship to products/services, customers, etc (*iii*) Its focus is on activities not resources. Therefore, it generates move relevant information for measuring performance. (*iv*) It helps in cost control by ascertaining costs of each activity and sub-activity.

   Activity-based costing suffers from many **limitations:** (*i*) It generates considerable information for which computer based information system is needed (*ii*) Its focus is on cost reduction and not on customer satisfaction, (*iii*) It is based on the assumption that the volume of activities is not dependent on the volume of operations.

11. Rubin Cooper and Robert S. Kaplan, "Measure Cost Right, Make the Right Decision," **Harvard Business Review,** Sept. Oct; 1988, pp. 96-103.

2. **Budgetary Control:** Budgetary control is the process of using budgets to control activities and performance of an organisation. Budgets are prepared to establish performance standards and actual performance is compared with budgetary standards. In case of undesirable variation between the two, necessary corrective actions are taken. Both overall performance and performance in functional areas can be controlled through budgets. Sales budget, production budget, finance budget, cash budget, etc, are functional budgets. Master budget is an integrated summary of all other budgets.

   Budgetary control offers many **advantages:** (*i*) Budgetary control helps in making judicious use of scarce resources (*ii*) Budgets provide quantitative standards of performance (*iii*) Budgeting involves people at all levels which facilitate mutual cooperation and coordination between different functions.

   Budgetary control suffers from some **limitations:** (*i*) Budgetary control tends to create rigidity in the functioning of the organisation (*ii*) Focus on budgeted figures rather than on results may hamper efficiency and effectiveness.

3. **Return on Investment:** The amount of profit in relation to total investment is known as return on investment (ROI). Thus,

$$\text{ROI} = \frac{\text{Net Profit}}{\text{Total Investment}}.$$

   Comparison of ROI over time period indicates trends in the firm's profitability. ROI of the firm can be compared with the ROI of similar firms in the same industry. ROI is a single comprehensive indicator of corporate performance.

   ROI offers many advantages: (*i*) It reflects the efficiency in the use of new resources (*ii*) It helps in rational allocation of resources (*iii*) It facilitates decentralisation of authority. (*iv*) It can be used as a total control technique.

   ROI suffers from several **limitations:** (*i*) Valuation of investment is difficult as it may be original cost, depreciated cost or replacement cost. During inflation the problem of price adjustment arises (*ii*) ROI is related to risk, higher the return higher the risk (*iii*) The focus on short run ROI may hamper R & D and other such areas which are necessary for longterm profitability (*iv*) ROI may lead to excessive focus on financial performance (*v*) In case one division sells to another, the problem of transfer pricing arises (*vi*) Business cycles and industry conditions affect ROI.

4. **Shareholder Value:** Shareholders contribute capital of a company and assume risk of business. Therefore, the value created by a company for its shareholders can be used to judge its performance. Shareholder value is the present worth of anticipated profits. In case of listed company, shareholder value is expressed in terms of Market Value Added (MVA). It is the difference between acquisition value and market value of shares. Shareholder value is derived from Economic Value Added (EVA) which in turn has been derived from Return On Value Added (ROVA). ROVA is expressed as profit before tax divided by value added. ROVA helps to identify the causes of decline. Necessary corrective actions can be taken on the basis of such early warning signals.

   EVA means excess of profit after tax over cost of capital. However, market price of shares fluctuates widely due to cyclical, seasonal and several other factors unrelated to corporate performance.

Shareholder value alone does not reflect organisational effectiveness. These are several stakeholder groups in addition to shareholders. Employees, customers, suppliers, dealers, government, local community are stakeholders. Value created for them should also be taken into account in assessing an organisation's overall performance.

5. **Ratio Analysis:** A financial ratio measures relationship between two financial variables. Financial ratios are commonly used to measure operating performance of business firms. These ratios are grouped into four major categories.

   (*i*) *Liquidity Ratios*: These ratios indicate a firm's ability to pay its short term debts **current ratio** (current assets/current liabilities) indicates the extent to which current assets are adequate to pay current liabilities. **Quick ratio** (liquid assets/current liabilities) better indicates ability to pay current liabilities.

   (*ii*) *Profitability Ratios*: These ratios indicate a firm's ability to earn profit in relation to its sales and investment. Profit margin (selling price-cost per unit) and return on investment are the main profitability ratios.

   (*iii*) *Leverage Ratios*: These ratios indicate ratio between equity (owners' funds) and debt. Debt-equity ratio (debt/equity), and interest coverage ratio (interest/profit) are the main leverage ratios.

   (*iv*) *Activity Ratios*: These ratios indicate how the firm's funds are being used. Inventory turnover ratio (sales/inventory) indicates how effectively the firm is managing its inventory. Receivable turnover ratio (sales/receivable) shows how promptly the firm is collecting dues form its debtors. Assets turnover ratio (sales/assets) shows how effectively the firm is using its assets to generate sales.

6. **Management By Objectives (MBO):** Peter Ducker developed the system of MBO. Under this system, superior and subordinates jointly decide the objectives through mutual consultation. Performance is continuousally evaluated against these objectives. MBO system operates on the basis of commitment and self-control.

7. **Network Techniques:** Programme Evaluation and Review Technique (PERT) and Critical path method (CPM) are two widely used network techniques. Both techniques use network diagram wherein activities and events are shown with their logical relationships. These techniques are used for control of time schedules and costs in projects.

8. **Key Success Factors:** Monitoring of key success factors helps in judgesting strategy implementation. Product quality, customer service, productivity, employee motivation and morale, market share are examples of key success factors.

   The techniques given above focus on financial performance. Some of the techniques used to judge social performance are as follows:

9. **Social Audit:** Corporate social audit means a systematic assessment of the social impact of an organisation's activities. On the basis of social audit, a social report is prepared to indicate the organisation's role in serving the society and in discharging its social responsibilities.

10. **Environmental Audit:** Sustainable development has become a key issue all over the world. Business firms are now expected to contribute to environmental protection and

sustainable development. Environmental audit is a systematic assessment of the impact of a firm's activities on the environment. It helps to provide accurate, comprehensive and meaningful information on the firm's role in sustaining the environment.

SUMMARY

Concept and Nature: Strategy evaluation and control is the process of determining the effectiveness of the chosen strategy in achieving the desired objectives.

Need: (*i*) verification of strategic choice (*ii*) congruence between strategy and decisions (*iii*) assessment of progress (*iv*) linkage between performance and rewards (*v*) feedback for future planning (*vi*) overcoming resistance to change (*vii*) functional coordination.

Participants: (*i*) board of directors (*ii*) chief executive (*iii*) other managers.

Systems: (*i*) information (*ii*) planning (*iii*) development (*iv*) appraisal (*v*) reward system.

Barriers: (*i*) resistance to evaluation (*ii*) problems in measurement (*iii*) limits of control (*iv*) shortterm focus (*v*) emphasis on efficiency.

Requirements: (*i*) relevant activities and results (*ii*) minimum information (*iii*) timely evaluation and action (*iv*) focus on exceptional outcomes (*v*) longterm and shortterm focus (*vi*) proper rewards.

Strategic Control: Monitoring progress of strategy (*i*) premise control (*ii*) implementation control: strategic thrusts and milestone review (*iii*) strategic surveillance (*iv*) special alert control.

Operational Control: Monitoring performance and use of resources. (*i*) setting standards (*ii*) measuring performance (*iii*) variance analysis (*iv*) corrective actions.

Techniques: For Strategic Control (*i*) strategic momentum control: responsibility centres, key success factors, generic strategies (*ii*) strategic leap control-strategic issue management, strategic field analysis, systems modelling, scenarios.

Making Strategic Control Effective: (*i*) commitment (*ii*) objectivity (*iii*) focus (*iv*) empowerment (*v*) incrementalism (*vi*) flexibility (*vii*) timing.

Criteria for Evaluation: (*i*) Rumelt-Consistency/consonance, advantage, feasibility (*ii*) Thompson and Strickland—industry attractiveness, competitive strength, strategic fit, resource•fit (*iii*) Tilles' internal consistency, consistency with environment, appropriateness, acceptable risk, appropriate time horizon, workability.

Strategic Audit: Comprehensive and systematic evaluation of all facets of strategic management.

Techniques for Operational Control: (*i*) activity based costing (*ii*) budgetary control (*iii*) ROI (*iv*) shareholder value—EVA, MVA (*v*) ratio analysis-liquidity, profitability, leverage, activity ratios (*vi*) MBO (*vii*) PERT and CPM (*viii*) key success factors (*ix*) social audit (*x*) environmental audit.

TEST QUESTIONS

1. Why is it necessary to evaluate and control strategy? Discuss the main elements in the strategy review and control process.
2. Explain Rumelt's criteria for evaluation of strategy.

3. Critically examine the criteria of evaluation of corporate strategy as given by Seymor Tilles. In real life if you want to find out if a particular strategy proved effective, what important parameters would you consider?
4. Briefly discuss important aspects of strategic control. Is it necessary to modify the process for accomplishing this type of control by including environmental and internal assessments.
5. Describe the evaluation and control process of an organisation. Also explain its importance. Is evaluation and control process appropriate for an organisation that emphasizes creativity? Discuss.
6. Do you agree with the criteria of strategy evaluation as given by Seymor Tilles? Discuss and indicate changes which need to be made in the criteria to be useful for new paradigm of strategy formulation.
7. Distinguish between strategic control and operational control.
8. Describe the different elements that constitute the evaluation process for operational control.
9. Differentiate between strategic momentum control and strategic leap control.
10. What is a responsibility centre in an organisation? List various types of responsibility centres of an organisation.
11. What do you understand by Management by objectives (MBO) and its importance in strategy formulation and implementation?
12. What is meant by shareholder value? How can shareholder value be measured through Economic Value Added and Market Value Added? Do you think that these two measures are an improvement over traditional measures of corporate performance like ROI, EPS and ROE?
13. Explain the Market Value Added (MVA) method of measuring corporate and divisional performance.
14. Define strategic control. Discuss its techniques.
15. What is meant by strategic control? Discuss the quantitative and qualitative criteria used for evaluation of strategy.
16. Describe the purposes of strategy evaluation. Outline different techniques of strategy evaluation and control.
17. Discuss five tools of external strategic audit which can be utilised for scanning the macro level environment of an organisation. Which of these tools would you recommend for use in an IT firm. Give reasons.

CASE STUDY

The directors of Zaveri Enterprises were very pleased with the performance of their company during the last four years. Today, Zaveri Enterprises was manufacturing more than 2 lacs television sets and was third largest in the country. About 40% production was to colour TVs and the company enjoyed a popular image all over the country.

Mr. Satish Shah, the Chairman of the group and an electronics engineer by training always emphasised the importance of profit and growth. Because of his initiative ZE had put up a plastic moulding shop to manufacture cabinets for TVs. In addition, ZE has an excellent R & D set up to improve the TV circuits and at the same time indigenise the components. The impact of this backward integration was felt all over the company. It not only made all the staff members and technicians highly cost conscious but actually resulted in higher profits. Almost all the leading TV manufactures acknowledged that ZE was the most profitable company and was marketing the best products in the market. ZE was amongst the few companies whose TVs were selling on cash basis. With factories located in 7 states, to get local sales tax advantage, ZE enjoyed the leaders position in the industry.

In January 1987, during one of the meeting of the directors, Mr. Shah informed the other directors about the growing tax liabilities and need for new investments. Mr. Niren Shah, one of the directors looking after the finance agreed and indicated that if everything goes well, the company would have an investable surplus of about ₹ 3 crores at the end of 1987. During that meeting it was tentatively decided that ZE should look for acquiring a sick or a troubled unit in related areas. ZE informed their associates to be on look out for any serious offer from banks or SIDCs or entrepreneurs.

Between March 1997 and May 1999, the directors of ZE had several meetings with various promoters of Ferrite India Limited, a joint sector project, for acquiring partners capital.

	Original		Revised		(₹in lacs) Increase (+) Decrease (–)		Raised upto July 31, 1989	
Share Capital –								
Promoters	104		139		35		89**	
Public	100	204	131	270	31+	66	–	89.0
Term Loans –								
R/L – IDBI	170						80.5	
– ICICI	15						7.0	
– IFCI	–	185		288		+103		87.5
F/E – ICICI	100		107*		7*		59.3	
– IFCI	70	170	70	177	–	+7*	24.2	85.5
Deferred Payment Guarantee from ICICI		16		16		–		15.0
State subsidy		15		15		–		–
		590		766		176		276.0

* National increase due to foreign currency fluctuation.

** By way of interest free advance against share capital

It may be mentioned that the cost overrun of ₹176 lacs comprises 7 lacs due to foreign currency fluctuation and actual overrun of ₹169 lacs. Thus the company's requirement of additional funds would be ₹169 lacs. The additional requirement of ₹169 lacs is proposed to be financed by additional share capital of ₹66 lacs and additional term loans of ₹103 lacs.

The directors of ZE have received the proposal from Ferrite India Limited. The directors of ZE are wonders whether to acquire this project or not.

A. FERRITE INDIAN LIMITED

Ferrite (India) Limited (FIL), a new company promoted in the joint sector by Electronics bevelopment Corporation of Orissa Limited (ELCO), Industrial Promotion and Investment Corporation of Orissa Limited (IPICOL) and Shankar Ghosh and associates is setting up a project for the manufacture of 1200 tonnes per year of hard ferrites a Chandaka Industrial Complex at Bhubaneswar, Orissa. The project would be implemented in technical collaboration with Krupp widia Gmbh () of West Germany. The project is in the initial stages of implementation and is expected to go into commercial production by July 1997 as April 1996 envisaged originally, indicating a delay of about 15 month in the implementation mainly due to delay in obtaining technical documentation from Krupp.

The cost of the originally estimated at ₹ 590 lacs (including margin for working capital of ₹ 21 lacs) has now been revised to ₹ 766 lacs (including margin for working capital of ₹ 30 lacs). Major areas of cost overrun are indigenous plant and machinery, miscellaneous fixed assets and interest during construction period and other pre-operative expenses. Additional requirement of ₹ 176 lacs is proposed to be financed by equity share capital of ₹ 66 lacs and term loans of ₹ 110 lacs (including ₹ 7 lacs in foreign currencies already sanctioned by IFCI and ICICI). FIL has approached institutions **for providing additional rupee loans of ₹ 103 lacs and for reivising the repayment schedule of the existing loans.**

In 1983, institutions sanctioned to FIL, foreign currency loans equivalent to ₹ 170 lacs (at the then rates or exchange), rupee loans of ₹ 185 lacs, deferred payment guarantee of ₹ 16 lacs, and underwriting assistance for drawn about ₹ 83.5 lacs and ₹ 87.5 lacs respectively against the foreign currency loans and rupees loans. The deferred payment guarantee of ₹ 16 lacs has also been provided.

B. REVISED COST OF PROJECT

As mentioned earlier, the cost of the project has increased from ₹ 590 lacs (including margin for working capital of ₹ 21 lacs) to ₹ 766 lacs (including working capital margin of ₹ 30 lacs), indicating on overrun of ₹ 176 lacs.

The details of original and revised cost of the project and expenditure incurred upto July 31, 1986 are given below:

(₹ in Lacs)

	Original	Revised	Increase Decrease	Incurred upto July 31 1996
Land and site development	4.8	12.2	7.4	7.3
Buildings	60.0	65.0	5.0	40.4
Plant and machinery Imported CIF	170.1	177.7	7.6	83.6
Duty & transportations	72.8	49.9	(22.9)	9.4
Indigenous	26.0	85.0	59.0	5.9
Foundation and installation	8.0	10.0	–	–
Technical know how fees	38.1	38.1	–	30.5

Technical consultancy fees Expanses on forelgn technicians and training of Indian technicians abroad	3.5	3.5	–	–
Miscellaneous fixed assets	60.3	113.3	53.0	10.1
Preliminary & Preoperative expensive	87.5	151.7	64.2	52.2
Provision for contingencies	37.9	14.6	(23.3)	–
	569.0	736.0	167.0	252.2
Margin money for working capital	21.0	30.0	9.0	–
	590.0	766.0	176.0	252.2

C. MEANS OF FINANCING

The original and revised means of financing and the amount raised upto July 31, 1996 are as follows:–

Share Capital: The company new proposes to raise additional share capital of ₹ 66 lacs as against the original proposal of ₹ 204 lacs. of the total equity share capital of ₹ 270 lacs, the promoters ELCO, IPICOL and Shanker Ghos and associates would subscribe to share capital of ₹ 54 lacs 20%, ₹ 17 lacs (6%) and ₹ 68 lacs (25%) respectively. The balance equity share capital of ₹ 131 lacs would be offered for public subscription.

Institutions had originally agreed to under write ₹ 100 lacs equity shares of the company's original public issue of ₹ 100 lacs. Of the proposed public issue of ₹ 131 lacs, FIL proposes to approach banks/brokers for underwriting ₹ 49 lacs equity shares. The balance ₹ 82 lacs would be underwritten by institutions. Thus, there would be a reduction of ₹ 18 lacs in the underwriting assistance of institutions.

Termloans from Institutions: FIL has approached the all-India financial institutions for providing additional rupee term loan of ₹ 103 lacs. It may be mentioned that due to currency fluctuations, the original foreign currency loans from institutions have escalated by about ₹ 7 lacs. The additional rupee loan of ₹ 103 lacs carry interest @ 14% per annum and would be secured by a first mortgage on the fixed assets of FIL pari passu with the charges created/to be created in favour of institutions for their earlier loans would be repayable in 16 half yearly and instalments commencing from the first half of 1988 and ending in second half of 1995.

Based on the proposes so far make it is expected that FIL and GF Electronics Ltd. (GPE) would commence productions by 1987. Thus the total installea capacity in 1998-99 would be 5480 tonnes against the projected demand of 4776 tonnes indicating about 87 capacity utilisations.

Prospects for FIL

FIL is a new company promoted by technocrats who are experienced in the field of hard ferrites. The marketing organisation of FIL is being set up to cope with the competitive market during the initial stages of operation. FIL will have adequate sales set up and undertake sales promotional activities to establish its product in the market. Taking into account the technological support from Krupp the collaborators, we feel that FIL would be in a position to stabilise its production level and market its products.

Selling Arrangements & Prices

FIL proposes to market its products directly through the net work of sales officers in the important cities in India. However, considering the need for accelerated sales promotion particularly during the initial stages of its operation, FIL will have to allow discounts, commissions and turnover bonus etc. These expenses have been provided for in our projections.

D. PROFITABILITY

The cost of production and profitability of FIL is given in Annexures.

E. MARKET

Hard Ferrites are basically manufactured by a metallurgical process. They are formed to various shapes depending upon application. Hard ferrites car either be oriented or non oriented. Oriented magnets are mainly used in the production of loud speakers, DC l' Motors and magnets, while non-oriented magnets are used in the production of cycle and two-three wheeler toys, novelties and refrigerators.

Hard Ferrites are manufactured both in the organised and the small scale sectors but generally only non oriented magnets are manufactured by the small scale sector. Presently there are nine unite in the organised sector with a licensed capacity of 5370 tonnes and installed capacity of 1670 tones. There is only one small scale sector unit of licenced and installed capacity of 150 tonnes producing hord ferrites of comparable quality. Thus, the total licenced and installed capacity works out to be 5520 tonnes and 1820 tonnes respectively. The total production hard ferrites in 1982 from these ten units was 1430 tonnes, an capacity utilisation of about 78%; However, only two units namely, permanent Magnets Limited (PML) and Morrn, Electronics Limited (MEL), with a combined installed capacity of 1400 tonnes, accounted for 95% of the industry's production in 1962.

Future Demand

The demand for hard ferrites is linked with the demand and growth of end user products. Loud speakers constituted a market share of about 71% of the total ferrite demand in 1992. The growth in the production of loudspeaker is estimated to be about 20% per annum. Based on this growth and the norms of consumption (depending upon the size of the speakers), the demand of hard ferrite for use in loudspeakers is expected to increase from 1010 tonnes in 1992 to 3687 tonnes in 1999. The other significant product requiring hard ferrites, is the magnets used in two and three wheeler industries. Judging from the future expansion plans of this industry, the demand for sector magnets for this market segment is expected to increase from 130 tonnes in 1992 to 391 tonnes in 1969. The demand from other miscellaneous applications for magnets like DC motors, refrigerators and magnetic applications is expected to increase from 291 tonnes in 1962 to 698 tones in 1969. Thus, the total demand for hard Ferrites is expected to increase from 1431 tonnes in 1982 to 4776 tonnes in 1989, indicating a growth rate of 16% per annum. It may be mentioned that the estimates made by the Electronic Commission for the ninth plan, indicates a demand of 5,500 tonnes in 1999.

Future Supply

As stated earlier, the total installed capacity for 1992 was 1820 tonnes. MEL and PML have completed their expansion projects with aggregate installed capacity of 1800 tonnes recently.

FERRITE INDIA LIMITED

Parameters for Profitability Projections (Updated)

Selling Price

Rings	₹ 30,000 per tonne
Segments	₹ 60,000 per tonne

Composition of Sales

	1st Year	2nd Year	3rd Year
Rings	100%	60%	50%
Segments	–	40%	50%

EXPORTS

Exports have been considered from the 2nd year onwards. The extent of exports 14.50% comprising 30% rings and 70% segments.

FERRITE INDIA LIMITED

CASH FLOW

(₹ in Lacks)

SOURCES OF FUNDS	Implementation Period	1998	1999	2000
Shares' Issue	270	–	–	–
Net Cash Accruals	–	(22)	138	201
Term Loan from Institutions	479	–	–	–
Deferred Credit for Technical known-how fees	16	–	–	–
Increase in Bank Borrowing	–	56	23	14
State Subsidy	15	–	–	–
Total	780	34	161	215
APPLICATION OF FUNDS				
Capital Expenditure				
Project	749	–	–	–
Normal	–	–	5	10
Increase in Current Assets	24	62	33	21
Decrease in Bank Borrowings	–	–	–	–
Decrease in Term Loan	–	–	58	59
Decrease in Deferred Credit for Technical known-how	–	3	3	3
Total	773	65	99	93
Opening Cash/Bank Balance	–	7	(24)	38
Add/Deduct Net Surplus/Deficit	7	(31)	62	122
Closing Cash/Bank Balance	7	(24)	38	160

FERRITE INDIA LIMITED

Projected Profitability

(₹ in Lacs)

Year ending 31st March,	1998	1999	2000
Production in MT	300	780	900
Utilisation of capacity	50%	65%	75%
Raw Materials	10	27	33
Consumable	8	29	33
Power, fuel and water	8	24	27
Salary and wages	12	29	33
Repairs and Maintenance	5	11	15
Administrative off	6	15	27
Selling and Distribution	3	17	21
Total Direct Costs	52	152	182
Interest	30	53	45
Depreciation	43	87	87
Total Cost of Production	125	292	314
Total Sales	60	343	428
Operating Profit/(Loss)	(65)	51	114
Profit/(Loss) before Interest and Depreciation	0	191	246

FERRITE INDIA LIMITED

Balance Sheet

(₹ in Lacs)

As at 31st March	Implementation Period	1998	1999	2000
CAPITAL & LIABILITY				
Equity Share Capital	270	270	270	270
Reserve & Surplus	–	(65)	(14)	100
State Subsidy	15	15	15	15
Term Loan from Institutions	479	479	421	362
Referred Cr. from Collaborators	16	13	10	7
Bank Borrowing for W.C	–	56	79	93
Total	780	768	781	847
Assets				
Net Fixed Assets	749	706	624	547
Net Current Assets	24	86	119	140
Cash & Bank Balance	7	(24)	38	160
Total	780	768	781	847

Questions

(*i*) What is the degree of synergy between the two companies in the areas of finance and marketing?

(*ii*) What other alternatives could the company have considered before deciding to go ahead with the given company?

(*iii*) If you were to head the company today what course of action would you recommend and why?

PART – VI

STRATEGIC ISSUES IN SPECIFIED AREAS

14. Strategic Management in International Business
15. Strategic Issues in E-Business or Digitalisation
16. Strategic Management of Technology and Innovations
17. Strategic Issues in Organisational Change
18. Strategic Management in Small Business, Family Business and Non-Profit Organisations

14

CHAPTER

STRATEGIC MANAGEMENT IN INTERNATIONAL BUSINESS

CHAPTER OUTLINE

14.1. MOTIVES FOR GOING INTERNATIONAL

Companies go international due to several reasons:

(*i*) Inadequate demand in the home market mainly due to low purchasing power.

(*ii*) Availability of low cost raw materials, labour, capital and other inputs abroad.

(*iii*) Rapid shrinking of distance and time across countries owing to modern transportation and telecommunication facilities.

(*iv*) Political stability in some nations and political disturbances in other countries.

(*v*) Need for diversification of risks in terms of markets.

(*vi*) Desire to avail economies of scale.

(*vii*) Desire to earn economic power and prestige.

(*viii*) Gradual decline in tariff and non-tariff barriers under globalisation.

Once a company decides to go global, it has to restate its corporate mission, objectives and goals. The restated mission and international involvement are connected through the comparative cost advantage. The company may enter markets/countries which have a cost advantage in producing certain products/services. For example, Saudi Arabia has a cost advantage in oil drilling. Some companies set up their production plants in other countries due to political reasons. For example, when the US government restricted imports of cars, Japanese car firms set up their plants in the USA.

Table 14: Four Stages of Internationalisation

	First-degree Internationalisation	Second-degree Internationalisation	Third-degree internationalisation	Fourth-degree Internationalisation
Nature of contact with foreign markets	Indirect, passive	Direct, active	Direct, active	
Locus of international operations	Domestic	Domestic	Domestic and international	Domestic and international
Orientation of company	Domestic	Domestic	Primarily domestic	Multinational (domestic operations viewed as part of the whole)
Type of international activity	Foreign trade of goods and services	Foreign trade of goods and services	Foreign trade, foreign assistance contracts, foreign direct investment	Foreign trade, foreign assistance contracts, foreign direct investment
Organisational structure	Traditional domestic	International department	International division	Global structure

Source: Stoner, **Management,** Prentice-Hall of India, New Delhi, p. 769.

After restating its mission, objectives and goals, an international firm conducts a global SWOT analysis. It attempts to identify opportunities and threats through analysis of economic, social, cultural, political and legal environment in a foreign country. The size, growth rate, nature of the industry are analysed to judge its attractiveness. Competitive situation in the foreign country is also assessed.

The company analyses its strengths and weaknesses in terms of its financial, marketing, technological, operations and human resource capabilities. The company then decides which markets to enter. A company usually enters the markets with high attractiveness, high competitive advantage and low risk.

14.2 MODES OF ENTRY INTO GLOBAL MARKETS

A company can begin its international operations in several ways which are called modes of entry into global market. Some of these entry modes are as follows:

1. **Exporting:** In this mode, the firm sells its home-made products/services in overseas markets. There are two methods of exporting:

   (*a*) *Indirect exports*: The firm exports through intermediaries. There are four types of intermediaries:

   (*i*) ***Domestic-based exporter:*** Domestic-based exporter buys the products from the manufacturer and he in turn exports them to various countries.

   (*ii*) ***Domestic-based export agent:*** Domestic-based export agent negotiates with domestic producers and foreign purchasers for exports. He coordinates the domestic producers and foreign purchasers. He collects commission for his services.

(*iii*) ***Cooperative organisation:*** A number of producers producing the same or similar products form into a cooperative organisation. This cooperative organisation will carry on exporting activities on behalf of the member producers. This type of arrangement is used by the producers of agricultural products.

(*iv*) ***Export-management company:*** This company manages the exports by charging a fee.

Indirect exports cost less to the producers and the producers can concentrate on the manufacturing as the export arrangements are taken care by the intermediaries.

(*b*) *Direct Exports:* Companies depend on indirect marketing during the early stage of their exports. Eventually, they may decide to export directly in order to get more benefits and economies of scale. The investment and risk will be greater compared to the indirect export. The methods of direct exports are as follows:

(*i*) ***Domestic-based Export Department or Division:*** A separate export department or an export division within the marketing department may be created by the company to look after the exports. This department/division will perform all the functions and completes the procedures relating to exports.

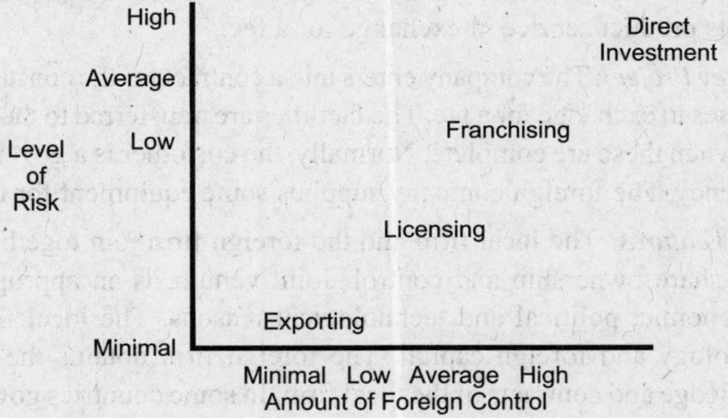

Fig. 14.1. Ways to Go International

(*ii*) ***Overseas Sales Branch or Subsidiary:*** The company may establish overseas sales branch(es) in one or more foreign countries. These sales branches perform the functions of export marketing and also fulfil the procedural formalities. These branches also make the host countries to feel the presence of the company. These branches perform customer service in addition to performing other marketing functions in the host country.

(*iii*) ***Travelling Export Sales Representatives:*** The company can send sales representatives to various foreign countries to explore business and also to execute the business.

(*iv*) ***Foreign-based Distributors or Agents:*** The company appoints foreign-based distributors or agents to deal with the exports and sell the company's products. These distributors or agents may be given exclusive right to represent the company and its products. Alternatively they may be given limited rights as well as responsibilities.

Companies have to participate in international exhibitions and trade fairs and exhibit their products.

(c) *Licensing*: Under this approach, the licensor licenses a foreign company to use its production process, trade mark, patent, trade secret or other item value for a fee or royalty. The manufacturer enters a foreign market with little risk. The foreign company gains the advantages of production expertise or technology, or a well-known product without having to start from scratch. Coca-Cola enters different foreign markets by licensing bottlers around the globe. It supplies them syrup, and trains the personnel of the foreign companies in producing and selling the product.

There are different forms of licensing agreement:

(a) ***Management Contract:*** Under this arrangement, the company enters into a management contract to manage its facilities (*e.g.* hotel, hospital, etc.) for a fee. The company offers managerial expertise.

(b) ***Contract Manufacturing:*** In this method, the company engages local manufacturers abroad to produce the product.

(c) ***Franchising:*** The company (franchiser) authorises an overseas firm to market its product/service in exchange for a fee.

(d) *Turnkey Project*: The company enters into a contract for the construction of operating facilities in exchange for a fee. The facilities are transferred to the host country or the firm when these are complete. Normally, the customer is a government department or agency. The foreign company supplies some equipment for the project.

(e) *Joint Ventures:* The local firm and the foreign firm join together to run business. They share ownership and control. Joint venture is an appropriate strategy due to economic, political and technological reasons. The local firm gets advanced technology and foreign capital. The foreign firm obtains the benefit of market knowledge and contracts of the local firm. In some countries government insists on domestic share in the foreign firm's entry. However the foreign firm may start its own independent business after gaining knowledge of market and culture. Similarly, the local firm may have complete ownership and control after getting technology. Cultural differences, different views on reinvestment of profits, desire to control management, etc. create problems in joint ventures. Lupin, Ranbaxy, Reddy and other pharma firms have adopted this strategy. Strategic alliance provides enormous scope for. Indian companies to acquire technology and to enter overseas markets.

(f) *Direct Investment:* Under this arrangement, the company sets up its own manufacturing and/or marketing facilities in the foreign country. This strategy enables the company to widen the market. The company gains access to low-cost raw materials, labour and other inputs abroad. Cost of transportation is also reduced. Incentives and subsidies from the foreign government can be availed of. Closer relationship can be established with host country's government, customers, suppliers, etc.

Direct investment strategy suffers from some **disadvantages:**

(*i*) The company exposes its large investment to commercial and political risks.

(*ii*) The host country may impose discriminative restrictions.

(*iii*) Political instability in the host country may affect business.

(*vi*) *Acquisitions:* A company may enter global market by acquiring firms abroad. It can secure synergistic benefits by acquiring a firm with a strong complementary product line, new technology and efficient distribution network. However, host country government may put restrictions on acquisition of local firms by foreign investors.

14.3 INTERNATIONAL PRODUCT PORTFOLIO

An international firm should match markets and products with its resources and capabilities. Portfolio analysis can be applied in international business. In Fig. 14.1 country attractiveness is shown on the vertical axis. Market size, market growth rate, government regulations, etc. determine a country's attractiveness. The competitive strength of the product shown on the horizontal axis, depends on market share, contribution margin, product fit and market support. In case of high country attractiveness and high product competitive strength growth strategy is appropriate. On the other hand, harvest or divest strategy is suitable in case of low country attractiveness and low product competitive strength. Firms falling in the upper right box can go for divestment or joint venture. Those falling in the centre or lower left boxes should think of 'milking' to generate strong cash flows in the short run.

High ← Competitive Strengths → Low

Country Attractiveness (High ↑ ... ↓ Low)

Invest/ Grow		Dominate/ Divest Joint Venture
	Selectivity Strategies	
		Harvest/ Divest Combine/ Licence

Fig. 14.2.

Source: G.D. Harrell and R.O. Kiefer, "Multinational Strategic Market Portfolios, "MSU Business Topics, Winter 1981, p. 7.

14.4 COMPETITIVE ADVANTAGE OF NATIONS

Just like each organisation, each country has its own competitive advantage. For example, USA has competitive advantage in computers, Germany has in machines, Japan has in electornics and automobiles, Switezerland has in pharmaceuticals and confectionary. How does a country acquire a competitive advantage? Michael Porter[1] has developed a model known as national diamond (Fig. 14.3) to answer this question. This model consists of four interrelated factors which together contribute to the competitive advantage of a nation.

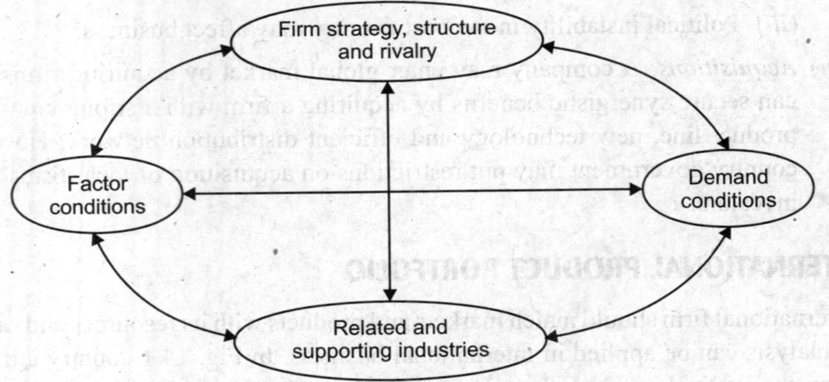

Fig. 14.3. Porter's Diamond of National Competitive Advantage

1. **Factor Conditions:** A nation may gain a competitive advantage because it is endowed with certain natural and/or manmade resources. Raw materials, labour, knowledge, capital, infrastructure are these resources. These special factors may enable a country to produce at a low cost or to produce a highly differentiated product/service. As a result a competitive advantage accrues to that country. Availability of low-cost and trained engineers and other professionals has enabled Japan to produce low-cost and high-quality consumer electronics and automobiles.
2. **Demand Conditions:** The nature and size of demand in a country determine the rate of innovation. Demand conditions may prompt or discourage organisations to be globally competitive. Three characteristics of home demand, namely, its composition, size and growth pattern and the means by which a nation's home demand pulls its products/services into foreign markets, are particularly significant for competitive advantage. Demand conditions which serve as incentives for continuous investment and innovations provide a competitive advantage. USA developed a competitive advantage in information technology largely due to its demand conditions.
3. **Related and Supporting Industries:** The existence of industries which are related to and support the main industry also determines the industry's competitive advantage. The relationship between the main industry and the related and supporting industries becomes reciprocal in the long run. When the main industry develops, related and supporting industries emerge after some time. The related industries in turn facilitate further growth of the main industry. For example, development of computer industry in the USA led to the emergence of computer software industry, which helped to increase demand for computers.
4. **Firm Strategy, Structure and Rivalry:** The way firms are created, organised and managed and the nature of domestic competition also determine a nation's competitive advantage. For example US companies give top priority to return on investment and

1. Michael E. Porter, **The Competitive Advantage of Nations,** Macmillan, London, 1990, p. 71.

quick decision-making whereas Japanese companies prefer market share and consensual decision-making.

Government exercises an important influence on the four variables given above. Government policies affect the manner in which these variables shape the country's competitive advantage.

For example, India has advantages in terms of market size and human resources. But India ranks lower than China in global competitiveness due to poor infrastructure and Government policies (before 1991).

The diamond of national competitive advantage is a valuable framework. On its basis, a country can determine the industry in which it can develop a competitive advantage. Porter's diamond is also useful in explaining why one or more industries from a particular country become globally competitive. For example, India has achieved remarkable growth in information technology and pharmaceuticals industries. Availability of low-cost technical skills, high domestic demand, existence of semiconductor and other supporting industries to manufacture computer hardware, presence of IT clusters, etc. led to the growth of IT industry. The pharmaceuticals industry owes its growth to huge domestic demand, government's protectionist policies (before 1991), and existence of upstream supplier industries.

Table 14.2: Arvind Mills Mantra for Globalisation

- Source raw materials wherever they are cheapest.
- Manufacture wherever in the world is most cost effective.
- Sell in those global markets where prices are highest.
- Raise finances globally.
- Forge international strategic alliances
- To manage all these, take on the best talent from all over the world. And you will have achieved the stature of a true multinational.

14.5 STRATEGIES FOR INTERNATIONALISATION

According to Bartlett[2] and Ghoshal, two sets of factors impinge upon a firm's decision to adopt strategies for global business—cost pressures and pressures for local responsiveness.

1. **Cost Pressures:** There are pressures on a firm to minimise its unit costs. The firm attempts to minimise costs through economies of scale and location economies. In order to achieve economies of scale, the firm may produce globally standardised products from a single low-cost location and market them widely around the world. Cost pressures are usually high in case of products that serve universal needs. Steel, petroleum, personal computers and camera are examples of such products.
2. **Pressures for Local Responsiveness:** The firm is under pressure to customise its products/services to the requirements of the individual country market it is serving. For example, cars, clothes, food, entertainment and other products are tailored to suit the preferences of customers in each country. A global firm has to tailor its strategies

2. C.A. Bartlett and Sumantr Ghoshal, **Managing Across Borders,** Harvard Business School Press, Boston, MA, 1989.

to country-level differences in customer preferences and tastes, business practices and government policies.

The two variables given above are contradictory because product/service differentiation increases unit costs. The juxtaposition of these two variables results in four types of strategies for international business (Fig. 14.4).

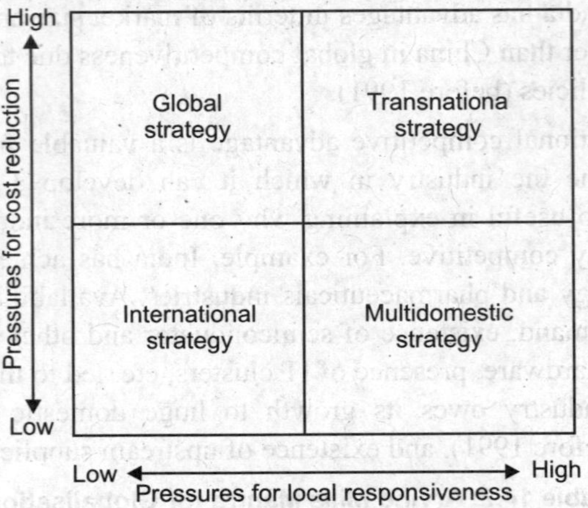

Fig. 14.4. Strategies for Internationalisation

(*i*) *Global Strategy:* Under this strategy, a firm sells standardised products on the assumption that customer needs are similar worldwide. Such a firm has competitive advantage in the form of low costs which are the result of economies of scale in product development, production and marketing. The firm leverages its expertise in producing standardised products at favourable locations. In order to implement the global strategy the firm may centralise its R & D facilities in one country but decentralises production in different countries to save transportation costs.

(*ii*) *MultiDomestic Strategy:* In multidomestic strategy, the firm attempts to achieve a high level of local responsiveness by matching its products or services to the requirements of the countries it operates in. Preferences and tastes of customers differ from country to country. Therefore, a multidomestic firm customises its products/services according to the local conditions in different countries. Such differentiation results in high cost structure due to duplication of R & D, production and marketing facilities.

3. **International Strategy:** In the early stage of globalisation, a firm may not be able to adopt global strategy or multidomestic strategy. Therefore, it adopts international strategy. In this strategy the firm exports goods produced in the home country. Once the firm achieves success in exporting, it might set up manufacturing and marketing facilities abroad. The firm retains tight control over its overseas operations. It offers standardised products/services in different countries. The main drawback of this strategy is that the firm reaps benefits of neither low cost nor product differentiation.

4. **Transnational Strategy:** Under this strategy, a firm adopts a combined approach of low cost and high local responsiveness simultaneously. It is difficult to integrate these

two contradictory approaches. Bartlett and Ghoshal[3] suggest the following actions to achieve combination of low costs and customisation.

(*a*) *Getting Inputs from Subsidiaries:* There should be multiple linkages between the head office and the subsidiaries. The subsidiaries should be involved in generating innovative ideas and disseminating them across the firm. The managers at the head office understand needs and opportunities in different counties. Country managers need to understand and be involved in decision-making processes at the head office.

(*b*) *Distribution of Interdependent Capabilities:* Various subsidiaries in different countries should be encouraged to achieve economies of scale. They need to perform an activity or produce a product that can be used in all the subsidiaries.

(*c*) *Flexible Integration Process:* The integration across the firm should be flexile. An environment that allows development of managers with a global mindset needs to be created.

Thus, a transnational firm should transfer expertise from its foreign subsidiaries to its headquarters and from one foreign subsidiary to another through the process of global learning.

SUMMARY

Motives: (*i*) inadequate demand at home (*ii*) low cost inputs abroad (*iii*) modern transportation and communications (*iv*) political conditions (*v*) diversification of risks (*vi*) economies of scale (*vii*) power and prestige (*viii*) removal of trade barriers

Modes of Entry: (*i*) exporting – direct and indirect (*ii*) licensing–management contract, contract manufacturing, franchising (*iii*) turn key projects (*iv*) joint venture (*v*) direct investment (*vi*) acquisitions.

International Product Portfolio: country attractiveness (high, low), and competitive strengths (high, low).

Competitive Advantage of Nations: (*i*) firm strategy, structure and rivalry (*ii*) demand conditions (*iii*) factor conditions (*iv*) related and supporting industries.

Strategies for Internationalistion: (*i*) cost pressures (*ii*) pressures for local responsiveness (*iii*) global strategy, international strategy, multi – domestic strategy, transnational strategy.

Guidelines for Low Cost and Customisation: (*i*) inputs from subsidiaries (*b*) distribution of interdependent capabilities (*c*) flexible integration process.

TEST QUESTIONS

1. What is the challenge of strategic management in the context of globalisation of modern business?
2. How has globalisation influenced Indian industries? Explain the strategies for global business.
3. Discuss various strategies adopted by the organisations to enter international markets.

3. C.A. Bartlett and Sumantra Ghoshal, **Transnational Management: Text, cases and Readings in Cross-Border Management,** Irwin, Chicago, 1995.

4. "Business firms having formal strategic planning system have a higher probability of success than which do not." Comment on this statement and explain how globalisation and internet are both providing challenges and opportunities to strategic managemnt in Indian companies.
5. What should be the corporate strategy of a firm having foreign collaboration? Discuss in detail supporting your suggestions with suitable examples.
6. Explain the strategic issues relating to foreign collaborations. What are the effects of liberalisation and globalisation on these issues?
7. How does a multicounty strategy differ from global strategy? Under what conditions would you recommend the use of these two strategies?
8. What strategic options can local companies adopt to compete against global companies in emerging markets?
9. Assume you are the CEO of a leading technology company. Your are currently manufacturing state-of-the-art notebook computers and have a highly successful brand name to your credit. A Japanese firm wishes to form an alliance with you. The proposed partnership would involve manufacturing a large portion of your notebook computers in Japan using the partner's factories and employees. The partner insists on using his or her factories in Japan because they have a reputation for quality products.

   In the light of the above situation, answer the following questions:–

   (*i*) What are some of the benefits and risks that you face in the relationship?

   (*ii*) How would you manage this relationship over the long term?

   (*iii*) Does manufacturing in Japan make a difference to your long-term competitive advantage?

   (*iv*) What are some key issues you need to think about when entering the alliance?
10. BioGene, an Indian pharmaceutical firm, a division of an Indian conglomerate, has grown from 3000 employees to 7000 in two years, serving Indian market. It has now decided to expand overseas.

    (*a*) Discuss how it should align its structure to its new strategy.

    (*b*) Develop a strategic evaluation and control mechanism for the firm.
11. In what way the practice of strategic management of multinational corporations differ from domestic companies? Explain.

CASE STUDY

IPCA was promoted as a pharmaceutical company by a group of medical professionals and businessmen. Incorporated in 1949, it was taken over by Amitabh Bachchan and his brother Ajitabh in 1975. The latter has been its chairman, while the co-promoters, Premchand Godha and M.R Chandurkar, have been the two Managing Directors. In early 1999, the Bachchans reduced their stake in the company from 36 to 1 per cent in favour of the promoters and some private investors. Reportedly the sell-off was caused by a cash crunch that Bachchan brothers were facing. Godha and Chandurkar now hold a 52 p.c. stake in the company.

In 1994, Ipca seemed to be in a position to emerge as one of the most successful Indian pharma companies by the turn of the century. But its overdependence on the anti-malarial range of drugs did not allow the expected growth. Being under Drug Price Control Order, the anti-malarial drugs did not have much scope for profits. Also cheap imports of chloroquin from China cut into its market and the company soon fell out of favour.

The financial performance of the company since 1993-94 was reasonably satisfactory, the turnover having more than doubled in 1997-97 from ₹ 142 crore in 1993-94 to ₹ 292 crore in 1997-98. Profit also doubled during the same period from ₹ 10.43 crore to ₹ 19.45 crore at a compound annual growth rate (CAGR) of 17 per cent. But the increase in profitability was not even. It was ₹ 10.00 crore in 1993-94, ₹ 18.54 crore in 1994-95 and ₹ 15.04 crore 1995-96; the drop was due to the excess interest costs that the company had to bear as a result of its borrowings.

In 1998-99, Ipca was the leader in anti-malarial products in the country with a market share of close to 40 per cent in the chloroquine bulk drug market. *Lariago* is the dominant product in its range of anti-malarial formulations. In November 1998, the company also launched *Larither*, a drug to treat *falciparum Malaria*. Its top five brands commanded 72 p.c. of the market for anti-malarials. However, profitability from this range was so low, that the company decided to reduce its dependence on them, and in 1999 launched 13 new products in the high-margin segments of macrolids, antidiabetics, and anti-obesity. This was to be followed by a few more in 2000 in the anti-bacterial, cardiovascular and cephalosporin therapeutic groups.

Despite the policy of lunching new products, Ipca's R & D budget has been only 1 p.c. of its total sales. The company did not get into basic research as it was too expensive. According to a private inventor with substantial investments in the pharma industry, "the less an Indian pharma company spends on basic research, the better. With venture-capital-funded bio-tech firms mushrooming in the United States, there is grave risk of basic research getting commoditised. In such a scenario, a pharma company investing in basic research is likely to lose out as it does not have the ability to handle the kind of risk that venture-capital funded firms do have. In any case, no Indian company can match the research facilities of players like Merck, which spends close to $ 2 billion annually on R & D."

Ipca had six plants located around the country and an employee strength of 3600. In-house production of bulk drugs had gone up substantially with expansion of capacity since 199-94, although it contributed only 28 p.c. to total sales. One of its plants at Ratlam received USFDA approval in 1999 and at least two more plants awaited approval. The plant at Athal, Silvassa, conformed already to FDA standards. The FDA approved plants were state-of-the-art and were automated to a great extent. The same facilities were expected to be extended to other plants as well. The company had decided to acquire approval for plants from those countries to which it intended to export its products. Besides the USFDA, the company also had approval from the regulatory agencies of Canada, the UK, Australia, Italy and France. The mangement decided to focus on exports and launching of new products for future growth.

Almost 50 p.c of Ipca's total sales has been from exports to 60 countries around the world, the major markets being U.K, the US, Israel, Italy and Russia. The focus on exports was aimed at achieving quick growth. Its revenue from exports in 1998-99 was about ₹ 160 crore with ₹ 65 crore coming from formulation exports. The company was also focused on increasing its contract manufacturing business, its clients including Smithkline, Beecham, Sinto farm, Hoechst, and Zeneca.

In 1998-99, new products contributed 10.14 per cent to domestic formulation sales compared to 5.78 per cent the previous year. It was estimated that turnover in 1998-99 would be ₹ 330 crore with a profit before tax of ₹ 20 crore. The profit was low as it was arrived at after taking into account a one-time ₹ 3.3 crore VRS settlement for 106 workers at the Kandivli plant which was shut down as it was operating at a very low efficiency level.

The company also initiated steps to operate its other plants at full capacity so as to achieve high levels of productivity. The reason why it continued to produce the anti-malarials of which contribution was negligible to the bottom line was that substantial investment had been made in the past on this range of products and it was not possible just to stop manufacturing them so long as they helped covering at least the fixed costs.

The company planned to increase its sales force by adding 200 medical representatives to its existing 600 by 1999-2000. It also intended to acquire exclusive marketing rights (EMRs) for products of different companies. It was not to engage in any more capital expansion for the time being, but planned to spend ₹ 5 to 10 crore on modernising its existing plants during 1999-2000 the funding of which would be from internal accruals.

Questions

1. Do you agree with IPCA's. strategy of growth through exports and new products?
2. Should the company set up manufacturing facilities abroad?

CHAPTER

STRATEGIC ISSUES IN E-BUSINESS OR DIGITALISATION

CHAPTER OUTLINE

Industrial Revolution led to **mechanisation** *i.e.* replacing physical labour with machines. Later on mental work was also shifted to machines which is called **automation**. Today, computers, mobile phones and Internet have become an essential part of our daily life as well as office life. Both business and non-business organisations have adopted mechanisation, automation and computerisation. Computers have become an integral part of information systems. **Computerisation** of data requires its electronisation. Transformation of physical data into electronic data is called **electronisation**. For example, in a physical watch the hands pointing to figures on the dial show the time. But an electronic watch shows the time in digits or numbers on the dial. But the electronic data has to be digitised. **Digitisation** refers to conversion of electronic signals into digital signals. For example, while recording music on a compact disk physical sound waves or electrical sound signals get converted into digital electronic signals.

Computerisation, electronisation, digitisation, telecommunications and networking have led to merging of all types of information into a common digital form. Such merging is called **convergence**. Organisations which use these five components are known as **digitised organisations** and the process of digital coding of information is called **digitatisation**. It offers considerable saving of time, space, efforts and money in the processing, storage and transmission of information. Digitalisation makes information available both within and outside an organisation quickly, widely, cheaply and efficiently. Availability of required information has significant implications for strategic management.

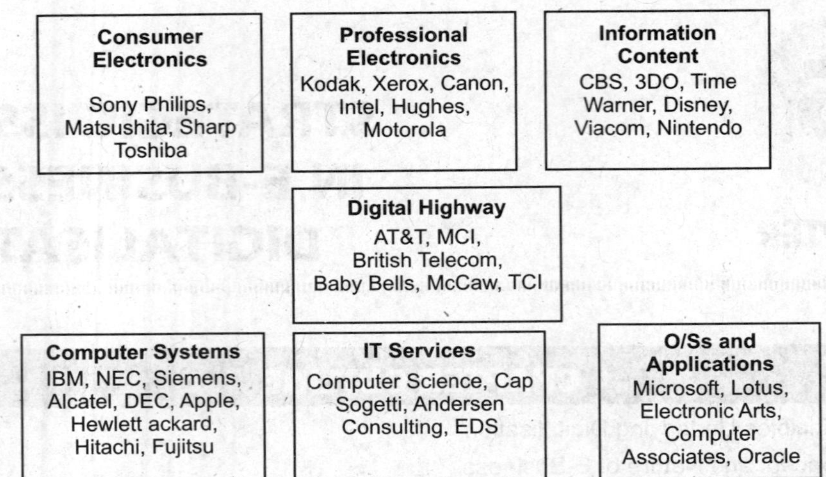

Fig. 15.1. Evolving Digital Space

Source: Gary Hamel and C.K. Prahalad, Competing for the Future Tata McGraw-Hill, New Delhi. 2002

15.1 PRINCIPLES UNDERLYING DIGITALISATION

In this information age, digitalisation can be used to create markets and to achieve market leadership. Downes and Mui[1] hence suggested the following principles for digitalisation strategies:

(*i*) Outsourcing to customers by letting them perform many of the service functions on their own.

(*ii*) Cannibalising their markets before their competitors do it.

(*iii*) Treating each customer as a market segment through mass customisation.

(*iv*) Creating communities of value by creating groups of like-minded people in cyber-space.

In the second stage, an organisation must link closely to customers in order to build new connection. This involves the next four principles:

(*v*) Replacing human interfaces with learning interfaces through customer-operated facilities.

(*vi*) Ensuring continuity for the customer by using e-commerce that helps customers perform their own service functions.

(*vii*) Giving away as much information as the organisation can be developing websites that are designed to be interfaces for the customer.

(*viii*) Structuring every transaction as a joint venture with the customer.

In the final stage, the organisation must redefine its interiors by the following steps:

(*ix*) Treating physical assets as liabilities to be replaced by virtual assets in the form of knowledge.

1. Larry Downes and Chunka, Mui **Unleashing the killer App: Digital Strategies for Market Dominance,** Harvard Business School, Boston, 1998.

(*x*) Deconstructing one's value chain.

(*xi*) Managing innovation as a portfolio of options so that risk is minimised.

(*xii*) Hiring children who instinctively understand digital technologies better as they are growing up with it.

15.2 CONCEPT AND NATURE OF E-BUSINESS

E-business or digitalisation refers to doing business over the Internet. According to IBM e-business is about using the Internet infrastructure and related technologies to enable business anywhere and anytime. An organisation that uses e-business is called net-enabled or web-enabled organisation. It is wider term than electronic commerce (e-commerce) which means buying and selling through the use of information technology. E-business involves not only buying and selling but also managing organisational processes needed for online transaction. According to the Organisation for Economic Cooperation and Development (OECD), "E-commerce refers to all the forms of transactions related to commercial activities, including both organisation and individuals, that are based upon the processing and transmission of digitised data, including text, sound and visual images."[2]

E-commerce has business-to-business (B2B) and Business to Consumer (B2C) model. In B2B model transactions take place between two or more business enterprises. In B2C model transactions occur between a business enterprise and consumers.

The process of e-commerce consists of the following steps: (Fig. 15.2)

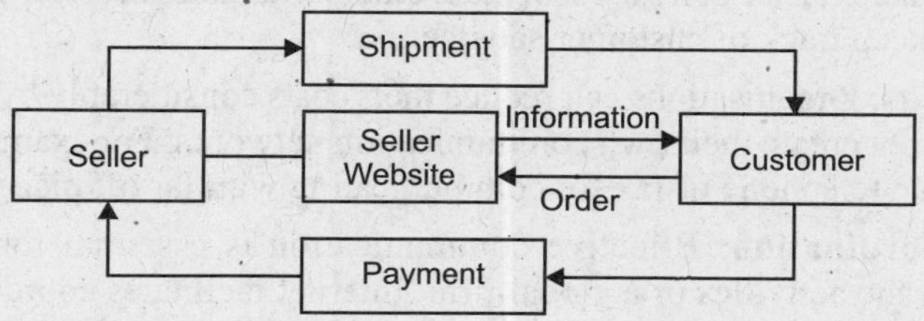

Fig. 15.2. E-Commerce Cycle

1. **Seller:** Seller is the firm which sells products and services. These products and services are those which can be provided online. These are standardised and with fixed prices. For example, Flipkart is a seller which sells books and other items online.
2. **Seller Website:** The seller develops a website on the Internet. The website provides information about products/services to customers and accepts orders from them.
3. **Customer:** Customer is an individual or organisation which wants to buy products/ services online. The customer places a purchase order and mentions mode of payment. On receipt of order, the seller's computer transmits the credit card details to his bank. The bank's computer takes authorisation from the card issuer. Once the payment is confirmed, the seller's computer confirms acceptance of the order to the customer's computer.
4. **Shipment:** The product/service may be sent to the customer electronically or through courier.

2. OECD, "Concept of Electronic Commerce," quoted in David Kosiur, **Understanding Electronic Commerce,** Microsoft Press, Washingtons, 1998.

5. **Payment:** Payment is usually made through the credit card. The amount may be debited directly to the customer's bank account provided the customer authorises such payment.

Table 15.1: Merits and Limitations of E-Commerce

Merits	Limitations
• Global market • Round-the-clock business • Convenience to both customer and seller • Low transaction costs • Minimum inventory • Shopping from home	• Technical problems • Lack of verification of product/service • Chances of fraud • Legal problem

15.3 IMPACT OF INTERNET ON BUSINESS

The main benefits of Internet for business organisations are as follows:

1. **Interactive Marketing:** Internet has enabled firms to adopt direct marketing. Online marketing allows customers to have interactive dialogues with sellers. E-commerce has reduced the costs of distribution and delivery time. Internet is an economical means of delivering customer service.
2. **Higher Customer Satisfaction:** Better customer satisfaction is a source of competitive advantage. Internet helps to improve customer satisfaction through better interaction with customers, faster delivery schedule, quick after-sales service, etc. Business firms, can better keep track of customer satisfaction.
3. **Lower Costs:** Organisations can reduce their costs considerably by using the Internet. They need not create their own communication networks. For example, e-mail is much cheaper than telephone or fax for communicating with far off places.
4. **Better Coordination:** Effective communication is essential for coordinating and controlling the activities of a global firm. Internet facilitates coordination and control of business operations in different countries. The headquarters can easily communicate with its subsidiaries and affiliates around the world.
5. **Efficient Management of people:** Internet is very helpful in recruitment and training of staff. Time and costs involved in human resource management activities can be considerably reduced.
6. **Faster Dissemination of Knowledge:** In today's knowledge economy, quick dissemination of knowledge throughout the organisation has become a critical success factor. Business enterprises now have instant access to information relating to business practices, technological breakthrough, government policies and procedures, etc. Availability of accurate and timely information helps to improve the quality of managerial decision-making.

STRATEGIC IMPLICATIONS OF INTERNET

- Alters market and competitive environment.
- Creates new strategic groups.
- Breeds new strategic groups.
- Reconfigures the value chain.
- Reduces entry barriers.
- Permits collaboration with best suppliers globally.

- Faster diffusion of new technology and ideas.
- Causes shifts in competitive forces.
- Affects company strengths and weaknesses.

An organisation can use the Internet for strategic advantage in the following ways:

(*i*) to enhance revenue
(*ii*) to generate synergies
(*iii*) to link with suppliers
(*iv*) to streamline distribution
(*v*) to reduce costs
(*vi*) to speed up delivery to customers

15.4 IMPACT OF E-BUSINESS ON VALUE CHAIN

E-busines or digitalisation can transform the value chain in the following ways:

1. **Deconstruction:** The process of breaking down the total product or service into components, delivering some of them digitally and thereby enhancing value to the customers is known as deconstruction. The physical product (*e.g.* a computer) may be delivered through traditional means. But other inputs in the value chain (*e.g.* instruction manual, warranty, customer support services, etc.) can be delivered digitally. Deconstruction makes it possible for a firm to outsource or enter into strategic alliance for increasing customer value.
2. **Disintermediation:** Disintermediation means elimination of some processes in the value chain. For example, a traveller can reserve a seat online instead of visiting a travel agent or the airline's office. In this way, buying tickets or making reservations from the travel agent or airline is eliminated. E-business allows online reservation and payment.
3. **Re-Intermediation:** Supplementing some processes in the value chain with one or more intermediaries is known as re-intermediation. These intermediaries provide information and are, therefore, known as infomediaries. For example, an online book-seller (*e.g.* Flipkart) provides considerable information to prospective buyers. They can view books online, buy them and pay for them online.
4. **Industry Morphing:** E-business has transformed traditional industries by redefining their boundaries. For example, online banking enables clients to do several banking transactions without visiting the bank. This process is called industry morphing. Online retailing, insurance, healthcare, etc. are influencing the strategies of firms operating in these industries.
5. **Cannibalisation:** The cannibalisation of value chain refers to replacing an old set of activities with a new set of activities. For example, the Internet is replacing digitally the functions of travel agents for making reservations.
6. **Techno-Intensification:** More intensive use of technology and reduced use of human resources is called technology intensification. This process has several implications such as higher capital investment in information technology, more reliance on third parties for outsourcing and alliances, and providing access to customers 24 hours a day, 7 days a week and 365 days a year (24 × 7 × 365).

7. **Re-channelling:** Under re-channelling a manufacturer specialistses in some activities in the value chain and the remaining components of the value chain are performed by others. For example, a firm may focus on manufacturing and outsource marketing to specialised agencies.

15.5 STRATEGIC GUIDELINES FOR THE INTERNET ECONOMY

1. **Develop an E-Business Strategy:** In order to compete successfully in the digital economy, an organisation must develop an e-business or digitalisation strategy. The strategy must describe how the organisation will leverage the Internet capabilities to create and sustain competitive advantage. Operational, functional, behavioural and other relevant aspects must be duly considered for this purpose.
2. **Build Talent:** Competent people must be hired and trained to handle the Internet infrastructure.
3. **Invest in Information Technology:** Adequate capital investment is necessary to develop the needed hardware and software.
4. **Knowledge Management:** Effective management of knowledge is essential in the digital economy.
5. **Focus on Innovation:** Both product and process innovation are required. Innovation does not always mean a new product. It may be a new way of performing a task or to interface with customers.

SUMMARY

Principles of Digitalisation: Outsourcsing, cannibalising, mass customisation, communities of value, interaction continuity.

E-Business: Seller, Website, Customer, Shipment, payment.

Impact of Internet: (*i*) interactive marketing (*ii*) customer satisfaction (*iii*) cost reduction (*iv*) coordination (*v*) efficient management (*vi*) faster dissemination of knowledge.

Impact on Value Chain: (*i*) deconstruction (*ii*) disintermediation (*iii*) re-intermediation (*iv*) industry morphing (*v*) cannibalisation (*vi*) techno-intensification (*vii*) Re-channelling.

Strategic Guidelines for Internet Economy: (*i*) Develop e-business strategy (*ii*) build talent (*iii*) invest in IT (*iv*) knowledge management (*v*) focus on innovation.

TEST QUESTIONS

1. What is e-business? Is it the same as e-commerce? Explain the cycle of e-commerce.
2. State the principles underlying digitalisation.
3. Explain the impact of Internet on business.
4. Describe how e-business influences the value chain.
5. Suggest strategic guidelines for the Internet economy or digital age.

CASE STUDY

Orient Cables has been in the business of making and marketing electrical cables for ten years. It makes paper-insulated cables, polyvinyl chloride cables, and cross-linked polyethylene (XLPE) cables. The company produces low-, medium- as well as high-voltage cables and is the only company in India producing 400-KV cables.

Orient has a technical collaboration with a Japanese company (Figuchi) which had given Orient access to their quality manuals. Kaizens and quality circles are in place and the company has obtained an ISO-9000 certification. With a 17 p.c. market, Orient ranked second in the cable industry.

In a meeting with the CEO, Abhay Shukla, the Vice-President Operations, Rahul Verma, has been offered an additional responsibility coordinating Orient's Total Quality Management (TQM) programme. Verma was hesitant in accepting the responsibility and was given a week's time to make up his mind.

Verma's hesitance was due to certain reasons. So far, the TQM project had been coordinated by Bharat Saxena, Vice-Presisdent, Human Resource Management (HRM), who has recently left Orient. It was Saxena who had introduced TQM a year-and-half ago, and as a member of the apex committee which was piloting the project, Verma was fully aware of its chequered progress. A change of guard at this juncture could make or break his career. He called on Varun Mitra, a TQM consultant, who had earlier taught him HRM in the college. Verma expressed his dilemma to Mitra when they met: "It is an opportunity that I would have jumped at. There are several positive elements. The company is young; the people are enthusiastic; and the rank and file are receptive to change. The CEO has assured me of his personal support. But I have an uneasy feeling about the whole thing. It could be something to do with the false starts we have had in implementing TQM."

Mitra became alert on hearing about false starts. They mean trouble. They may turn the clock backwards. He wanted to know about the company and why it thought of TQM. Having heard about the company's performance, Mitra remarked, "That is quite impressive. You have the right ambience for TQM. Now tell me, who are your customers?" Verma explained that Orient was largely dependent on State Electricity Boards (SEBs) for the offtake of its products. The main problem with the SEBs has been the collection dues which took anywhere between 6 months and year. There was little control on prices which were negotiated annually. The company was compelled to absorb hikes in input prices since there was an escalation clause in the agreement. The biggest constraint was the fluctuation in the prices of raw materials like copper and aluminium 70 p.c. of which were imported. Hence, the only way to get a grip on the costs-revenues-margins chain was to tighten up production processes and secure efficiencies in internal operations. That was why TQM was thought of.

According to Mitra, that was the classic trap that most companies fell into; there was no link with the customer. But the *raison d'etre* of TQM movement was customer satisfaction. Without that linkage, TQM becomes merely process-oriented.

At this stage, Verma informed Mitra that the decision to go for TQM was also influenced by the emergence of a new market, that of industrial cables, during the last 3 years. Orient was selling nearly 30 per cent of its output to the industrial sector through a dealer network. The share of industrial power cables in the turnover was likely to go up to 50 per cent in the next two years. The specialised requirements of industrial uses had ensured higher margins. Besides the dealers, the company was also talking directly to the customers to ascertain their needs, and had developed customised products for several customers. So, the TQM movement did also have its origin in the needs of a growing customer segment.

How did the company go about implementing the TQM process. As Verma put it, "We began by asking ourselves several questions. What does the customer want? The answer was self-evident: high-quality output at competitive prices. What drives prices? Raw material costs, interest, and employee costs. What was the most critical issue that needed management attention? Reducing the lead time of the production cycle by bringing down the down-time for imports of copper and aluminium. All that was part of an attempt to identify processes that would give us a tight control over costs. Simultaneously, we started looking at the key result areas: commodity trading skills that would enable us make timely purchases of copper and aluminium, and inventory and receivables management."

How was the TQM coordinated? There was an apex committee headed by Saxena, former Vice-President, HRD. He had some experience of TQM in his earlier job. He was also a qualified trainer. So it was not necessary to enlist any external consultants except for some of the training programmes.

Mitra thought it was a basic mistake. The apex committee should have been headed by the CEO, with the Vice-President, HRD, acting as Convener.

Any way, the committee would meet once a month with a structured agenda. The idea was to examine the feedback on some of the internal training programmes on building, of continuous improvement programmes, and experimental workshops. The cost of poor quality was also being computed, and one of the tasks of the apex committee was to keep track of such costs regularly. There was a cascading organisation structure for TQM, wherein the Vice-President, HRD, was the head of the apex committee, and each member of the apex committee was the head of a sub-committee pertaining to his department. Thus, for example, Verma, Vice-President (Operations) headed the sub-committee for TQM.

Why was Verma in two minds about accepting the offer? As he explained to Mitra: "The CEO's intentions are right, but I don't think he is clear about. The change he wants. TQM needs sustained backing of the CEO. The change initiated must be the personal responsibility of the CEO; the role of the coordinator is merely to facilities change. The CEO has not spelt out the factors that drive him personally towards TQM. If he withdraws the mandate at a late stage, overtly or covertly, the change process would collapse. That is my biggest concern."

Further, as Verma explained, "There were some false starts." He cited two examples. After some initial hesitation, which was quite natural, people at Orient were enthused with the team concept. Everybody plunged into the new style of working, and a number of small improvement projects took off. Once the team members got to the root of the problem that they were asked to solve, they become confident. They believed that any problem at any level of the organisation, however formidable, could, indeed, be tackled. Surprisingly, Orient's line managers started feeling uncomfortable when teams were uncovering major problems, and people went around seeking information from sources they had no access to earlier, the line managers felt that the situation was getting out of control. Long used to screening information before it went outside their departments, they found the new openness quite daunting. As a result, departmental heads started pulling out their subordinates from various cross-functional teams on seemingle valid grounds. This led to a backlash. Employees felt bitter at having their hopes raised only to be let down. Perhaps the mistake lay in not securing the buy-in of line managers right at the beginning of the programme.

Another example was with regard to capacity utilisation. As attempts were made to develop customised products, Orient's capacity utilisation level started falling. It fell from 60 to 45 p.c. within the first five months. While catering to customised demand, an increase in cross-sectional area and voltage requirements of finished cables became the new value drivers, not output as measured by cable length. The overall output measured by tonnage of metal drawn would increase but the output in terms of kilometres of cables–the conventional measure of capacity utilisation–would decrease. It took time for people to realise that capacity utilisation is not a true indicator of productivity of fixed assets in customised manufacture. But the decline in plant capacity was attributed to TQM.

The third reason behind Verma's apprehension was that he considered TQM to be essentially a staff role, not a line function, and he was a line manager. "In my 20-year-long career," he said, "I have been used to issuing instructions and commanding action by allocating responsibility and ensuring accountability from people on the shop floor. I am used to chasing results on a day-to-day basis. It is a mindset unsuited to a staff function like TQM, where the role of a coordinator is not to hand out instructions, but to facilitate change through a slow and steady process of individual transformation. I have seen it happen in many companies; any attempt by a staff functionary to chase result is doomed to fail."

According to Mitra, Verma was over-reacting. "Let me address each of your concerns," he told Verma. "The best way to ensure the continuing support of CEO is to make him the sponsor of the apex committee. The false starts are, of course, alarming. The line managers, in particular, should be put through development sessions," Mitra added Further, he said, "there is no reason why you can't hold on to two contradictory roles simultaneously. It depends on the kind of person you are. Three issues are relevant here: Are you likely to be biased towards your traditional function? You should avoid giving too much attention to operations in implementing TQM. Secondly, can you build trust among your people easily and establish your credibility with them without the backing of the authority? And, thirdly, if the change process derails for some reason, do you still have a job at Orient? My own feeling is that you have good opportunity to add value to the company."

Upon enquiry from Verma, what other specific issues he should look for, Mitra replied, "I think what Orient needs is a change driver. Something that provides a compelling need for change in the company. It could be a vision that was just out of reach unless a radically new thinking was applied. It could be some signs of decline within the company. It could be the fact that a competition was closing in. If people do not see a fundamental reason for change, the leader's commitment, however genuine, may be discounted by them as one person's eccentricity."

Along with these observations, Mitra advised Verma to take a decision keeping in view the fact that TQM is not an employee-motivation programme, nor is it a panacea or a guarantee of success. Mitra said, "In its very nature, quality transformation is a team effort, and not everyone starts off with the same enthusiasm. Unless someone takes responsibility for masterminding the whole affair, either nothing gets done or there is complete chaos. This is where the skill and dedication of the change agent is a key success factor. You cannot succeed as a TQM coordinator if you are inclined to hogging the limelight."

The choice of Verma was tough. He was not going to start on a clean slate. He would have to galvanise an entire organisation which had lost faith in the abilities of TQM to bolster its performance. It would mean changing his own approach to achieving results by being facilitator rather than an instructor.

Questions

1. How can Qrient get back on the TQM track?
2. How can Verma ensure that the quality movement will not be derailed in the company?
3. What are the initial hurdles that a company should guard against?
4. Should TQM be a staff function?

16 CHAPTER

STRATEGIC MANAGEMENT OF TECHNOLOGY AND INNOVATION

CHAPTER OUTLINE

Technology is needed to convert inputs into outputs. An organisation can develop competitive advantage through strategic management of technology because technology has far reaching effects on cost, productivity and quality. Similarly, innovation helps an organisation to satisfy needs of its customers in new and better ways. Management of technology and innovation has become critical for success in business due to global competition, increasing aspirations of customers and shortening product life cycles.

16.1 MANAGEMENT OF TECHNOLOGY

The key strategic issues involved in the management of technology are as follows:

1. **Source of New Technology:** There are two broad sources of technology – internal and external. Internally, an organisation can develop new technology through research and development (R & D). How much investment an organisation should make in R & D depends on nature of its business and its approach towards R & D. In industries characterised by fast technological changes and high product innovation (*e.g.* pharmaceuticals, information technology, fast moving consumer goods, etc.), high R & D outlay is needed. Organisations which seek to be trend setters and market leaders also spend more on R & D.

   An organisation must formulate **R & D policy** which provides guidelines for undertaking R & D activities. An organisation that gives high priority to R & D will place its R & D division at high level in the organisation structure.

   Product-market combination also influences R & D investment. Evolution stage requires more R & D effort than the maturity or declining stage.

Outside sources of technology consist of (*a*) **licensing** from domestic and foreign research agencies such as Council of Scientific and Industrial Research, (*b*) copying simple technologies of **competitors**, and (*c*) **consultants** who provide technology blue-prints.

2. **Choice of Technology:** While acquiring technology from various sources, an organisation must evaluate such technology on the following criteria:

   (*a*) relevance of the technology for the company's existing and proposed businesses;

   (*b*) cost of the proposed technology;

   (*c*) impact of the technology on costs of production and distribution; and

   (*d*) effect of the technology on quality and performance of the product/service.

   Business strategy determines the choice of technology. A company which competes on the basis of cost leadership will select technologies that enable mass production of standardised products at low cost. On the other hand, a company having differentiation strategy will look for batch production based technology.

3. **Transfer and Diffusion of Technology:** When a new technology is acquired from an outside source, it requires adaptation. Developing a new technology inhouse is called technological development. Different components of new technology need to be synthesised.

4. **Application of Technology:** A new technology results in a new or improved product and/or process which adds value to the organisation and its customers. For example, use of information technology helps to reduce the time and cost involved in order processing, delivery and payment. Online marketing has proved beneficial to both the sellers and the buyers.

5. **Timing of Introduction:** When to adopt a new technology to develop a new/improved product/process is an important decision. There is a time gap in adoption of new technologies both within a company and among firms in an industry. Technological innovations take time to yield results. The firm which is the first to adopt new technology gains a competitive advantage. But such an advantage gradually disappears when competitors also adopt the new technology.

Technology strategy deals not only with the decision to be a leader or a follower in terms of technology and market entry but also with the source of the technology. Should a company develop its own technology or purchase it from others? The strategy also takes into account a company's particular mix of basic versus applied and product versus process R & D. The particular mix should suit the level of industry development and the firm's particular corporate and business strategies. In addition, R & D strategy in a large corporation deals with the proper balance of its product portfolio based on the life cycle of the product.

Each and every organisation is not able to take the full advantage of advances in technology due to barriers in management of technology. Lack of long range planning, lack of top management support, inadequate investment in R & D, lack of risk taking, shortage of well qualified technical staff are some of these barriers.

16.2 TECHNOLOGICAL FORECASTING

An organisation needs to continually scan the environment for new developments in technology that may be relevant to its present and prospective businesses, customers, suppliers, distributors, and research agencies. It must also predict new technologies that are likely to. emerge in future and the time when these are likely to be economically feasible. Advances in technology create both opportunities and threats for organisations. Therefore, every business organisation must predict likely developments in technology so that it can take proactive action to remain competitive.

Technological forecasting is necessary due to the following reasons:

(*i*) Technological forecasting enables an organisation to understand future scenario in the field of technology. With the help of such understanding, the organisation can evaluate threats and opportunities likely to occur in future. It can then take appropriate actions to exploit the opportunities and to avoid the threats.

(*ii*) Technological changes cause changes in the nature of business and competition in the market. Technological forecasting helps an organisation to redefine its business properly to compete in a better manner.

(*iii*) Technological forecasting enables an organisation to avoid costly mistakes and wastages in the areas of R & D, modernisation and upgradation of production facilities, etc.

16.3 MANAGEMENT OF INNOVATION

Innovation means the process of introducing new ways of doing things. It is different from invention. An invention is a new concept, device or idea. On the other hand, innovation is the application of the concept or idea to develop a new product, service or process. Innovation may be in several forms *e.g.* a new marketing method, new method of production, new organisation system or process, etc.

Innovation is of the following types:

(*i*) Incremental Innovation: Such innovation involves continuous and minor improvements in products/services, processes, etc.

(*ii*) Radical Innovation: A major breakthrough which changes a whole industry is called radical innovation. For example, introduction of microchips changed the computer industry. Small-sized chip-based computers have much more memory and data processing capability than large-sized card-based computers.

(*iii*) Systems Innovation: Use of radical innovation in a new way to create new functions is known as systems innovation. For example, combination of automobile engine with bicycles led to the creation of various types of two-wheelers.

Innovation helps to reduce costs, improve quality, widen product range, reduce consumption of energy and minimise pollution. Therefore, innovation is a major driver of growth in business.

Management of innovation involves generation and diffusion of innovations:

1. **Generation of Innovations:** There are four main stages in the process of generating innovations:

   (*i*) *Identifying Need for Innovation:* All innovations are made to satisfy human needs in a better way. Therefore, needs of customers create the need for innovation. Any unsatisfied or poorly satisfied need requires an innovation.

(*ii*) *Generating Ideas:* Creativity helps to generate ideas. Brainstorming, delphi-technique, market research, intuition, etc. are the techniques used to create new ideas. At this stage an attempt is made to generate as many ideas as possible.

(*iii*) *Evaluating Ideas:* All the generated ideas are evaluated against predecided criteria. The criteria may be objective (*e.g.* feasibility of the idea) as well as subjective (personal preferences).

(*iv*) *Choice of Idea:* The idea which best meets the set criteria is selected for implementation.

2. **Diffusion of Innovation:** The process of applying the innovation is called diffusion of innovation. This process consists of the following steps:
   (*a*) awareness about innovation occurring outside the organisation.
   (*b*) assessing the relevance of the innovation to the organisation
   (*c*) trying the innovation to judge its feasibility.
   (*d*) adoption of the feasible innovation.

Effective management of innovations requires knowledge management and learning organisation.

16.4 KNOWLEDGE MANAGEMENT

In this knowledge economy, knowledge has become the key source of creating wealth. Knowledge means information, enlightenment, skill and experience. Knowledge management may be defined as the process of creating, sharing and utilising knowledge.

1. **Creating Knowledge:** There are several methods of creating knowledge such as experimentation, R & D, creative thinking, customer feedback, benchmarking, etc. An organisation can acquire knowledge. from outside and generate it inside through individuals and groups. Explicit knowledge that is embedded in policies, procedures, reports, etc. can be harnessed through information technology and other mechanisms. But it is difficult to harness **tacit or implicit** knowledge that resides in the minds of people.

2. **Sharing Knowledge:** It is necessary to communicate and disseminate knowledge throughout the organisation. Knowledge stored in the database of the organisation can be delivered to the individuals and groups which need it. Information technology, process engineering and organisational dynamics are the main methods of knowledge sharing. Information technology (Intranet and Internet) enables an organisation to capture; store and transfer knowledge to its units all over the world. Process engineering involves knowledge sharing through employee rotation, education and training, site visits, etc. Organisational dynamics involves formal and informal interactions among employees for sharing knowledge.

3. **Utilising Knowledge:** Utilisation of knowledge to solve problems and create value is the most important phase of knowledge management. Unlike other resources that deplete with use, knowledge grows with sharing and utilisation. Knowledge is self regenerative and feeds on itself.

16.4.1 Requirements for Effective Management of Knowledge

1. **Knowledge Culture:** First of all, a culture that allows and encourages creative thinking must be created and nurtured in the organisation. Often employees are reluctant to share knowledge for fear of losing power and control. Therefore, suitable incentives and rewards are needed to motivate employees to share knowledge. Promotions and other employee benefits should be linked to contributions towards creation, sharing and utilisation of knowledge for the benefit of the organisation. Everybody in the organisation must understand the value of creating and sharing knowledge, how it will benefit them and the organisation and how to share knowledge. Commitment to knowledge management must be developed at all levels of the organisation. Psychological support should be provided to employees for knowledge sharing.
2. **Knowledge Strategy:** Every organisation must develop an appropriate strategy for knowledge management. Such a strategy should lay down guidelines concerning why to share knowledge, what knowledge to share, with whom to share knowledge, and how to share knowledge. Knowledge should be shared to enhance success of the organisation. Technical know-how, managerial know-how, competitive intelligence, operational processes are the main aspects of knowledge to be shared. Knowledge should be shared with all those who need and can use it for the organisation. Knowledge can be shared by means of face-to-face contacts, meetings, computer networks, etc.
3. **Knowledge Team:** It is necessary to create a key team for continuous generation and sharing of knowledge under the leadership of chief knowledge manager. A knowledge centre is needed to capture personal expertise into organisational knowledge and allow people access to such knowledge. The centre would serve as a repository of business solutions. This centre can organise workshops, etc. to teach knowledge sharing.
4. **Technology for Knowledge Sharing:** Technology is a key enabler for knowledge management. Information technology used for knowledge sharing consists of computer hardware, computer software, database and telecommunication. Information and communication technology (ICT) can be used in all stages of knowledge management. The selected technology must the fit with organisation's needs. Adequate investment in physical facilities, ICT and personnel must be made.

HOW TO MAKE KNOWLEDGE MANAGEMENT SUCCESSFUL

(*i*) Define the organisation's mission, purpose and industry position in terms of knowledge.
(*ii*) Develop a culture conducive to learning and knowledge sharing.
(*iii*) Create commitment to creating and sharing knowledge.
(*iv*) Provide incentives for sharing knowledge.
(*v*) Integrate knowledge management with the systems, processes and practices of the organisation.
(*vi*) Formulate a suitable strategy for knowledge management
(*vii*) Create necessary infrastructure and technology for knowledge management.

16.5 LEARNING ORGANISATION

A learning organisation is an organisation that can create, acquire and transfer knowledge and also modify the behaviour of its members to reflect new knowledge and insights. It has knowledge as its edifice and builds its core capabilities through advancing knowledge. The unique characteristics of a learning organisation are as follows:

(*i*) Members of a learning organisation share a common vision of the future.

(*ii*) The learning organisation believes that continuous learning is the source of competitive advantage.

(*iii*) It nurtures creative thinking and innovative ideas at all levels.

(*iv*) It encourages its members to experiment and learn continually.

(*v*) It develops new capabilities and renews itself from time to time.

(*vi*) Its outlook is futuristic.

(*vii*) It empowers its people.

(*viii*) Its focus is on teamwork and assimilation of varied viewpoints.

(*ix*) There is high level of trust and mutual understanding among people at all levels.

(*x*) Members are free to share their personal feelings and ideas with one another.

Table 16.1: Comparison between Traditional and Learning Organisations

Basis of Comparison	Traditional Organisation	Learning Organisation
(*a*) Determination of overall direction	Vision is provided by top management.	There is a shared vision that can emerge from many places, but top management is responsible for ensuring that this vision exists and is nurtured.
(*b*) Formulation and implementation of ideas	Top management decides what is to be done, and the rest of the organisation acts on these ideas.	Formulation and implementation of ideas are placed at all levels of the organisation.
(*c*) Nature of organisational thinking	Each person is responsible for his or her own job responsibilities, and the focus is on developing individual competence.	Personnel understand their own jobs, as well as the way in which their own work interrelates and influences that of other personnel.
(*d*) Conflict resolution	Conflicts are resolved through the use of power and hierarchical influence.	Conflicts are resolved through the use of collaborative learning and the integration of diverse viewpoints of personnel through the organisations.
(*e*) Leadership and motivation	The role of the leader is to establish the organisation's vision, provide rewards and punishments as appropriate, and maintain overall control of employee activities.	The role of the leader is to build a shared vision, empower the personnel, inspire commitment, and encourage effective decision-making throughout the enterprise through the use of empowerment and charismatic leadership.
Source: Peter Senge: **The Fifth Discipline: The Art and Practice of the Learning Organisation,** Doubleday, New York, 1990.		

A learning organisation enjoys the following advantages:

(*i*) It achieves a sustainable competitive advantage that helps it to survive and grow in a highly competitive world.

(*ii*) It can successfully face the challenges of a turbulent environment.

(*iii*) It does not face obsolescence of management practices.

(*iv*) It can maintain good relations with all the stakeholder groups.

NEED FOR LEARNING ORGANISATION

1. To survive in the knowledge-based economy of 21st century.
2. To cope with rapid changes in technology.
3. To manage global competition in future.
4. To handle tomorrow's demanding and fragmented markets.
5. To build people-based systems.
6. To lead to Holistic values.

16.5.1 Developing a Learning Organisation

1. **Top Management Commitment:** In order to develop a learning organisaton major changes are needed in the existing beliefs, values, goals, structures, systems and processes. Such changes cannot be made without full support from top management. Commitment of top management ensures the availability of resources required for implementing the change and participation of everyone in the change process.
2. **Shared Vision:** All members of the organisation must share the vision of learning organisation. The vision needs to be communicated to all so that everyone accepts the need for utility of learning. People at all levels understand the types of changes to be made and their role in creating the learning organisation. Such acceptability and common understanding helps to overcome resistance to change.
3. **Learning Culture:** Top management must create and sustain a culture wherein experimentation, risk taking, creative thinking are encouraged. Suitable incentives and rewards may be offered for self-learning and assisting others in learning.
4. **Introducing New Structures, Processes, Etc:** Existing structures, processes, values, beliefs, etc are transformed to meet the needs of the learning organisation. This is the most crucial and difficult step in creating a learning organisation.
5. **Reinforcement:** The new systems, processes, etc. must be reinforced so that these become a permanent part of the organisation. Steps are taken to ensure that employees do not revert back to the old ways.

SUMMARY

Management of Technology: (*i*) source of new technology (*ii*) choice of technology (*iii*) transfer and diffusion of technology (*iv*) application of technology (*v*) timing of introduction.

Technological Forecasting: (*i*) to understand likely developments in technology (*ii*) redefine business (*iii*) avoid costly mistakes.

Management of Innovation: incremental, radical and systems innovations.

Generation of Innovation: (*i*) identify need (*ii*) generate new ideas (*iii*) evaluate ideas (*iv*) choice of idea.

Diffusion of Innovation: awareness, relevance, feasibility.

Knowledge Management (KM): creating, sharing and utilising knowledge.

Requirements For KM: (*i*) knowledge culture (*ii*) knowledge strategy (*iii*) knowledge team (*iv*) technology for knowledge sharing.

Learning Organisation: (*i*) sustainable advantage (*ii*) facing challenges of environment (*iii*) avoid obsolescence of knowledge (*iv*) stakeholders value.

Developing Learning Organisation: (*i*) top management commitment (*ii*) shared vision (*iii*) learning culture (*iv*) new structures and processes (*v*) reinforcement.

TEST QUESTIONS

1. Explain the strategic issues in the management of technology.
2. What is technological forecasting? Why is it needed?
3. What is meant by innovation? Describe the three types of innovation.
4. "Management of innovation involves generation and diffusion processes." Explain.
5. What is knowledge management? Explain the steps involved in it.
6. Discuss the requirements for effective management of knowledge.
7. What is a learning organisation? How does it differ from a traditional organisation?
8. Why is learning organisation needed? How can such an oragnisation be developed?
9. "Customer driven quality, innovation and the learning mechanism are particularly important in the development of corporate strategy." Discuss.

CASE STUDY

Early in the financial year 1996-97, Auto-Samurai (India) Ltd., (ASL) confronted one issue more than any other, *viz*., how to survive and maintain the company's growth in a market of growing competition and changes all around.

ASL's performance for the year ending 31 March 1996 recorded a turnover of ₹ 850 crore gross profits of ₹ 85 crore, and net profits of ₹ 64 crore—the highest ever achieved by the company. Its production performance during the previous year was also impressive. Production of its two-wheelers increased by 18 p.c. in the case of scooters, 24 p.c. in the case of motorbikes, and 31 p.c. in the case of mopeds. The company continued to lead in the mopeds segment with 41 p.c. market share while its ranking in the motorbikes business stayed No. 4, with a 16 p.c. market share. However, in the scooters market, the company came in only fifth, with an 8 p.c. market share. It was way behind the market-leader Supreme Auto, with an edge both in respect of price-points and volume.

When the company started its business fifteen years ago, it had no marketing department.

It sold everything that was produced. Presently, inventories proved to be the biggest drain on working capital. According to the CEO, ASL can survive the competitive times if it can become an innovation-led corporation, and react to the changing market by changing methods, achieving breakthrough goals, and taking greater risks.

The company had adopted the Japanese quality practice—*Kaizen*—which helped it to bring about incremental improvements in routine tasks in the workplace, and there had been regular gains in areas like safety, process quality, waste control, cost reduction, energy conservation, and even productivity. But *Kaizen* was a gradual process—subtle, undramatic, one step at a time. It involved low investment high, involvement and high effort. The company had also brought about technological improvements. For instance, it had introduced 60 c.c. Scobike—a cross between a scooter and a motorbike—which was developed entirely in-house, and had become ASL's showpiece in the marketplace. In addition, the company had put in place several good organisation development tools as a part of its TQM (Total Quality Management) drive, such as Sensitivity Training Experiential Workshops, and Survey Feedback. During the previous two years, it had also conducted Employee Satisfaction Surveys aimed at improving morale and conflict resolution.

It was admitted that *Kaizen* was a good enough change-force. At the same time, it was agreed that innovative changes were needed in many critical areas, and innovation should be declared by the company as one of its strategic intents in view of the ongoing liberalisation process, flow of foreign investment and joint ventures coming up in the automotive sector.

The question remained of identifying the most appropriate change-agents. Top management, it was argued, were by and large trapped in the successes of the company in the past. Innovative ideas were expected to be generated by middle-level managers. The fact that middle-level managers could rise to the occasion when required was evidenced during the recession in 1991-92. The company set a cost reduction target at five per cent of the previous year's turnover, *i.e.*, ₹ 25 crore over two years. Within six months, the target was found unachievable. So, the management was asked to "Eliminate what Annoys the Customer, Both Internal and External". It worked and the company achieved savings in excess of ₹ 100 crore.

Even with this example in the background, it was recognised that recession in 1991-92 was one thing, and the challenge of 1996-97 was something different. Now, the company needed to change and keep on changing. The CEO felt that instead of management-led initiative one should think of creating an appetite for innovation. One suggestion was that financial outlays could serve the purpose. Suppose, each profit centre contributed 1 p.c. of its annual earnings into a central corpus to be called (say) New Concept Fund, and it was agreed that it would be entitled to use the amount for innovative projects, the fund could support development of ideas that could not be anticipated in routine budgetary projections. Allocation could be enhanced from the annual budget if the project showed commercial promise.

Another suggestion was that the company may adopt an annual corporate theme, like productivity, product quality, after-sales service, etc., and have a benchmark of best-in-class. All efforts could then be targeted to tackle that problem area, so that in a year or two a new benchmark would have been internalised by the employees: to ensure motivation, that parameter could be included in the employee's annual appraisal and rewards assured.

With the TQM in place, the company had the practice of inviting dealers, customers and suppliers in small groups every month to discuss their development plans. In that context, a third suggestion was that every employee should be encouraged to spend two weeks in a year in the field talking to customers suppliers, dealers, and competitors. Innovations which have a bearing on market needs could flow from there as well.

The CEO meanwhile had informal discussion with management experts and executives from other industries. Their observations were as follows:

1. To transform itself from a good enterprise to an aggressive competitor, ASL must create an organisation that not only values better performance, but also sustains commitment. That means a major shift in values, and not just an incremental step-up in the number of new ideas generated. To sharpen ASL's receptivity to change, the basic prerequisite is that its top managers must be personally involved in the process. Their task must be to nurture a climate conducive to people who are willing to anchor new ideas, and eager for an opportunity to turn germane ideas into new divisions new businesses, and even new industries. So top management should—(*a*) Encourage individuals and groups to be forthcoming with new ideas, be creative, and exercise initiative. (*b*) Individuals with creative ideas must not be looked down upon as troublesome. (*c*) Equally necessary is an atmosphere that tolerates mistakes and failures; most ideas don't pan out, but the organisation learns a great deal for the future from a good attempt that fails. (*d*) Strategy managers should be willing to use all kinds of *ad hoc* organisational forms to support ideas and experimentation—venture teams, task forces, performance shoot outs—in different groups working on competing approaches. (*e*) Strategy managers must see that the rewards for successful champions are large and visible, and that people who champion an unsuccessful idea are encouraged to try again.
2. To conduct an organisational stock-taking in a rapidly changing environment is timely, but the urge to declare innovation as strategic intent for ASL appears to be premature. The top management should first evolve a formal and widely-held strategic business intent for the company. This is fundamental. The process of defining what ASL stands for will be, in itself, the effective launch of innovation, which is essentially a mindgame creativity. Over the next six months, the agends for action by ASL should be to: (*a*) Draw up a vision and strategy statement highlighting where ASL wants to position itself in the transportation industry 15 years from now. (*b*) Secure its acceptance by employees through intensive communication. (*c*) Evolve a five-year plan, breaking it down by milestones of growth and financial performance that can be monitored every quarter. (*d*) If everyone at ASL cannot play innovator, examine the option of identifying areas of activity where innovation is most required and can generate critical mass. (*e*) Create an Idea Bank as a strategic asset led personally by the CEO and coordinated by an insider. (*f*) Use every alternate meeting of top executives to discuss new ideas, evaluate the results of experiments, share learning and celebrate Idea Champions. (*g*) Review the onging quality initiatives, both to reinforce them and to look critically at the Ideas Checklist still awaiting approval. (*h*) Monitor the feedback from organisational climate surveys to formulate a policy framework to make innovation and learning a matter of habit at ASI. (*i*) Customerise the corporation by making every function attuned to the needs of the customer, internal and external. (*j*) Encourage extensive employee interaction with customer groups to gain insight into areas of customer dissatisfaction.
3. ASL does have serious problems but they are not insurmountable. The most critical long-

term issue facing ASL is that it can no longer make what it likes, when it likes, and sell it to whoever it likes. Therefore, there is an urgent need to undertake market research with a view to ascertaining where in the two-wheeler market, should ASL position its products even while phasing out those rendered redundant by the customer-driven environment. The suggestion that all employees should spend time in the field meeting customers and other stakeholders is an excellent one. It is important for ASL's management to feel confident about the strength of its internal processes, which should be disciplined enough to provide warning signals in advance and flexible enough to respond adequately to changing market demands. The problems of rising inventories requires that rolling sales forecasts, monthly at least, should be demanded from marketing and passed on to Operations for compilation into production plans. Then operations requirements can also be identified, and vendor schedules provided to suppliers to enable them to plan their own requirements to ensure timely supplies to ASL. Finance can plan the funds and close the loop. This would not, of course, solve ASL's larger problems of product portfolio, pricing and customer needs, but will place the company in a better position to address them.

Questions

1. Does ASL need to become an innovative organisation?
2. Should ASL become more customer focussed?
3. What should be the strategic intent of ASL?
4. Can innovation, by itself, be a strategy of ASL?

17

CHAPTER

STRATEGIC ISSUES IN ORGANISATIONAL CHANGE

CHAPTER OUTLINE

Change is the only permanent thing in this world. Organisations which fail to change and adapt themselves to the changing environment decline or disappear. When changes occur in economic, social, political, legal and technological environment, an organisation requires changes in its structure, processes, systems, goals, etc. in order to survive and grow. Changes also take place in an organisation when its top managers change. Changes are also made to remove weaknesses such as too many levels of authority, poor communication system, lack of cooperation and coordination, etc. Thus, forces both outside and inside the organisation create the need for organisational change.

17.1 CONCEPT OF ORGANISATIONAL CHANGE

Organisational change means alteration in any component of an organisation such as structure, technology, job design, people, etc. Major features of organisational change are as follows:

(*i*) Change may occur in any part of the organisation. But change in one part influences other parts because all the parts are interrelated. However, some parts may be affected more than other parts.

(*ii*) Change disturbs the equilibrium between the organisation and its environment and creates a new equilibrium, depending on the degree of change and its impact on the organisation.

(*iii*) Organisational change is a continuous process.

(*iv*) Organisational change is necessary for strategy implementation. Success in strategy implementation depends partly on effective management of change.

(*v*) Managers act as change agents. They identify the need for change, overcome resistance to change, introduce the change, and monitor the progress towards change.

(vi) Organisational change may be reactive or proactive. When an organisation change is due to pressure from external forces, it is called **reactive change**. For example, many companies started contributing to Corporate Social Responsibility (CSR) when such contribution became mandatory under the Companies Act, 2013. **Proactive change** is made by an organisation on its own initiative in anticipation of opportunities and threats that are likely to arise in future. Proactive change is planned change and it is anticipatory in nature.

(vii) Different people may respond to the same change in different way. Some employees may willingly accept it, others accept under pressure, still others resist it and a few may altogether reject the same.

17.2 MANAGEMENT OF STRATEGIC CHANGE

Strategic change is the process of deliberately changing one or more aspects of an organisation to improve its future position. It may be a change in the values, goals, strategy, structure, technology, systems or processes of the organisation. The main purpose of change is to make the organisation more effective. The process of strategic change consists of the following steps:

1. **Identifying the Need for Change:** Change for the sake of change is meaningless. The gap between the existing position and the desired position can be one indicator of the need for change. Any major change in the external environment that creates an opportunity (*e.g.* announcement by government to grant licences for new banks) or threat (*e.g.* entry of a new competitor) is another trigger for change. Any deficiency in any dimension of the organisation (*e.g.* frequent inter-group conflicts) also necessitates organisational change. Continuous monitoring of internal and external environment is necessary to identify the need for planned change.

2. **Formulating the Change Strategy:** The major issues involved in planning for change are: how much change, when to change and which element to change.

   (a) *Degree of change:* According to the degree, changes can be classified as follows:

   - ***Incremental changes:*** These are small, piecemeal, gradual and routine changes that take place over a long time period. Revision of sales policies, regular improvements in quality, tapping new sources of recruitment are examples of incremental changes. Incremental change is an adaptive process in a continually changing environment.

   - ***Transformational changes:*** These are radical changes involving a major transformation of the organisation. Changing the top management team, diversification into unrelated businesses, entering overseas markets are examples of transformational changes.

   (b) *Areas of change:* Which element of the orgnaisation should be changed depends on the need and objectives of change. Organisation structure, technology and people are the three major areas wherein changes are made. Structural changes may include job design, span of control, power structure, policies and procedures, etc. Technological change may consist of changes in production methods, information technology, plant and machinery, etc. Changes in attitudes, behaviour, leadership style, etc. are people-related changes.

(*c*) *Timing of change:* An organisation can change either as a reaction to some threat (reactive change) or foresee the threat and change in anticipation of it (proactive change). Strategy implementation may require both types of changes. While deciding the timing of change, time required to prepare people for change, time needed to raise resources for change, urgency of change, etc. must be considered.

In addition to the issues given above, planning for change involves questions such as who will bring the change and how to carry out change.

3. **Assessing Change Forces:** In any organisation some forces facilitate change while other forces restrain it. Kurt Lewin[1] has developed a model, called **forcefield analysis,** to analyse these forces.

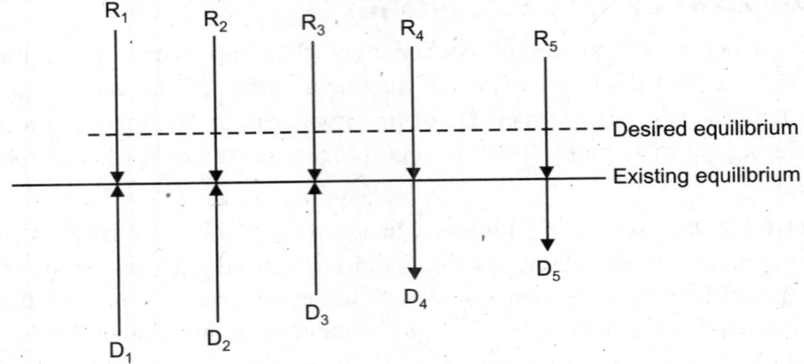

Fig. 17.1. Forcefield Analysis.

Restraining forces are obstacles to change while driving forces stimulate change. Management has to take steps to eliminate or minimise the restraining forces and to boost or maximise the driving forces.

4. **Implementation of Change Strategy:** Lewin[2] has suggested three stages in the implementation of planned change.

(*i*) *Unfreezing:* First of all, the existing processes, systems, behaviour, etc. which are inappropriate, inadequate or irrelevant to the new situation are cast aside. Just as a farmer clears the field before planting new seeds, a manager has to remove old attitudes, goals and roles from the minds of his employees. Some of the measures that are helpful in unfreezing are as follows:

(*a*) The physical removal of the individuals being changed from their accustomed routines, sources of information, and social relationships.

(*b*) The undermining and destruction of social support.

(*c*) Demeaning and humiliating experiences to help individuals to see their attitudes or behaviour as unworthy and think to be motivated to change.

(*d*) The consistent linking of reward with willingness to change and of punishment with unwilling to change.

1. Kurt Lewin, "Frontiers in Group Dynamics: Concept, Method and Reality in Social Science, Social Equilibria and Social Change", **Human Relations,** June 1947, pp. 5-41.
2. Ibid.

(*ii*) *Changing:* In this stage the individuals learn new thinking, new roles, new work methods, etc.

Some guidelines for changing are as under:[3]

(*a*) Recognise that the primary purpose of change is to improve performance results.

(*b*) Make individuals responsible for their own change.

(*c*) Encourage improvisation, team performance and coordinated initiatives.

(*d*) Ensure that people see how they fit into the larger organisational picture.

(*e*) Encourage learning by doing, and provide just-in-time training for performance.

(*f*) Use positive energy, meaningful language and courageous leadership to drive change relentlessly.

(*iii*) *Refreezing:* In the last stage, internalize the new beliefs, thinking and behaviour. What is learned during the changing phase is integrated into actual practice. Suitable reinforcements are needed to ensure that people do not revert back to their old behaviour.

5. **Monitoring and Feedback:** Regular monitoring and follow-up actions are taken to ensure that the change programme is progressing in the right direction. Any problems and dysfunctional effects created by the change must be tackled immediately. Feedback obtained from the initial efforts may be used to improve the change programme.

17.3 CAUSES FOR RESISTANCE TO CHANGE

Changes, particularly major ones, are usually resisted due to various reasons. The reasons causing resistance to change arise at individual, group and organisation levels.

17.3.1 Individual Resistance to Change

Individuals resist change due to several reasons:

1. **Economic Reasons:** These include:

(*a*) Fear of technological unemployment, *i.e.*, loss of job due to new technology.

(*b*) Fear of reduced work hours and consequently reduced pay.

(*c*) Fear of demotion due to obsolescence of skills.

(*d*) Fear of higher job standards and reduced incentive pay.

2. **Social Reasons:** These consist of:

(*a*) People working together develop informal or social relationships. Introduction of change often disturbs or **interrupts these social relationships.** Employees dislike breakup of friendships with colleagues. They try to maintain friendship and fight **social displacement** by resisting change.

(*b*) Sometimes an individual is willing to accept change but resists it due to **peer pressure.** His co-workers pressurise him to oppose change.

(*c*) Individuals resist changes which are introduced **abruptly** without consulting them.

(*d*) Changes are also resisted because workers fear that the **new social setup** will be less satisfying than the existing set-up.

---

3. Douglas K. Smith, **Taking Charge of Change,** Addison Wesley, Reading Mass, 1996.

3. **Psychological Reasons:** These comprise:
   (*a*) Individuals attach great importance to **status quo.** Change creates uncertainty which is inconvenient and uncomfortable to them.
   (*b*) Change implies that the present behaviour is not adequate and suitable. Employees do not like such **criticism.**
   (*c*) Change is resisted due to the **fear of unknown.** People fear the consequences of change and therefore oppose it. For example, an employee may refuse promotion which requires transfer to an unknown place.
   (*d*) Sometimes an individual resists change due to **ego-defensiveness.** For instance, a good suggestion made by a salesperson to increase sales is rejected by the sales manager who feels accepting the suggestion will hurt his ego.

17.3.2 Group Resistance to Change

Informal groups often resist change when they fear that it threatens their unity and existence. This is more likely when members have a strong sense of belonging to the group[4]. A study on the impact of technological change in the coal mining industry in England highlighted group resistance to change. Under the old system (shortwall method) miners worked in small independent teams. Each team was responsible for the total operation of cutting, loading and removing coal from a small section of coal face. The introduction of mechanical equipment for coal cutting and conveyors disrupted these small groups. The new system (longwall method) required large groups each consisting of 40 to 50 workers. The workers were so located that face-to-face relationship and communication was obstructed. Workers felt uprooted from their workgroup mooring, experienced loss of meaning in work and a sense of being unrelated to one another. They developed attitude of passivity and indifference and productivity suffered.[5]

17.3.3 Organisational Resistance to Change

Resistance to change may also occur at organisational level. Organisational resistance to change is caused by:

(*a*) **Threat to Power and Influence:** Top executives may resist a change which is a potential threat to their position and influence in the organisation. Novel ideas and new use of resources can disrupt power relationships.

(*b*) **Resource Constraints:** An organisation may resist change when it lacks resources which are essential for implementing the change. For example, a company may not have adequate funds needed to invest in new technology.

(*c*) **Sunk Costs:** The huge capital blocked in fixed assets may cause a problem in automation. Sunk costs are not restricted to physical assets. The knowledge and skills of employees may become redundant and retraining may be essential for introducing information technology.

---

4. D.A. Trumbo, "Individual and Group Correlates of Attitudes Towards Work-related Change", **Journal of Applied Psychology,** 1961 (45), pp. 338-344.
5. E.L. Trist and K.W. Bamforth, "Some Social and Psychological Consequences of the Longwall Method of Coal-getting", **Human Relations,** 1951 (4), pp. 346-348.

(*d*) **Organisation Structure:** Some organisation structures have built-in mechanism for resistance to change. For example, in a typically bureaucratic structure jobs are narrowly defined, lines of authority are clearly spelled out and the flow of information is top to bottom. In such an organisation new ideas do not flow upwards the hierarchy. One study[6] of twenty companies in England revealed that 'mechanistic' organisations tend to resist change.

17.4 OVERCOMING RESISTANCE TO CHANGE

Managers can adopt the following techniques to overcome resistance to change by employees:

1. **Education and Training:** Many people resist change because they do not understand its consequences. Such misunderstanding can be removed by educating the people. Employees must be taught new skills and oriented in new relationships.
2. **Communication:** Communication helps people to understand the need and logic of change. It is an effective method when resistance is caused by inadequate or inaccurate information. Two-way communication is useful in removing fear and insecurity of employees. Managers should explain:
   (*a*) What the change is?
   (*b*) Why the change is needed?
   (*c*) How it will be implemented?
   (*d*) When it is be introduced?
   (*e*) What will be its benefits to the employees?

   Once the employees are persuaded, they will help in the implementation of change. However, this method involves considerable time and effort.
3. **Participation and Involvement:** Employees can be actively involved in the design and implementation of change. A dialogue with the employees allows them to express their doubts and view. Such involvement and participation clears misunderstanding and satisfies the ego of employees. Labour leaders who are taken into confidence can convince the workers to accept change. Participation also increases commitment of those who have considerable power to resist change. The relevant information which they provide can be integrated into the change plan. But participation and involvement is very time-consuming.
4. **Facilitation and Support:** This method involves listening, providing emotional support, giving training in new skills and allowing employees time off after a difficult period. Support may be facilitative and emotional. Facilitative support implies removing physical barriers in implementing change by providing appropriate tools, materials advice and training. Emotional support involves compassionate listening and helping people overcome their anxiety and stress. Facilitation and support are most helpful when resistance arises due to fear, anxiety and adjustment problems. But this method can be time-consuming and expensive with no guarantee of success.

---

6. Tom Burns and G.M. Stalker, **The Management of Innovation,** Tavistock Publication, London, 1961.

5. **Negotiation and Agreement:** This method is helpful when the group has considerable power to resist change. It is relatively easy to avoid major resistance through negotiation and incentives.

   For example, agreement with labour union, promotion of union nominees and sharing gains of change with employees can overcome major resistance to change.

6. **Manipulation and Cooptation:** In rare cases managers may use covert methods to overcome resistance to change. Manipulation involves conscious structuring of events and the very selective use of information. Under cooptation key persons are given a desirable role in design or implementation of change. This method is relatively quick and inexpensive. But it may backfire if people feel they are manipulated.

7. **Explicit or Implicit Coercion:** Managers may force people to accept change through explicit or implicit threats. Withholding promotion, dismissal, transfer are examples of such threats. This method is less time-consuming and is used when speedy implementation of change is essential.

   Managers often commit the mistake of using only one method. For example, a **people-oriented** boss adopts participation and involvement while a **task-oriented** boss often coerces people. A combination of two or more methods may be more effective. But the combination or mix must be appropriate to the specific situation.

SUMMARY

Concept of Organisational Change: Alteration in any part of an organisation to make it more effective, can be reactive or proactive.

Management of Strategic Change: (*i*) identify need for change (*ii*) change strategy-degree of change (incremental/transformational), areas of change, timing of change (3) assessing change forces – forcefild analysis (*iv*) strategy implementation – unfreezing, changing and refreezing (*v*) monitoring and feedback.

Causes of Resistance to Change: Individual level, group level, organisation level.

Overcoming Resistance to Change: (*i*) education and training (*ii*) communication (*iii*) participation (*iv*) facilitation and support (*v*) negotiation and agreement (*vi*) manipulation and cooptation (*vii*) coercion.

TEST QUESTIONS

1. What is organisational change? Describe its features.
2. Explain the process of managing strategic change.
3. Why are changes in organisations resisted? Explain with examples.
4. Suggest strategies that can help organisations in overcoming resistance to change.
5. Write notes on:
   (*a*) Forcefield analysis
   (*b*) Strategy for change
   (*c*) Implementation of change strategy

CASE STUDY

RHL was founded by Richardson Vicks Inc. (RVI) of USA in 1964 to oversee the construction of a pharmaceutical plant and to take over the marketing efforts then handled bya small RVI branch. Today RHL is well known as the producer of Vicks Vaporub, Cough Syrup, Cough Drops, etc., and Clearsil, the beauty face cream. The company had a phenomenal growth in sales since its inception but stagnation set in by the end of 1970s. The build-up of an extensive distribution and effective advertising campaigns were at the core of its growth. When Gurcharan Das took over as RHL's president in 1981, the company was in a real mess. It had seen a 77-day strike by workers of its Kalve plant caused mainly by "poor personnel management and industrial relations." The company was cash poor, morale was low, labour was hostile, and labour-management relations were advertorial. Turnover in management ranks was very high because the company was stagnating, lacked any clear direction for the future, and the working environment was conflict ridden. There was very poor communication between functional heads, and it appeared that their commitment was not to the company as a whole, rather it only extended to their own domains.

Among the factors that contributed to this situation was the fact that RHL basically had a dominant marketing orientation. RVI, the parent company, was itself a marketing-oriented company which favoured investments marketing over manufacturing. With the tight centralised control of RVI over its subsidiaries, RHL's top management tended to be bureaucratic and procedure-oriented, and seen by the parent company as implementators of RVI's decisions and not independent decision-makers. The top executive's style of functioning tended to be authoritarian, highly resistant to delegating authority, and inclined towards creating functional empires. Their interpersonal relations and conflict resolution abilities were poor. Non-marketing managers perceived themselves as second class citizens of the company, which led to their being defensive about their jobs and to inter-departmental rivalry.

The company showed poor financial results after 1977. The major indicators of performance declined in 1978, and dipped further in 1979. While increased profitability was to receive top priority, the president felt that an equally important task was to create a "people-oriented culture" within RHL, with a consultative and participative management style promoting ideas at all levels and pushing decision making down to the lowest levels.

As a first step to initiate and then to follow through the processes of change, the president required the services of a full-time professional committed to organisational development (OD). He created a senior post for the purpose, vice-president—personnel, and selected for the position Shirodkar, who had 20 years' experience in personnel functions.

The OD programme was launched in March 1982 when the president of the company along with senior executives sent into 'retreat' in Hyderabed to explore what the company's future was to be. The objectives wet for this meeting were: (*i*) to reflect on culture, ethos, values and behaviour; (*ii*) set organisation change goals for the team; (*iii*) raise the level of people and task-orientation, and (*iv*) build a managements team. Dharani Sinha of the Administrative Staff College, Hyderabad, was the facilitator for the meeting, and continued to be RHL's consultant and senior facilitator of senior management programmes.

This 'unstructured' meeting proved to be 'pretty explosive' with members of the team reflecting completely different perceptions of the problems of the company, its goals and objectives. But the meeting was also a catalyst for airing personal problems and interpersonal grievances. The outcome of this interaction, besides thrashing out the differences in perception, were as follows:

1. The company was reorganised—the number of people directly reporting to the president was reduced from 11 to 5 which was to enable the chief executive concentrate on major issues and delegate authority and responsibility;
2. A decision was made that RHL would give high priority to developing people in the company and would aim for high growth through consultative and participative management; and
3. The executives came away with improved trust and understanding.

Reorganisation of the company at the top level was a difficult decision which required delicate manoeuvring and sensitive handling if it was not to result in a flood of resignations. Sinha opened the session by a recorganisation exercise. Each of the top 12 executives was asked to design a smaller top management team stating why they were including or excluding the people they listed. The decision which followed was highly emotional but it was to the credit of participants that they were able to constructively discuss the problems, resolve some of them and begin the process of change. To keep the team building at the top going, workshops were again held in September 1982 and February 1983. The workshops also included sensitivity training as a means of helping individuals to become aware of and change their style of interpersonal behaviour. In addition, Sinha used to meet those executives every six months to facilitate desired changes.

Though the OD processes began with top management, it touched all levels of management and workers at RHI during the next two years. The OD efforts included: residential workshop for field sales supervisors and managers which focused on people management and selling skills; residential programme for senior and middle managers with emphasis on development of general management skills; personal growth laboratories for union leaders, workers, supervisory staff and executives; team building workshop for manufacturing managers and sales and marketing managers; performance appraisal workshops; union leadership workshops; supervision skills workshops, etc.

In a move to diffuse the hostile and adversarial labour-management relations, RHL's top management visited the factory in 1982 and sat down with workers to explain the company's new purpose and goals. They stressed their desire to improve relations. This meeting did not achieve much but the workers started asking questions. Union-management negotiations revealed that there was lot of internal dissent among the union leaders although the workers were not affiliated to any external union. A strong union leadership team would represent a more uniform view of union members as well as be able to easily implement decisions taken. It was felt that a personal growth lab would help sensitise union leaders to their inter personal problems. G.K. Datey, a management consultant, was invited to conduct a three-day lab. A wide range of issues were brought up and discussed at the lab and appropriate strategies for change were agreed upon. In the end the union leaders were pleased with the lab and came out of it with a sense of camaraderie. This lab was followed by further inputs to improve productivity, cost consciousness and leadership skills.

But all this had a twofold effect: 1. the Union Committee's new way of working was perceived by workers as being too close to the management; (2) sensitive to the worker feeling of distrust, the Union Committee decided to relegate their leadership role and give an opportunity to the younger workers. A new committee was thus elected in 1983. As it happened, this was a difficult year for personnel with respect to union-mangement relations. Shortcomings in not being able to reach a productive relationship were recognised by both parties. However, confrontation was not resorted to by either of them. Management remained determined to continue training workers to be strong and committed negotiators and leaders.

The continued attempts at building trust paid off in 1984. In September 1984, the Union Committee went through a six-day residential training programme which included a four-day personal growth lab. Their response to the programme was overwhelmingly positive, which showed signs of growth and maturity: consideration among leaders, less reliance on senior managers for conflict resolution, and decision-making together with front-line supervisors and line managers.

In view of the higher aspirations of the average worker and the proneness of new workers to take a belligerent stance against management in the face of problems, it was felt that the motivating factors could only be, improved working conditions and higher wages. To this end, besides programmes to improve interpersonal relation, the classification structure within the plant, which was pretty flat with few opportunities for promotion, was restructured. The company introduced job rotation and created more job levels, thereby opening up more supervisory positions. Equity participation was also offered to increase worker identification with the company.

Management's relations with sales personnel also improved as a result of the steps indicated with decentralised team building workshops held for all the 150 salesmen. The sales people had a feeling that they were highly pressurised by the head office to sell and their contribution to the company was not recognised. In response to this, management for the first time started communicating to sales representatives what they did with the feedback they gave them. To relieve their 'pressured' feelings, management arranged to have them set targets for themselves in consultation with sales managers. New systems were set up to facilitate communication; and managers from all departments were required to spend time in the field to understand the vital role selling plays in the company's operations. To improve the traditionally adversarial relations between sales and marketing personnel, a three-day team building workshop for sales and marketing managers was held in November 1984. Managers at the meeting felt that apart from pre-arranged exercise, what they wanted to do was to understand the two groups' perception of each other.

Overall Results

More important than the impact of individual workshops and programmes was the overall change in the company's working environment achieving its stated goals. First of all, the way top management interacted with each other changed considerably and this began filtering down. Senior managers who had been dictatorial and quite unapproachable began to open up and began to listen to other people's opinions. Tensions between senior executives began diffusing. The quality and quantity of information company plans and strategies given to middle and lower management increased which gave them all a sense of involvement. That contributed to greater motivation. Supervisors were recognised to be the key link in the management-worker chain. They were given training in motivation skill and effective decision-making, how to manage the boss, conflict resolution and negotiation, and various functional operations. Supervisors were thus involved in decision-making and planning, and realised that labour relations were a part of their responsibility and not that of the personnel department alone. All this reduced the previously high turnover of supervisors. Shirodkar and other members of the personnel department kept a highly visible profile in the company, meeting constantly with both staff and workers, to ensure that they got constant feedback on the working environment.

Questions:

1. Did RHL succeed in achieving a strategic breakthrough on a durable basis?
2. What were the basic factors that underlay the breakthrough?

CHAPTER

STRATEGIC MANAGEMENT IN SMALL BUSINESS, FAMILY BUSINESS AND NON-PROFIT ORGANISATION

CHAPTER OUTLINE

A small business is established by a single person or a small group of close friends/family members. In India, small scale sector has been defined as follows[1]:

1. **Manufacturing Enterprises:**
   (i) *Micro enterprise:* investment in plant and machinery up to ₹ 25 lakh.
   (ii) *Small enterprise:* investment above ₹ 25 lakh and up to ₹ 5 crore.
   (iii) *Medium enterprise:* investment above ₹ 5 crore and up to ₹ 10 crore.
2. **Service Enterprises:**
   (i) *Micro enterprise:* investment up to ₹ 10 lakh.
   (ii) *Small enterprise:* investment above ₹ 10 lakh and up to ₹ 2 crore
   (iii) *Medium enterprise:* investment above ₹ 2 crore and up to ₹ 5 crore.
3. **Small Scale Unit Owned and Managed by Woman Entrepreneur:** An enterprise promoted by a woman entrepreneur and in which women own not less than 51 per cent share capital.
4. **Village Industry:** An industry located in a rural area which produces any goods, renders any service with or without the use of power and wherein investment does not exceed ₹ 50,000 per head.

18.1 STRATEGIC ISSUES IN SMALL BUSINESS

The strategic issues involved in small business are as follows:

1. **Nature of Business:** First of all, the small entrepreneur has to decide the type of business to be undertaken. The entrepreneur usually chooses a line of business in which he has knowledge, skill, aptitude and experience. For example, a person with a degree in

1. The Micro, Small and Medium Enterprises (MSME) Act, 2006.

information technology may set up a small firm to offer software services. An individual who has worked in a retail chain may start a retail store. The individual must also keep in mind the degree of risk involved in the proposed business and his/her capacity to bear the risk.

2. **Scale of Operations:** The size of business to be undertaken will depend on the managerial' financial, risk-bearing capabilities of the entrepreneur. It is preferable to begin with small size and gradually expand the operations.
3. **Form of Ownership:** A small scale business may be organised in either of the three forms—sole proprietorship, limited liability partner-ship, and one person company. In sole proprietorship, the single owner controls the business. It offers benefits of quick decisions, ease of formation, uniform policies, tight control and secrecy of business. But the single owner may be unable to finance and manage the business and assume the risk beyond a certain size. In limited liability partnership (LLP), there are benefits of limited liability, pooling of managerial skills and funds and sharing of risk. But there are chances of conflicts among partners. One person company (OPC) offers similar benefits but involves legal formalities.

   Sole proprietorship is suitable when the business requires one type of skill and can be managed and controlled by one person. In case complementary skills and pooling of funds are necessary, limited liability partner-ship is appropriate. Businesses involving more risk and of a medium size can better be organised as one person company or private limited company.
4. **Sources of Funds:** Small firms may raise funds from the following sources:
   (*a*) Self-financing – funds contributed by the proprietor or partners
   (*b*) Loans from relatives and friends.
   (*c*) Loans from banks, financial institutions and venture funds.
   (*d*) Incentives and subsidies from government agencies.

   In the initial stage it is preferable to depend on owned funds. Once the business begins to generate profits external funding may be used.
5. **Marketing Methods:** The marketing mechanisms depend on the type of business. For example, a grocery shop sells directly to consumers. On the other hand, a small manufacturing unit may supply all its output to a big buyer. Such a captive arrangement relieves the small firm from marketing problems and it can focus on technical competence in manufacturing. But the firm's future is dependent on the buying firm and on the terms it gets due to its weak bargaining power. In auto, fast moving consumer goods and engineering thousands of small firms act as captive units of multinationals. Alternatively, a small scale manufacturer may focus on a niche market. Small firms can formulate their marketing strategy on the basis of analysing competition dynamics in niche markets.
6. **Process of Learning:** A small scale entrepreneur is inspired mainly by the desire to be his own boss. Therefore, his focus is on survival and organic growth rather than rapid or major growth. The organic or incremental growth is a source of learning for the entrepreneur. The owner may learn by solving problems, getting advice, attending

training sessions, etc. A small firm usually does not have a formal training system. Therefore, its staff must share their knowledge and experience for mutual learning.

7. **Succession Planning:** When a small firm expands beyond the managerial capacity of the owner, it requires additional executives. Generally, family members are roped in because they are trusted by the owner. But the business may suffer in case the family members do not work as a close team. Another alternative is to employ professional managers. This will enable the owner to concentrate on strategic issues. The professional has expertise and can better handle operational issues. But he may lack personal stake in the success and growth of business.

   Small firms usually lack formal system to monitor the environment, make forecasts, or evaluate and control strategy. They depend on experience and intuition. Therefore, strategic planning in small firms tends to be less formal and systematic. But strategic planning is no less important in small business. Owners of small firms gradually become familiar with opportunities and threats in the environment and their strengths and weaknesses. To begin with, strategic planning in small firms may be based largely on judgment, experience and well-guided discussion. It can become systematic and complex as the owner acquires the necessary skills. Strategic planning is easier in small firms because strategies can be implemented effectively through face-to-face interactions. Moreover, for small business strategic planning is a learning process.

18.2 STRATEGIC ISSUES IN FAMILY BUSINESS

A business owned and controlled by members of a family/extended family is called family business. Family business firms are common in both developed and developing countries. It is estimated that 97 per cent of all registered firms in India are family-owned. Tatas, Birlas, Bajajs, Singhanias, Ambanis, Mittals are some of the family business groups in India. Family business houses dominate business in India and control more than 75 per cent of the country's GDP.

Strategic issues in family business are as follows:

1. **Integration of Family and Business:** In a family business the family and its business interact and depend on each other. Family structure affects the degree and continuity of family involvement in ownership and management of business. Family values shape governance of the business and management of the family shapes operating leadership. There exist considerable differences between family system and business system. By its very nature, family gives top priority to stability, consistency, enduring values, traditions and harmony. On the other hand, family business needs to be flexible and adaptive and customer-oriented so as to succeed in a competitive and turbulent environment. The head of the family continues to be the chief executive officer (CEO) of family business for a long period in case the owner CEO is very dynamic, rigidity arises in business. Therefore, the basic problem in family business is to reconcile the need for stability of the family system with the need for change of the business system. In order to overcome this problem, two alternatives have been adopted. Most owners of family business send their wards to best business schools for professional education and training in management. Under the second alternative, family business owners appoint professional CEO (*e.g.* Dabur India).

2. **Sustainability:** Most family businesses do not survive after the third generation. The main causes of low survival rate are as follows:
   (*i*) Rigid family values.
   (*ii*) Break up of business into separate units to accommodate members of the family.
   (*iii*) Conflicts among family members due to generation gap. The patriarch wants to keep control over the business he founded and nurtured. On the other hand, the next generation seeks independence to run the business in its own way. There are several court cases involving father-son, brother,-brother-sister, etc. over control and division of family business.
   (*iv*) Top management positions in family business are decided on the basis of an individual's seniority in the family rather than on merit. Even when professionals are appointed on these positions, personal relationship between family members and the professional is given priority over competence.
3. **Right Strategic Intent:** A large number of family business houses in India have functioned in an opportunistic manner. They have used financial, ethnic and political connections to accumulate domestic and foreign resources at low costs. Before economic liberalisation, they diversified into entirely unrelated areas. Now they have to change this mindset and focus on their core capabilities. They can do so in the following ways[2]:
   (*i*) *Cost Leadership:* Family business can achieve cost leadership in the following ways:
      (*a*) developing a core competence *e.g.* Reliance Industries in polymer intermediaries, Arvind Mills in denim and Ranbaxy in generic drugs.
      (*b*) leveraging pre-eminent position in the domestic market to increase business volume.
      (*c*) leveraging cost advantage to gain share in the global market.
      (*d*) leveraging large market size to set up world-scale and world-class plants so as to gain entry into the world market
      (*e*) forging alliances and subcontracting relationships with multinational corporations to gain access in the world market.
      (*f*) lowering financial costs by raising funds abroad.
      (*g*) employing world-class consultants to help improve strategies, costs, design, and performance.
   (*ii*) *Service Leadership:* Serving customers in a better way creates value to them and provides service leadership. In the past most family businesses were not service-oriented. Now the situation is changing due to information technology and growing competition. Knowledgeable and well trained employees and information technology are needed to deliver superior value-added services to customers. This is the key to service leadership.

2. Gurcharan Das, "Family Business: A Symposium on the Role of the Family in Indian Business," October 1999, www.indian-Seminar. com

(*iii*) *Technology Leadership:* Collaboration with multinational corporations can help family business acquire leadership in technology. But for this purpose they must access competitive technology and absorb it as early as possible. For example, Hero Corp. gained technology leadership by collaborating with Honda Motors of Japan.

4. **Corporate Governance:** Family business houses in India have had poor governance practices. Lack of transparency, related party transactions, siphoning of funds, etc. have been quite common. But the situation has improved since SEBI regulations on listed companies. However, regulations alone cannot ensure good corporate governance. Indian family business must change their mindset.

5. **Succession Planning:** Founders and owners cannot control and manage family businesses for ever. They must groom competent successors through formal education and training and experience. Heads of family business groups have realised that in the era of globalisation developing the second and third generation for business is essential. Their wards join family business after acquiring formal degrees/diplomas in management and gradually rise to the top positions. Professional managers are being appointed at top and middle levels to ensure continuity and growth.

18.3 STRATEGIC MANAGEMENT IN NON-PROFIT ORGANISATIONS

Public needs many services which neither private sector nor government provides in sufficient volume. Social sector or third sector has grown over the years to fill this vacuum. This sector consists of non-profit or not-for-profit-organisations. A non-profit organisation is formed and works for public benefit rather than for earning profits or acquiring wealth. Such organisations function in the fields of art, culture, education, public health, environment, religion, animal care, etc. HelpAge, CRY, Red Cross are examples of non-profit or non government organisations (NGOs). Non-profit organisaitons are organised in the form of trusts, societies, foundations, etc.

Table 18.1. Difference between Profit and Non-Profit Organisation

	Profit Organisations	Non-Profit/Private Organisation
Ownership	Private	Private
Funding	Sales revenue	Membership fee, contributions from public and/ or private sources, sale of products or services
Stakeholders	Few	Many
Types	Sole proprietorship	Floated by members
Activities	Production and/or Marketing of goods and/or services	Educational, charitable, social service, Health service foundation, cultural, religious, and recreational
Main objective	Profit maximization	Service to public

Concepts and techniques of strategic management were developed mostly for business organisations. But these are also necessary and useful for non-profit organisations.

1. **Defining Mission, Objectives and Goals:** A well-defined mission helps to provide direction to a non-profit organisaiton. Therefore, the best non-profit organisations devote considerable thought to formulate their mission statements. The mission statement of management institute may be "to develop as a centre of excellence for education, research and consultancy in management."

A non-profit-organisation may formulate its objectives keeping in view the interests of donors, founders and clients. It has to maintain a balance among the conflicting interets of different stakeholders. Goals of non-profit organisations are often vague (e.g. to protect environment) due to several reasons: (*a*) goals are value laden, (*b*) goals often involve trade offs.

2. **Strategy Formulation:** The strategies of non-profit organisations often complement those of government agencies. For example, NGOs in the health sector supplement the efforts of Ministry of Health. Non-profit organisations face political constraints while making their strategic choices. The process of strategy formulation becomes complex due to several rules, regulations, procedures and formalities. Newman and Wallender point out the following **constraints on strategy formulation** in non-profit organisations:
   (*i*) Service is often intangible and hard to measure. This problem is compounded by the existence of multiple service objectives developed in order to satisfy multiple sponsors.
   (*ii*) Client influence may be weak. Often the organisation has a local monopoly, and payments by customers may be a very small source of funds.
   (*iii*) Strong employee commitment to profession or to a cause may undermine their allegiance to the organisation employing them.
   (*iv*) Resource contributors – notably fund contributors and government – may intrude upon the organisation's internal management.[3]

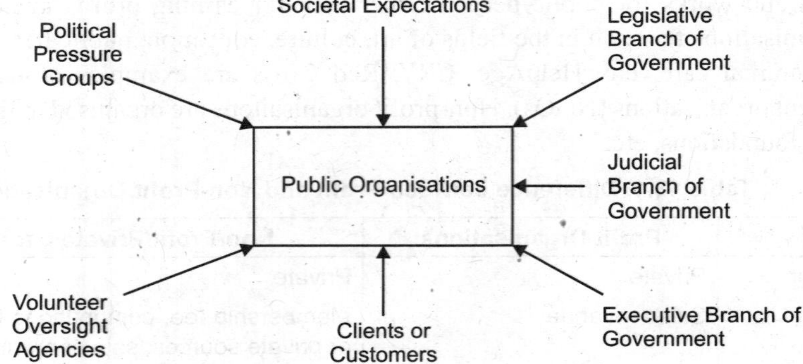

Source: Wright, Pringle and Kroll, *op., Cit.*, P. 250.

Fig. 18.1. Stakeholder Constraints on Public Organisations

The constraints given above create the following **problems in strategy formulation:**

(*a*) There is lack of a single clear cut goal. Donors have more influence than clients in goal setting. Divergent objectives create a conflict and rational planning becomes difficult.

(*b*) Resource inputs become more important than service outputs because it is difficult to measure the service outcomes.

3. W.H. Newman and H.W. Wallender III, "Managing Non-Profit Enterprises", **Academy of Management Review,** January 1978, p. 26.

(c) Vague objectives and concern for resources create scope for goal displacement and power politics. The organisation may focus on satisfying the sponsors rather than the clients. Ability to mobilise funds rather than managerial competence may become the basis for selecting the trustees.

(d) Professionalisation of management may help to improve efficiency but creates rigidity in operations.

3. **Strategy Implementation:** Execution of strategy is also affected by the constraints.

   (i) Decision-making is often centralised due to the absence of clear cut goals and non-measurability of output.

   (ii) Non-profit organisations depend too much upon the external sources for funds. (Sponsors and donors). Therefore, executives act as **linking pins** between the internal operations and external sponsors. Some non-profit organisations employ public relations experts or funds-raisers for this purpose.

   (iii) There is limited scope for job enrichment and executive development because these may be viewed as encroachment into the authority of higher level managers.

4. **Strategy Evaluation and Control:** In the absence of clear cut goals and performance standards, evaluation and control becomes difficult. Constraints on strategic management create two main problems in evaluation and control of strategies in non-profit organisations:

   (i) Rewards and penalties have little linkage with performance.

   (ii) Emphasis is more on controlling costs (inputs) than on performance (outputs).

In order to overcome the constraints, non-profit organisations may adopt the following measures:

1. Select a dynamic and forceful leader who has (a) values to be used in decision-making, (b) enough power to make strategic choices, and (c) influence to get the choices accepted by the employees.
2. Develop a 'mystique' that can (a) attract the sponsors, (b) set the character of decision, makers, and (c) motivate client satisfaction through shared objectives.
3. Formulate rules and regulations so that employees pay adequate attention towards the clients.
4. Appoint a strong board of trustees which can look after strategic as well as operational issues *e.g.* hiring, directing and budgeting.
5. Establish performance-based budgets that link measurable goals to budget items. Such a system involves[4]:

   (a) Specify objectives as clearly as possible in quantitative measurable terms.

   (b) Analyze the actual output of the non-profit organisation in terms of the stated objectives.

   (c) Measure the cost of the particular programme.

   (d) Analyze alternatives and search for those that have the greatest effectiveness in achieving the objectives.

   (c) Establish the process in a systematic way so that it continues to occur over time.

---

4. Keating B.P. and Keating M.O., **Not For Profit,** Thomas Horton and Daughters, New Jersey, 1980, pp. 140-141.

18.4 POPULAR STRATEGIES AND ISSUES IN NON-PROFIT ORGANISATIONS

1. **Strategic Piggybacking:** When a non-profit organisation develops a new activity to generate funds needed to make up the deficit in its budget, it is known as piggybacking. The new activity is undertaken mainly to subside the primary activities. The new activity may be related directly or indirectly to the existing activities. The non-profit organisation invest in new, safe cash cows to funds its current cash-hungry stars. Before taking up a revenue-generating activity, a non-profit organisation must consider the following:
   (*i*) Finding a market for its products/services
   (*ii*) Enough people must be available to nurture and sustain the income-earning venture over the long term.
   (*iii*) Trustees must support the income-earning venture.
   (*iv*) Management must adopt an entrepreneurial attitude and take interest in innovative ideas which are practical.
   (*v*) Enter into a joint venture with a business organisation to secure necessary funds, marketing and management support for the new activity.
2. **Inter-Organisational Linkage:** Another strategy adopted by non-profit organisations is to develop cooperative ties with other organisations so as to acquire resources and increase the ability to serve clients efficiently. For example, a hospital may cooperate with other hospitals to cope up with rising costs or declining revenues.
3. **Linkage with a Profit-Making Organisation:** This strategy is employed to augment funds, marketing and management. Educational institutions, particularly business schools, adopt this strategy. They get funds, guest faculty, jobs for their graduates, etc. Therefore, management and engineering institutes tie up with business houses.
4. **Mission-Driven Work Culture:** In order to be successful, a non-profit organisation must develop mission-driven work culture. Clients or beneficiaries of such an organisation have no control over its activities. Therefore, managers and employees of the organisation must decide and act not in their self-interest but in the interest of beneficiaries.
5. **Managing Multiple Stakeholders:** There are several stakeholders in a non-profit organisation and each stakeholder group tries to influence its decision-making in its own favour. Founders/trustees, government agencies which provide grants, major donors, employees and recipients of paid services are these stakeholders. The final outcome depends upon the relative power of various stakeholders.

   This situation may lead to goal displacement which means displacement of original goals by goals of most powerful stakeholders. For example, several educational institutions set up as non-profit organisations focus on earning money for their founders/trustees.
6. **Mobilisation of Resources:** A vast majority of non-profit organisations face shortage of funds. In order to generate funds they can take the following steps:
   (*a*) Finding new donors and persuading the existing donors to contribute more.
   (*b*) Persuading government agencies to give more grants.
   (*c*) Collaborating with other organisations having similar goals.
   (*d*) If possible, taking up income generating activities.

7. **Generating Institutional Advantage:** A non-profit organisation is said to have an institutional advantage when it performs its tasks more effectively than other comparable organisations. Leaders of non-profit organisations can develop institutional advantages by performing the following roles:[5]

8. **Overcoming Institutional Disadvantages:** Non-profit organisations suffer from some institutional disadvantages. They must recognise and employ appropriate strategies to overcome these disadvantages According to Salamon[6] institutional disadvantages for non-profit organisations arise from the following sources:

   (i) **Philanthropic Insufficiency:** A non-profit organisation may be unable to generate sufficient sources needed to provide relevant services to public. During recession donations decline while demand for services increases.

   (ii) **Philanthropic Particularism:** Too many non-profit organisations may try to serve a particular religious, ethnic or caste group. In such a situation they waste their energy and funds, for other groups may dry up causing an imbalance in the non-profit sector.

   (iii) **Philanthropic Paternalism:** Too much reliance may be put on the governing boards to define needs of the community. This situation may encourage the governing boards to define the activities of the organisation in a self-serving manner. To overcome this danger the mission must be quite specific so as to empower the target group.

   (iv) **Philanthropic Amateurism:** A non-profit organisation suffering from shortage of funds may rely too much on volunteer staff which may adopt amateurish approach towards clients. Newly recruited employees tend to leave after getting some experience while passionate employees may get frustrated due to very demanding and taxing activities.

SUMMARY

Strategic Issues in Small Business: (*i*) Nature of business (*ii*) scale of operations (*iii*) form of ownership (*iv*) sources of funds (*v*) marketing methods (*vi*) learning process (*vii*) succession planning.

Strategic Issues in Family Business: (*i*) Integration of family and business (*ii*) sustainability (*iii*) right strategic intent (*iv*) corporate governance (*v*) succession planning.

Strategic Issues in Non-Profit Organisations: (*i*) Defining mission and goals (*ii*) strategy formulation (*iii*) strategy implementation (*iv*) strategic evaluation and control.

Popular Strategies and Issues in Non-Profit Organisations: (*i*) Strategic piggybacking (*ii*) inter-organisational linkage (*iii*) linkage with a profit-making organisation. (*iv*) mission driven culture (*v*) managing multiple stakeholders (*vi*) resource mobilisation. (*vii*) generating institutional advantages (*viii*) overcoming institutional disadvantages.

---

5. B.Hanns and S. Dobbs, **Leaders Who Make a Difference,** Jossey Bass, San Francisco, 1999.
6. Laster M. Salamon, **America's Non-Profit Sector: A Primer,** The Foundation Centre, New York, 1999.

TEST QUESTIONS

1. Explain the strategic issues involved in small business.
2. Discuss the strategic issues in family business.
3. "A majority of family businesses do not survive beyond the third generation." Explain why?
4. What is a non-profit organisation? How does it differ from a profit-making organisation?
5. Explain the constraints faced by non-profit organisations in their strategic management.
6. "Some non-profit organisations focus on serving their founders rather than the public." Give reasons for this phenomenon and suggest measures to overcome it.
7. Discuss the strategic issues in and strategies of non-profit organisations.
8. Write notes on:
   (*a*) Strategic piggybacking
   (*b*) Institutional advantage
   (*c*) Sources of institutional disadvantages for non-profit organisations.

CASE STUDY

KinderCare Learning Centres had been founded to take advantage of the increasing number of dual-carrer couples who were turning to day-care centres to watch their children while they were at work. In comparison to some centres that were nothing more than baby sitting services providing only minimal attention to the needs of the children, KinderCare offered pleasant surroundings staffed by well-trained personnel. Soon KinderCare had over 1,000 centres in almost 40 cities in the United States. Not satisfied with its success, however, KinderCare's top management decided to take advantage of its relationship with working parents to diversify into the somewhat related businesses of banking, insurance, and retailing. Financed through junk bonds, the strategy failed to bring in enough cash to pay for its implementation. After years of losses, the company was driven to bankruptcy in the late 1980s. It emerged from bankruptcy in 1993, divested itself of its acquisitions and pledged to stay away from diversification. The new CEO initiated a concentration strategy with emphasis on horizontal growth. KinderCare opened its first centre catering expressly to commuters in renovated supermarket near the Metro line to Chicago. It also offered to build child-care centres for big employers or to run existing facilities for a fee. It opened its first overseas centre in Britain. By 1996, the company was earning $21.7 million on revenues of $506.5 million with centres in 38 states and the United Kingdom.

Question:

(*i*) What did this company do right?
(*ii*) What mistakes did it make?
(*iii*) Do you think it made the right decision to grow internationally?
(*iv*) Should it expand further? If so, what corporate strategy should it use?